Manuel de Falla:
his Life
&
Works

p o e s í a

REVISTA ILUSTRADA DE INFORMACIÓN POÉTICA Nº36–37

Manuel de Falla: his Life & Works

Edited by Gonzalo Armero
and Jorge de Persia

MINISTERIO DE CULTURA
SPAIN

OMNIBUS PRESS

poesía

REVISTA ILUSTRADA DE INFORMACIÓN POÉTICA

This edition copyright © 1999 Omnibus Press
(A Division of Book Sales Limited)

First published 1996 in *Poesía*,
a publication of the Spanish Ministry of Culture,
by Ediciones Opponax, C/ Campomanes,
8. 28012 Madrid, Spain.

Supervision: Jorge de Persia
Edited by: Manzani Díaz Agero
            Juan Pérez de Ayala
Production: Chiqui Abril
Photography: Javier Campano
             Mariano Cano
             Gerardo Kurtz
             Pedro Albornoz

Translation: Tom Skipp

ISBN: 0.7119.6909.4
Order No: OP 48071

Exclusive Distributors:
Book Sales Limited,
8/9 Frith Street,
London W1V 5TZ, UK.

Music Sales Corporation,
257 Park Avenue South,
New York, NY 10010, USA.

Five Mile Press,
22 Summit Road,
Noble Park,
Victoria 3174,
Australia.

To the Music Trade only:
Music Sales Limited,
8/9 Frith Street,
London W1V 5TZ, UK.

© Ministerio de Cultura, Spain
© Gran Vía Gestión Artística y Editorial, s.a.
© Opponax, s.l.

Photo credits:
p. 18, Calle Ancha, No. 19, José María García de Paredes;
p. 36, Calle Serrano, no. 70, Nené García de Paredes;
p. 61, Comic Opera Theatre in Paris, Harlingue-Viollet;
p. 94, previously unpublished photo of Manuel de Falla,
Ballesteros Ledesma's family album; p. 102, portrait of
Manuel de Falla, Dover Publications, New York; p. 113,
Antonia Mercé, Paris 1936, Monique Paravicini; p. 127,
Léonide Massine, 1938, Crown Theatre Museum, London;
p. 181, Manuel de Falla shakes hands with Don Quixote,
Giacomelli, Venice. © of the photographs of works by
Santiago Rusiñol (p. 71, pp. 88-89, p. 144), Pablo Picasso
(p. 103, p. 129, p. 130, p. 131, p. 132), Michel Larionov
(p. 123), Daniel Vázquez Díaz (p. 144, p. 199), Ignacio
Zuloaga (p. 158, p. 180, p. 279) Manuel Ángeles Ortiz
(p. 165, p. 175, p. 176, p. 177, p. 178, p. 180), Hernando
Viñes (p. 178, p. 180, p. 201) and Juan Gris (p. 189),
Vegap, Madrid, 1996.

While every effort has been made to trace and acknowledge
all copyright holders, we would like to apologise should
there be any omissions.

Poesía is a publication of the Spanish Ministry of Culture,
which started in 1977 under the editorship of Gonzalo
Armero. 42 titles have so far been published in the series,
including monographs on Fernando Pessoa, Juan Ramón
Jiménez, Rubén Darío, Vicente Huidobro, Salvador Dali,
Federico Garcia Lorca, José de Almada Negreiros, José
Martí, Picasso's 'Guernica' and Manuel de Falla.

Printed and bound in Singapore.

A catalogue record for this book is available from the
British Library.

Visit Omnibus Press at http://www.omnibuspress.co.uk

INTRODUCTION

ONLY the wealth of documents in the possession of the Manuel de Falla Archives (currently at Granada, near the house, now a museum, where the famous Andalusian composer used to live) made the publishing of this issue of *Poesía* possible.

Precisely one of the problems that arose when deciding on the final design for this issue was the selection of the documents and their presentation in such a way as to give them meaning.

The option chosen was that of using extracts from contemporary accounts of the events mentioned. These are either by Falla, in the form of short autobiographical pieces, letters, etc., or by others who played a part. The aim was, in one way or another, to let the main actors speak for themselves, lending a hand on some occasions with short editorial comments that would help to place the situations in perspective.

Theoretical articles and current lucubrations on different subjects were ruled out, giving strict priority to historic texts.

Likewise, it will be seen that photographs are used whenever possible, chronologically, in order to complement the written narrative. In many cases previously unpublished material is used.

The chronology, especially drawn up for this occasion, is a necessary basis for each chapter, which in turn consists of two areas: a biographical album and appendices about the composer's most important works.

Many of the texts used have been taken from books published during Falla's lifetime (1876-1946) and not reprinted, and nearly all of them belong to musicians, researchers, writers, artists, etc., who had a personal relationship with Manuel de Falla.

One of the challenges facing us was that the final result had to be not an "illustrated biography", but rather consist of original sketches about the concerns, circumstances, thoughts, work, hopes and biographical data of the brilliant composer from Cadiz.

JORGE DE PERSIA

Contents

CHAPTER 1... 13
1876-1899
CADIZ

CHAPTER 2... 31
1900-1907
MADRID

CHAPTER 3... 47
1907-1914
PARIS

COMPOSITIONS. Appendix I 57

CHAPTER 4... 79
1914-1920
MADRID

COMPOSITIONS. Appendix II 105

CHAPTER 5 147
1920-1929
GRANADA

COMPOSITIONS. Appendix III 171

COMPOSITIONS. Appendix IV 185

CHAPTER 6 213
1930-1939
GRANADA

CHAPTER 7 237
1939-1946
ARGENTINA

COMPOSITIONS. Appendix V 243

INDEXES
1. Bibliographical index of texts by Manuel de Falla 297
2. Bibliographical index of texts about Manuel de Falla 297
3. Names index 300

1
C A D I Z
1876-1899

CADIZ AT THE END OF THE 19TH CENTURY. CHILD-
HOOD AND ADOLESCENCE. FIRST LETTERS. MUSICAL
BEGINNINGS. COLÓN, IMAGINED CITY. *EL CONDE DE
VILLAMEDIANA*. LITERARY LOVES. THE SALVADOR VI-
NIEGRA MUSICAL SALON. FATHER FEDRIANI. MUSIC,
THE DEFINITIVE VOCATION. MUSIC STUDIES IN MADRID.
CONCERTS IN CADIZ.

C H R O N O L O G Y

1876-1896. ■ MANUEL DE FALLA Y MATHEU WAS BORN IN THE FAMILY HOME, N°. 3, PLAZA DE MINA, IN CADIZ, ON THE 23rd OF NOVEMBER 1876, SON OF JOSÉ MARÍA FALLA AND MARÍA JESÚS MATHEU; HE WAS BAPTISED IN THE PARISH CHURCH *NUESTRA SEÑORA DEL ROSARIO.* ■ HE WAS EDUCATED IN AN APPROPRIATE ATMOSPHERE FOR A WEALTHY CADIZ FAMILY OF THE TIME, GROWING UP WITH THE TALES AND POPULAR SONGS OF HIS NANNY "*LA MORILLA*" AND THE LOVE OF MUSIC OF HIS MATERNAL GRANDFATHER, WHO PLAYED THE HARMONIUM, AND HIS MOTHER, WHO TAUGHT HIM TO PLAY THE PIANO. ■ HIS PRIMARY SCHOOL EDUCATION WAS PROVIDED BY PRIVATE TUTORS AND HE LEARNT FRENCH. ■ AS A CHILD HE WANTED TO BE A WRITER AND STARTED SOME HOME-MADE MAGAZINES WITH FRIENDS. HE WROTE SHORT ARTICLES FOR THEM, DREW, AND EVEN APPEARED AS THE DIRECTOR IN SOME VOLUMES. SOME EXAMPLES OF *EL BURLÓN* FROM 1889 AND *EL CASCABEL* FROM 1891 HAVE BEEN PRESERVED. ■ OWING TO HIS TALENT FOR THE PIANO, HE RECEIVED LESSONS FROM HIS FIRST MUSIC TEACHER ELOÍSA GALLUZZO, AND WENT, WITH HIS PARENTS, TO CHAMBER MUSIC MEETINGS HELD IN THE SALONS OF SALVADOR VINIEGRA AND SEÑOR QUIRELL. ■ HIS RELIGIOUS EDUCATION INTENSIFIED AFTER ATTENDING THE MEETINGS FOR YOUNG PEOPLE ARRANGED BY FATHER FEDRIANI, WHO BECAME HIS SPIRITUAL GUIDE THROUGHOUT HIS ADOLESCENCE AND EARLY LIFE. ■ ELOÍSA GALLUZZO ENTERED A CONVENT AND FALLA CONTINUED HIS STUDIES OF HARMONY AND COUNTERPOINT WITH LOCAL TEACHERS ODERO AND BROCCA. ■ FINANCIAL PROBLEMS WITH THE FAMILY BUSINESS AROSE.

1897-1899. ■ HE BEGAN TO COMPOSE HIS FIRST WORKS AND TO PARTICIPATE ACTIVELY IN SALVADOR VINIEGRA'S CHAMBER MUSIC SESSIONS. FROM THIS PERIOD ARE: *NOCTURNE* FOR PIANO, *MELODY* FOR CELLO AND PIANO, JUNE 1897 AND *ROMANZA*, 1898, BOTH DEDICATED TO VINIEGRA; AS WELL AS *SCHERZO* AND *MAZURKA*, FOR PIANO, 1898 AND 1899. ■ HE WENT TO MADRID TO CONTINUE HIS PIANO STUDIES WITH JOSÉ TRAGÓ. ■ IN 1898 HE PASSED WITH DISTINCTION, THE FIRST THREE YEARS OF MUSICAL THEORY AND THE FIRST FIVE OF PIANO. ■ IN 1899 HE WAS AWARDED THE FIRST PIANO PRIZE AT THE MADRID CONSERVATORY OF MUSIC AND DECLAMATION.

CADIZ WAS a colonial city, that is, linked to Spain's immense American colonies and to the Pacific; port of call on the journey to America and to the West, to the Philippines, the Mariana Islands, the Palau Islands, the Caroline Islands... and to the far East before the new route through the Suez canal was opened. For this reason, since olden days, people from other countries, merchants and ship owners –from Italy, England, northern Europe and from other regions within Spain itself: the Basque Country and in particular Catalonia– had settled in the city. In Cadiz there are numerous Catalonian and Basque surnames along with others from outside Spain: Italian, English, German, and Danish; the surnames of families that had come to the city because of its trade with America and had settled there for several generations. Falla's surnames are an example of this: Falla –his father's name– is Valencian and Matheu –his mother's name– Catalonian.

JAIME PAHISSA

PLAZA DE MINA, CADIZ. MANUEL DE FALLA WAS
BORN AT N°. 3.

THE PLAZA DE MINA in Cadiz is colonial style and decorated with white marble statues, which stand out against the well cared for gardens; the Levant –an easterly wind common in this area– sometimes lashes across its every nook, and when not withering the flowers, it bothers all who frequent the place.

JUAN J. VINIEGRA

JOSÉ MARÍA DE FALLA FRANCO AND MARÍA JESÚS MATHEU ZABALA, THE PARENTS OF MANUEL DE FALLA.

CALLE ANCHA , N°. 19, CADIZ.

AT FIRST the family lived in a house on calle Ancha. Falla spent the first years of his childhood there. People called it calle Ancha even though this was not its official name. It was a street for walks every evening at dusk, lit by the glow from the window displays of the best shops. After leaving that house they spent a long time in Fonda de Cádiz, located in the Plaza de San Antonio.

JAIME PAHISSA

FALLA IN THE ARMS OF HIS NANNY, "*LA MORILLA*".

THROUGHOUT my early
childhood (I must have been
two or three years old) Ana *"la
Morilla's"* songs and stories
led me into a marvellous world.
Later, when I could read, story
books with their beautiful
drawings added to her spell.

MANUEL DE FALLA
Letter to Roland Manuel

THE CHILDREN did not attend school: they had a private tutor at home. This man wore a frock coat and a top hat, had a black moustache and hairy hands, and was tall and strong. This master penman of English letters was called Clemente Parodi, another of Cadiz's Italian surnames.

Falla learned to read and write with this man and his first musical notes with his mother. Falla's father was no musician; he was a merchant like his mother's father. However, his mother was an excellent pianist. At home, Falla heard her play not just the fashionable operas of the moment, but works by Chopin and sonatas, such as the *Pathetique* and the *Moonlight*, by Beethoven.

JAIME PAHISSA

AT A FANCY DRESS PARTY DRESSED
AS A HUGUENOT AND, A PAGE FROM THE PUBLICATION *EL CONDE
DE VILLAMEDIANA* BY DUQUE DE RIVAS,
A TEXT ON WHICH FALLA BASED ONE OF HIS FIRST
MUSICAL COMPOSITIONS.

CHILDHOOD and youth until he was twenty went by for him with the ease and carefreeness of someone who has no need to think about earning his keep. He was an "Andalusian gentleman" redeemed from the frivolity of his peers by his love of music and his desire to do something grand in the realms of divine art. He carried the songs of Andalusia in his blood and had a Moorish nanny who sang him to sleep with sweet sounding Arabian melodies and, to amuse him, told him tales worthy of inclusion in *The Arabian Nights*. Thus, in his imagination, which would later become his inspiration, this bewitching Flamenco-Moorish combination took root. A combination which would fire his singular and moving music more than any other abundant sensual source.

MARÍA MARTÍNEZ SIERRA

MANUEL DE FALLA, AROUND 1890.

SIGNATURE ON A PAGE OF THE "OLLENDORF FRENCH METHOD".

THE REAL ACADEMIA of Santa Cecilia had at the time a fine group of select pupils, but did not include little Manuel de Falla. His mother, a true artist, was his first teacher. But a deep interest began to take possession of the little lad and led him to Santa Cecilia.

While the other children could only think about games and being mischievous, little Manuel, with a seriousness unsuited to his age, spent his time listening to the lessons that were given to the other children.

JUAN J. VINIEGRA

ELOÍSA GALLUZZO, HIS FIRST PIANO TEACHER.

IT WAS THEN that Eloísa Galluzzo, a friend of my good mother and, what is more, an excellent pianist, took charge of my initiation into music to develop the improvisations I enjoyed playing on my grandfather's harmonium..., the kitchen and *"la Morilla"* were far away now.

Eloísa Galluzzo, for whom I felt great affection in spite of the raps with a baton that she gave my unobediant fingers, taught me for two or three years, with help from my mother, (right up until she entered a convent caring for old people). Then Alejandro Odero, who had been her teacher (an outstanding artist, who studied piano and harmonium with his father and at the Paris Conservatory), took it upon himself to continue my musical education.

MANUEL DE FALLA
Letter to Roland Manuel

FALLA'S MUSIC BOOKS.

THE SEVEN WORDS OF JESUS CHRIST, BY J. HAYDN, A WORK WHICH FALLA INTERPRETED AT THE AGE OF NINE, ACCOMPANYING HIS MOTHER, IN THE SAN FRANCISCO CHURCH IN CADIZ; AND THE SCORE *FAUST* BY GOUNOD.

AT THE AGE OF NINE FALLA VISITED SEVILLA.

BACK AGAIN in Cadiz, despite the tenderness he felt for his native town, the city of beautiful nights, he shut himself up with his dreams in a secluded chamber that he called "Eden". There he built a utopian city, which compensated for all the charms of the lost city [Seville]. It is *Colón*, which he populated and governed with his imagination, as well as defending it from the curiosity of the outside world. For six years, this thoughtful and taciturn child gravely undertook the execution of the diverse tasks that the government of his metropolis entailed. The town council, newspaper editors, academics and company administrators entered "Eden" through his wardrobe door. Musicians too, because *Colón* had a magnificent theatre where the Maestro Manuel de Falla was both the applauded composer and irresistible conductor of the successful *El Conde de Villamediana, ópera seria*. Nothing could be less childlike, or more removed from caprice and play than this life in a two-sided game, played in strictest secrecy, with extraordinary perseverance and naturalness. One carnival day, they searched for Manuel high and low to show him the masks that were passing beneath the windows of the house. But Manuel remained hidden, busily occupied fixing the rates of individual tax for his administrators.

Every spiritual acquisition and piece of school material found an immediate and appropriate application in the invisible city. Neither his parents, nor his eminent professors Odero and Brocca, who were teaching him the rudiments of harmony, suspected anything. Music, secretly favoured above all *Colón's* delights,was still no more than an adornment to its charms. The repertory of Cadiz's theatre was neither varied nor rich enough to outshine that of the Grand opera of *Colón*. Though *Faust* was able to beguile and possess the composer of *El Conde de Villamediana, Lucía di Lammermoor* distressed and bored him. On the other hand, in his opinion, nothing was nearly as good as an old French minuet that he found in the *Journal des demoiselles*. He analysed it –a practice that he would fruitfully employ in the future– and, using the same model, composed another dedicated to his *Colonian* music lovers.

ROLAND MANUEL

IN SPITE of my vocation and my love for certain music (not all!), I have always felt myself drawn to the literary side (prose, rather than verse). To this could be added my interest in history, in particular Spanish history, wherein I discovered a kind of continuation of the old legends that thrilled me as a child. Its study had a growing effect on me that increased with good exam results. Thus, at that time, my ambitions for the future did not include music as a singular profession. These things and the city of *Colón* were my joy.

I still set up my performances in a small puppet theatre whose only audience was my sister, and in which Don Quixote and his adventures took first place.

MANUEL DE FALLA
Letter to Roland Manuel

PAGES OF THE CHILDHOOD MAGAZINES WHICH HE MADE IN 1889 AND 1891. THEY ARE HAND-MADE MAGAZINES WHICH DESCRIBE STORIES ABOUT AN IMAGINARY STAFF OF COLLABORATORS.

In Don Salvador Viniegra's musical salon

FROM THE age of ten onwards I often attended, with my parents, Señor Viniegra's musical evenings; where chamber music was mainly played. It was there that I received my first initiation into classical music, but to no immediate avail. My definitive vocation truly awoke during the symphonic concerts at the Cadiz museum.

MANUEL DE FALLA
Letter to Roland Manuel

WE LIVED, then, at number 4 in the Plaza de la Candelaria and its beautiful drawing room became a concert hall. I still remember it, even though many years have gone by; those first impressions of life are not easily forgotten. At one end, there was a big grand piano; in the centre, a magnificent Erard harp and, on the left, a harmonium; it was ideally decorated, and from its walls hung paintings which came from the house of the marquises of Ureña, ancestors of our family. The sofa, the armchairs and chairs were black wood with red upholstery.

There, in that drawing room, Manuel played the piano for the first time in front of a select audience, which was the kind that came to the concerts held in our house. He never forgot that, his first performances.

J. J. VINIEGRA

RECOMMENDATIONS FROM HIS SPIRITUAL
GUIDE, FATHER FEDRIANI.

YOU SHALL devote the days of the week to the following purposes:

Sunday to the Holy Trinity.
Monday to the Blessed Sacrament.
Tuesday to the Holy Virgin.
Wednesday to Saint Joseph.
Thursday to all the Angels and Saints.
Friday to the Lord's Passion.
Saturday to the Holy Virgin.

All the works of charity and religion and all your good acts will be dedicated in penance for your sins and in demonstration of your love of God and his Holy Mother, and they will be dedicated too to the well-being of the members of your family and friends, devoting one or more days of the week for each one or to various people, and when you wish to receive some benefaction from the Lord, you will dedicate one or various days of the week towards this purpose according to the instructions of your Spiritual Guide who Blesses you.

The 8th of December, 1892.

MOMENTO OF HIS FIRST CONFESSION.

WITH HIS PARENTS AND HIS BROTHER GERMÁN.

FROM this time, at the age of seventeen, something of a conviction both frightening and profound, drove me to drop everything to devote myself definitively to the study of composition. That calling was so strong that it even made me feel afraid, because the ambitions it filled me with were well beyond what I believed myself capable of achieving. I do not mean from a purely technical point of view, as I knew that with time and effort that could be attained by anyone slightly gifted; but in terms of INSPIRATION, in the truest and noblest sense of the word; that mysterious force without which –as we all know so well– it is impossible to realise anything truly useful. I felt I did not have it. So, had it not been for the great support of my religious convictions, I would never have had the courage to follow such a foreboding path. Nevertheless, curiously, in my first calling [literature], fear was completely absent, no doubt because it was simply a childish whim. In truth, unfounded fear has never played a dominant part in my personality.

MANUEL DE FALLA
Letter to Roland Manuel

DURING THE last years of the century a young man from Cadiz resided for short periods in Madrid in order to work at the piano with José Tragó, a fellow pupil of Albéniz in the classes given by old Compta, who later gained first prize at the Paris Conservatory, from where he returned to become professor at the Madrid Conservatory, after a brilliant soloist career which he postponed for the pedagogical profession. The young man from Cadiz, just turned twenty, was called simply Manuel Falla, but later he called himself Manuel de Falla, which was his real name.

ADOLFO SALAZAR

AS WELL as my studies of harmony and counterpoint which I later continued by myself, I would analyse with avid curiosity every musical piece that really interested me because of a certain secret affinity with its aims. Its execution, however, I thought practically impossible.

MANUEL DE FALLA
Letter to Roland Manuel

OUR FRIEND Falla set (as you have undoubtedly heard) a very high standard in the last end of term exams and competitions. He is a very studious and conscientious boy, with a good artistic nature, for whom a gratifying future surely awaits in our difficult art.

JOSÉ TRAGÓ
Letter to Salvador Viniegra
[Madrid, 17 December 1899]

JOSÉ TRAGÓ, HIS FIRST TEACHER IN MADRID: "TO MY ADMIRABLE PUPIL DON MANUEL MARÍA DE FALLA, WINNER OF THE 1905 ORTIZ Y CUSSÓ COMPETITION, AS A TOKEN OF MY TRUE AFFECTION AND ADMIRATION. JOSÉ TRAGÓ. MADRID, MAY, 1905"; AND THE CERTIFICATE OF STUDIES UNDERTAKEN AT THE MADRID CONSERVATORY OF MUSIC AND DECLAMATION.

ABOUT 1895.

MANUEL FALLA.

En las *Actualidades* publicadas el 29 de Marzo último en el DIARIO DE CÁDIZ, se hizo un cumplido elogio de un joven pianista y compositor, que fué la admiración de cuantos lo oyeron en una velada musical, á la cual concurrieron distinguidos artistas y notables aficionados.

Por causa que desconocemos, se reservó el nombre del joven artista. Hoy que está próximo á marchar á Madrid, y no puede darse á conocer públicamente en Cádiz, como se indicaba en aquél suelto, al menos por ahora, nos creemos obligados á descifrar el enigma y decir, *que el genio musical que está en la aurora de no lejanos triunfos, es, Manuel Falla, hijo de Cádiz*, discípulo de Odero y de Tragó: su escuela de piano es correctísima y hace honor á sus notables maestros; pero hay en él personalidad propia que recuerda á Pianté más que á Rubinstein.

Ejecuta los pasos más difíciles sin esfuerzo alguno, y con la misma aparente naturalidad que los fáciles; pero lo mismo en unos que en otros, demuestra verdadero sentimiento artístico y delicadeza exquisita.

Sorprende oírlo buscar á primera vista obras llenas de dificultades, pero no sorprende menos en la música de conjunto, ó cuando acompaña á concertistas. En estos casos su estudio ya, es, no sobreponerse á los demás, antes al contrario, y seguro estamos que el concertista á quien Falla acompañe alguna vez, no lo olvidará, porque no es fácil encontrar artistas que se despojen de su propia personalidad cuando acompañan á otros.

Tal es el pianista.

En cuanto al compositor, en pocos renglones lo presenta de relieve el discreto redactor del suelto á que se alude.

Cuanto íbamos escuchando, dice, era inesperado. ¡Qué frescura en la preparación del tema; qué gusto en su forma; cuánta gallardía en su desarrollo; cuánta originalidad en las modulaciones y cuánta pureza de estilo y ejecución!

Es la verdad.

En las pocas composiciones que de él conocemos, lo que más descuella es la espontaneidad.

Ha escrito una "Melodía" para un principiante de violoncello; no sale de la primera posición, pero tan inspirada, tan espontánea es, que ha tratado de cambiar el tono en que está escrita ó introducir en ella algunas dificultades de ejecución, y no ha podido conseguirlo sin desvirtuarla por completo: tal cual la concibió es, y no puede dejar de ser; y lo mismo la toca y goza con ella el principiante que el concertista. *Esto solo es dado al genio.*

En época remota anticipábamos que Hierro llegaría á ser en España el segundo Sarasate, y que Jerónimo Jiménez, apesar de la guerra sistemática que se le hizo, se abriría camino y ocuparía lugar distinguido en la esfera del Arte. No nos equivocamos entonces.

Continúe Falla por el camino que para gloria suya ha emprendido, no se engría con los triunfos que hoy alcanza; estudie, hágase dueño de los secretos del Arte, y no creemos equivocarnos hoy, como no nos equivocamos ayer, al asegurar que Falla no solamente llegará á ser un pianista eminente, sino que tiene genio y talento sobrados, para figurar entre los buenos compositores contemporáneos.

V.

ARTICLE FOR THE NEWSPAPER *EL DIARIO DE CÁDIZ* REVEALING THE PERSONALITY OF A YOUNG PIANIST FROM CADIZ, WHO TOOK PART IN A CONCERT, AND PRAISING HIS MANY TALENTS: HIS SELECTION OF VERY DIFFICULT PIECES PLAYED EFFORLESSLY WITH GREAT DELICACY; HIS DISCRETION WHILE ACCOMPANYING OTHER ARTISTS; THE SPONTANEITY OF HIS COMPOSITIONS WHICH, WITHOUT A SHADOW OF A DOUBT, WILL MAKE HIM STAND OUT AMONG THE BEST MODERN COMPOSERS.

PROGRAMMES OF HIS FIRST CONCERTS AND, *ABOVE,* NEWSPAPER CUTTING FROM *EL DIARIO DE CÁDIZ* SUMMARIZING *CANTO V* OF THE POEM *MIREYA* BY FEDERICO MISTRAL ON WHICH FALLA BASED ONE OF HIS FIRST COMPOSITIONS

Concierto Falla 10-9-1899

Esta noche, como está anunciado, se verificará en el Teatro Cómico el concierto de aquel afamado pianista y compositor gaditano.

El interesante programa del mismo ya lo dimos á conocer ayer, si bien hay que hacer alguna alteración.

Por una mala inteligencia apareció incluido en dicho programa el nombre del Sr. Gallego, siendo así que este señor, según se nos manifiesta, aunque sintiéndolo, no ha podido aceptar el número que en dicho programa se le destinaba.

Tenemos noticias muy favorables de la aceptación de los billetes que se han enviado á domicilio y se nos ruega por los señores que patrocinan con sus firmas la velada artística, recomendamos á las familias que por lutos ú otras circunstancias no pudieran asistir, que devuelvan los billetes hoy mismo con antelación á la hora de comenzar el concierto, al despacho del Teatro Cómico, para ponerlos á la venta.

Para poder saborear con mayor gusto el *quinteto* que figura en la segunda parte del programa, damos á continuación una idea del Poema provenzal Mireya, de Federico Mistral (Canto V.), en que está inspirada la composición musical del Sr. Falla.

Elzear, después de haber herido traidoramente á su rival Vicente, que le disputaba el amor de Mireya, llega á las orillas del Ródano, *"que dormita en su lecho descubierto rielando en sus aguas tranquilas el resplandor de la luna."*

Salta en la barca en la que bogan tres remeros fantásticos, atando su yegua por el cabestro á los estrovos de la barca.

Los grandes peces de lucientes escamas, dejando las profundas grutas, saltan en torno de la proa y remueven el agua calmosa. La barca comienza á hacer agua y el piloto exclama: Es la noche de San Mednardo; ved los míseros ahogados cómo salen de las profundidades del río formando larga procesión. *¡Pobres almas llorosas! Vedlos allá, cómo suben destilando de su revuelta cabellera gruesas gotas de agua turbia.* Ya hacen oscilar la barquilla *con sus piernas contraídas y sus brazos lívidos como lo haría una tempestad. Piloto,* dice Elzear presa de indecible temor, *la barca hace agua. Ahí tienes el achicador, le contesta tranquilamente el Piloto.* Y Elzear trabaja sin descanso, hasta que ya extenuado vuelve á decir: Piloto, el agua llega al último tablón. ¿Salvareis la barca?

No, contesta fríamente el piloto y la barca se hunde con Elzear en las aguas del Ródano, al mismo tiempo que se destaca en la obscuridad un largo rayo de luz, por el que suben los tres remeros, y que sale de *las pálidas y temblorosas lámparas de los muertos del río.*

Aquella noche los duendes y las brujas del Rodano bailaron sobre el puente de Trinquetalla.

2
MADRID
1900-1907

FIRST WORKS. THE *ZARZUELA*. FELIPE PEDRELL. *LA VIDA BREVE*, PRIZE-WINNER. THE ORTIZ Y CUSSÓ PIANO PRIZE. ROMANCE WITH MARÍA PRIETO LEDESMA.

18. - MADRID
Calle de Sevilla y Banco Hispano

C H R O N O L O G Y

1900-1902. ■ HE SETTLED IN MADRID WHERE HE MET AMADEO VIVES, WITH WHOM HE COLLABORATED ON SOME SHORT COMPOSITIONS FOR *ZARZUELAS*, AND JOAQUÍN TURINA. ■ HE WROTE SHORT CHAMBER PIECES, CONTINUED HIS STUDIES WITH TRAGÓ AND GAVE PRIVATE PIANO CLASSES TO SUPPORT HIMSELF AND TO SEND FINANCIAL HELP TO HIS FAMILY AS THEIR BUSINESS WAS ON THE VERGE OF BANKRUPTCY. ■ FREQUENT TRIPS TO CADIZ WHERE HE GAVE CONCERTS AND PRESENTED HIS FIRST WORKS. IN APRIL 1900 HE COMPOSED *SONG FOR PIANO*, AND THE FOLLOWING MONTH, THE MADRID ATENEO PRESENTED THE PREMIÈRE OF *LA SERENATA ANDALUZA* AND *VALS CAPRICHO*, FOR THE SAME INSTRUMENT. HE ALSO WORKED ON TWO SONGS WITH TEXTS BY G. A. BÉCQUER AND ON ANOTHER TO A POEM BY ANTONIO TRUEBA. IN 1901 HE COMPOSED *CORTEJO DE GNOMO* AND A *SERENADE* FOR PIANO, AND OTHER PIECES ABOUT WHICH THERE IS NO DEFINITIVE INFORMATION. ■ SOON AFTER HE TRIED HIS LUCK IN THE TERRAIN OF *ZARZUELA* AND WROTE *LA CASA DE TÓCAME ROQUE*, *LIMOSNA DE AMOR*, AND OTHERS WHICH WERE NOT PRESENTED. THE ONLY ONE TO REACH THE STAGE WAS *THE LOVES OF INÉS*, PERFORMED WITH SOME SUCCESS AT MADRID'S TEATRO CÓMICO, IN 1902. ■ IN THIS YEAR HE BEGAN HIS STUDIES WITH FELIPE PEDRELL, WHICH WERE SPONSORED BY A FRIEND IN CADIZ UNTIL 1904, THE YEAR THAT PEDRELL WENT BACK TO BARCELONA.

1903. ■ HE COMPOSED *ALLEGRO DE CONCIERTO*, WHICH HE PRESENTED AT A COMPETITION FOR PIANO COMPOSITIONS HELD AT THE CONSERVATORY, THE PRIZE WAS AWARDED TO ENRIQUE GRANADOS. ■ FALLA'S SONG TO A POEM BY CRISTÓBAL DE CASTRO, *TUS OJILLOS NEGROS*, AND HIS *NOCTURNE* WERE PUBLISHED IN MADRID.

1904. ■ HE COMPOSED *CANTARES DE NOCHEBUENA*. ■ IN JULY THE SAN FERNANDO ACADEMY OF FINE ARTS HELD A COMPETITION TO GIVE AN AWARD TO SPANISH OPERA. FALLA WORKED INTENSIVELY IN COLLABORATION WITH CARLOS FERNÁNDEZ SHAW AND FINISHED *LA VIDA BREVE*, WHICH HE ENTERED IN THE COMPETITION.

1905. ■ ON THE 31 OF MARCH THE ACADEMY OF FINE ARTS AWARDED FIRST PRIZE TO *LA VIDA BREVE*. IN APRIL HE WON THE ORTIZ Y CUSSÓ PRIZE. ■ A DIFFICULT ROMANCE WITH HIS COUSIN MARÍA PRIETO LEDESMA.

1906-1907. ■ HE GAVE A SERIES OF CONCERTS AND BEGAN TO FEEL DISAPPOINTED BECAUSE OF THE IMPOSSIBILITY OF SHOWING HIS PRIZE-WINNING OPERA. ■ FIRST DISILLUSION WITH MADRID. HE APPLIED FOR OFFICIAL AID TO STUDY IN FRANCE AND THIS WAS REJECTED. ■ HE WAS OFFERED THE OPPORTUNITY TO GIVE A SERIES OF CONCERTS THERE AND DECIDED TO GO. HIS FRIEND JOAQUÍN TURINA, ALREADY LIVING IN PARIS, ENCOURAGED HIM IN THIS DECISION.

MY DEAR FRIEND:

For some time now I have wished to write to you to thank you for your kindness, and to send you, as I do today, my two published piano compositions. However, I have been exceedingly busy, firstly, with the première at the *Cómico* and secondly, preparing another piece. So, until today, I have not had the pleasure of doing so. If I tell you that the *fiestas* at this time of year have passed me by almost unnoticed, you will be able to imagine the work I have had and still have, because at the beginning of next week is the debut of the *Zarzuela* which I spoke to you about earlier, whose libretto is by Jackson. Let us see how that turns out.

Moreover, I am preparing a concert which I want to give here this summer, and which I would like to give in better conditions than the ones before in terms of venue; but to that end I will need the help of the City Council, and if possible for them to include it in the programme of festivities in August, for which I would be very grateful to you should you deem it opportune to say something about it in *Actualidad*.

There is no lack of good music here at the moment, and at the *Lírico* they are presenting the operas they had prepared, though the audience does not respond as it should to these works, and I do not think they will be able to give all the performances announced, which means, unfortunately, that national opera will continue to be a pipedream in Spain.

I do not need to remind you that if there is any way that I can avail myself to you here I should have great pleasure in doing so, because, please believe me, I am very grateful for your many favours, and I hope that you will ask whatever you wish of your affectionate and true friend.

MANUEL DE FALLA
Letter to José J. Rodríguez y Fernández
[Madrid, 22 May 1902]

COVERS OF THE FIRST EDITIONS OF FALLA'S WORKS WHICH COULD BE SEEN IN SHOP WINDOWS IN CADIZ IN 1903.

UNTIL 1904 I wrote dramatic music, for chamber instruments, piano, diverse instruments, voices, etc...

What I published before 1904 has no value whatsoever. It is all nonsense, some of it was written when I was 17 to 20 years old, though published later. A *Nocturne*, for instance, which I wrote when no more than a child. When I showed it, a long time after, to a publisher in Madrid, I thought they might be interested and publish it, and that was all... It might be possible to find things of more interest among the things which have remained unpublished; but among the published works there is nothing, nothing...

MANUEL DE FALLA

COVER OF *MAZURKA, IN C MINOR* FOR PIANO, 1899.

Amadeo Vives and the *Zarzuela*

AMADEO VIVES

DEAR FAYA [*sic*]: I would be infinitely grateful if you would be kind enough, simply for tonight no more, to study piano with the damper pedal, because I have to finish a prelude for the rehearsal tomorrow. I won't bother you ever again; just today, no more, because of the urgency of the work that I have to do. Forgive my boldness and I will be eternally grateful, your good friend and companion.

AMADEO VIVES
Letter to Manuel de Falla

COVER OF THE COLLECTION OF
"ORIENTAL SONGS".

DEAR FAYA [*sic*]: Yesterday I had to speak to Berges about another affair and, in passing, I asked him about ours [*El corneta de órdenes*] and he told me that he has a piece by Dicenta and Chapí he is going to put on stage directly; another by a lady, which will come after, and another, by Villa, and that the season lasts only until Epiphany. He even doubts that he will be able to present all the works he has engaged. In view of this I consider our efforts are in vain and that we can save ourselves the trouble of visiting him today. Do you not agree? Know that I am your true friend.

AMADEO VIVES
Letter to Manuel de Falla, 1904

FRONT ENTRANCE OF CALLE
SERRANO 70, FIRST DWELLING IN
MADRID, WHERE HE COMPOSED
LA VIDA BREVE.

DEAR FRIEND Vives:

   As the collection of oriental songs is of the utmost importance to me, I beg you to ask Benavente for them and next Tuesday, at about one, I will come to collect them at your house, as on the same day I have a class next door, so you need not send me them.

   Your ever affectionate and good friend.

MANUEL DE FALLA
Letter to Amadeo Vives
[Madrid, 4 April 1904]

MY DEAREST child: I arrivcd safcly and only hopc that you are having a good time and are being very careful with the motorcars and of the many other things to look out for in that wicked Madrid, which you are so fond of and I so little. But in short, you like it and thus should take this opportunity to enjoy it.

Address yourself to the Lord and the Holy Virgin and remember me well and receive the best wishes and blessing of your Father.

FATHER FEDRIANI
Letter to Manuel de Falla

ABOUT 1904.

DEAR FALLA:

I had a pleasent conversation with Señor Arregui, owner of the work that I planned to base a *zarzuela* on and give to you to compose its music. He answered that he had no reservations as to my arranging it, but said that the music must be set by a well-known composer. As you understand, I can not change this.

If I did not have to write *six librettos* in March when we leave for Mexico, I could try to find a spare moment to write you a book, but under the present circumstances it is impossible for me to do so and I shall not deceive you with promises that I cannot keep.

I believe that you will not doubt that I have tried to serve you by looking for something to use, but *this something* cannot disagree with the author of the work.

I will recommend you to my friends to see if one of them can give you a book. When October comes and I return from my expedition I shall write you a book, as I wish, and promised to do.

At the moment with the rehearsals and arrangements for *La Cariñosa* I do not have a free moment and consequently will not be able to see you to give you this explanation.

Have a little patience and in the meantime start some light work on polkas, waltzes, etc., which we can use later.

I repeat that I am not to blame for what has happened and I give you my word, once again, that I will give you a book as soon as is humanly possible.

JOSÉ JACKSON
Letter to Manuel de Falla
[Madrid, 4 December 1901]

COVER OF *LA CHAVALA*, A *ZARZUELA* BY MAESTRO CHAPÍ.

THE SCORE OF *THE LOVES OF INÉS*, THE ONLY *ZARZUELA* BY FALLA TO BE PERFORMED.

I REFER to our so-called *"great" zarzuela*, which, as anyone can easily confirm, is nothing but a copy of Italian opera in vogue at the time these works were produced. In a certain sense it was natural as the dramatic elements used to create comic operas or *zarzuelas* could not possibly have a national character, the great majority of them being simple adaptations of foreign works.

Barbieri with his desire to "hispanize" our music, broke with that precedent, and *El barberillo de Lavapiés* and *Pan y toros* are the illustrious proof of his noble enterprise. But even in these works of a sincerely national nature, the musical techniques used rarely escaped the customary Italian influence.

MANUEL DE FALLA

WHEN he [Falla] was last in Madrid he told me that he came full of a real desire to work. He also showed me the ideas contained in his compositional work and in his decision to set out to write something for the theatre. I could do no more than applaud him, as this is the only way for a musician in Spain to ensure a secure material future.

JOSÉ TRAGÓ
Letter to Salvador Viniegra
[Madrid, 17 December 1899]

WHEN I DID *zarzuela*,
something which went against
my sensibility, it was not just to
gain material benefits, but
rather to enable myself to study
and work in Paris. Not to make
myself popular in Madrid.

What I would like to make
known is that my music was
good enough for an orchestra.
Back then, before my classes
with Pedrell, I hardly knew
anything about instrumentation.

MANUEL DE FALLA
Letter to Jaime Pahissa

Felipe Pedrell

PEDRELL was a musician in the highest sense of the word, because through his doctrine and his example he showed and opened, for Spanish musicians, the way that would lead them to create a noble and deeply national art, a way which at the beginning of the last century they believe closed forever.

Having said this, I do not intend to deny that some of the works of our 19th century composers (preceding or coinciding with the second great period of Pedrell's output) are worthy of respect and even some admiration in certain cases. They cultivated a musical genre in which they distinguished themselves brilliantly: the *zarzuela*. But this genre was a mixture of Spanish tunes and Italian opera and never went further than being an artistic product for national consumption, when not purely local. On most occasions, both its musical content and its structure had to

MY TEACHER was Don Felipe Pedrell, to who I owe my initiation to a broad, sincere art based on popular songs. I studied with him for two years, receiving his precious council and glimpsing, under his wise and tender tutoring, new and far reaching horizons.

MANUEL DE FALLA

be fatally modest, as they were generally works which were written with inadequate technical preparation and in an incredibly short space of time. Their authors rarely pursued any other artistic goal than their prompt and easy execution and their equally easy understanding by the audience, and when, once in a while (in the so-called great *zarzuela*, in opera and evenin religious music), composers attempted to raise themselves to higher artistic spheres, they fell, apart from a few occasional and famous exceptions, into a puerile travesty of that Italian style which marks the beginning of that great country's period of musical decline.

Within this state of affairs the trilogy *Los Pirineos* and the pamphlet *For Our Music*, by Felipe Pedrell, were published. In them the author convincingly demonstrates that Spanish lyrical drama, and any musical work which aspires to be universal art, must take its inspiration from both the deep and varied Spanish tradition and from the admirable legacy which we have inherited from our 16th, 17th and 18th century composers.

Nine years after the appearance of *Los Pirineos* and during his prolonged residence in Madrid, Pedrell composed *La Celestina* and *El Conde Arnau*, which along with *Cancionero Popular Español* form the rich heritage which the Maestro left us and which resumed our interrupted musical history.

The period in which he composed the second and the third of the works mentioned, marks one of those decisive moments in my life, because it was at that time that I was taught by the Maestro.

It seems –sad to say– that some of his old disciples have made it known that they did not find his teachings very fruitful. Perhaps they did not know how to benefit from them or they sought to learn from them what was completely contrary to the Maestro's strong aesthetical convictions; perhaps they came to him without the technical preparation needed by anyone who looks to a great artist for advice; but whatever the reason, in my case I can state that I owe my artistic direction, indispensable for any well-intentioned apprentice, to Pedrell's teachings and the strong effect his works had upon me.

Our Maestro lived a life of hard work. At the time that I am referring to, apart from his constant work as a composer and musicologist, he was the teacher of the History and Aesthetics of Music class at the National Conservatory, and at the Ateneo's School of Advanced Studies he continued to give courses about "Spanish popular song". Extremely interesting and educative, these courses were preceded by others no less memorable in which our religious and profane musical riches were studied by the Maestro with his unique blend of devotion and conviction. Pedrell loved his art with a passion which has rarely been equalled. "A work of art", he used to say," is engendered by love: love of God, of our country and our fellow men."

I imagine him in his work place in Madrid (an entresol apartment on calle de San Quintín, opposite the gardens of the Plaza de Oriente), touched by children's singing in a ring which wafts in from the adjacent garden, or engaged in friendly conversation with a blind singer of old Romances or with a Galician bagpipe and drum player.

And with what joy he informed us of the discovery of one of those old manuscripts that revealed the eternal character of our art, and how his eyes shone as he explained those qualities, tracing with his finger the curves of a musical line ideally sketched in space!

Manuel de Falla

La vida breve

[SEE *COMPOSITIONS*, APPENDIX I, PAGE 57]

CARLOS FERNÁNDEZ-SHAW, AUTHOR OF
THE LIBRETTO OF *LA VIDA BREVE*. "TO
DON MANUEL DE FALLA A TOKEN OF MY
SINCERE ESTEEM FOR THE FRIEND AND

EDITION OF *LA VIDA BREVE*, PARIS, 1913.

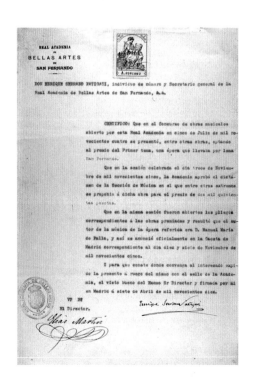

COMPETITION NOTICE, 1904, AND THE
JURY'S DECISION, 1905.

Premio Ortiz y Cusso

27-4-1905

EL GADITANO FALLA

Ocupándose en *La Época* el competente crítico Sr. Roda de esos actos, escribe entre otras cosas lo que á continuación copiamos:

«Hasta el día en que terminaron los ejercicios entre los aspirantes al piano gran sola de la casa Ortiz y Cussó, era indiscutible el triunfo del joven pianista catalán Francisco Marshall. Pero ayer actuó el último número de la lista, Manuel María de Falla, y su ejercicio fué de tal calidad, que el Tribunal lo propuso para el premio, agregando al fallo unas cuantas menciones, en las que luego me ocuparé.

....

Marshall es todo un artista. Mecanismo, desenvoltura, fuerza, expresión, todo lo reune. No le oí; pero he hablado con él sobre el arte de interpretar, sobre el sentido poético de las obras, y sus convicciones son las de un artista, las del que tiene ya un criterio y una orientación fija. Ha estudiado con Granados, con Bauer y con Rišler, y no ha desperdiciado el tiempo. Su éxito mayor lo obtuvo aquí en las obras de Chopin, de Schumann, de Scarlatti y en la *Campanella*, que tocó de un modo maravilloso.

Manuel Falla actuó ayer. Su arte es completamente interior, sin concesiones al efecto, sin exterioridades deslumbradoras, sin la brillantez y la fuerza que tan fácilmente conquistan al auditorio. Ni llega al pianísimo esfumado, ni trata siquiera de abordar el fortísimo de sonoridad poderosa. Sus ejecuciones se mueven siempre en una media tinta; pero en ella, ¡cuánta poesía, cuánta intención, y qué estado de alma tan hermoso y tan penetrante! Bach, Beethoven, Chopin y Schumann desfilaron en sus versiones con un espíritu austero, narrativo y poético. Las de Scarlatti y Saint-Saens fueron inferiores en gracia y finura á las de otros muchos opositores.

Todo lo que procede, exceptuando las primeras líneas, lo tenía escrito antes de conocer el fallo del Tribunal. Para mí era muy interesante problema. ¿Se pronunciarían los jueces, entre dos artistas de igual talla, por el arte más interior, ó preferirían el de más refinamiento?

Mis convicciones artísticas me hacen aplaudir sin reservas el fallo que adjudica el premio al señor Falla, y pido una mención honorífica para el Sr. Marshall al ministro de Fomento, aunque el tal ministerio no tenga nada que ver en un premio que ha establecido un particular por su voluntad propia y libérrima. Pero se menciona al Sr. Marshall, y esto es lo justo.

ARTICLE FROM *EL DIARIO DE CÁDIZ* (27-IV-1905)
COMMENTING ON THE TECHNICAL PROWESS OF CATALAN PIANIST FRANK MARSHALL WHO SEEMED A SURE WINNER OF THE ORTIZ Y CUSSÓ COMPETITION UNTIL FALLA PERFORMED HIS VERSIONS WITH AN AUSTERE, NARRATIVE AND POETIC SPIRIT. HE WAS AWARDED THE PRIZE.

IN 1905 I was awarded the Ortiz y Cussó Prize, by unanimous decision, in the public competition between Spanish pianists organised by the Conservatory, in which there were more than thirty participants and a very demanding programme. As far as my pianistic virtuosity goes, in reality it has never existed, because my assiduousness and patience in "purely musical" studies have at no time been shared by instrumental ones.

MANUEL DE FALLA
Letter to Roland Manuel

CONSERVATORIO
DE
Música y Declamación.
1904 Á 1905

CONCURSO DE PIANO
para la adjudicación del
PREMIO ORTIZ Y CUSSÓ
Día 17 de Abril de 1905 y siguientes.

Invitación personal.
(Permanente.)

PROGRAMME OF THE PIANO COMPETITION FOR THE ORTIZ Y CUSSÓ PRIZE. THE PARTICIPANTS HAD TO INTERPRET WORKS BY BACH, BEETHOVEN, SCARLATTI, CHOPIN, SCHUMANN, SAINT-SAËNS, PAGANINI AND LISZT. THE JURY WAS FORMED BY BRETÓN, TRAGÓ AND PELLICER, AMONG OTHERS. MANUEL DE FALLA WAS AWARDED THE PRIZE ON THE 24TH OF APRIL 1905.

Fran Hung   PRINCIPE 33 MADRID

AT THAT time, Manuel de Falla sported a bushy moustache and wore a bowler hat. He was going through a period of abject poverty. Whenever he could he gave piano lessons for two pesetas an hour, and if the applicant tried to bargain, he reduced his price to six *reales*. His awful situation was somewhat diminished when he won first prize as a pianist in the Ortiz y Cussó competition. The prize consisted of a grand piano.

MARIO VERDAGUER

Father Fedriani councils
Manuel de Falla in affairs of the heart

WHAT YOU are doing is truly ridiculous and inappropriate. If you do not wish to speak to her, because you fear that it is still not the right moment, or whatever, then do not speak. But put an end to this foolishness and childish nonsense of being like this and that. I assure you that if she is not crazy like you (and if she is she is completely unsuitable for you) she will finish by giving you your marching orders.

I absolutely forbid you any kind of apprehensions and similar feelings which can seriously impair your mind. Thus, either you declare your intentions for once and for all, or you leave it for the moment and without bothering yourself with the matter or being with her in this or that way; but rather show her constant affection, etc., and that is that for the time being. Or desist completely.

Seville, 5 April 1905

MY PRECIOUS child. What has happened in this matter was what I expected. That was the reason why I wanted you to find out soon. I think that I told you that one of the reasons (for me the foremost) was to know if she thought or rather felt as you believed, or not; and there had been wishful thinking on your part.

You should continue with her as if nothing has happened. In spite of what has occurred one day you might be able to fulfil your dreams. I should like to know whether she has said anything, as that would help me know her better. It would make me even happier if she has said nothing.

Be very calm, my son, stop that nonsense, you will see that if and when God wants it, it will be, and if it does not happen, it will be for your good, so tranquillity and absolute indifference. Perhaps she plans to return your feelings in the future. But do not speak of this to anyone if they do not mention it first. If they mention it do not deny it but say that it was your former intention, etc., and that you will wait until you have obtained a position and then you will return and if not, God will decide.

MARÍA PRIETO LEDESMA, FATHER
FEDRIANI AND MANUEL DE FALLA.

Cordova, 25 April 1905

MY PRECIOUS child. What can I say, my child, that you knowing all the sincere fondness I feel for you do not already know and understand?

I can tell you that the telegram which I was indeed waiting for (I do not know why) has been the only thing to make me joyful for a moment and has delivered me some consolation in my deeply bitter and sad state of mind. May God reward you, my son!

I await your letter which will arrive tonight, for more details.

You told me in one of your letters that the mother of that person was now all right with you. You attributed this change to various causes which you explained to me. Perhaps it is not any of those which you placed before me. It occurs to me (just an idea) that it might well be because she knew what had happened. It is possible that this opposition to you visiting her house was caused by her belief that you were a strange man and having noticed in her daughter a hint of affection towards you (if this is true) fearing that you would not notice it or would not pay her any attention..., etc. Tell me what you think about this if you have understood me, I believe you have.

14 November 1905

THE THING is eminently practical and important and therefore one must treat it as such. If because of her character or any other circumstance she seeks enigmas like you, that is unfit for you. You can delay your proposal. So too can you do it now... As you wish. But foolishness, deductions, interpretations, suppositions, conjectures, apprehension, and any other of this ridiculous and idiotic sort, no, a thousand times no.

TOMÁS BRETÓN: "TO MANUEL MARÍA FALLA Y
MATHEU HIS FRIEND AND ADMIRER. MADRID.
XI. 1905."

MANUEL DE FALLA INTERPRETED "THE DANCES", BY CLAUDE
DEBUSSY, FOR PIANO, WITH STRING ORCHESTRA CONDUCTED BY
TOMÁS BRETÓN. CONCERT PROGRAMME, TEATRO DE LA COMEDIA,
MADRID, 4 FEBRUARY 1907.

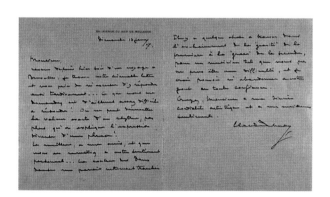

CLAUDE DEBUSSY'S ANSWER TO A LETTER FROM MANUEL DE FALLA ASKING
HIM FOR TECHNICAL ADVICE ON THE EXECUTION OF HIS WORK: "MY DEAR
SIR, I FOUND YOUR KIND LETTER LAST NIGHT ON RETURNING FROM BRUSSELS
AND I BEG YOU TO FORGIVE THE TARDINESS OF MY REPLY... MOREOVER WHAT
YOU ASK ME IS QUITE DIFFICULT TO ANSWER! ONE CANNOT DEMONSTRATE
THE EXACT VALUE OF A RHYTHM JUST AS ONE CANNOT EXPLAIN THE DREAMY
EXPRESSION OF A PHRASE! THE BEST THING, IN MY OPINION, IS TO REFER IT
TO ONE'S OWN FEELINGS... FOR ME, THE COLOUR OF THE TWO DANCES IS
CLEARLY CONTRASTED. YOU MUST FIND SOME WAY OF LINKING THE
"SERIOUSNESS" OF THE FIRST WITH THE "HUMOUR" OF THE SECOND. FOR A
MUSICIAN LIKE YOURSELF IT SHOULD NOT BE DIFFICULT, AND I BELIEVE
THAT I CAN SURRENDER MYSELF TO YOUR JUDGEMENT WITH COMPLETE
CONFIDENCE.
ACCEPT, SIR, MY SINCERE CORDIALITY AND MY BEST WISHES. PARIS,
13 JANUARY 1907."

3
PARIS
1907-1914

PAUL DUKAS. CLAUDE DEBUSSY. ISAAC ALBÉNIZ.
RICARDO VIÑES. MAURICE RAVEL. JOAQUÍN TURINA.
PREMIÈRE OF *LA VIDA BREVE* IN NICE AND PARIS.
MARÍA AND GREGORIO MARTÍNEZ SIERRA. THE
GREAT WAR.

85 — PARIS.   Le Pont d'Arcole et l'Hôtel de Ville.   ND Phot

C H R O N O L O G Y

1907. ■ ARRIVAL AT THE HEIGHT OF SUMMER. DISCONCERTING AND UNCERTAIN WORK PROSPECTS. ■ HE JOINED A DRAMA COMPANY AS ACCOMPANIST AT THE PIANO AND TOURED FRANCE, BELGIUM, GERMANY AND SWITZERLAND. ■ PAUL DUKAS RECEIVED HIM AT HIS HOUSE AND, AFTER HEARING FALLA'S PIANO VERSION OF *LA VIDA BREVE*, DECIDED TO HELP HIM. HE INTRODUCED HIM TO ISAAC ALBÉNIZ. THROUGH THE PIANIST, RICARDO VIÑES, HE ESTABLISHED CONTACT WITH THE FRENCH GROUP OF AVANT-GARDE MUSICIANS: MAURICE RAVEL, ENRIQUE GRANADOS, M. P. CALVOCORESSI, ROLAND MANUEL, JOAQUÍN NIN AND FLORENT SCHMITT. ■ FOLLOWING PAUL DUKAS' ADVICE, FALLA SPENT MANY HOURS STUDYING, TAKING NOTE OF THE RECOMMENDATIONS WHICH, IN EVERY INSTANCE, HIS MAESTRO AND CLAUDE DEBUSSY GAVE HIM.

1908. ■ IN JANUARY HE TOOK PART IN A CONCERT TOUR OF THE NORTH OF SPAIN TOGETHER WITH MIRECKI AND FENÁNDEZ BORDÁS. ■ HE VISITED HIS FAMILY IN MADRID, BUT SOON RETURNED TO PARIS.

1909. ■ ALBÉNIZ MANAGED TO SECURE HIM FINANCIAL AID FROM THE SPANISH ROYAL HOUSE WHICH ENABLE HIM TO WORK ON *FOUR SPANISH PIECES* FOR PIANO. ON THE RECOMMENDATION OF ALBÉNIZ, DEBUSSY AND DUKAS, THE *PIECES* WERE PUBLISHED BY THE PARISIAN FIRM DURAND & FILS AND ON THE 27TH OF MARCH RICARDO VIÑES PLAYED THEM FOR THE FIRST TIME AT THE SALLE ÉRARD IN PARIS. ■ HIS BROTHER GERMÁN SETTLED IN PARIS WITH HIM. ■ HE BEGAN MAKING SKETCHES FOR THE *NOCTURNES* DEDICATED TO VIÑES. ■ ON THE 18TH OF MAY ISAAC ALBÉNIZ DIED.

1910. ■ ON THE 4TH OF MAY FALLA HIMSELF PLAYED THE FIRST PERFORMANCE, AT THE SOCIÉTÉ MUSICALE INDÉPENDANTE, OF HIS *THREE SONGS* BASED ON POEMS BY THÉOPHILE GAUTIER, ACCOMPANIED BY MME. ADINY-MILLIET. THE PUBLISHERS ROUART, LEROLLE & CIE. ISSUED THESE PIECES. ■ HE GAVE SOME CONCERTS OF SPANISH MUSIC IN PARIS AND LE HAVRE, WHERE HE MET G. JEAN-AUBRY. ■ HE CONTINUED WORK ON *NIGHTS IN THE GARDENS OF SPAIN*. ■ HE MET IGNACIO ZULOAGA AND WANDA LANDOWSKA.

1911. ■ HE TRAVELLED TO LONDON AND OTHER EUROPEAN CITIES. HE GAVE A CONCERT AT THE AEOLIAN HALL IN LONDON. ■ CARLOS FERNÁNDEZ SHAW DIED IN MADRID.

1912. ■ HE CONCENTRATED HIS EFFORTS ON THE PRESENTATION IN FRANCE OF *LA VIDA BREVE*, WHICH WAS TRANSLATED INTO FRENCH BY PAUL MILLIET. ■ HE GAVE SOME CONCERTS. ■ HE MET THE MARTÍNEZ SIERRA COUPLE IN PARIS. ■ HE TRAVELLED TO SWITZERLAND AND MILAN. ■ IN NOVEMBER, RICARDO VIÑES PRESENTED *FOUR SPANISH PIECES* AT THE MADRID PHILHARMONIC SOCIETY .

1913. ■ AT LAST, AFTER MUCH HARD WORK, ON THE 1ST OF APRIL THE FRENCH VERSION OF *LA VIDA BREVE* RECEIVED ITS FIRST PERFORMANCE AT THE MUNICIPAL CASINO IN NICE. OWING TO THE GREAT SUCCESS THAT GREETED IT, PREPARATIONS BEGAN FOR ITS DEBUT IN PARIS AT THE COMIC OPERA, WHICH TOOK PLACE ON THE 30TH OF DECEMBER. ■ HE CONTINUED WORK ON *NIGHTS IN THE GARDENS OF SPAIN*. ■ THE PREMIÈRE OF STRAVINSKY'S *THE RITES OF SPRING*.

1914. ■ HE STARTED WORK ON *SEVEN SPANISH POPULAR SONGS*, WHICH HE FINISHED IN THE MIDDLE OF THE YEAR. ■ THE 1ST WORLD WAR BROKE OUT AND HE RETURNED WITH HIS BROTHER GERMÁN TO MADRID.

WITHOUT PARIS, I would have stayed buried in Madrid, interred and forgotten, leading a gloomy life, living miserably off of a few lessons and keeping the prize, like a family momento, in a picture frame, and my opera in a drawer.

MANUEL DE FALLA

DEAR ALL, I barely have time, but I do not want another day to go by without writing.

When I arrived I received the postcard from mamma and Germán, and I am pleased to hear that all is well. I continue in very good health, thank God, and the journey has agreed with me excellently, and I am in much better spirits than last month. You ask me for newspaper cuttings, but I cannot send them as I have not read any. Moreover, my work has been limited to *L'Enfant Prodigue*, in which I have had real success, but it was impossible for me to play concert works because the pianos were awful and on top of this, which is already reason enough, I had no time to practice, so it was a cinema trip. In Martigny there was no orchestra for the overture and I had to play it alone at the piano, with great success, so much so that the applause continued even after the curtain rose.

I have also received personal congratulations at various places. But this *tournée*, like the second series which we began on the 21st or 22nd, cannot be considered anything other than a stepping stone to more important things, and I already have

another truly artistic tour planned for October, from which I hope to earn some thousand five hundred francs or a little more. This is also an affair of Sandrille and will be performed with a singer of Lieders (Schumann, Schubert, Grieg, etc.). It may be a wonderful *tournée*. I need you to send me one of the Franzen portraits, so in my next letter I will send instructions, in case, as I believe, there isn't one at home.

It would be a good idea to take down the diploma and photographs in my room, so that they do not get spoilt by the sun. This morning I have been studying at the Pleyel Concert Hall, where I will continue every day. Mr. Lefetrure, who is one of the bosses at the hall, is very friendly with me. Who would have believed that I would end up studying at the very Pleyel, in Paris? Here we have a much better climate than in Switzerland because, incredibly enough, it is very hot in Geneva. But what a country! Whatever you imagine falls short of the truth. Before I leave I will tell you more about it, but I must finish for today.

I send you all my best wishes. Your son and brother,

MANOLO

Letter from Manuel de Falla to his family

[Paris, 16 August 1907]

SALVADOR VINIEGRA, 1903.

DEDICATION FROM PAUL DUKAS,
AUTHOR OF *THE SORCERER'S
APPRENTICE*, TO MANUEL DE FALLA,
AUTHOR OF *LOVE THE MAGICIAN*. PARIS,
NOVEMBER 1924.

I AM more and more pleased to have decided at last to leave Madrid, because there was no future for me there. The piano and harmonium lessons, that I had there, I am beginning to have here too and better paid (10 francs a lesson). On Monday the 23rd I will make my debut as a conductor in Luxembourg. Let us see how this new phase of my work turns out, because although I have conducted before in rehearsals, it will be the first time in public.

My warm regards to Joaquina and all the rest and to you, Don Salvador, for who I have the sincerest esteem yours truly,

MANUEL DE FALLA
Letter to Salvador Viniegra
Paris, 13 December 1907

My first big satisfaction in Paris, an hour after my arrival, was to visit Dukas. (Debussy was not present at the time.) During that first visit I explained to Dukas the reasons which brought me to Paris: to work and to study in order to familiarise myself with the technical methods of the modern French school, as I found them applicable to my manner of perceiving music. He asked me to let him hear some of my work to see which direction would be best for me: I played him *La vida breve*, and I will never forget the generosity and interest with which he attended my reading. Until then he had been reserved (naturally so, because not only was this the first time that we had spoken, but also I went to see him without even a presentation card); but when he had heard my work everything changed, and his words filled me with such encouragement that, as I told him, I had the impression of waking from a bad dream. He advised me emphatically to take great care not to change my personal feeling for music and to continue working alone, as I did then. He indicated with immense precision the plan that I should follow, placing himself at my disposal for any questions I might have, and prepared to examine all that I continued to write. He introduced me to Albéniz, who welcomed me in a truly magnificent fashion.

[...] Later, when I heard that Debussy was back in Paris, I went to see him, because I had to recite what we could call a litany of gratitude, as I owed him so much for the interest he had taken in my work and for the artistic protection which, like Dukas, he had had the goodness to grant me, and guiding me in my work, like Dukas, getting it published and unceasingly encouraging me to press on with my plans and projects. At the same time I visited Ricardo Viñes, the distinguished Spanish pianist, and through him I met Maurice Ravel, Florent Schmitt, Calvocoressi, etc., and to all of them I have countless reasons to feel grateful.

MANUEL DE FALLA
Letter to Carlos Fernández Shaw
[Paris, 31 May 1910]

Claude Debussy

HE ALSO got to know Debussy personally (he had already corresponded with him). At first, on seeing him, Falla did not recognise him. He had seen some portraits of him with sunken cheeks. The man who stood before him cut a robust figure; he looked like a sailor, as he had actually been.

"C'est moi, c'est moi-même", said Debussy, before Falla's uncertainty, with the customary irony he used when speaking.

In order to say something –like we all do at times, making use of a platitude or a little flattery, to keep the conversation going– Falla said to him:

'I've always liked French music.'

'Well, I haven't', responded Debussy with his cutting irony.

Debussy had already been informed, by Dukas, about Falla and his opera –Dukas had told Debussy: *"Un petit espagnol tout noir* has been to see me". Debussy wanted to hear the opera and Falla played it. And the situation with Dukas and Albéniz was repeated: he had to play the entire piece, to the end. And he received the praise of the eminent French composer.

JAIME PAHISSA

PORTRAIT OF CLAUDE DEBUSSY WITH THE FOLLOWING INSCRIPTION: "FOR MANUEL DE FALLA, EXCELLENT MUSICIAN, TRUE FRIEND, EMMA AND CLAUDE DEBUSSY".

AND FALLA recalled that Debussy, like himself, admired Grieg. And he stated that the Norwegian composer's music had an influence on Debussy, and that at some concerts he had played, alongside his own works, others by Grieg. Falla commented on Debussy's way of playing the piano at the time, a full and sonorous touch. He said to Falla: "I like it to be the piano's hammers that sound; I don't hammer with my fingers." His execution was exact and precise; it did not allow any other interpretation than that written in the original score. And Falla went on to speak about Debussy. He said that what is valuable in his work is not the novelty of its style –Impressionism– but the music in itself, the purely musical ideas. The same applied to the rest of the schools –continued Falla– like the school of musical nationalism: what was worth-while was not contained in the typical, the specific or the new, but in the music.

JAIME PAHISSA

FALLA BY BAGARÍA.

Isaac Albéniz

AROUND the year 1907 I was listening to a concert given by the Parent quartet, at the Aeolian Hall in Paris, when two gentlemen who were speaking Spanish sat down beside me. Naturally, I listened to what they said. For the first time that night Parent and his colleagues played a modernist quartet with horrendous dissonances. "This sounds awful!", exclaimed one of my neighbours. "Well, what do you expect?", the other replied, "these things are fashionable now and I myself am writing a series of pieces in which I use the same method". That was Albéniz, who was referring to his series of pieces entitled *Iberia*.

Nothing more occurred that night, but in October of the same year, and at the concerts in the October Room, held at the Grand Palais, on the Champs Elysées, I played my *Quintet for piano and strings* with the Parent quartet. This quintet was deeply rooted in the studies I had done at the Schola Cantorum, in other words, based on César Franck's forms. At the end of the concert Albéniz introduced himself to me, resolute and friendly. Without more ado he took me and Manuel de Falla by the arms and led us to my Maestro, Vincent d'Indy, who was shouting for all his worth from one end of the room: "The barbarians are here!"

From that moment I struck up a strong friendship with him, which did not last long, because soon after he was taken ill and died. There was nothing more friendly and attractive than Albéniz's house. On one of my first visits there I met another

prominent musician: Paul Dukas, kindly retained in the house after a misfortune in his family. A Catalonian, versed in Andalusian, Albéniz showed off his southern-ness, calling his daughters, with an exaggerated accent, for "fresh drinks", lavishing his attention on his friends and sitting at the piano, not to play, which he was hardly able to do anymore, but to perform a strange version of his *Iberia,* in which his hands, his voice and even his Cuban cigar which, in complicated spirals of

smoke, resembled the garland of notes which decked the pretty melodies of *Triana*, all played a part.

This does not mean that there was any scarcity of good music in Albéniz's small drawing room. Blanca Selva, at the height of her fame, played the *Iberia* pieces at the same rate that they were published. Conscientiously studied, the poor woman really had to slave. Albéniz listened to her all satisfaction and he winked an eye at us as if to say: "Look, look at her work". Gabriel Fauré, as well, attended these gatherings and one could understand the enormous distance which separated those eminent musicians: Fauré, courtly and quintessential composer; Albéniz, vibrant and a plethora of ideas. One night Ángel Barrios appeared there with two other friends from Granada. They came equipped with guitars, lutes and *bandurrias*. They played skilfully pieces from Albéniz's first period: *Cordova, Granada, Prelude.* Albéniz defended his first born with ardour: "Well now, undeniably, these little pieces have got a certain something. I don't reject them, not at all".

JOAQUÍN TURINA

DEAR MAESTRO:

If I were *Uncle Sarvaor* I would say that I am cursed to not be able to work in peace, or even without peace, which is worse, because you should know that for almost a month and a half I have scarcely had a free day in which to take up my pen. First, there were those damned rehearsals for *L'Enfant Prodigue* and company, to prepare the performance which Mlle. Sandrini gave in Luxembourg, where I had to conduct the orchestra, and now the preparation for the concerts in Bilbao and Oviedo, where I will have to play six trios at the end of the month with Mirecki and Bordás.

I am desperate, believe me.

Here I am, after having left Madrid because lessons did not leave me time for anything else, worse off than I was there in this respect and all my hopes of working under your guidance and that of Mr. Dukas have come to nothing. For the time being Bilbao will earn me a few months respite, but then I will have carry on as before, accepting anything which comes my way in order to continue *vegetating*, which is the only thing that this way of life achieves.

Though I still hope that you can obtain something from the Royal Household (that would be my salvation). Have you received an answer from Princess Isabel yet?

Milliet is as excited as ever with *La vida breve*, but told me that it is impossible now to show it this season at the Comic Opera, as they are planning another opera with a Spanish subject, *La Habanera*, by Laparra.

I considered the *Opera House*, but I do not think that it is the right place for it and I imagine you will agree with me. Anxiously awaiting news from you.

Wishing you and your family a very happy 1908. Yours truly, your grateful friend,

MANUEL DE FALLA
Letter to Isaac Albéniz
[Paris, 11 January 1908]

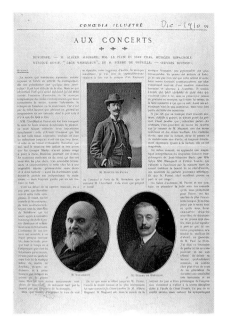

ARTICLE BY M. P. CALVOCORESSI, *COMOEDIA
ILLUSTRÉ*, PARIS, DECEMBER 1910. ONE OF
THE FIRST REFLECTIONS OF FALLA'S SUCCESS
IN THE FRENCH PRESS.

PORTRAIT OF RICARDO VIÑES: "TO MY DEAR FRIEND
MANUEL DE FALLA WITH MY MOST FERVANT
ADMIRATION AND AFFECTIONATE SUPPORT, RICARDO
VIÑES. MADRID, 17 MAY 1915 ".

FAÇADE OF THE FIRM MAX ESCHIG, PARIS,
PUBLISHERS OF FALLA'S FIRST
COMPOSITIONS.

OIL PAINTING BY GEORGES D'ESPAGNAT, 1911. RICARDO
VIÑES AT THE PIANO AND SURROUNDING HIM
MAURICE RAVEL, DÉODAT DE SÈVERAC, ALBERT
ROUSSEL, FLORENT SCHMITT, CYPRIEN GODEBSKI, HIS
SON AND M. P. CALVOCORESSI.

COMPOSITIONS

Appendix I

LA VIDA BREVE

FOUR SPANISH PIECES

THREE SONGS

SEVEN SPANISH POPULAR SONGS

NIGHTS IN THE GARDENS OF SPAIN

Score of the first definitive version of *La vida breve*, act II, first scene, with text in French.

LA VIDA BREVE

LA VIDA BREVE BEGAN TO TAKE FORM IN 1904. ON THE OCCASION OF THE COMPETITION ORGANISED BY THE SAN FERNANDO ROYAL ACADEMY OF FINE ARTS TO AWARD A SPANISH OPERA, FALLA DECIDED TO INTENSIFY HIS WORK WITH THE LIBRETTIST CARLOS FERNÁNDEZ SHAW, BASED ON THE PLOT OF ONE OF HIS POEMS, *"EL CHAVALILLO"*, WHICH FALLA HAD READ SHORTLY BEFORE IN THE MAGAZINE *BLANCO Y NEGRO*.

THE FIRST DATED MANUSCRIPT THAT WE KNOW OF, WITH MUSICAL SKETCHES, DATES FROM THE 24TH OF AUGUST 1904. THE FIRST VERSION OF THE PIECE, IN ONE ACT, WAS PRESENTED TO THE JURY BY FALLA ON THE 31ST OF MARCH 1905 AND THE ACADEMY AWARDED HIM FIRST PRIZE ON THE 13TH OF NOVEMBER THE SAME YEAR.

A FIRST PERFORMANCE IN MADRID WAS DELAYED, WHEREBY FALLA CONTINUED TO WORK ON IT THROUGHOUT HIS RESIDENCE IN PARIS. PAUL DUKAS, CLAUDE DEBUSSY, MAURICE RAVEL AND ISAAC ALBÉNIZ ENCOURAGED HIM IN THE TASK. PAUL MILLIET TOOK CARE OF ITS TRANSLATION INTO FRENCH AND IT WAS PRESENTED AS "A LYRICAL DRAMA IN TWO ACTS AND FOUR SCENES" AT THE MUNICIPAL CASINO IN NICE ON THE 1ST OF APRIL 1913. AFTERWARDS, THE NATIONAL THEATRE OF COMIC OPERA OF PARIS, PREMIÈRED THE PIECE ON THE 30TH OF DECEMBER THE SAME YEAR.

ON FALLA'S RETURN TO MADRID, HE SUCCEEDED IN RAISING THE CURTAIN ON *LA VIDA BREVE*, SUNG IN SPANISH, AT THE TEATRO DE LA ZARZUELA ON THE 14TH OF NOVEMBER 1914.

CARLOS FERNÁNDEZ SHAW, AUTHOR OF THE LIBRETTO, DIED IN MADRID IN 1911 WITHOUT HAVING LIVED TO SEE THE OPERA'S FIRST NIGHT AND ITS SUCCESS.

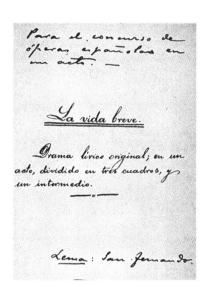

Cover of the libretto of *La vida breve*, presented for the Spanish opera competition by Manuel de Falla and Carlos Fernández Shaw in 1905, under the motto, San Fernando.

HONOURABLE lady and friend: I have the pleasure of informing you that in the middle of next February *La vida breve* will receive its first performance in Nice, represented in magnificent conditions and part of a season which is exceptional in artistic importance, considering that the programme includes such pieces as *Pelléas*, by Debussy, *Ariane*, by Dukas, *Don Giovanni*, by Mozart, etc. The Nice Opera intends, from this year on, to compete with Montecarlo, and thus it is that, as the saying goes, they have thrown the house out through the window.

Naturally, it will be a great pleasure for me to keep you up to date with everything that happens, as well as the other plans which arise regarding the future of *La vida breve*. Much of this we owe to the extraordinary interest with which our adapter, Mr. Paul Milliet, has taken in the affair for some time.

MANUEL DE FALLA
Letter to C. F. Shaw's widow
[Paris, 12 October 1912]

AT LAST the date of the début of *La vida breve* at the Casino in Nice had been decided upon and Falla had to move to the beautiful city on the Côte d'Azur in order to prepare the rehearsals and the performance. He was there three months, lodged in the room reserved for the Casino's director and engaged in revising the pages of the score, with exaggerated care and improved wherever possible every single detail, whereby he sent them to publisher Max Eschig to produce the orchestral material.

As the first day of rehearsal approached, his anxiety and worry about how it would sound increased daily. One must bear in mind that he had never heard any of his pieces played by an orchestra, other than his *zarzuela* which Loreto Prado and Chicote had shown at the Comic in Madrid. Before leaving Paris he had been to visit Debussy and Dukas to consult them about orchestration, as he felt an unconquerable fear due to his inexperience in this branch of composition. In spite of all Dukas' attempts to calm him, Falla refused to be convinced, to the extent that the Maestro had to tell him:

"But, I'm telling you it will sound fine. Do you think I have no practice at reading a score?"

And he gave him a highly beneficial piece of advice: "If the conductor of the orchestra, at some point during the rehearsals, says to you that such and such a passage has to be altered or changed, because he thinks it won't sound good, you only need answer him with this: that they must play it once again, executing 'exactly what is written'; and if it still doesn't sound good, 'they must repeat it once again'; and then let's see if in the end it doesn't sound just as you had imagined."

And sure enough, that is what did happen; on the day of the first rehearsal, in the Casino's attic, the place set aside for preparatory rehearsals, they had barely reached page 10 or 12 of the sheet music when the conductor stopped the orchestra, and said to Falla, who was standing behind him:

"You will have to change this."

To which Falla replied:

"Repeat it exactly as it is written."

And in effect, the second time the passage came out perfectly. From this moment the conductor made no other observations throughout the entire rehearsals. After this small incident, the music was read without any major mishaps. Falla was delighted, hearing the wonderful reality of his imagined sounds. Because it is true —the fact he had heard Debussy claim— that there is no greater pleasure than to hear, for the first time, an orchestra play your work. The orchestral rehearsals were followed, as is customary, by the artists' and group ones. Everyone who took part in the opera was nice to him, and worked on it happily and devotedly. The first night arrived, and *La vida breve* was very well received, and was performed various occasions until the end of the season, which was already ending, as it was April, and, as usual, the high season in the Côte d'Azur is in winter.

JAIME PAHISSA

ESTEEMED SIR and friend:

Taking advantage of the offer which you made me with such kindness in Paris and according to the arrangements we made then, I have the pleasure of writing to you to announce the visit of my brother Germán, who will take some photographs of your suits so that they can be used as models here in Nice. I would also be very thankful for a photograph of your commendable gypsy as we also agreed back then. Rest assured that your name will not appear in any way in the advertisements for the piece. One of the photographs that interests me most is the jacket which they are going to use as a model for the tenor.

A thousand sincere thanks, your affectionate friend and humble servant.

MANUEL DE FALLA
Letter to Ignacio Zuloaga
[Nice, 11 March 1913]

I am at your service in Nice:
Casino Municipal
Chez Monsieur de Farcounet.
The opera's début will be on the 28th of this month, according to their reckoning.

DINSTINGUISHED friend:

Let me begin by expressing my abundant and sincere gratitude.

Last night I received the clothes, which the stage manager is looking after in order to make copies, giving me a detailed receipt for them.

The receipt consisted of:

3 scarves: dyed; red and white, and frothy yellow.

2 complete suits.

1 dressing gown.

A jacket, waistcoat and riding breeches.

A thousand thanks too for you offer to send me the photograph of your gypsy and for the generosity you show with your concern about the success of the piece. Let us see...

MANUEL DE FALLA
Letter to Ignacio Zuloaga
[Nice, 13 March 1913]

THE MATINÉE tomorrow will be the first performance at a party held by *Le Figaro*, the Parisian newspaper, and on the following day, Wednesday evening, the first public performance will take place.

Everything is going well and we have just finished the dress rehearsal. I have no words to express my gratitude for the affection with which the artists, from the first to last have worked on the opera. As far as the orchestra is concerned, anything I say falls short, because they break into applause in the rehearsals as if they were the audience. I thank God who has felt fit to guide me and give me strength to work, because if not, I do not know what I should have done, poor me! For the last month I have hardly slept and sometimes I do not even have time to eat. Lately, even more so, because I have had to orchestrate a new dance to add to the opera in just a week. Most of the work is done at night and most nights I go to bed at about four in the morning, then I have to get up early to begin rehearsing at ten. Nevertheless, I am in good health and feel better than I have done for a long time. I do not understand this. I marvel at it and I do not know how to thank God.

MANUEL DE FALLA
Letter to Leopoldo Matos
[Nice, 31 March 1913]

Programme of the première of *La vida breve*, Casino Municipal, Nice, 1st of April 1913. French version by Paul Milliet. The rôle of Salud was played by the soprano Lillian Grenville.

AT LAST, the first night arrived. Its success was greater than I could have hoped, and even greater at the public première than at the *Figaro* party, which was considerable. Outstanding interpretations. Mlle. Lillian Grenville made an absolutely glorious "Salud". She is going to study her rôle in Spanish now, because I am determined that if *La vida breve* is performed in Madrid it should be sung by her. I beg you not to forget this and that her name should go alongside the work's in the negotiations made to perform it at the Real, which I hope are successful. I would be grateful to know what you think about these arrangements. I think that this is the right moment to start work on it, while at the same time we are going to deal with Paris, where I am going in some twelve days time.

MANUEL DE FALLA
Letter to C. F. Shaw's widow
[Nice, 4 April 1913]

THE PIECE was performed for the first time last week and I am very pleased with the result. The last performance will be on next friday as the season finishes a few days later. In the middle of the month I am going back to Paris and will have the gratification of telling you all the details, personally.

You cannot imagine how useful your clothing consignment proved, and I do not know what we would have done without it. Thanks to your kindness the piece was represented with a faithfulness which the audiences of this country are not accustomed to, and the effect was perfect.

In all respects the interpretation was excellent. Mme. Grenville has made the heroine an unforgettable part.

In short, I will tell you all about it when I go to Paris. Meanwhile, accept a million repeated thanks, your ever faithful friend and sincere admirer.

MANUEL DE FALLA
Letter to Ignacio Zuloaga
[Nice, 6 April 1913]

MY DEAR Maestro, you cannot imagine how much it delights me that you remember me, and that you are interested in hearing about the première of *La vida breve*... By this post I will receive a copy of the opera and some of the newspapers which mention the performance. I believe that there is no need for me to say with what pleasure and deep affection I send them... I always feel a thrill when I remember that first reading of the poem, which our poor friend Fernández Shaw delivered at your house in Madrid, and the encouragement you gave me in the work I was to embark upon.

MANUEL DE FALLA
Letter to Felipe Pedrell
[Madrid, May 1913]

Report about the première of *La vida breve* at the Comic Opera of Paris. *Comœdia*, 31 December 1913.

Poster of *La vida breve*, Paris, Comic Opera, 1914. The part of Salud was played by Marguerite Carré.

Paris National Theatre of Comic Opera.

WHAT CAN I say about the music? That it is worthy of the deep affection I feel for Falla, a modest, ever humble, but remarkable composer. He is part of the musical family which I have watched, with satisfaction, grow up beside me and I will simply state that I have no claim on his talent and mutual affection that I am shown by an honest man and eminent artist who will bring honours to his country, in spite of the fact that Falla is one of those silent artists who neither beg nor demand positions.

FELIPE PEDRELL

Set by M. Bailly for the first act of *La vida breve*, Comic Opera, Paris, 1914.

A moment from the second act of the performance of *La vida breve*, Paris,

THE VICTORY of a Spaniard. The première of *La vida breve*, Paris. Last night, before a select audience, the dress rehearsal of the opera *La vida breve*, in one act, lyrics by the late and much lamented Carlos Fernández Shaw, translation by Paul Milliet, and music by the notable young composer Manuel de Falla, took place at the Comic Opera. The success which greeted *La vida breve* in Paris is more resounding and enthusiastic than that which met it at its première in Nice last spring. It is a great honour, not often granted to foreigners, unless they are among the world's most famous composers, to receive a first night at the Paris Comic Opera. And this honour was justly bestowed upon Falla. Albert Carré, who today retires from the management of the Comic Opera, and who recognised the great artistic merits of *La vida breve* did not wish to leave the theatre of his successes without showing Falla's opera, which he judged to be a work of extraordinary qualities. His wishes were granted. The select audience that attended last night's dress rehearsal of *La vida breve* warmly applauded Manuel de Falla's work, proclaiming the singular talent of the illustrious Spanish composer. The newspapers are full of praise for the score of *La vida breve*.

AMADEO VIVES

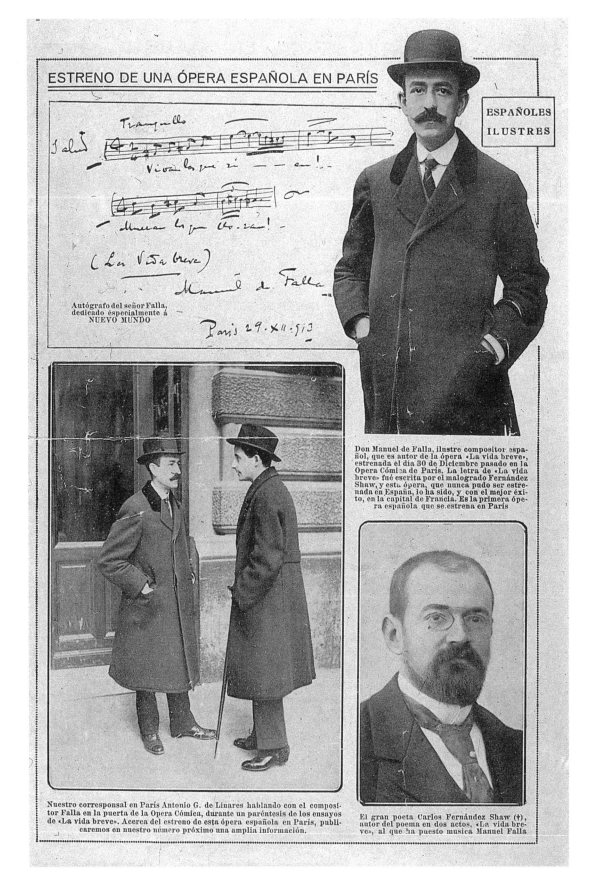

ESTRENO DE UNA ÓPERA ESPAÑOLA EN PARÍS

ESPAÑOLES ILUSTRES

Autógrafo del señor Falla, dedicado especialmente á NUEVO MUNDO

Don Manuel de Falla, ilustre compositor español, que es autor de la ópera «La vida breve», estrenada el dia 30 de Diciembre pasado en la Opera Cómica de París. La letra de «La vida breve» fué escrita por el malogrado Fernández Shaw, y esta ópera, que nunca pudo ser estrenada en España, lo ha sido, y con el mejor éxito, en la capital de Francia. Es la primera ópera española que se estrena en París

Nuestro corresponsal en París Antonio G. de Linares hablando con el compositor Falla en la puerta de la Opera Cómica, durante un paréntesis de los ensayos de «La vida breve». Acerca del estreno de esta ópera española en París, publicaremos en nuestro número próximo una amplia información.

El gran poeta Carlos Fernández Shaw (†), autor del poema en dos actos, «La vida breve», al que ha puesto música Manuel Falla

Article published in the newspaper *Nuevo Mundo* under the title: "première of a Spanish opera in Paris". The top photograph is of Falla. The photograph on the left is of Falla talking with Antonio G. de Linares by the door of the Comic Opera, during a break in rehearsals of *La vida breve*. Below, poet Carlos Fernández Shaw author of the libretto.

Manuel de Falla, autor de la ópera española «La vida breve»

Una escena de «La vida breve», admirable ópera española aplaudida ya en París, y que ha obtenido un éxito clamoroso en el Teatro de la Zarzuela, de Madrid   FOT. DEL RÍO

I HAD FOUR aims in mind while making *La vida breve*.

1. To make a Spanish opera in dramatic form, something which I could find no example of in the entire history of Spanish lyrical theatre.

2. To compose the music from a series of popular songs and dances.

3. To try, above and beyond all else, to evoke the feelings of fear and joy, of hope and torment, of life and death, of exultation and depression, all linked to certain personal images of places, moments, landscapes, etc.

4. To notch up some money in order to carry on working.

MANUEL DE FALLA

THE PLOT: A gypsy, Salud, lives with her Grandfather and aunt in Granada, in the Albaicín district. She has been seduced by Paco, an elegant, fashionable young man. They both swear undying love, but Paco abandons Salud for a rich woman, Carmela, who he is set on marrying. On the day of the wedding, Salud, followed by her family, bursts into the middle of the celebration and reproaching her lover's behaviour falls dead at his feet.

Repercussions in Madrid's press after the first night of *La vida breve* at the Teatro de la Zarzuela in Madrid, 14 November 1914 and two moments from the performance.

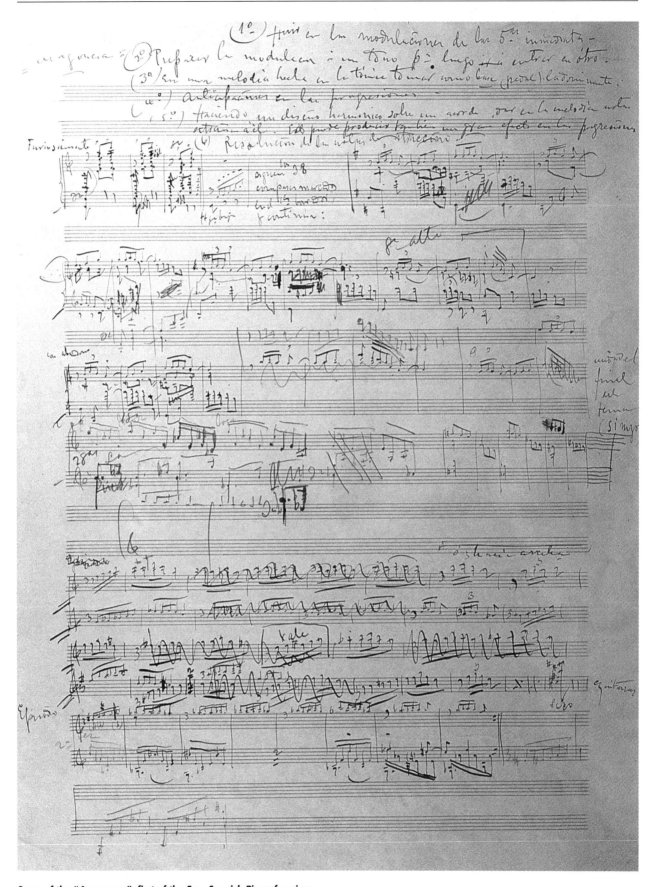

Score of the "Aragonesa", first of the Four Spanish Pieces for piano.

FOUR SPANISH PIECES

THE *FOUR SPANISH PIECES* WERE WRITTEN AND REVISED ALMOST ENTIRELY IN PARIS –THERE ARE PRELIMINARY SKETCHES DATING FROM 1908– AND WERE DEDICATED TO ISAAC ALBÉNIZ. THEY WERE FIRST PERFORMED BY THE PIANIST RICARDO VIÑES AT THE SALLE ÉRARD IN PARIS DURING A CONCERT ORGANISED BY THE SOCIÉTÉ NATIONALE DE MUSIQUE, ON THE 27TH OF MARCH 1909. THEY ARE FOUR PIECES FOR PIANO: "ARAGONESA", "CUBANA", "MONTAÑESA" AND "ANDALUZA". THEY WERE PUBLISHED BY THE PARISIAN FIRM DURAND IN PARIS AT ABOUT THE SAME TIME THEY WERE PERFORMED IN PUBLIC.

Poster of the première of *Four Spanish Pieces*, interpreted by Ricardo Viñes, organised by the Société Nationale de Musique, Salle Érard, Paris.

WHEN FALLA came to Paris he brought with him, well underway, the first, the second and part of the third of the *Four Spanish Pieces* for piano. He finished these in Paris and composed a fourth. He played them to his friends. Then, with enormous surprise, he received a letter from the publisher Durand, which said: "Messers. Dukas, Debussy and Ravel have spoken to us about your *Four Spanish Pieces*, for piano. If you so wish we would gladly publish them". There is no need to describe the impression that news caused. A famous publisher asking for his pieces! It seemed to him that the world was at his feet. He hastened to send them. Durand bought them for 300 francs, and moreover asked him to consider whether he had any other pieces ready for publication. Brimming over with happiness and hopefulness, he went to tell his friends. After listening to him Debussy said:

"So, they've paid you 50 francs more than they gave me for my *Quartet*."

"And the same amount that they gave me for *The Sorcerer's Apprentice*," Dukas said, joining in.

"Well, they didn't give me anything for my composition, *Catalonia*," added Albéniz.

"They didn't even want my *Quartet* given away free," finished Ravel.

JAIME PAHISSA

MY DEAR Sir and friend: I have not replied earlier to your kind postcard firstly because I have been ill and latterly because I have not found the right moment to write with the necessary calm. Today I do so very willingly and begin by thanking you once again and heartily for the kind concern and encouragement you have shown for my work.

To answer your questions about my thoughts on writing *Four Spanish Pieces* I can tell you that, in both these, and La vida breve and in all I write, my main aim is to translate my feelings into musical terms with the greatest possible fidelity, making use of musical methods only as a means of acheiving this end. And therefore, what I have attempted to do in the composition of the *pieces*, is to express musically the impressions that the character and atmosphere of these four very different branches of the Spanish race produce in me.

My idea of music is to be able to speak and paint with it. I am interested in the relation between colours and sounds and often my melodic ideas and harmonic combinations have been suggested by a painting or an old stained glass window. These ideals have led me to consider music as an art of evocation; but I am not trying to tell you that I think I have achieved this. Far from it, as we say in Spain, between words and action there is more than a fraction.

The *Aragonesa* is based on the first two bars of its first movement, from which I borrow elements later on for the second (which I have structured according to popular melodic tradition) the coda and, needless to say, for the piece's thematical development.

The form of the accompaniment is another consequence, and by making it like this I have been inspired (among other reasons of an artistic nature) by the bands of street musicians in Aragon.

The spirit of the coda contains a certain personal statement. In parenthesis, I can say that I hope you hear Viñes play it. What a reading he gave it the other evening at the *Nationale*!

In the *Cubana* everything changes, necessarily so, as I had to attempt to express a completely different character and atmosphere. Let us put it like this as regards popular music: I do not consider that melody, modality and rhythm can express any better than the ornamental formulas of accompaniment, which have as much or practically as much importance (at least as a complement) as those primordial factors.

And I consider all this to be simply the meeting of internal elements which have to be placed at the service of innermost feelings.

The themes of the *Cubana* are based on the *guajira*, the first, and the *zapateo*, the second. Both have a similar rhythm. The formulas of accompaniment are an imitation of folk ones.

And now we reach the *Montañesas*, quite different from the other two. Its themes are a major alteration of two folk ones. I wrote this Piece in Paris after returning from a stay in the north of Spain the previous winter. What an effect the atmosphere and the landscape of that part of my country had on me!... The church bells ringing in the distance, slow and sad songs, dances, and all this with a superb backdrop of imposing snow topped mountains... Truly, there is material there to make not just one piece, but a whole musical world.

As for the *Andaluza*, we have already spoken. Thankyou very much for your answer to my question about the scene of the crime, which is wholly true; but not with pride, rather with artistic integrity I will say that what has happened here is like two portraits of the same person made by different painters, though unfortunately I take second place and am, in many ways, leagues apart from the art of the first... Happily no one has noticed, not even I, until you drew my attention to it. The *Fandangos*, *Polos* and *Malagueñas* are the real materials which have served to make *Andaluza*.

Viñes played this piece as an encore at the *Nationale* concert which I mentioned earlier. Following on from this, he has played it at the *Libre Esthétique*, in Brussels.

Do not forget to notify me in good time of your visit to Paris. It goes without saying that I am at your complete disposition.

My kind regards to Mr. Lambinet. I was very pleased to receive his letter and will soon have the gratification of replying, I remain your sincere and affectionate friend,

MANUEL DE FALLA
Letter to H. Collet
[Paris, 15 April 1909]

Score of "Séguidille", third song of the _Three Songs_.

THREE SONGS

FALLA WORKED IN PARIS ON TEXTS BY THÉOPHILE GAUTIER BETWEEN 1909 AND 1910. THEY WERE THREE SONGS WITH PIANO ACCOMPANIMENT: *"COLOMBES"*, *"CHINOISERIE"* AND *"SÉGUIDILLE"*. THEY WERE PERFORMED FOR THE FIRST TIME IN PARIS AT A CONCERT OF THE SOCIÉTÉ MUSICALE INDÉPENDANTE, ON THE 4TH OF MAY 1910 INTERPRETED BY FALLA, AT THE PIANO, AND SUNG BY ADA ADINY–MILLIET, TO WHOM THE FIRST WAS DEDICATED. THE SECOND SONG WAS DEDICATED TO MME. R. BROOKS AND THE THIRD TO CLAUDE DEBUSSY'S WIFE, EMMA. THEY WERE PUBLISHED BY THE PARISIAN FIRM ROUART, LEROLLE AND CIE.

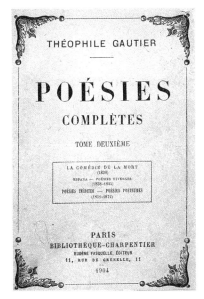 

Cover of the *Poésies complètes* by Théophile Gautier, 1904, and a page of the poem "*Séguidille*", 1843.

IMMEDIATELY after finishing the four Spanish pieces for piano, Falla composed the *Three Songs* for voice and piano, based on poems by Théophile Gautier: *Les colombes*, *Chinoiserie*, and *Séguidille*. The last was, in fact, a simple translation of a poem by Bretón de los Herreros, which retained some Spanish words, as the French were in the habit of doing when they wanted to create a "Spanish flavour". They bore the date 1909. At that time Falla lived on the fourth floor of a small, but very respectable and comfortable hotel in the Rue Belloy. The Guimet Museum of Oriental Art, which contained some Egyptian mummies and wonderful Chinese objects, was situated near his house. It was there that Falla went to savour this atmosphere of Orientalism which he would reflect in *Chinoiserie*. As soon as he had finished the *Three Songs*, he went to show them to Debussy. Debussy liked them and praised them; but, in the case of *Chinoiserie*, he found that the preparation, that is the recited part which precedes the *machine chinoise* —which was how Debussy, with his ever sharp humour, referred to this genre of music— had nothing to do with the real song in his opinion. Falla, feeling bad about having to revise a piece he had considered finished, asked him:

"What can I do?"

"I don't know", replied Debussy. "You should know, 'Look and you will find', as Jesus said."

Falla went home and started to look and to search, until at last he realised that the entire, heavily laden, piano part, which he had written to accompany the spoken introduction, was unnecessary, and he found that by simply cutting the piano part and leaving nothing but the melodic line with a chord to begin and another to lead to the *machine chinoise*, as Debussy called it, he could put it right. This is exactly what he did, and Debussy was very satisfied with the result.

●

FALLA'S *THREE songs* were played for the first time at the second concert held by the *Société Musicale Indépendante* (S. M. I.), of Paris. This society had been founded recently and one of its founders was Falla. It happened in the following way. At the house of the composer Delage —a good musician and, like Roland Manuel, one of Ravel's disciples— some friends gathered, once a week. Some musicians and a poet. Among them were, Florent Schmitt, Viñes, Déo-

dat de Sèverac (before he went to live in Provence), and the abbé Petit, who was so mad for music that when a worthwhile piece was played at the opera he attended the performance hidden at the back of a box. To avoid being seen, he arrived and sat down before anyone else and he left after everyone else had gone. He claimed that his keen enthusiasm had enabled him, by introducing him to artists, to attain some conversions. One day Falla received a letter from Delage which asked him not to miss the meeting that evening at his house —he lived in a small hotel in Auteil— because they had to prepare the audition, for four hands, of a symphonic piece, by Delage, that he had just finished orchestrating. Falla and Ravel had been chosen to play it. Sure enough, that evening the rehearsal took place with Falla and Ravel playing while Delage orchestrated, in pencil, what was lacking on paper. The audition was to be held the next day, before a jury which would select the pieces for the concerts of the *Société Nationale de Musique*, of Paris. Vincent d'Indy was the president of the Society and also presided over the jury, of which Florent Schmitt was also a member. It is worth pointing out that many people have the impression that Vincent d'Indy was Falla's Maestro, but this was never the case.

On the following day, the time arrived (unfavourably so, on one of those disagreeable, cold and wet, Paris mornings) for Ravel and Falla to play the version for four hands of Delage's symphonic poem, *Conté par la mer*, before the jury. D'Indy was a man who was very set in his artistic convictions and uncompromising with anyone else's views. With the score in front of him he noted down his impressions. Florent Schmitt had placed himself behind him in order to see what he wrote. After the audition, the friends met at a nearby café. Not much later Florent Schmitt arrived and told them:

"We haven't got a hope. Over Delage's score D'Indy has written: '*pas de musique, pas d'orchestre, jolis coins*'."

This caused general outrage.

"Things have to change," they all agreed.

And there and then began the process of the foundation of a new society: the *Société Musicale Indépendante*. A great effort was made to do everything better than with the *Nationale*. The concerts were held at the Salle Gaveau. At the first one, with an orchestra, Ravel's *Ma mère l'oie* and Delage's *Conté par la mer*, which made their début, were a huge success.

At the second concert, the aforementioned, Falla's *Three Songs*, based on poems by Gautier, were first performed.

JAIME PAHISSA

Score of "El paño moruno", first of the *Seven Spanish Popular Songs*.

SEVEN SPANISH POPULAR SONGS

THE *SEVEN SPANISH POPULAR SONGS* FOR VOICE AND PIANO WERE COMPOSED BY FALLA AT THE END OF HIS STAY IN PARIS, AFTER THE PREMIÈRES OF *LA VIDA BREVE*. THE SONGS WERE: *"EL PAÑO MORUNO"*, *"SEGUIDILLA MURCIANA"*, *"ASTURIANA"*, *"JOTA"*, *"NANA"*, *"CANCIÓN"* AND *"POLO"*. AND THOUGH THEY WERE FINISHED IN JULY 1914, WITH PLANS FOR THEIR IMMEDIATE PEFORMANCE, THE DÉBUT HAD TO WAIT UNTIL THE 14TH OF JANUARY 1915 AS PART OF THE HOMAGE WHICH THE MADRID ATENEO GAVE JOAQUÍN TURINA AND FALLA, WHO HAD RECENTLY ARRIVED FROM PARIS. THEY WERE SUNG BY LUISA VELA ACCOMPANIED BY FALLA HIMSELF AT THE PIANO.

Aga Lahowska with Falla, Granada, 1933.

Cover of the programme and order of the performance.

Miguel Salvador, Joaquín Turina, Manuel de Falla and Luisa Vela after the homage which the Madrid Ateneo gave the two composers.

ATENEO DE MADRID

Falla y Turina.—La sección de Música del Ateneo de Madrid organizó, con el concurso de la eminente artista doña Luisa Vela, un homenaje dedicado á los ilustres jóvenes compositores D. Manuel Falla y D. Joaquín Turina.

Este homenaje se celebró anoche en la docta Casa. Los nombres de Falla y Turina son ya suficientemente conocidos y reputados en el mundo del Arte: han traspasado las fronteras; y la "élite" musical y el gran público han saboreado sus espléndidas composiciones.

El homenaje celebrado anoche en honor de tales artistas era una deuda del Ateneo, y la ha sabido pagar generosamente. En la Casa de la calle del Prado se hace siempre justicia.

En la primera parte de la interesante velada, el culto presidente de la sección, D. Miguel Salvador, ofreció la fiesta en un bello discurso.

En la segunda parte, el maestro Falla interpretó al piano piezas españolas (aragonesas, cubanas, montañesas, andaluzas), presentadas al editor por Dukas, Debussy y Ravel, y estrenadas por Viñas en la Société Nationale de París. El autor se propuso expresar en ellas el alma de cada una de las regiones indicadas, imitando los ritmos y modalidades, la línea melódica, la ornamentación y cadencia de sus aires. El maestro Turina ejecutó al piano, acompañado por Luisa Vela, una "Rima" de Bécquer.

En la tercera parte, el maestro Falla tocó, cantadas por Luisa Vela, siete canciones populares españolas (primera audición pública), evocando también la región á que pertenecen, el carácter propio de la música y el texto de cada canción popular. Y, por último, Turina interpretó al piano, y por primera vez públicamente, "Recuerdos de mi rincón" (tragedia cómica), "Petenera" y "Rueda de niños".

La velada fué sencillamente deliciosa. Luisa Vela cantó de un modo encantador, y Falla y Turina dejaron oir sus más bellas composiciones, obras maestras de colorismo, de delicadeza, de espiritualidad, de españolismo, de inspiración y de estudio. Exquisitos compositores, nos dieron la expresión viva de sus obras en momentos de imborrable delectación artística. ¡Una gran noche para el Arte español!

El público distinguido é inteligente que llenaba el salón salió encantado y aplaudió calurosamente á los artistas, elogiando á la sección de Música del Ateneo por esta obra de cultura y de homenaje á dos grandes artistas que por todo el mundo llevan muy alto el nombre de la España musical.

D. de V.

A press cutting about the homage in the newspaper *Mañana*, Madrid, 16 January 1915,

Now HIS name takes first place in universal appreciation, undoubtedly the first among 20th century Spanish composers. Even Music Hall singers and artists sing, and receive the sincere and enthusiastic applause of the most common audiences, his *Seven Spanish Popular Songs*, interpreted for the first time in 1915 by Luisa Vela, with her wonderful voice and perfect style, for a Madrid forum, music experts, select and ultra sophisticated, the cream of connoisseurs, who greeted them with clear indifference, with polite scorn and complete incomprehension... Today they are the record maker's most profitable business. The amount their author earned from them altogether in rights over fifteen years would not even have bought him a bottle of champagne.

MARÍA MARTÍNEZ SIERRA

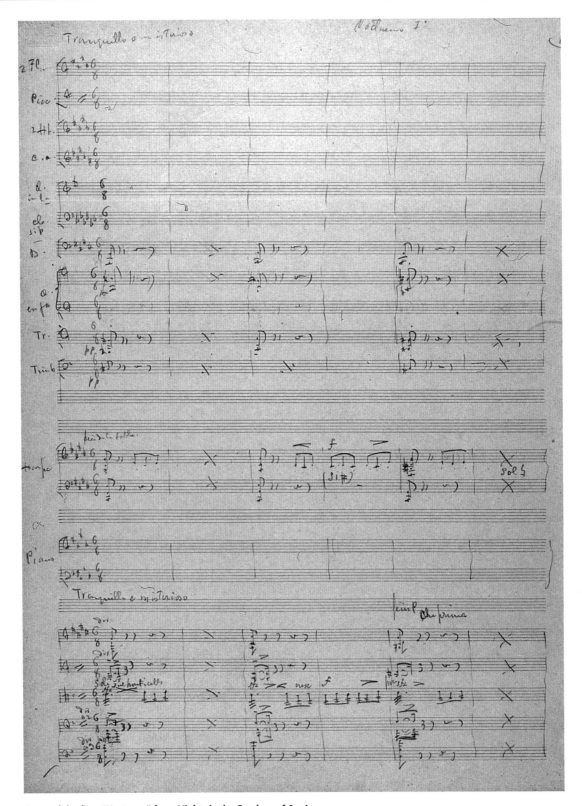

Score of the first "Nocturne" from *Nights in the Gardens of Spain*.

NIGHTS IN THE GARDENS OF SPAIN

FALLA WORKED ON THIS PIECE WITH MANY INTERRUPTIONS, FROM THE YEAR 1909 TO 1916. IT AROSE FROM THE IDEA OF COMPOSING FOUR "NOCTURNES", DEDICATED TO THE PIANIST RICARDO VIÑES, AND INSPIRED BY "THE GARDENS" BY SANTIAGO RUSIÑOL. IN THE YEARS UP TO THE FIRST PERFORMANCE OF *NIGHTS...*, FALLA DEVOTED HIMSELF TO *LA VIDA BREVE*, THE *THREE SONGS*, THE *SEVEN SPANISH SONGS* AND *LOVE THE MAGICIAN*, AS WELL AS WORKING ON A SERIES OF SHORT COLLABORATIONS WITH THE MARTÍNEZ SIERRA COUPLE. THE FINAL PIECE, FOR PIANO AND ORCHESTRA, WAS MADE UP OF THREE NOC-TURNES: *EN EL GENERALIFE*, *DANZA LEJANA* AND *EN LOS JARDINES DE LA SIERRA DE CÓRDOBA*. IT IS PLAYED FOR THE FIRST TIME AT THE TEATRO REAL IN MADRID, ON THE 9TH OF APRIL 1916, BY THE SYMPHONIC ORCHESTRA OF MADRID CONDUCTED BY FERNÁNDEZ ARBÓS AND WITH JOSÉ CUBILES AT THE PIANO.

An Alhambra garden by Santiago Rusiñol.

FALLA REACHED Paris, and his translator Milliet took him to see publisher Max Eschig. He auditioned the work, and the outcome was exactly the opposite of what had happened in Milan [with Ricordi]. Max Eschig asked him for the score and offered him a contract for the publi-cation of *La vida breve* and *Nights in the Gardens of Spain*, which he had begun to compose, and for any-thing else that he might write during the time period which the contract would cover. Falla would receive, in exchange, a monthly wage, fixed and secure, on account from publishing rights. In this way, he could devote him-self to his work with relative calm, leaving aside other activities which occupied his time and energy. And later on he could even turn down offers, like that of a rich and elderly jewish lady, who offered to pay him whatever he wished —as had been the tragic case with Albéniz— to set her librettos to music.

JAIME PAHISSA

Santiago Rusiñol by Ramón Casas.

An Alhambra garden by Santiago Rusiñol, from the book *Jardines*.

ONE DAY, during one of his rambles where he tried, through exercise, to temper his inner troubles, he halt-ed at Rue Richelieu in front of the display in the Spanish Bookshop. There looking out at him from the display —or at least, that is what he imagined— was a book: *Granada (Emotional Guide)* , by Martínez Sierra. He spent the few francs he had with him on the book, and he spent the night reading it. The next morn-ing both he and his inspiration woke up. His forgotten Muse had taken her place once again at the head of his humble bed. The power of creation filled him again. And his mind was agitated by the beguiling melodies, con-fused, insistent and eager to burst into song, of one of his greatest works: *Nights in the Gardens of Spain*.

This Andalusian from Cadiz had never been in Grana-da: he knew neither the Alhambra nor the Generalife, nor its enchanted wood, nor its fountains; and we can-not tell what polite and intellectual sorcery he used to make his own the emotions that others had felt, for no one has expressed like him the murmur of the fountains and the pungent and sensual fragrance of the myrtles. Thus the Muses aided him, enlightened and guided him jointly, to give us ignorant humans lessons in solidarity.

MARÍA MARTÍNEZ SIERRA

WHEN FALLA returned to Spain, the three *Nocturnes*, which he brought with him, were almost finished. After the première of *Love the Magician*, in Madrid, Falla went to Barcelona. He spent two or three months in Catalonia's capital during the season that Martínez Sier-ra's company performed at the Teatro Novedades. It was during that time that we got to know each other. Falla lived in a flat on calle Rosellón, two blocks from my house. Sometimes I went to see him at his flat, and he came to mine as well. During this theatrical season Shakespeare's *Othello*, with some short but beautiful musical sketches by Falla, was performed. I recall one day, in the evening, with my friend Peypoch —who had spoken highly about the music of *Love the Magician* when it was shown by Pastora Imperio in Barcelona and had taken me to hear it— strolling along the *Rambla*, when we met Falla and told him how much we had en-joyed his delicate sketches in *Othello*, like Desdemona's very sensitive and dainty *Willow Song*.

"And the noble and original sound of those trum-pets?" asked my friend.

Falla rapidly claimed authorship:

"The trumpets are mine too" he said.

During this period, in Barcelona and at the pretty beach nearby in Sitges, Falla finished composing the *Noc-turnes*. In Sitges, in that merry fishing town, so bright and clean that even the pavements are whitewashed, Falla lodged at the old Subur Hotel. His room looked out onto a beaming inner-courtyard, with blue-painted walls covered with tiny pieces of mirror that reflected the marvellous sky, where some hens roamed freely and even entered his room. This patio had inspired Rusiñol's painting *El pati blau* (The blue courtyard). The owner of the hotel, who as well as being an excellent cook, was a philosopher, had covered the walls of the lounge with the sayings of renowned Greek and Roman authors. Falla worked in El Cau Ferrat, Santiago Rusiñol's house, full of *objets d'art*, especially iron ones, a true museum which was bequeathed to the people of Sitges. The Cau

The kitchen of Santiago Rusiñol's house, Cau Ferrat, in Sitges, where Falla spent some days finishing *Nights in the Gardens of Spain*.

Programme of the première of *Nights in the Gardens of Spain*, with the participation of the pianist José Cubiles, Teatro Real de Madrid, 9 April 1916.

Ferrat piano was very old and out of tune. He had to call the piano tuner, and when he had finished working, Falla asked him:

"Do you think that the piano will bear it?"

"If you play according to your fancy don't blame me for what might happen," the piano tuner answered.

Thus Falla, with certain reserves about the piano, but surrounded by an ideal environment with old paintings by El Greco, priceless glassware, medieval metalwork, the bluest sea beneath the very balcony of the house, and with blissful peace, was able to put the finishing touches to one of his most superb compositions, *Nights in the Gardens of Spain*.

JAIME PAHISSA

DEAR FRIEND, your letter and your telegram have arrived at the same time. I am truly sorry to hear the news about your health and the difficulties which you have been through. Are you and your daughter completely recovered now? I most certainly hope so.

It is true that Ricardo Viñes will play the *Nocturnes* in Barcelona with the Arbós orchestra in a few days time and he will bring you the material and a score you will recognise, the original written in pencil... I have not had time to make a copy.

I would be *very* grateful if you could send me the material (at least the score) in the diplomatic pouch you suggested. I need it as soon as possible for rehearsals here and... I am very scared of losing it, because the original is the only existing copy...

The Magistrate advances. I hope to finish the music soon.

See you soon!

MANUEL DE FALLA
Letter to Ernest Ansermet
[Madrid, 19 October 1916]

THE *NIGHTS in the Gardens of Spain* was published by Max Eschig. And if Eschig did Falla a favour by publishing his work, we should not forget the favour which Falla did him too. After a charge of suspicion of spying was made against him, Eschig was imprisoned in a concentration camp during the 1914 war. Consequently, his firm closed. At the end of the war, released from the concentration camp, Eschig found himself on the street, minus his firm, without resources, without a thing. Falla gave him all he had, his compositions for publication, and he helped him to rebuild the firm. After this they would become even closer friends. Eschig treated Falla

well, at least for the time being, though later things would change a bit. But his widow has not forgotten, and she had good reasons not to forget, what Falla did for Eschig.

JAIME PAHISSA

THE AUTHOR of these symphonic impressions for piano and orchestra considers that, if his aims have been successful, the simple ennunciation of their titles should be guidance enough for their listeners.

Even though the composer of this piece —as must occur with any work which legitimately aspires to be musical— has followed a strict plan in terms of tonality, rhythm and motifs, a detailed analysis of its purely musical structure might perhaps divert us from the real reasons it was written, which were none other than to evoke places, sensations and feelings.

Let us merely point out that the second and third nocturnes are joined without interruption by a period which scatters the notes beginning the main theme of the *Danza lejana* like distant echos under a melodic tremolo at the violins' upper register, bringing the period to an end with an ascending pattern of octaves on the piano, resolved in the *tutti* which begins the third and final nocturne: *En los jardines de la Sierra de Córdoba*.

The thematic element of this work is based (as is generally the case with this author's compositions, *La vida breve*, *Love the Magician*, etc.) on the rhythms, modalities, cadence and ornamental factors which characterise Andalusian folk songs, but which are rarely used in their original form; and the instrumental work is often marked by certain effects unique to folk instruments.

Bear in mind that the music of these nocturnes does not try to be descriptive, but rather simply expressive, and that something more than the echos of *fiestas* and dances has inspired these musical evocations, in which pain and mystery also play a part.

Programme note of the première

Maurice Ravel

I MET Ravel a few days after my arrival in Paris in the summer of 1907, and that was the beginning of a sincere and heartfelt friendship. The only composition of his that I knew, from my Madrid days, was the *Sonatine*, which had greatly impressed me. For this reason, later, when I was able to carry out my unchanging dream of visiting Paris and getting to know my favourite composers, I wanted to meet Ravel from the very first moment. This was easily arranged, thanks to Ricardo Viñes, brave champion of the artistic currents that had carried me to Paris. He gave me the warmest welcome when I introduced myself to him, attracted by his unusual artistic prestige which, as a fellow Spaniard, gave me such pleasure. I did not realise at that time just how much I would be indebted to his art and noble friendship.

I feel moved when I think of those first times in Paris, where I went to seek my fortune, but found what became an extension of my home country.

But let us return to the day on which I met Ravel for the first time. He and Viñes played a sight reading of *Rhapsodie espagnole* which Ravel had just published in its original version for four hands and which would first be performed at a concert at the Nationale. The *Rhapsodie*, apart from musically confirming my impression of the *Sonatine*, surprised me with its Spanish character. That character, coinciding with my own aims –unlike what Rimsky had done in his *Caprice*– was not attained by simply arranging folk themes, but rather by the liberal use (except for the fair *jota*) of the rhythmic, modal-melodic and ornamental elements of our popular lyrical music. These elements did not alter the composer's idiosyncracies, in spite of his use of a melodic language that differed notably from that employed in the *Sonatine*. Incidentally, the idea of orchestrating the piece, which was rapidly and effectively done in a rough version, came to Ravel when Ricardo Viñes raised doubts about the practical difficulties which certain passages presented for a clean execution with four hands. Thus, that admirable series of transcriptions from piano to orchestra, proof of unsurpassed inventiveness and virtuosity, was unveiled.

However, back then, how was I to account for the composer's subtly authentic Spanishness, knowing, by his own admission, that the only link he had with my country was to have been born near its border? I soon solved the mystery: Ravel's Spain was an ideally felt Spain inherited from his mother. Her cultured conversation, always in fluent Spanish, brought me so much pleasure when, recalling her youth spent in Madrid, she spoke to me of a time prior to mine, but which I found familiar because of the vestiges of customs that remained. Then I understood how fascinated her son must have been since childhood to hear these often repeated memories that were enlivened, undoubtedly, by the strength inherent in and inseparable from any recollection connected with song and dance. This explains both the attraction that Ravel had felt, since childhood, for this frequently dreamt of country and his later predilection for the *habanera* rhythm, the most fashionable of the songs his mother had heard sung in the old days at gatherings in Madrid.

I shall not insist on the delicate sensitivity beating in the 'child prodigy's' melodic expression: a sensitivity which similarly affects the unmistakable accent and inflection of his lyrical declamation. I simply wish to state that whoever has seen him at crucial moments of his life, has no doubt about the emotional capacity of his spirit. I will never forget just how clearly I came to see it the day I had to accompany him across Paris, when his father was gravely ill, nor how, when we reached his house, seeing that all human hope was lost, he begged me with urgency to find our abbé friend (who has sadly also passed away) Petit to attend to the dying man's Christian needs. Only on such occasions did Ravel's reserved and good soul burst out, with the sole, but constant exception of his music, wrought in that inner world which serves as shelter for any spiritually beneficial deed against a disturbing reality.

MANUEL DE FALLA

13/XI. Last night we went to Schola, to Parent's second concert devoted to Franck, in order to hear the famous *quintet* again, which you already know.

As it is impossible for Falla and me to live together because we can't study, he is thinking about moving and, although it is probable that he will go, if I found a place with room and board, I might move.

16/XI. Falla has already moved to his new place, leaving me alone, though the truth is that I was expecting it, because it was completely impossible to study in peace, apart from the fact that we wasted a lot of time on pointless conversations.

20/XI. Last night I had supper at Franck's and I think that next week I will go with Falla, who was also invited yesterday, but did not want to go because he had not shaved.

8/XII. Today, Sunday, after lunch I will go to the Colonne concert with Falla, then to Nin's house.

14/XII. I have not got much news today, because my "Sonata" has been blocked for days. I have spent the week revising and retouching the first movement.

I think I will go to Colonne tomorrow with Falla, as they are going to play Beethoven's *Ninth Symphony*, with choirs.

JOAQUÍN TURINA

PORTRAIT OF JOAQUÍN TURINA: "TO MANUEL DE FALLA FROM HIS OLD FRIEND AND BUDDY WITH GREATEST AFFECTION, JOAQUÍN, 1927."

AFTER FALLA left Turina's hotel he went to live at a nearby boarding house on the Bois de Boulogne Avenue. He took a room on the first floor, at the end of a corridor, which was always dark, day or night. Falla stayed there until the end of summer, when a violinist, who rented the adjoining room, returned from his holidays and he or one of his disciples, played from dawn to dusk. It was impossible to live there. Falla had to move again, and he went to Neuilly. In the meantime, Turina, who had recently married, returned from his summer holidays in Spain and gave up the hotel room where he had lived as a bachelor. Thus, Falla was able to settle once more in that excellent hotel. However, soon after this, a singer arrived and then a child pianist who practised the whole day long. In desperation Falla turned to the hotel owner and he, very kindly, took the matter into his hands, arranged for the boy pianist to move to a groundfloor flat, and promised not to accept any more musicians in the hotel. Thus Falla, at last, concluded his continual house moving –Debussy had started to say that Falla moved house more often than Beethoven– and he stayed at the hotel until, at the outbreak of the 1914 war, he left Paris for Spain.

JAIME PAHISSA

THE FAÇADE OF THE KLEBER HOTEL,
PARIS, WHERE MANUEL DE FALLA LIVED.

COVER OF A COPY OF THE *SONATE ROMANTIQUE*, BY JOAQUÍN TURINA, WITH AN ACROSTIC POEM DEDICATED TO FALLA: "**M**ODESTLY / **A**ND TO YOU I OFFER / **N**EW NONSENSE / **U**LTIMATELY / **E**XCAVATED / **L**IBERALLY FROM OUR / **D**EAR LAND / **E**NRICHED BY SUN. / **F**IERY / **A**ND TO YOU I ASK / **L**AUDABLE FALLA / **L**OOK ON THEM ALWAYS / **A**FFECTIONATELY. / AMEN. PARIS, 29-JANUARY-1910"

A WEAK figure, with two broken teeth, always wearing a well worn, but very smart black suit, complimented by a black tie, Falla did not have the look of an extraordinary person. I confess that at the time he looked more like, truth be told, a domestic delivery boy or a monastery verger. He spoke little and about things of no interest, smiling once in a while, showing the gaps in his teeth. Between pauses he told me, without any apparent enthusiasm, of his preference for French composers, in particular Debussy, over German ones. He also informed me of his desire, which he uttered passionately, though he used cold words, to reside for the rest of his life in a villa in Granada.

We had finished our frugal meal. We went out. The Maestro distributed the bread which was left over among his friends the sparrows and blackbirds, who waited everyday for him, perched on the avenue's trees. A mad fluttering formed around Falla, on whose face, until this moment inexpressive, was etched an angelic smile which emanated an ineffable light. Then I realised that this man was like a hard shell of timidity and coldness, inside which a great soul burned. At that moment Falla's aspect resembled the expression of tenderness which I have contemplated before in some of the Saints by divine Fra Angélico. It was as if "the *poverino* Saint Francis of Assis" had been brought to life in the present day, in an over long and excessively wide secular suit.

MELCHOR ALMAGRO SAN MARTÍN

DEAR ALL: I suppose you have received the letter and money I sent last week. Your postcard arrived afterwards, which made me feel doubly content at having written before, but very sorry, needless to say, that you, mother, do not feel well. I hope that your next letter will bring as good news (as far as possible) as I desire. I imagine that Germán must be about to arrive home. I have not heard from him since the postcard he sent from Huesca that I told you about.

When I set off for Evian and we said goodbye, he told me to write to him at his Paris address, as I have done, and that is all that I can tell you. I do not know if he has received two postcards that I sent him there. In short, I suppose that he will be preparing to arrive in Madrid, and let us see when I can do the same. I hope that God will wish it soon, because everything is going well, better than ever, and just to prove it I enclose the paragraph of a letter from Milliet which arrived today: "*Voilà longtemps que j'attends pour vous cette heure de justice; elle sonne enfin, et les mauvais moments d'espérances qui désespèrent sont oubliés*". I am convinced, like he, that better times are near, and if I do not give you more details it is because it would be very complicated and I think it better to wait a few days before breaking the news *directly*, because really the truth is that at this point in time I have nothing definitive to say, and whatever I could tell you might sound like just another *reworded version* of sentences said a while ago, which does not mean in the least that they were untrue. In short, I know what I am talking about and prefer to wait a little. Next week, probably on Thursday, I leave for Milan, where I will stay for three or four days. As you see the railway has become one of my collaborators and for free because, naturally, none of these trips cost me a penny. Of course, if that were not the case I would not be able to go. And I wind up this *chapter* repeating that I do not want to be mysterious or any such thing by not saying more, but that I prefer to wait a little in order to speak to you with complete certainty.

Let us turn to my trip to Evian. That sweet land seems to grow more beautiful every day. *You have to see the Lake of Geneva to believe it*, and the absolutely silver light, created by the lake's blue reflections and the snow on the mountain tops is marvellous.

I lodged at *l'Ermitage*, the same hotel as the Milliets, to whom I feel most grateful. How could I have gone there had it not been for them! Imagine it (it terrifies me just to say it), the hotel costs 50 francs a day... I felt like asking them to give me the money and find myself a place in a nearby inn. This Ermitage is located at quite a high altitude, so much so that one has to take the cable car (rack railway) to reach it. From my room I could see the magnificent lake and all its shores, Lausane, Ouchy, Vevey, which looked like the scenery of an enormous theatre lit up at night. On the other side, in front and all around, mountains. There was one in particular that I did not tire of seeing. Its peaks were completely silver, and the clouds seemed to amuse themselves playing there. Believe me, I could write twenty pages about Switzerland, but I have to finish.

The weather is impossible, last night it snowed! I hope I can spend winter outside Paris, because if it's already snowing here imagine what will it be like then! Moreover, I have not forgotten the damage the last two winters caused me.

I await your news, with best wishes from your ever loving son and brother,

MANOLO
Letter from Manuel de Falla to his parents
[Paris, 9 September 1912]

EVEN though I planned to go to Spain, I do not think I
shall and, thus, will invite my family in September, not
here to Paris, but to a healthy, peaceful, happy and
picturesque town which is a hour from Gare Saint Lazare,
where I intend to shut myself up to work like a fiend from
dawn till dusk.

I have a lot of ideas for work! I will tell you about them
here later.

The best one is a lyric drama based on Calderon's
Devotion to the Cross, a splendid piece, as you know.

MANUEL DE FALLA
Letter to Leopoldo Matos
[Paris, 20 July 1914]

PARIS DURING THE WAR.

PORTRAIT OF MAURICE RAVEL DURING THE
FIRST WORLD WAR, WITH THE FOLLOWING
DEDICATION: "TO MANUEL DE FALLA WITH
WARM REGARDS. MAURICE RAVEL".

I MET Manuel de Falla in Paris, in 1913, a few months before the First World War. Joaquín Turina, our friend and later our collaborator, had spoken to us about him, and thanks to him we met. He lived then in one of those sad, sordid and disgusting hotels –as Cervantes would have said, "there was room for all discomforts"– in which Paris has harboured such artistic dreams and hopes for future glories. In the small and not very clean room with a worn carpet, faded and frayed curtains, a suspicious looking bed and scant light, the only luxury was a piano, rented at the cost of God knows what privations. A piano which the Maestro explained, with a bitter smile, sounded more like scrap metal than an upright... Luckily, his inner song and his zeal to get it written down and allow the world to share it, let this solitary man forget the sadness of his forced asceticism.

Forced? Not completely. Manuel de Falla, if he had wished, could have condescended, like many, to come down to earth once in a while to easily earn the necessary francs... He could have given lessons, written an ingratiating song for his publishers, an ordinarily jolly waltz, that little piece for piano which sounds like all the others, but without too many technical difficulties so that romantic girls can play it without ruining it. The market was open, and it would have been childishly simple for Falla to contribute to its demand, but the author of *Love the Magician* showed a rare loyalty to his Muse, and preferred hunger to abandoning his principles: yes hunger, because during his stay in Paris –he told me this himself when we became friends– in order to eat he was often obliged to resort to the "food trials" which food manufacturers advertised, and thus, filling in and cutting the coupons out of newspapers he would receive, now and again, a sample of powdered cocoa, canned food, or a packet of lacteous flour. And when, at times, invited to supper at a rich acquaintance's house, he managed to eat normally, he was so accustomed to not eating that he was ill the next day.

We found the "Maestro" seated at the piano decyphering the score of Stravinsky's *The Rites of Spring*. The remarkable Russian composer was greatly admired then by the Spanish composer. In fact, the two often coincided in terms of quality and technique and it would have been strange had they not felt

a mutual respect. Moreover, as they were perfectly aware of their own worth they did not lower themselves to feel pangs of jealousy. And I think that, on many occasions, they willingly allowed themselves to be reciprocally influenced.

He received us with the refined politeness which was one of his characteristics, but he absolutely refused to play us any of his music... the reservations of a father to show his beautiful daughter to some strangers? Distrustful pride? Fear of not being understood? Who can tell! I have mentioned earlier that Manuel de Falla was nearly always a bundle of nerves. But he delighted us for more than an hour –he was a prodigious pianist– with a formidable interpretation at the piano of the score which he had been savouring alone when we rang at his door.

Though Falla's politeness and Stravinsky's music had formed a liking between us, I felt strangely uncomfortable. Something in me said: "There is something false about this man; there is something untrue here". And I was anxious to find the reason that prevented me from falling under the spell of a growing friendship... Before we separated, enticed by the musical entertainment, we implored him to play a little more as a farewell. He consented and sat at the piano once again. I, following a habit acquired in my childhood, approached him and remained standing beside him in order to turn the sheets of music. At that very same moment a stray, pale beam from the setting sun entered the room piercing the balcony's dirty muslins and lit up the pianists head. At once the disturbing mystery was solved: the raven black hair which, seemingly, grew from the composer's cranium acquired the tell–tale shininess and roughness of a dead thing... The musician was bald and tried to remedy the damage with a hair piece. The falseness which had bothered me was not, fortunately, in Falla's soul, but in his toupée. Which, moreover, soon disappeared. When war broke out in August 1914, Falla escaped France as quickly as possible. In his hurry to catch a train he lost his toupée. And thus, he arrived in his home land once more parading, with complete frankness, the copious ivory patch, which heightened his ascetic appearance.

MARÍA MARTÍNEZ SIERRA

4
MADRID
1914-1920

THE FIRST PERFORMANCE OF *LA VIDA BREVE* IN
MADRID. HE VISITS GRANADA. TOURNÉE WITH THE
MARTÍNEZ SIERRAS. ARTHUR RUBINSTEIN. *LOVE THE
MAGICIAN.* ENRIQUE GRANADOS. IGOR STRAVINSKY
AND THE RUSSIAN BALLET. *THE MAGISTRATE AND
THE MILLER'S WIFE.* DEATH OF HIS PARENTS. *THE
THREE-CORNERED HAT.* J. B. TREND. GRANADA AND
EL POLINARIO.

MADRID. — Plaza de Canalejas

1914. ■ IN SUMMER HE ARRIVED IN MADRID AND SETTLED IN A FLAT AT Nº. 24, CALLE PONZANO. HE ATTEMPTED TO CON-TINUE WORKING AND HELP HIS FAMILY. ■ ON THE 14TH OF NOVEMBER *LA VIDA BREVE* APPEARED AT THE TEATRO DE LA ZARZUELA. ■ HE STRENGTHENED HIS FRIENDSHIP WITH MR. AND MRS. MARTÍNEZ SIERRA AND WORKED ON HIS FIRST COL-LABORATIONS WITH THEM: MUSICAL FRAGMENTS FOR *LA PASIÓN*, WHICH WERE PLAYED ON THE 30TH OF NOVEMBER, AND IN DECEMBER HE COMPOSED *ORACIÓN DE LAS MADRES QUE TIENEN A SUS HIJOS EN BRAZOS*, A SONG INSPIRED BY THE EUROPEAN WAR.

1915. ■ ON THE 15TH OF JANUARY THE MADRID ATENEO HELD A HOMAGE TO JOAQUÍN TURINA AND MANUEL DE FALLA. THE *SEVEN SPANISH POPULAR SONGS* WERE SUNG BY LUISA VELA. ■ THE RECENTLY FORMED NATIONAL MUSIC SOCIETY, FOUNDED BY MIGUEL SALVADOR AND ADOLFO SALAZAR, AMONG OTHERS, GAVE ITS INAUGURAL CONCERT ON THE 8TH OF FEBRUARY AT THE RITZ HOTEL. ■ THE DÉBUT OF *ORACIÓN DE LAS MADRES QUE TIENEN A SUS HIJOS EN BRAZOS*. ■ THE IDEA OF WRITING A MUSICAL SPECTACLE FOR THE DANCER PASTORA IMPERIO, CALLED *LOVE THE MAGICIAN*, OCCURED TO HIM. ■ HE ACCOMPANIED MARÍA MARTÍNEZ SIERRA ON A TOUR OF GRANADA, WHICH HE SAW FOR THE FIRST TIME, RONDA, ALGECIRAS AND CADIZ, DURING THE MONTHS OF MARCH AND APRIL. MARÍA MARTÍNEZ SIERRA AND MANUEL DE FALLA WORK ON THE PROJECT *PASCUA FLORIDA*. ■ ON THE 15TH OF APRIL, A WEEK AFTER A BRIEF COLLABORATION IN *AMANECER*, AND IN THE TEATRO LARA, *LOVE THE MAGICIAN* WAS PERFORMED FOR THE FIRST TIME INTERPRETED BY PAS-TORA IMPERIO, AND RECEIVED A VARIED RESPONSE FROM THE AUDIENCE. ■ PIANIST ARTHUR RUBINSTEIN WAS IN MADRID ON ACCOUNT OF THE WORLD WAR. ■ MARTÍNEZ SIERRA'S COMPANY MOVED TO BARCELONA WHERE THEY REMAINED A NUMBER OF MONTHS. ■ HE FINISHED THE DEFINITIVE VERSION OF *NIGHTS IN THE GARDENS OF SPAIN*, PRE-PARED A NEW ORCHESTRATION OF *LOVE THE MAGICIAN,* CONTINUED TO COMPOSE INCIDENTAL MUSIC FOR MARTÍNEZ SIERRA'S PIECES (*OTHELLO*) AND SPENT TIME ON THE *PASCUA FLORIDA* PROJECT, BY MARÍA MARTÍNEZ SIERRA. ■ SANTIA-GO RUSIÑOL INVITED HIM TO WORK AT "CAU FERRAT" IN SITGES. HE MET RAFAEL MORAGAS AND FREQUENTED ART NOU-VEAU CIRCLES IN BARCELONA. ■ HE SAID GOODBYE TO ENRIQUE GRANADOS WHO LEFT FOR NEW YORK.

1916. ■ IN MADRID ONCE MORE HE WORKED ON THE IDEA OF *THE MAGISTRATE AND THE MILLER´S WIFE*, IN COLLABO-RATION WITH MARÍA AND GREGORIO MARTÍNEZ SIERRA. ■ ON THE 28TH OF MARCH *NIGHTS IN THE GARDENS OF SPAIN* APPEARED AT THE TEATRO REAL, WITH THE MADRID SYMPHONIC ORCHESTRA AND JOSÉ CUBILES AT THE PIANO, CON-DUCTED BY ENRIQUE FERNÁNDEZ ARBÓS. ■ THE RUSSIAN BALLET LED BY SERGE DIAGHILEV WAS IN MADRID, DIAGHILEV PROPOSED AN ADAPTATION OF *NIGHTS IN THE GARDENS OF SPAIN* FOR HIS BALLET. FALLA TURNED DOWN THE OFFER BUT SIGNED A CONTRACT TO PREPARE A VERSION OF THE DRAMA *THE MAGISTRATE AND THE MILLER´S WIFE*, WHICH HE WAS PREPARING WITH THE MARTÍNEZ SIERRAS. ■ ENRIQUE GRANADOS DIED. ■ HE PARTICIPATED IN A SERIES OF CONCERTS IN SEVILLE, CADIZ AND GRANADA IN SPRING AND SUMMER. ■ ON FELIPE PEDRELL'S RECOMMENDATION AND AFTER OBSERVING HER PIANO PLAYING, HE ACCEPTED THE CHILD ROSA GARCÍA ASCOTT AS HIS APPRENTICE.

1917. ■ ON THE 7TH OF APRIL *THE MAGISTRATE AND THE MILLER´S WIFE*, PANTOMINE IN TWO SCENES BY GREGORIO MARTÍNEZ SIERRA AFTER THE NOVEL BY PEDRO ANTONIO DE ALARCÓN *EL SOMBRERO DE TRES PICOS*, WAS PERFORMED FOR THE FIRST NIGHT AT THE TEATRO ESLAVA, MADRID. ■ ON THE 29TH OF APRIL THE CONCERT VERSION OF *LOVE THE MAGICIAN*, FOR SMALL ORCHESTRA, WAS PLAYED AT THE TEATRO REAL. ■ DIAGHILEV'S RUSSIAN BALLET TRIUMPHED IN MADRID. IGOR STRAVINSKY WAS IN MADRID TOO. FALLA WORKED WITH LÉONIDE MASSINE AND PICASSO ON THE ADAP-TATION OF A NEW *MAGISTRATE*. DUE TO FINANCIAL DIFFICULTIES AFFECTING DIAGHILEV'S COMPANY BECAUSE OF THE WAR, THE PLANNED PREMIÈRE WAS POSTPONED. ■ AT THE END OF THE YEAR HE SET OFF ON A CONCERT TOUR WITH SINGER AGA LAHOWSKA.

1918. ■ HE WORKED WITH THE MARTÍNEZ SIERRAS ON THE PROJECTS *EL FUEGO FATUO* AND *DON JUAN* WHICH LED TO FALLA'S BREAK WITH THE COUPLE. ■ CLAUDE DEBUSSY DIED. ■ ON THE 27TH OF APRIL A "HOMAGE TO DEBUSSY" WAS ORGANISED AT THE MADRID ATENEO, WITH THE PARTICIPATION OF: AGA LAHOWSKA, ARTHUR RUBINSTEIN, THE PHILHAR-MONIC ORCHESTRA AND FALLA WHO READ HIS LECTURE ABOUT "CLAUDE DEBUSSY'S PROFOUND ART". ■ RUBINSTEIN, ON REALISING IGOR STRAVINSKY'S FINANCIAL PROBLEMS, SENT HIM, THROUGH FALLA, SOME MONEY IN RETURN FOR A COM-POSITION. HE ASKED THE SAME OF FALLA, WHO RESPONDED TO THE COMMISSION THE FOLLOWING YEAR BY WRITING *THE FANTASIA BÆTICA*, WHICH HE DEDICATED TO THE PIANIST. ■ THE PRINCESS OF POLIGNAC ASKED FALLA FOR A COMPOSI-TION TO BE PERFORMED IN HER SMALL DRAWING ROOM THEATRE.

1919. ■ IN FEBRUARY HIS FATHER, JOSÉ MARÍA DE FALLA, DIED. ■ HE WENT TO LONDON TO PREPARE THE PREMIÈRE, BY DIAGHILEV'S COMPANY, OF *THE THREE-CORNERED HAT*, WHICH TOOK PLACE ON THE 22ND OF JULY AT THE ALHAMBRA THEATRE WITH GREAT SUCCESS. ON THE DAY OF THE PREMIÈRE HE RECEIVED NEWS OF THE SERIOUS CONDITION OF HIS MOTHER'S HEALTH. HE RETURNED URGENTLY TO MADRID AND, EN ROUTE, HEARD OF HIS MOTHER'S DEATH. ■ IN SEP-TEMBER HE SPENT A FEW DAYS IN GRANADA WITH HIS SISTER MARÍA DEL CARMEN AND MR. AND MRS. VÁZQUEZ DÍAZ. ÁNGEL BARRIOS, A MUSICIAN FROM GRANADA AND ONE OF FALLA'S PARIS FRIENDS, INVITED THEM TO THE HOUSE OF HIS FATHER, ANTONIO BARRIOS *"EL POLINARIO"*, WHO MANAGED A TAVERN IN THE ALHAMBRA WHERE VISITORS LIKE SANTIA-GO RUSIÑOL AND JOSEPH SARGENT FREQUENTLY LODGED. THE ENGLISH HISPANIST, J. B. TREND, MET MANUEL DE FALLA ON HIS WAY THROUGH GRANADA.

1920. ■ IN JANUARY THE FIRST PERFORMANCE OF *THE THREE-CORNERED HAT* TOOOK PLACE IN PARIS, WITH FALLA PRE-SENT. ON THE 20TH OF FEBRUARY ARTHUR RUBINSTEIN PLAYED THE NEW YORK PREMIÈRE OF *FANTASIA BÆTICA*. ■ ON THE 3RD OF JUNE, AT THE SOCIÉTÉ MUSICALE INDÉPENDANTE OF PARIS, FALLA PLAYED A SHORTENED VERSION OF *NIGHTS IN THE GARDENS OF SPAIN* FOR TWO PIANOS WITH HIS PUPIL ROSA GARCÍA ASCOTT. ■ ON THE 9TH OF JUNE PABLO PICAS-SO FINISHED HIS PORTRAIT OF MANUEL DE FALLA. IN AUGUST FALLA FINISHED *POUR LE TOMBEAU DE CLAUE DEBUSSY*, FOR GUITAR. ■ IN THE MIDDLE OF SEPTEMBER HE TRAVELLED TO GRANADA WITH HIS SISTER AND J. B. TREND. HE STAYED AT THE CARMONA GUEST HOUSE IN THE ALHAMBRA.

WHEN HE arrived the whole of Spain clamoured with the success of *Las golondrinas*. That success had to a certain extent opened the way for Spanish dramatic music sweeping aside

FALLA AT MR. AND MRS. MARTÍNEZ SIERRA'S HOUSE, WITH THEM, MARÍA MARTÍNEZ SIERRA'S SISTER AND, *BELOW*, WITH JOAQUÍN TURINA.

the idea that, to be happily heard by an ordinary and troublesome audience, *zarzuela* music had to be superficial and easy to understand. José María Usandizaga, with his wise and youthful inspiration, had brilliantly demonstrated that a *zarzuela* could triumph along any lines... even with first class music.

There remained, however, another prejudice to break: that which considered Spanish folk music as "vulgar" and solely suitable for common peoples' revels and for avid tourists on the look out for anything "picturesque". This prejudice had, by dint of distain, distanced the great Spanish musician Isaac Albéniz from Spain –and ironically brought him success in the rest of the world–. The subject of *La vida breve* was, as I mentioned before, Andalusian, and themes

of Andalusian music were written in the score. For this reason, when, after arduous negotiations, the moment of its début at Madrid's theatre of Zarzuela arrived, we felt obliged to publish an article titled "The Magic Guitars" the day before the première, in one of the biggest selling newspapers in Madrid, to advise the audience, and perhaps the critics that such "popular and vulgar" subjects were what, in Germany, Beethoven had extolled and sublimated in his *Pastoral Symphony*. Falla was doing something similar with the folk rhythms of *La vida breve*, but in a Spanish context. The fact is that the respectable audience liked every last one.

So now, the name of this new Spanish composer was on everyones' tongue, and some of the loudest bells began to ring his praises... But one opera alone, even if it is a great success, does not solve the problem of an author's material life... If only Falla had been able to take advantage of his good fortune by writing a few more *zarzuelas*! But that was like asking an elm tree to bear pears. At that moment he was busy finishing the instrumentation of the *Gardens of Spain*. But financial worries, his family problems –father, mother, sister, submerged in complete ruin and whom he alone had to support, inexorably, day after day– prevented him from finishing his work and made it impossible for him to begin anything new.

MARÍA MARTÍNEZ SIERRA

FALLA WITH CARLOS FERNÁNDEZ-SHAW'S CHILDREN AND THE PRINCIPLE ACTORS OF THE PREMIÈRE OF *LA VIDA BREVE* AT THE TEATRO DE LA ZARZUELA, MADRID.

El maestro FALLA, autor de «La vida breve», estrenada con ruidoso éxito en el teatro de la Zarzuela. (Caricatura de BAGARIA)

CUTTING FROM *LA TRIBUNA*, MADRID, 15-XI-1914.

ONE APRIL morning –crystal clear, enamelled sky, smell of victory– I said "let's go to the Alhambra today". And there we went climbing the enchanted hill, beneath the elms planted by Wellington. As we arrived at the doors of what was palace and fortress, I said to my fellow traveller: "Give me your hand, close your eyes and don't open them again until I say so". He complied with my wish, enjoying himself like a child who pretends to be blind, and I led him quickly through the myrtle courtyard, where beneath the water of its pond sleeps a heart, through the "Hall of the Boat", through the prodigious Comares Hall, the ambassadors hall of olden days whose ceiling imitates a starry sky. I led him to the central window –the one opposite the door crowned with golden and blue stalactites– whose inscription reads: "We are all the daughters of this proud cupola..."

"You can look now!", I said dropping my companion's hand. And he opened his eyes. I shall never forget the Aaah!, which he let out. It was almost a shout. Simple admiration? Satisfaction at having guessed, with the help of some book, the charm which he had never seen before? Pride at having known what to expect? Elation at having subtly pin-pointed in rhythm and sound this unknown wonder? Perhaps all these things together. I believe that that

WINDOW OF THE COMARES HALL IN THE ALHAMBRA. DETAIL OF AND ENGRAVING BY LEISNIER AND VAUZELLE, 1818.

moment of complete happiness –his shout left no doubt– was one of the raptures which compensated for the torments of his existence surrounded by so much meaness and, at times, dullness. He looked and contemplated with eagerness. I, leaving him in his "trance", also looked. I knew this room by heart, but I never tired of watching the "smiling valley" which the superb window looked out over, the river at the bottom, the bordering hill, the prickly pear trees hiding and protecting the gypsies' caves, whose burnished trunks reflected the midday sun like mirrors... On the right hand, the Generalife, orchard of orchards, climbing up to the summit in carefully cultivated terraces... "Thank you!", said the musician simply, returning to himself. The emotion did not let him say anything else. And we went home, leaving our visit to the rest of the palace for another day.

MARÍA MARTÍNEZ SIERRA

AT THAT time, my husband, Gregorio Martínez Sierra, established, in association with the distinguished actor Enrique Borrás, his first theatre company. For this purpose we had to travel throughout Spain and North Africa on tournée, as we had the habit of saying. Wishing to help his friend, who he esteemed highly and of whose music he was a staunch enthusiast, Martínez Sierra invited him to travel with us. And thus we lived together for almost a year, a few winter months in Barcelona, others spent travelling from city to city in Adalusia and Levant; two short excursions to Melilla, Ceuta and Tetuan. In that kind of mobile home, Falla worked on his "Orchestration"; my husband took charge of rehearsals and performances, making his début in the profession –which was his number one passion– as a stage director. I added the finishing touches to our dramatic comedy (Elegy, we subtitled it) *El reino de Dios*, planned in Madrid, begun in Paris, continued in Munich and which would be completed and performed in Barcelona.

MARÍA MARTÍNEZ SIERRA

AS THERE was neither music nor pianola in *La Puñalada*, in the autumn of 1915 Manuel de Falla joined Rusiñol, Catalina Bárcena and Martínez Sierra who acted at the Novedades Theatre, where they produced *Amanecer* and re-

hearsed the translation of *Othello* by Ambrosio Carrión and José María Jordá, with incidental musical sketches for small orchestra by Falla.

One night we surprised Falla with his musical notebooks.

"It's for Gregorio," said Falla "who insists that we make a gypsy ballet, but with the racket at the guest house where I live, I can't write. I need a quiet place."

"If you need a quiet place," re-

marked Rusiñol, "Falla my friend, I offer you 'Cau Ferrat' in Sitges. No other sound than the sea at the foot of its old iron."

"Good grief! I must be dreaming!" exclaimed Falla.

"Not at all. Tomorrow morning you're going to Sitges. What's the piece to be called?"

"*Love the Magician.* The action takes place on the Sacromonte in Granada. Gypsy men and a gypsy woman, Pastora Imperio, who will perform the *Fire Dance.*"

In this way Falla went to Sitges where he wrote *Love the Magician*, which has been played the whole world over.

MARIO VERDAGUER

PORTRAIT OF MANUEL DE FALLA
BY F. SANCHA.

MARÍA DE LA O LEJÁRRAGA, GREGORIO
MARTÍNEZ SIERRA'S WIFE.

Usually, every morning we performed a sketch from a tragicomedy. I, who had always played my role as a housewife with amusing indulgence, and similarly have always gone to great efforts to make sure that our table was as well prepared for as our means allowed. And as in Barcelona, it is not considered dishonourable, like in Madrid, but rather the opposite, like in France, a laudable custom for the wife to go shopping; I went to the market everyday early in the morning. As I opened the door to go out to the street, I invariably heard Manuel de Falla's voice calling from his room: "Wait for me! I'll go with you."

Why should the prominent composer go with me, forever lost in the labyrinth of his mathematical sounds, on a seemingly prosaic and practical excursion to buy vegetables and fish? Had he done so, hypersensitive and self-tormented by nature, he would have made me, such a healthy, practical and trustworthy person, into the ghost of a fragile being, unable to defend itself from the dangers of street traffic. He would have decided to walk on the other side of the street, "In order to save my life", making it more likely for me to be run over by a motorcar.

Evidently I did not wait for him –he was, thank goodness a late sleeper, slow to dress and get ready... and to complete his gymnastic weights session–. I ran to the market to do my shopping. As he was not able to accompany me, he set off after me. Sometimes we met each other on my way back. Then he scolded me for my imprudence. I made fun of his fears. We walked for a while together until, at the first church we passed, he entered to say his prayers, and I returned home alone... and defenceless.

MARÍA MARTÍNEZ SIERRA

PRESUMED PORTRAIT OF MANUEL DE FALLA
ATTRIBUTED TO SANTIAGO RUSIÑOL.

THE PIANO at *Cau Ferrat* is an authentic relic. For forty years, every important musician who went through the country used it. But perhaps the person who used it longest was Don Manuel de Falla when he composed *Love the Magician*.

JOSEP PLÁ

ARTHUR RUBINSTEIN.

Love the Magician

[SEE *COMPOSITIONS*, APPENDIX II, PAGE 105]

PASTORA IMPERIO, MANUEL DE FALLA
AND ARTHUR RUBINSTEIN.

ORIGINAL COVER OF AN EDITION OF
LOVE THE MAGICIAN BY NATALIA
GONTCHAROVA, LONDON 1921.

IN THE end, in Madrid, almost everyday I saw Manuel de Falla and the celebrated gypsy dancer and singer Pastora Imperio who danced in *Love the Magician*. After the performance at midnight Falla and I had the custom of taking her to *La Mallorquina*, famous for its hot chocolate. On most occasions she was escorted by a whole group of hungry relations: cousins, neices, nephews, and the rest –and I was paying–. Convinced that no man could approach her without falling in love at first sight, Pastora said to me with her eyes ovewhelmed by compassion: "Tut, tut, my poor thing".

ARTHUR RUBINSTEIN

"GYPSY", DESIGN BY YVES BRAYER FOR
LOVE THE MAGICIAN AT THE NATIONAL
THEATRE OF THE OPERA OF PARIS.

Enrique Granados

I BEGIN to write with deep emotion. Enrique Granados' music has spoken to me on his behalf. That music which has so often evoked people and things from the past has helped me now to evoke the presence of the great artist who composed it. The fact is that those of us who have had the good fortune to hear him play his own works, will never forget the strong artistic effect that we experienced.

Consequently, while playing my favourite piano pieces by him, I have unconsciously reproduced the rhythmic accents, the nuances, the inflexions which he stamped his music with, and in doing so it seemed to me that Granados' soul vibrated along the sound waves which his judgement had fixed forever in staves, like a testament.

I'll never forget his reading of the first part of his opera *Goyescas* which he offered us at Joaquín Nin's house in Paris.

That dance of *Pelele*, so brightly rhythmical, with which the work begins; those dittylike phrases translated with such delicate sensitivity; the elegance of certain melodical changes, sometimes impregnated with simple melancholy, at others with joyful spontaneity, but always distinguished and, above all, evocative, as if they expressed the artist's inner visions..., all this I have felt once more while playing his music.

But then how differently we trusted in the success to come: the opera was to be shown in Paris at the Opera, the coming winter; no one suspected that a barbarous and unjust war would be triggered a few weeks later by a neighbouring State which still called itself friend...

Now our hopes and our desires have been partly realised: the opera was performed; it was a great success, but Paris was not there to see, and the composer –victim of what were then only hidden enemies– was not able to celebrate it with his friends in his homeland.

We who have felt honoured by the friendship of this notable musician and who admire his talent, must demand justice from those who snatched away one of our artists who so brilliantly represented Spain abroad, and after carrying out this duty to humanity and patriotism, unite to praise and preserve as a precious treasure the heritage that Enrique Granados left us when he died, the highest and noblest heritage a man can leave his country: one created with the strength of his intelligence and his will.

MANUEL DE FALLA

Igor Stravinsky and the Russian Ballet

THE RUSSIAN BALLET IN MADRID. *SEATED FROM LEFT TO RIGHT*, CONRADO DEL CAMPO, ERNST ANSERMET, SERGE DIAGHILEV, MIGUEL SALVADOR, IGOR STRAVINSKY AND MANUEL DE FALLA, 1916.

FROM LEFT TO RIGHT, ROBERT DELAUNAY, BORIS KOCHNO, IGOR STRAVINSKY, SONYA DELAUNAY, SERGE DIAGHILEV, MANUEL DE FALLA AND BARACCI, IN MADRID, 1918.

SCORE OF *THE RITES OF SPRING* BY IGOR STRAVINSKY WITH A DEDICATION TO FALLA.

THE RUSSIAN ballet troupe, which the noble artist Serge Diaghilev directs so magnificently, has arrived, at last, to this corner of Europe, converted into a peaceful refuge by the sad force of circumstances. This troupe advertised and is giving a programme in which music occupies the main position, and in order to direct the premières of the two works advertised –*The Firebird* and *Petrushka*– their composer, who is called Igor Stravinsky, has come.

I know perfectly well that for those in Madrid who take an interest in the European artistic movement the name is familiar and, by many, admired. But does the anonymous mass, which make up what we could call the great public, know how important it is for us that an artist of Stravinsky's stature comes to renew our corrupted musical environment with his severe and subtle, but always refreshing art? Does Madrid know that one of Europe's greatest artists is its guest? Will it know, in short, how to reject those who say that the art of this composer serves to disorientate rather than to guide to the path of truth? More than anything, I hope it does! Because Stravinsky's work is imbued with the brave and courageous sincerity of one who says what he feels, fearless of what people, who do not feel or think like him, will say.

Stravinsky's music sometimes seems to me like a challenge aimed at those timid people who flee from a path which has not been trampled beforehand by a few generations. The author of *Petrushka* wants, on the other hand, to open new paths or, at least, to clean up the old ones, and the success of that resonant avalanche called *The Rites of Spring* justifies him completely.

MANUEL DE FALLA

IT IS difficult to imagine a man like Manuel de Falla, Spain's greatest composer, in the midst of a noisy café. Nevertheless, sometimes Falla goes to a café.
   But whilst the customers shout, gesticulate, cough, growl and expectorate,
he sits back thoughtfully in his chair, waiting perhaps for an opportune moment
of silence to secure a melody in his mind. But it is not easy to find silence in
modern Madrid.

WALTER STARKIE

I saw Stravinsky again some time later, one March night, in Madrid.

The formidable composer had just given a concert, in which he had been outstanding and afterwards, we waited for him at the Circle of Fine Arts: Manuel de Falla, Joaquín Turina, Enrique Fernández Arbós, Gustavo Pittaluga, José Cubiles, Conrado del Campo, Eugenio d'Ors, the violinist Corvino, the painter Ricardo Baroja, the critic of *El Sol*, Adolfo Salazar, Ricardo Viñes and I.

We ate, chatted and, after the coffees, at almost three in the morning, improvised a piano session.

Ricardo Viñes interpreted compositions by Federico Mompou, by Rocafort and Joaquín Rodrigo, which Stravinsky thoroughly enjoyed.

Then Viñes played *Petrushka*. The remarkable pianist from Lérida played masterfully, and when he had finished, Stravinsky hugged him saying enthusiastically:

"*Très cher Ricardo, vous êtes magnifique.*"

Then Manuel de Falla sat at the piano and let us hear *Love the Magician*. Afterwards Turina played the "Orgy" from his *Danzas fantásticas*.

Four o'clock came, then five o'clock. The wind had died down. The morning commenced quietly and shyly.

We decided to go on a walk before going to bed.

Some of the spectators of the improvised concert disappeared, leaving only the hardiest.

At nine in the morning we were still to be found at a bakery located in calle Ciudad Rodrigo, which is off the old calle Mayor. How strange things are. We were in the same establishment where in 1872 some gunmen had tried to assassinate Amadeo Ist of Savoy.

Spanish doughnuts and brandy, which made no visible impression on the revolutionary composer of *The Rites of Spring*.

Manuel de Falla was dismayed, seeing himself obliged to indulge in this binge, as he drank his second bottle of Mondariz mineral water.

Timidly, he asked Ricardo Baroja's advice:

"Tell me. I think this would be a sensible time to retire. My body can't take any more... I don't think Stravinsky will mind..."

"But don't you see that Stravinsky is having a good time?"

And addressing himself to the author of *Petrushka* he said:

"Maestro, what about another doughnut?"

Stravinsky looked around him, his eyes shining joyfully, and exclaimed in Spanish, without knowing what he was saying, repeating a phrase he had heard a moment before:

"*Olé, olé*, terrific!"

MARIO VERDAGUER

IGOR STRAVINSKY BY PICASSO, 1917.

I will never forget the performance of *Schéhérazade* at the Alhambra in Granada. The atmosphere and the effect of the arab costumes with the marvellous palace in the background was unique.
JOAQUÍN TURINA

WE DECIDED to hire some mules and visit the Alhambra palace and the Generalife gardens. With Félix (Fernández) and Falla as guides, we began to climb the first hills: but Falla noticed that Diaghilev had disappeared. We went back and found him at the bottom of the hill leading his mule which had collapsed under his weight.

●

We had stopped to listen to a blind man who played guitar. Falla spoke with the man and he asked him to play the melancholy melody once more which he had interpreted a number of times before. While the guitarist played again, Falla stood still with his eyes shut. He hummed it and finally wrote it down in his notebook. Later he used it for the *sevilla-na* in the second act of our ballet.

LÉONIDE MASSINE

FALLA IN THE NEIGHBOURHOOD OF THE STUDENTS' RESIDENCE IN MADRID (AN INSTITUTION WHICH
LODGED FIGURES OF GREAT CULTURAL IMPORTANCE SUCH AS FEDERICO GARCÍA LORCA, SALVADOR DALÍ
AND LUIS BUÑUEL).

NOW FALLA'S nature was not just nervous, but rather "oversensitive". His exaggerated sense of self-dignity, his faith in the quality of his composi-tions, his obsessive need to perfect them to the tiniest detail, turned his work into a kind of torture, a kind of self-torment which both destroyed and gratified him. I, who had seen him work for many years and had pre-tended to laugh at his meticulous self-criticism in an attempt to lighten his bitter existence a little, know the fever and spleen that went into those heartbroken and heartbreaking melodies which today seem so natural, the fruit of a happy flourishing tree, daughters of super-abundant inspi-ration. True, Falla always possessed fresh and clear inspiration, without hesitation or doubt, by means of divine communication, immediate and right. But the realisation, writing it down on staved paper, with his care-ful and elegant musical caligraphy, the imperitive orders of his inner voice, was not an easy or God given thing. Like a meticulous potter, he turned the wheel shaping a phrase, tuning the vase's contours, and once finished, he smashed it on the floor, and began all over again. "Is it better like this? Or that? Or this way?", he asked himself, as there was nobody else who could bear to stay beside him while he worked. To be truthful, on the many occasions that I was witness to his doubts, because we were collaborators and he granted me the honour –perhaps just for appearances sake– to trust not my opinion, but my taste, I never noticed any difference between one version and another and replied, suspecting that he was not listening: "I think that's much better". My layman's opinion seemed to calm him for a moment, but he soon returned to his self-contradiction and inner strug-gle. Manuel de Falla's perfect art was no easy task.

MARÍA MARTÍNEZ SIERRA

The Magistrate and the Miller's Wife

[SEE *COMPOSITIONS*, APPENDIX II, PAGE 105]

ABOVE, PEDRO ANTONIO DE ALARCÓN, AUTHOR OF *EL SOMBRERO DE TRES PICOS* ON WHICH GREGORIO MARTÍNEZ SIERRA BASED HIS LIBRETTO OF *THE MAGISTRATE AND THE MILLER'S WIFE*; POSTER FOR THE PERFORMANCE OF *THE MAGISTRATE AND THE MILLER'S WIFE*; IN MADRID (7-VI-17); AND MR. AND MRS. MARTÍNEZ SIERRA, 1915: "FOR MANUEL DE FALLA OUR ILLUSTRIOUS AND GYPSY COLLABORATOR A TOKEN –A PROVISIONAL ONE– OF OUR ADMIRATION AND FRIENDSHIP. MARÍA AND GREGORIO".

Letters to his family

Barcelona, January 1918

DEAR ALL: I see that tomorrow is your (mamma) saint's day which I thought was later, and I want to take advantage of the first post to send you my best wishes and happiness. I was very pleased today to receive your news and to know that you are recovering from your troubles.

Last night Gregorio and María's play was performed with great success. They send you warm and kind regards.

I will write soon. Until then. Meanwhile accept all best wishes from your loving son and brother,

MANOLO

30 January 1918

DEAR ALL: Thank you very much for your letters. I did not answer because I was hoping to announce my arrival which has been delayed a few days. I will arrive next Wednesday or Thursday, and in view of the postal service sent twenty coins yesterday which you should have received today. Go (papa) to the Society on the 1st, because there should be something worth collecting. See you very soon. Very best wishes from you son and brother who is anxious to see you all,

MANOLO

El Escorial, 13 June 1918

DEAR ALL: I received your postcard and was relieved that nothing new or unpleasant, has happened. The only guest I have received was Mme. Lahowska who was here for two days on which, incidentally, the wind blew more furiously than I have known it to do since those Puerto Real days... It has calmed down since yesterday and the fine temperatures have returned. I work a lot, but as I am sparing with the intervals and sleep more than before, I feel wonderful.

I still do not know if I will leave this Saturday. If I do not, I will send the money by post. Regards from these ladies and best wishes from your son and brother,

MANOLO

El Escorial, Sunday, 4 August 1918

DEAR ALL: I can now imagine everything that awaits me! The Alpujarra rising before me!..

We still have not finished working. I think we will tomorrow and if so I will return by the evening train. But as I am not sure of this, I will warn you by telegram whether it will be tomorrow or later. Yesterday it was cold here, but today the temperature is fine.

Warmest wishes from your loving son and brother,

MANOLO

On the death of his parents

MY DEAR FALLA:

I would have written to you days ago, but I did not know your address. In the end I decided to send this letter to the Spanish Musical Union, trusting that it will reach you.

I only want to send you my sincerest wishes, my deep estimation for your immense talent and the expression of my old and heartfelt friendship; my congratulations for your great success in London and my deepest sympathy for the misfortune you are suffering with the loss of your good father.

I consider it useless to write vain words. For you, personal immortality is not an unmeaningful word: in it your pain will find its only respite.

In any case I imagine that the death of a father must be a little easier for him, if he has the certainty of knowing that his son's work ennobles his name and his country as your's indeed does.

You must realise how nobly dramatic your triumph seemed to your father and how extremely triumphal his death appears to you, when both things happen at once. Even more so if the word triumph expresses, as is your case, not just the consequence of success, but the full realisation of a new sense of ideal perfection.

With the greatest admiration and friendship, accept my warmest regards, your ever affectionate and humble servant,

AMADEO VIVES
Letter to Manuel de Falla
[San Pol de Mar, 22 August 1919]

JOSÉ MARÍA FALLA, THE COMPOSER'S
FATHER, WHO DIED IN 1919.

MY DEAR FRIEND:

On the same day I read in *El Sol* of the sadness of a son and the success of a musician. I send you all my sympathy, and I hope you feel it with the same intensity that I have sent it. My admiration and happiness, mixed with fondness and sadness.

Yours always,

JUAN RAMÓN JIMÉNEZ
Letter to Manuel de Falla
[Madrid, 27 July 1919]

MY HEARTFELT thanks dear friend for your words of friendship, which I feel so honoured to receive and deeply esteem.

My sincerest friendship and admiration always, your affectionate,

MANUEL DE FALLA
Letter to Juan Ramón Jiménez
[Madrid, 3 August 1919]

MARÍA JESÚS MATHEU, HIS MOTHER,
DIED IN 1919.

DEAREST brother Germán:

Early this morning we received your telegram and at the moment I am still wondering whether I should send you another or not.

We did not want to write to you before you had received Pedro's letter. You are suffering like I suffered in London with the difference that I was able to return as soon as I received María del Carmen's alarming telegram; but the Lord decided it should be in vain. Once more this is tremendous proof that we are God sent and the only consolation for us is the Christian certainty that death is none other than the beginning of true life and that in this new life we will soon meet all those who we loved in the love of God.

Of course suffering is always horrible, but how different it is for those who have no hope!

Imagine my dreadful entrée to Madrid. An hour before I had learned from a newspaper that all was in vain. Poor mother had died on the day I left London and had been buried the day before I arrived...

From the moment I left Madrid the strong premonition that I would not see her again was with me constantly, because though she had recovered from the attacks she suffered, the way mamma said goodbye, with a sadness I had never seen in her before, impressed me deeply. I have tears in my eyes on telling you and my only comfort is the thought that I will see her again soon in the true life, which both she and papa are enjoying. The two are at rest now and will be petitioning the Lord for us.

What a grievous year we are undergoing! I hope you can come soon so that the three of us that remain in this world can be together.

With my warmest wishes and affection your brother,

MANOLO
Letter from Falla to Germán de Falla
[Madrid, 1 September 1919]

The Three-cornered Hat

[SEE *COMPOSITIONS*, APPENDIX II, PAGE 105]

LONDON, THE CITY WHERE ON 22 JULY 1919, THE RUSSIAN BALLET GAVE A FIRST PERFORMANCE TO *THE THREE-CORNERED HAT* AT THE ALHAMBRA THEATRE; COSTUME AND SET DESIGNS BY PABLO PICASSO FOR THE PERFORMANCE OF *THE THREE-CORNERED HAT* AT THE PARIS PREMIÈRE IN JANUARY 1920.

My much longed for "quiet retreat" in San Sebastián metamorphosed into a senseless carrousel. The greatest attraction was to attend, in the morning, the rehearsals of the dancers and exquisite ballerinas in their tights.

I loved the long sessions with the painters and Ansermet on a café terrace and our hurried meals at the hotel; I also loved to hear Falla play passages from his new ballet, *The Three-cornered Hat*. Well into the evening, Lydia Lopokova, Bolm and other music amateurs dragged me to the Casino's big empty hall and made me play for hours, sometimes even until after midnight. Everyone showed tremendous courage. The dancers often spent days without eating properly, not able to pay their hotels and without a penny in their pockets. But this did not make them lose any of their natural joy. They were always ready to have fun and they never would have allowed their difficulties to interfere in their work.

What an extraordinary personality Manuel de Falla had! He looked like an ascetic monk dressed in ordinary clothes. He always wore black, and something melancholic flowed from his bald skull, his black and piercing eyes and his thick eyebrows. Even his smile was sad. However his music revealed such intense passion that it seemed to represent the absolute antithesis of the man. Nervous and full of complexes at the idea of writing the music for a ballet, he had introduced antiquated airs of min-

uets and gavottes which Diaghilev had no intention of using.

"I want everything to be Spanish! Not old relics!" He shouted.

The following day, poor Falla came back with a short sketch for a *jota*, the classical Spanish dance.

"That is exactly what I wanted!" said Diaghilev as Massine nodded his head in agreement. "Bring us more like this!"

Thus, day after day, much to the satisfaction of his torturers, Falla's *jota* became the long passionate dance at the end of the ballet. The finished work was striking: *The Three-cornered Hat* was, definitively, one of the greatest successes of the ballet's repertory.

Arbós arrived in Madrid for the summer season and chose me to be soloist for the first recital, a new performance of Tchaikovsky's *concerto*, which he gave to an audience that yelled with enthusiasm.

Among the most responsive were Diaghilev and his lady friend, Mrs. Misia Sert. They both adored the concert and my interpretation. In reality, my great friendship with Diaghilev, dates from this day. Up until that moment the tokens of attention that he had paid me were mainly due to my Spanish accomplishments and to the fact that I might have proved useful to him in that country.

ARTHUR RUBINSTEIN

COMPOSITIONS

Appendix II

LOVE THE MAGICIAN

Compositions in collaboration with

María and Gregorio Martínez Sierra

THE MAGISTRATE AND THE MILLER'S WIFE

THE THREE-CORNERED HAT

POUR LE TOMBEAU DE CLAUDE DEBUSSY

FANTASIA BÆTICA

Score of *Love the Magician*.

LOVE THE MAGICIAN

DURING THE FIRST YEAR OF HIS RETURN TO MADRID, FOR A LITTLE MORE THAN THREE MONTHS, MANUEL DE FALLA WORKED ON THE MUSIC OF *LOVE THE MAGICIAN* WITH TEXTS BY MARÍA MARTÍNEZ SIERRA.

LOVE THE MAGICIAN GYPSY DANCE IN ONE ACT AND TWO SCENES, WAS PERFORMED FOR THE FIRST TIME BY PASTORA IMPERIO ACCOMPANIED BY A FAMILY GROUP FORMED BY HER MOTHER, "*LA MEJO-RANA*", HER BROTHER, VITO, HER SISTER-IN-LAW, AGUSTINA, AND HER COUSIN, MARÍA DEL ALBAICÍN. THE PREMIÈRE TOOK PLACE ON THE 15TH OF APRIL 1915 AT THE TEATRO LARA IN MADRID, WITH SET DESIGNS BY NÉSTOR DE LA TORRE. IN SPITE OF ITS SUCCESS WITH AUDIENCES, THERE WERE FEW PERFORMANCES.

NOT LONG AFTER THIS FALLA PREPARED A VERSION FOR SEXTET AND, NOT CONTENT WITH THE STAGE VERSION, ARRANGED A SUITE FOR ORCHESTRA WHICH WAS FIRST PERFORMED AT THE RITZ HOTEL, CON-DUCTED BY ENRIQUE FERNÁNDEZ ARBÓS, IN A CONCERT ORGANISED BY THE NATIONAL MUSIC SOCI-ETY ON THE 28TH OF MARCH 1916.

ON THE 29TH OF APRIL 1917 THE CONCERT VERSION FOR SMALL ORCHESTRA WAS PLAYED AT THE MADRID TEATRO REAL.

ANOTHER LATER VERSION FOR BALLET, BASED ON THE EARLIER SCORES, WAS FIRST PERFORMED BY ANTO-NIA MERCÉ "*LA ARGENTINA*" AND VICENTE ESCUDERO AT THE TRIANON LYRIQUE IN PARIS ON THE 22ND OF MAY 1925.

The dancer Pastora Imperio, for whom the Martínez Sierra couple and Manuel de Falla wrote *Love the Magician*.

ONE DAY, not long after his return to Madrid, Martínez Sierra said to Falla: "Pastora Imperio wants us to write her a song and a dance". Pastora Imperio was one of the best Andalusian gypsy dancers and, at that time, she was the most important dancer of that authentic and typical, but deeply serious dance. Falla liked the idea. He did not know Pastora personally. When he met her, and in particular her mother, his interest grew, and the composition as well; what had begun as a song and a dance turned into *Love the Magician*.

From Pastora's mother —Rosario "*la Mejorana*", who had been a fine artist— Falla heard *soleares* and *seguiriyas*, *polos* and *martinetes*, of which he captured *la almendrilla*, as she put it, that is, the essence, the nucleus, the seed of the music, and later incorporated into the pages of his score; and Martínez Sierra, from the stories, tales and legends, that Rosario told, was able to built the plot of a new work.

Falla set to work enthusiastically on *Love the Magician*. He began in November and finished in April. He had room and ease to work because his financial problems had been solved by the authors' rights he had earned. He was thus able to devote himself completely to the composition of this piece. He worked on it the whole winter long; at night, in a closed room, full of cigarrette smoke and fumes from the gas stove, with a small glass of Málaga wine beside him, which he sipped from time to time. Thus he worked every day until three in the morning. In this way he was able to finish the composition in a relatively short period of time, bearing in mind that his method of composing was extremely meticulous and slow. So much so that the publisher

Eschig, who continued to publish during the war, wrote to him demanding the work, because he did not believe that Falla could have written it so quickly, and thought that he must have begun and composed it earlier, in other words, during the time that Falla was pledged by contract to Eschig. In the end *Love the Magician* was published by Chester, of London; the piano version, in 1921, and the pocket score, in 1924.

JAIME PAHISSA

THE PLOT: a love-stricken gypsy woman whose feelings are not returned by the object of her attentions resorts to magic arts, sorcery, witchcraft and suchlike, to soften the unresponsive man's heart... and she suceeds. After a night of spells, conjurations, mysterious charms and more or less ritual dances, Aurora wakes at dawn along with Love, which had been sleeping soundly, and bells ring out the morning's victory.

MARÍA MARTÍNEZ SIERRA

Manuscript of the "Song of anguished love" from *Love the Magician*, written by María Martínez Sierra. [Aaaay! (*With anguish*): I don't know what I feel / don't know what's wrong with me. / When he's manly / I need that gypsy... (*Approaching the candle*): Ay! (*With fear*): Candle that burns... / (*With wrath*): Hell burns more hotly / burns my blood / searing with jealousy! / Ay! / (*With anguish*): When the river speaks / what does it say? / (*With bitterness*): For want of another / he forgets about me! / Ay! (*Raving*): When the fire sears... / When the river speaks... / (*Madly*): If the water kills not the fire / my sorrows will kill me! / My sorrow condemns me! / My desire poisons me!]

Pastora Imperio, caricature by Fresno.

Martínez Sierra, enthusiast producer, enthusiastic both about the composition itself and about the possibilities of a beautiful production that needed, in his opinion, as was his laudable custom, a fresh approach in order to assure a splendid performance. At that time, the dancer, Pastora Imperio was at the height of her maturity. She was truly the empress of all the Spanish dancers who have shaken the floor boards with the drumming of their heels during the 20th century. Pastora Imperio was no longer, as in her adolescence, the slender serpent coiling through the rhythm of the dance not only into the flesh, but also into the heart of every spectator, revealing all the sensuality and hypersensitive anguish which are and always will be an enigmatic cry untranslatable into any language (these inner cries use an inhuman or infrahuman language whose unknown words are both daggers' wounds and honeycombs). When she moved it was as if a perfect living sculpture, took over her; it was like a natural force which triumphed effortlessly and dominated by the mere virtue of existing. She was the interpreter Martínez Sierra chose and confirmed for *Love the Magician* surrounding her with a select group of pretty gypsy girls. And to frame the work and create the atmosphere, he commissioned costumes and scenery from the ill-fated Nestor, a painter from the Canary Islands and a wizard of impossible colours and phatasmagorical light. The stage performance of *Love the Magician* was unforgettable for those of us who were lucky enough to see it.

María Martínez Sierra

LOVE THE MAGICIAN.
CONVERSATION WITH MANUEL DE FALLA

The famous musician, who with just one admirable composition, *La vida breve*, has won an international reputation, shows his *Love the magician* for the first time tonight at the Lara.

This première is an exceptional artistic event, because it brings together four people, prestigious in their individual fields. Pastora Imperio, the great, unique, brilliant and extraordinary dancer; Martínez Sierra, who has really fought for his literary reputation; Manuel de Falla, eminent musician, and Néstor de la Torre, a painter whose scenery is unequalled in Spain. Convinced that an interview with the musician would be interesting, we requested one, though we never imagined that it would be so kindly granted.

Sheltered in a café, Manuel de Falla, simple, modest, friendly, without the slightest affectation, answered our questions.

—...?

—*Love the Magician* is a work which was suggested to Martínez Sierra and myself by the extraordinary Pastora Imperio. Such a singular artist and brilliant dancer should create a genre able to show her many facets. We have created a strange new work, and we are ignorant of the effect it might have on an audience, but we have "felt" it.

—..?

—As regards my work I have to confess that I have never worked with more enthusiasm or satisfaction than during the three months that it took me to write *Love the Magician*. Martínez Sierra has produced a libretto in which everything is designed so that the music can take the front line, standing out from all the rest. The gratitude I feel towards my collaborator is infinite. He delved into my temperament, my tastes and my way of experiencing art, and adapted himself to them completely, providing me with the means to "express liberally". At no point did he imagine that his personality could take form. And it takes it, colossally, in a libretto such as this, with a rounded "musical sense", though the audience is unfair and never manage to understand this. Martínez Sierra's work, when he collaborates with musicians, can only be fully appreciated by those who have collaborated with him. Let time pass, and when we are able and "know" how to appreciate, justice will be done.

—...?

—The work is an eminently gypsy piece. To write it I employed only ideas of a popular character, some of them borrowed from Pastora Imperio herself, who has the custom of singing them, and whose "authenticity" cannot be denied. In the forty minutes that the work lasts, I have attempted to "live it" like a gypsy, to feel it passionately, and I have used only those elements which I believe express the soul of that people.

Popular motifs, at all times, filled out with a technique suited to their character to form a homogenous "whole". That is my artistic conviction and I did the same in *La vida breve*.

—...?

—All that is said about Pastora's artistic intuition falls short. Her ear for music is such that at first one takes her to be a trained musician, when she knows not a single note.

—...?

—I have had to limit and control myself a lot with the orchestration, but as the work is written for a few musicians I attempted to use them to create the greatest possible range of sounds and expressions.

—...?

—Whatever the result of the first night might be, I have had the satisfaction of having worked happily, with real enthusiasm, and I repeat that, in every sense, the libretto has provided me the means to do so.

Rafael Benedito
Interview with Manuel de Falla
La patria, Madrid, 15 April 1915

MY DEAR Manuel: I have learned with gladness and satisfaction of this adventure *Love the Magician*, which deserves a fresh and ringing triumph. It is known that your presence in Madrid has bothered musicians, shaking up yesterday's and today's alike, all keen to show their failures at odds with artistic modesty, or to show their abilities and effort, in the case of those who still have strength to fight.

Bravo Manuel, now you can see with what interest and attention I follow your author's feats, because in you I have always recognised a sincere, high-minded composer, a faithful, honourable man and an ever dignified, ever deserving, praiseworthy artist.

Thus accept the enthusiastic, fervent regards and devoted esteem of your admiring friend,

FELIPE PEDRELL
Letter to Manuel de Falla
[Barcelona, 6 May 1915]

BUT, IN any case, thank God life goes on, and there is no lack of purpose, which is the main thing.

I wish you could hear *Love the Magician*, because in writing it I have tried to follow many of your noble teachings. Here it was shown some thirty times in twenty days, and then, when Pastora Imperio went to Valencia, it was performed six times there; but she had the misfortune to argue with the conductor (the only person able to conduct it, as he knows this difficult work very well) and Martínez Sierra and I have been obliged to beg Pastora not to perform it in Barcelona. But if things can be sorted out by some other means and I go there for the première, I do not need to assure you, Maestro, what a great pleasure it would be for me to embrace you after so many years and to speak at length about so many things past and present.

Laura Albéniz has written to me with news about you; I have promised to visit them in Majorca if I make a trip to Barcelona; but I believe it difficult.

Anyhow, if I cannot now I shall do so next winter,

MANUEL DE FALLA
Letter to Felipe Pedrell
[Madrid, 1915]

ANOTHER CURIOUS musical anecdote that I have to tell: Manuel de Falla and I had become very good friends and one night he took me to see Pastora Imperio, the famous gypsy singer and dancer, in her dance called *Love the Magician*. The performance took place very late, at a theatre, after the work they were showing finished. The dance told the story of a girl, victim to the charm a man had over her (the man was an excellent dancer). The music was played by six or seven musician —the type of group that tends to play in night clubs— and the pianist had an upright piano. But that music fascinated me —in particular the dance called "The Fire Dance" which Pastora executed so marvellously.

'Could you lend me the score of the music of that dance?' I asked Falla, 'I'd like to do an arrangement for piano to play at a concert'.

He replied smiling:

'Of course I'll give it to you. Though I strongly doubt that the music will have the least effect'.

I did the arrangement basing myself solely on the original. And when I played it as an encore at my next concert, the audience literally went mad. I had to repeat it three times.

ARTHUR RUBINSTEIN

THE FINAL touches to the orchestration of *Love the Magician* was the excuse for another visit to Granada. Taking advantage of the Easter week and Easter day, librettist and composer set off for Granada. We lodged within the Alhambra wood, where the path begins to level out, at a modest boarding house frequented mainly by elderly English lady tourists who liked peace and quiet. We went in silence searching too, as we had to listen first and then make sound the magical melody enveloped and sustained by bewitched melodies. It might appear that I was out of place there: the libretto was written; the action and the words decided... What remained for me to do? Something that the composer considered very important and highly amusing. We still needed to agree upon the most efficient way of communicating the emotion to the audience by means of aural sensation. Falla was an unmatched master of instrumentation. This was due not only to a God-sent gift, but to stubborn and fierce work. With his meticulous obstinacy, he devoted the best part of the seven years he spent in Paris to the complete study

of the technique of all the instruments which make up an orchestra, as well as the organ, compendium and sum of the orchestra. There was thus no problem of notation and interpretation that he was not able to solve satisfactorily. At first glance his scores can look as though there are too many difficulties of execution; however, that is not the case. I have heard many interpreters say: "It is a pleasure to play Falla's music. It is true that it demands everything that each instrument can give, but it never requires the impossible virtuosity of many great composers, like Wagner on more than one occasion".

Gregorio and María Martínez Sierra in San Sebastián. Photo dedicated to Manuel de Falla in 1915.

This complete mastery of the means of expression would convert a common piece into a perfect delicacy. I was sure, while working with him, that there was no shade of emotion or whimsical fancy that, once understood, he could not reproduce exactly and clearly. In that boarding house which was so humble that its roof leaked when it rained and the guests had to run with buckets and basins to catch the water to avoid the tiled floor flooding, in that kind of Bedouin tent raised in the desert, we sat before the piano, which sounded awful! He, with his pencil and paper; I, with my imagination and eagerness. And I spoke and he worked.

"Here I'd like a faint tremor of anguished hope..."

"Broken arpeggios?", he murmured "... Listen... Like that? or this?"

"Here, a rending cry..."

"Clarinet? or this?"

One should point out that Falla, thanks to the accomplished execution of his art, managed to reproduce the sound of any instrument on the piano.

"A little more harsh, because within the shout, I want it to show the tears this woman swallows and how her voice falters..."

"The oboe is just the thing... Like this?"

"Yes." "Let's have a look at the ballad... You've written: 'with a folk feel'. Is this alright?"

"Yes, wonderful. But I'd like the music to pause for a fraction of a second on this word, as if the woman who is singing so as not to cry were to say to herself: 'I can't go on!'"

"Of course. Like this?"

"Yes."

That is how we spent the evening until the sun went down, and on leaving our work, we climbed to the roof terrace to look over towards the Sierra at the golden, topaz and blood coloured citadel is reflected by the king of stars as it sank behind the clouds.

It was here that our spiritual communion would break and in absolute silence we both turned back to face our problems separately.

MARÍA MARTÍNEZ SIERRA

LOVE THE MAGICIAN

(THE TEXT of these notes, published by Adolfo Salazar in the programmes for the Sociedad Nacional de Música and Madrid's Symphonic Orchestra, has been edited in order to adapt it to the new stage version of the composition.)

Notes

The first version of *Love the Magician* was written for Pastora Imperio, who performed it on the 15th of April 1915 at the Teatro Lara in Madrid.

The theatre production used a new musical method which, in spite of the fact that it was inspired by the deepest and most southern musical feeling, adopting techniques and modes of expression hitherto unknown in Spanish music, was greeted with diverse opinions. Later on, Manuel de Falla wrote a new version of the work, stripping it of some of the recitative fragments and expanding its instrumentation, which had been too small in the original version because of the practical neccessities of the theatre for which it was written.

Now the orchestra consists of flute, piccolo, oboe, two clarinets, bassoon, drums, piano and string quintet.

Programme of the début of the orchestral version of *Love the Magician*, conducted by Serge Koussevitzky with Serge Prokofiev at the piano, at the National Opera House, Paris.

This orchestral expansion does not affect the character of the first version in any way, as regards its special tone and its evocation of primitive Arabian-Hispanic instruments: the instrumentation is subordinate to the composer's emotional and artistic desires which he has achieved by his use of melodic and harmonic means and simply enhances what he had in mind to express.

The action takes place inside an Andalusian gypsy cave. There is a strong atmosphere of witchcraft and mystery. It is night. At the end of the cave through the opening which is used as the entrance, a path can be seen lit up by the moon. *Candelas*, seated on the floor and by candlelight, deals out cards in order to read her fortune. Other gypsy women murmur spells. A voice inside the cave sings *Song of Wounded Love*.

The Spectre. The cave is filled with a mysterious light and *the Spectre* appears.

One motif of gypsy origin is played by a muted trumpet, a motif which is developed later in the *Dance of Terror*. Muffled violins, in a spasmodic theme, express the gypsy's terror as she is chased by the *Spectre*. While these themes are being developed, another characteristic folk tune joins them.

The Fisherman's Ballad. Candelas hums the ballad while she tries with spells and sorcery to free herself from the curse of the *Spectre*.

The orchestra plays a subtly mysterious and evocative motif.

Midnight. In the distance a clock strikes twelve. The gypsy women, who left the cave at the end of the first dance, return to carry out the midnight rites. Some of them carry lit oil lamps; others, tambourines and cauldrons.

Candelas throws a handful of incense on the fire, and as the smoke rises, she dances the Fire Dance, to Ward off Evil Spirits. This dance is musically based on an old gypsy tune, which the oboe plays, and on a theme (trumpets) which clearly echoes, despite its two-four rhythm, the first theme of *Love the Magician*.

After a short scene between *Candelas* and the *Spectre*, who reappears surrounded by will-o'-the-wisps, a ray of moonlight illuminates the inside of the cave making the *Spectre* and the wisps vanish.

Lucía appears on stage dancing the *Song of the will-o'-the-wisp*.

Pantomime.

The original motif with a new optimistic tone (Cello 7/8) sets the music for this scene.

Dance of the Love Game. The music of this dance is built from the base of a theme played solely on viola. The progress of the dance is interrupted by songs, which are played by solo instruments in the concert version. Rhythms and popular Andalusian melodic turns create this scene, which is linked to the *finale* (the Dawn Bells).

The new day arrives. The second theme of the dumb show is heard once more, with a growing fullness.

Candelas, victorious against the spells of the *Spectre* leaves the cave with her lover through the path which leads to the entrance. Sunlight illuminates the path and the piece finishes with the sound of bells pealing joyfully.

Antonia Mercé *"La Argentina"* performed the ballet version of *Love the Magician* on the 25th of May, in 1925, at the Trianon Lyrique, Paris. **"To the Maestro, and my friend Falla, so that he shall not forget this Candelas from his** *Love the Magician.* **With devotion, Argentina. Paris, September, 1925.**

Various moments from the performance of the ballet version of *Love the Magician,* **performed by Antonia Mercé** *"La Argentina"* **and Vicente Escudero. Stage design by Gustavo Bacarisas.**

ANTONIA MERCÉ, *"LA ARGENTINA"* AND THE BALLET VERSION OF *LOVE THE MAGICIAN*

ANOTHER RECOLLECTION of my travels with Falla which also came about by chance, is of the première of *Love the Magician*, at the "Trianon Lyrique", in Paris in 1925. The French capital was hosting the Exhibition of Decorative Arts and the première of the work was planned for the Exhibition theatre. But when the time came for the performance the new theatre was still being built. That was why the performance took place at "the Trianon Lyrique".

That evening was very moving. The first work to be played was by an English composer. Following this, *The Soldier's Tale* by Stravinsky, which caused a clamour of protest and applause. Madame Debussy, María del Carmen Falla —the composer's sister—, the poet Eduardo Marquina and I sat in one of the boxes; Marquina said to me:

'What will happen to us now?'

The 'us' he referred to were Falla and *Love the Magician.*

I answered Marquina that I had every faith in Don Manuel's composition and was sure that it would be extremely successful. Sure enough, that is what happened. The response of the audience, which had shown its restlessness earlier, was full of unrestrained enthusiasm, applause and more applause.

At last it was time for the "Fire dance". Antonia Mercé, "*La Argentina*", fell down on stage at the last bars of the music following the marvellous choreography. The "Trianon Lyrique" resounded with an unending and indescribable explosion of applause. She had to repeat the last number. Once again the applause was tremendous, interminable. Manuel de Falla, Antonia Mercé and Vicente Escudero were the great victors that unforgettable night at the "Trianon Lyrique".

Thus, *Love the Magician* commenced a career of uninterrupted success on stages the whole world over. It was performed again at the Comic Opera, along with *La vida breve*, by La Argentina. It was always greeted with tremendous success.

JUAN GISBERT

Cover of the *Revue Internationale de Musique et de Danse*, **Paris, 15th of March 1928. Photograph of Vicente Escudero.**

MY DEAR friend:

What you have done and what you are still doing with *Love the Magician* is so magnificent that I doubt that anyone could surpass it, even if they did excellently. For this reason I do not understand your repeated desire to have its exclusive rights. Moreover, in my opinion, the best guarantee of sustaining your interest in *Love the Magician* is the fact that this exclusive right does not exist. My own experience and the experience of others has convinced me that the absolute ownership of performance rights (with the exception of certain cases which have nothing to do with this one) make one lose interest in the object one possesses. In this manner, almost or completely without realising it, you would gradually lose the fondness with which you honour my composition and the joy that brings me. Please consider this and you will see that I am right, even though what I say at first might induce you to vigorously object...

Consider too, my esteemed friend, that you and *Love the Magician* are virtually the same thing. This is recognised by everyone. What better "exclusive right" could there be than this? I insist that I speak to you "*à coeur ouvert*" and in a way that one can only use when addressing a true artist and someone with as bright an intelligence as yours. This fact gives me the assurance that on this occasion —as always— you will understand me.

MANUEL DE FALLA
Letter to Antonia Mercé
[Granada, 30 August 1929]

Antonia Mercé surrounded by her dance ensemble. An Argentinian press cutting about the production of *Love the Magician* at the Teatro Colón in Buenos Aires in 1933.

« L'Amour sorcier »...
Un ouvrage qu'il faut « vivre »

L'Amour Sorcier !... Peu de choses peuvent me procurer un plus profond plaisir que de commenter ce chef-d'œuvre, si plein des beautés d'une race. Chef-d'œuvre qui, en quelques mesures, suggère au profane les mystères si humains de la gitanerie andalouse et qui, de son fouet sonore, éveille en tout Espagnol, avec un maximum d'intensité, les aspects spirituels d'un peuple autant fort dans sa race comme faible dans ses superstitions, d'un peuple qui crée et aime la beauté comme le prouvent ses faits et gestes dans. l'Histoire et qui, plus matériel que cérébral, n'a jamais pu cependant se libérer d'un goût inné pour le magique et l'irréel : son folklore musical en porte le reflet. « L'Amour Sorcier » traduit à la perfection la psychologie des gitans du Sud ; il est fait de la chair déchirée d'un peuple et, d'un bout à l'autre, il décèle les marques si frappantes de son âme pétrie d'amour, de passion, de fougue, de superstition religieuse.
Je me suis pénétrée si intimement de cet ouvrage qu'il est comme incorporé à moi-même. Ce n'est pas seulement le résultat des dix années de travail que je lui ai consacrées, m'émerveillant chaque jour davantage des beautés qu'il renferme, mais surtout l'effet d'une connaissance et d'une communion qui datent de son origine. Il me semble que cette musique pénètre en moi avec la force irrésistible d'un premier amour, elle en rejaillit en mouvements inéluctables. Je lui ai tout donné de moi, tout ce que je suis capable de donner et, en échange, elle m'a procuré, tandis que je découvrais ses secrets les plus subtils, la sensation de ce que peut être quelque chose d'immortel.
....
ARGENTINA.

LOVE THE MAGICIAN...
A COMPOSITION WHICH MUST BE "LIVED"

LOVE THE MAGICIAN!... Few things can bring me greater pleasure than to comment upon this masterpiece, so full of the beauties of a race. It is a masterpiece that, in some way, presents the uninitiated with the very human mysteries of the Andalusian gypsies and which musically, with incredible intensity, brings the spiritual aspects of a people vividly to life for any Spaniard. A people who are a strong race, but weak in superstitions, a people who make and worship beauty, as can be seen from the deeds and events which mark their history, and who, though more material than cerebral, have never been able to free themselves from an innate inclination for magic and the unreal: their musical folklore is a reflection of this. *Love the Magician* perfectly translates the psychology of the southern gypsies; it is made from the torn flesh of a people and, from beginning to end, reveals the palpable marks of their soul, mish-mash of love, passion, spirit and religious susperstition.

I have delved so deeply into this work that it has practically become part of me. Not just because of the ten years of work that I have devoted to it, startled each new day by the beauty it contains, but mainly because of a knowledge and a communion which were there at the start. It is as if that music entered me, with the irresistible effect of a first love, and branched out in unavoidable movements. I have given it all I had, everything that I was able to give it and, in exchange, it has given me, whilst I discovered its subtlest secrets, a sense of something which could be eternal.

ANTONIA MERCÉ, "*LA ARGENTINA*"

Poster for the première of *Love the Magician*, Teatro Español in Madrid, 28th of April 1934. A new version of the ballet for the Festival of Spanish music and dance organised by the National Council of Music.

I HAVE TOLD you before about the marvellous success which met *Love the Magician*, staged by *La Argentina* in Madrid. I do not think that Madrid has ever before witnessed such a beautiful ensemble or such a complete manifestation of art. I had never seen Antonia perform previously and I was really moved along with the rest of the audience who filled the theatre for five days consecutively (at 20 pesetas a seat). It would have been possible to give three of four more performances but we had to leave Madrid on the 3rd and Antonia had other engagements. Madrid will not easily forget Antonia, in the first place, or Pastora and the girls, who made such an admirable ensemble. The songs were sung by Conchita Velázquez (who I think unsurpassable). The Fire Dance, the Terror and the second song (danced by Pastora) were performed as an encore every night. It is a pity that you were not able to be here with us. Antonia was full of enthusiasm, art and energy to show this brilliant ballet and on the last night received an ovation such as I have never seen before. She had to make ten or twelve curtain calls...

I tell you all this so that you can hear *the truth* and because, after the many difficulties there were to overcome (you know what Madrid is like), I wanted you to hear about the audience's warmth and enthusiasm and the moving way they reacted. I send you my heartfelt admiration and congratulations.

ENRIQUE FERNÁNDEZ ARBÓS
Letter to Manuel de Falla
[Madrid, 21 May 1934]

(*Above, from the right*) Vicente Escudero, Pastora Imperio and Antonia Mercé "*La Argentina*", Madrid, 1934 and two moments from the performance of *Love the Magician*, Madrid, 1934.

DANCE IS the expression of my life. I put the best of myself into it. I give it my soul, my sensitivity, my intelligence: it possesses me and I think only about how to perfect it. I create my dances from suffering. The qualities for which I have been praised are due to this suffering. In fact, it is my soul which is expressed in my dances. One has to suffer to reveal what the soul hides.

ANTONIA MERCÉ, "*LA ARGENTINA*"

THE HUMAN body is at its purest and most beautiful when it dances. Because the sadness of the mortal and corruptible stuff of which we are made can only be evaded by the pure spirit of rhythm, clean, incorruptible and immortal.

FEDERICO DE ONÍS

Dances from *La vida breve* and *The Three-cornered Hat* at one of Antonia Mercé's last performances. Salle Pleyel, Paris, 5 June 1936.

From left to right: Manuel de Falla, Miguel Salvador, Adolfo Salazar and Salvador Bacarisse.

ORACIÓN DE LAS MADRES QUE TIENEN A SUS HIJOS EN BRAZOS

THROUGHOUT THE YEARS 1915 AND 1918, RELATIONS BETWEEN MANUEL DE FALLA AND MARÍA AND GREGORIO MARTÍNEZ SIERRA WERE VERY INTENSE. ESPECIALLY WITH MARÍA, WHOM HE WROTE TO ALMOST EVERY DAY DURING THOSE YEARS. FROM THAT TIME ARE THE SHORT PIECES WHICH THEY WROTE TOGETHER SUCH AS THE SONG *ORACIÓN DE LAS MADRES QUE TIENEN A SUS HIJOS EN BRAZOS*, FIRST PERFORMED AT THE RITZ HOTEL, MADRID, ON THE 8TH OF FEBRUARY 1915. THIS "CAROL" WAS WRITTEN FOR VOICE AND PIANO AND WAS DEFINITELY INSPIRED BY THE WAR IN EUROPE.

SEÑORES
QUE TOMAN PARTE EN EL CONCIERTO DE INAUGURACIÓN
DE LA
SOCIEDAD NACIONAL DE MÚSICA

QUINTETO DE PIANO

Piano .... D. Joaquín Turina.
Primer violín ... D. Abelardo Corvino.
Segundo violín ... D. Moisés Aranda.
Viola .... D. Enrique Alcoba.
Violoncello ... D. Domingo Taltavull.

Solista de piano, D. Francisco Fúster.

CANCIONES

D.ª Josefina Revillo.
D. Manuel de Falla.

CONCIERTO DE BACH

Director ...... D. Bartolomé Pérez Casas.
                 { D. Joaquín Turina.
Solistas ...... { D. Manuel de Falla.
                 { D. Miguel Salvador.

ORQUESTA:

              { D. Abelardo Corvino.
              { D. Fermín Fernández Ortiz.
              { D. Odón González.
Violines ...... { D. Augusto Repullés.
              { D. Moisés Aranda.
              { D. Joaquín Grandal.
              { D. Juan Valdés.
              { D. Conrado del Campo.
Violas .... { D. Enrique Alcoba.
              { D. Julio Soto.
Violoncellos .. { D. Luis Villa.
              { D. Domingo Taltavull.
Contrabajo ... D. Sebastián Ruiz Pardo.

On the 5th of February 1915, the inaugural concert of the National Society of Music was held in the drawing room of the Ritz hotel in Madrid. The Society was presided over by Miguel Salvador y Carreras and the artistic committee consisted of the musicians Conrado del Campo, Bartolomé Pérez Casas, Joaquín Turina, Francisco Fúster, Amadeo Vives and Manuel de Falla.

PROGRAMA

Primera parte.

Quinteto en *sol menor*, para piano e instrumentos de cuerda (primera vez en España) .... J. TURINA.

   I.   *Fuga lenta.*
   II. *Animado.*
   III. *Andante.—Scherzo.*
   IV. *Final.*

Piano, Sr. Turina; *primer violín,* Sr. Corvino; *segundo violín,* Sr. Aranda; *viola,* Sr. Alcoba; *violonchelo,* Sr. Taltavull.

Segunda parte.

Impromptu de la codorniz .... ⎫
Paisaje .... ⎬ GRANADOS.
Impromptu .... ⎭

   Pianista, D. Francisco Fúster.

Oración de las madres que tienen a sus hijos en brazos (poesía de Gregorio Martínez Sierra; primera vez en España) .... ⎫ FALLA.
Siete canciones populares españolas .... ⎭

   a) *Seguidilla murciana.*
   b) *El paño moruno.*
   c) *Asturiana.*
   d) *Jota.*
   e) *Nana.*
   f) *Canción.*
   g) *Polo.*

Por la Srta. Revillo, acompañada por el autor.

Tercera parte.

Concierto en *do,* para tres pianos y pequeña orquesta (primera vez en España) .... J. S. BACH.

   Solistas, Sres. Turina, Falla y Salvador; *Director,* Sr. Pérez Casas; doce profesores de orquesta.

Descansos de quince minutos.

Los tres pianos para el concierto de Bach son de **ERARD** (Unión Musical Española).
El piano de gran cola, **RÖNISCH** (casa Navas).

Programme of the first concert given by the National Society of Music at which *Oración de las madres que tienen a sus hijos en brazos,* based on a poem by Gregorio Martínez Sierra, was first performed with Falla at the piano.

PASCUA FLORIDA
EL PAN DE RONDA

ALL THAT REMAINS OF THE MUSICAL VOYAGE CALLED *PASCUA FLORIDA* IS THE SONG, *EL PAN DE RONDA*, WRITTEN BY MARÍA MARTÍNEZ SIERRA IN BARCELONA ON THE 18TH OF DECEMBER 1915 AT THE END OF FALLA'S STAY IN THE CITY WITH THE MARTÍNEZ SIERRAS.

Score of *El pan de Ronda, que sabe a verdad*, based on a poem by María Martínez Sierra.

ON OUR travels through Andalusia, one evening we reached Ronda. Strolling along the badly-paved streets of the picturesque city, feeling a little worn out, we bought some ring-shaped rolls. Before the war, Ronda's bread was food fit for gods, dipped in flour, golden and crispy. We ate and we walked, admiring the pretty wooden doors brought from America at the time our country was rich in colonies; the protruding grilles of the windows adorned by florid flower pots... The appeasing virtue of the bread combined with the peacefulness of the empty streets filled me with the desire to break out singing, a desire which is like the soul's incense thanking Destiny for a moment of tranquillity. As I did not feel able to write verses —my poetry was all in prose—, I wrote some simple couplets capturing the peaceful moment that inspired them. The couplets went:

> The bread of Ronda, that tastes of truth.
> ... And, even if everything in the world was a lie,
> we still have the bread,
> golden, toasted, that smells of oven wood,
> that tastes of truth!
> And, even if everything in the world is a lie,
> the bread is not!
> We enjoy to the utmost the good times
> sad ones are coming after!

This is what the couplets said, but they still had to sing. Falla made them sing by composing one of his clever and heartrending pieces for them. In the piece, under the serenity of the melody dictated to a certain extent by the words, he placed bitterly lonely and darkly melancholic harmonies. Back in Madrid, he wrote them out with his lovely, fine and clear musical hand on a small piece of parchment which he tied with a silk ribbon. Flattered —why not admit it—, I placed the exquisite page on a little table beside a group of Sèvres porcelain... Those couplets gave us the idea of composing some more travel recollections and I already had some written: in

Granada, *Darkness at the Convent* and *Rest at San Nicolás*; in Cadiz, home of the composer, *Cadiz has taken to the Sea*, and others that I do not remember... But one fine Madrid morning when he found out, because I told him, that I was writing some notes for our friend Joaquín Turina, with whom I had also visited Andalusia and North Africa, to use for his *Travel Album*, Falla was possessed by the devil and, in a fit of black rage, he wrenched the painstakingly written parchment from me and tore it into a thousand pieces without saying a single word. My pity won over my natural anger, and I said nothing... Thus perished an enchanted page of music..., unless the original is among the composer's papers. I believe him completely capable of destroying it, in furious revenge for the injury which, in his opinion, I had inflicted on our friendship.

MARÍA MARTÍNEZ SIERRA

Scheme of the poetic-musical cycle *Pascua florida*. María Martínez Sierra's manuscript. [6 April 1915. For the Maestro who is so fond of collecting old papers. *Pascua florida*. The poisoned garden. Rest at San Nicolás. The heart that sleeps beneath the waters. The gypsy district. Charles 5th's drawing room. Darkness at the convent. The bread of Ronda, that tastes of truth. The Gibraltar net. Oriental cities. Cadiz has taken to the sea.]

MY ADMIRABLE friend:

I liked *El pan de Ronda* to an extraordinary degree. I think that the music works as if by magic with your words. I really want to work with you once again!

How enjoyable it was to read your letter! A thousand thanks for sending it! The part about *Madame* made me laugh a lot...

Gregorio had told me about *El pan de Ronda* some time ago. I read it while we lunched the day before yesterday and yesterday he told me that you were planning to go to Tangier with the Maestro Turina, which you did not like because of the sea, and I can see why after Gregorio told me about the dramatic episode in a Swiss lake.

Gregorio is very satisfied with how the rehearsals for *Love the Magician* are going. I am satisfied too, but somewhat less so. It is true that because I hardly sleep I am becoming absolutely stupid and insensitive. Imagine that yesterday we rehearsed at one, at four and at two o'clock in the morning and apart from lunch with Gregorio where we laughed and chatted about loads of silly things, the rest of the day was taken up by *hard* work because, when I was not rehearsing, I was composing. At midnight I finished the *finale* of *Love the Magician*, and I have still got the Interval and a minute for Pastora's rest... and the curtain goes up the day after tomorrow, horror, terror, etc., etc.!

Gregorio informed me yesterday that you will reach Madrid at almost the same time that the show begins. There is no need to tell you how pleased that made me.

Now I have to end to eat a small lunch before going to the rehearsal. Curse the man who fried the lard, as the saying goes! Ah, *Mamma* is admirable. Know that *Amanecer* continues its triumphant run!...

Until very soon, *n'est ce pas?*

With all my friendship!

With all my gratitude!

D. Manué.

I suppose you received my letter from the day before yesterday, crossed by yours.

À bientôt!

MANUEL DE FALLA
Letter to María Martínez Sierra
[Madrid, 13 April 1915]

EL FUEGO FATUO

EL FUEGO FATUO WAS A MORE AMBITIOUS PROJECT. FALLA HAD A HIGH OPINION OF CHOPIN AND USING HIS MUSIC ALMOST TEXTUALLY, HE ORHESTRATED VARIOUS NUMBERS, WRITTEN BY MARÍA MARTÍNEZ SIERRA, FOR A COMPOSITION PLANNED IN THREE ACTS. ON THE VERGE OF ITS PERFORMANCE BY PENELLA THE IDEA WAS DROPPED, THOUGH THE REASON FOR THIS IS NOT KNOWN. THANKS TO PAPERS WHICH HAVE BEEN RECENTLY DISCOVERED, FALLA LEFT THE SECOND ACT UNORCHESTRATED. IN 1976, ANTONI ROS MARBÁ REVISED THE WORK AND THE SPANISH NATIONAL ORCHESTRA PLAYED A SELECTION OF THE NUMBERS AT THE GRANADA FESTIVAL.

THESE WORKS WERE COMPOSED BETWEEN 1918 AND 1919 AND PROBABLY ARE THE LAST COLLABORATION BETWEEN FALLA AND THE MARTÍNEZ SIERRA'S.

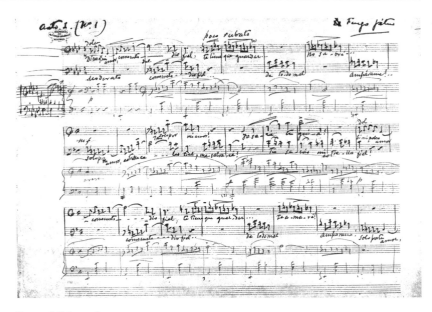

Score of *El fuego fatuo*.

FALLA, a great admirer of Chopin, had the idea of orchestrating some of his best pieces —ballads, noturnes, mazurkas and études— with the intention of stringing them together in a performable unity which, in his opinion and in mine, could prove highly successful. To think, in questions of art, is to do. To work. Imagine a "plot" as romantic as the music and the age in which it was written. The work inspired by Chopin was to have three acts. Two were already finished and Falla had genuinely achieved prodigious emotional results, both artistic and human, with his masterful orchestrations. But at this stage, the author's famous scruples started to trouble him. The dramatic conflict was, inevitably, caused by love. The librettist was a woman and, because of this, instead of writing about two men who fight for the love of the same woman, as is customary in librettos written by men, she had written about two women who yearned for the love of the same man. It followed, also inevitably, that one of the "sopranos" would play a typically conventional "angel", so dear to male imaginations, while the other would embody the character of a lady... we will simply call her frivolous to avoid offending her. Dear God, they certainly know how to wear a man out! Falla's sense of decency was acutely distressed, his natural gallantry could not conceive even for a moment of debasing the ideal "Eternal female" with guilty motives. Although I went to every length to try to explain to him that between two angels in a state of grace conflict cannot exist and that, if the two sopranos were saints, the respectable audience would be bored to death, he would not be convinced. Thus the work remained unperformed and months of work were lost.

MARÍA MARTÍNEZ SIERRA

THIS WAS NOT the first time that the pen of the composer of *Love the Magician* had been entertained in happy courtship with Chopin's music. During the years 1918 and 1919 he had written an interesting piece called *Fuego fatuo*. It was a comic opera in three parts, a lyrical and orchestral adaptation of piano compositions by Chopin, with a libretto by Gregorio Martínez Sierra. At the beginning of the year 1931 I asked to produce it at the first of our festivals. María del Carmen answered me: "My brother has read your letter with interest and does not reply in person for reasons that you are already familiar with. He asks me to tell you that he will consider the possibility of allowing you to use something from *El fuego fatuo* at the '32 festival. Twenty years have passed since he last saw this music and he would have to revise it, etc., before taking a decision. Thus, when his health permits, he will happily deal with the matter." Years went by and he never once spoke to me about it nor did I remind him of my request.

JUAN MARÍA THOMÁS

Costume designs for *El fuego fatuo*, by Manuel Fontanals.

THE MAGISTRATE AND THE MILLER'S WIFE

THIS DRAMA IN FOUR SCENES WAS COMPOSED BY MANUEL DE FALLA IN 1916 BASED ON A LIBRETTO WRITTEN BY GREGORIO AND MARÍA MARTÍNEZ SIERRA, IN CLOSE COLLABORATION WITH GREGORIO AND MARÍA WHO WERE INSPIRED BY THE POPULAR ROMANCE OF THE SAME TITLE WHICH PEDRO ANTONIO DE ALARCÓN HAD TRANSFORMED IN HIS NOVEL *EL SOMBRERO DE TRES PICOS* (*THE THREE-CORNERED HAT*). IT WAS FIRST PRODUCED AT THE TEATRO ESLAVA IN MADRID IN 1917.

MARÍA: I am thrilled to see that you are happy. Gregorio was happy yesterday as well. We were together from half-past one until half-past six. I played him the work I have done on the Drama. I was happy too when I saw his reaction. Let us see if all the rest runs as smoothly. I have finished the theme which identifies the Magistrate, Frasquita's greetings and some parts of the grape dance.

I have not received nor has Gregorio given me the *Song of Five* you refer to and that I am longing to see.

We thought that in the first scene some bird could sing (a blackbird, for example) and in the second scene the cuckoo clock and above-mentioned bird could perform a duet. Also we have often spoken, yesterday and beforehand, about the opera. The libretto is going to be magnificent. Gregorio has thousands of ideas to work on. I have encouraged him to produce the comedy you spoke to me about in Alicante with you.

His eyes are better and, though not completely recovered yet, he says they hardly bother him now and he has stopped using his eye drops.

Yesterday we ate lunch at Botín's . Among other delicacies a lamb whose head I ate in *votre souvenir,* because Gregorio said that had you been there you it would not have been wasted as it was upon him. I hope that the three of us will be eating lamb, or any other dish, I do not mind what, as long as we are together again...

I laughed a lot at all the things you tell me in you very special and unique manner...

Have you received my last two letters? I sent the first to the post office and the second to your hotel. On consecutive days.

I like that about Señor, Mister and Monsieur *ne me va pas du tout...*

This evening I am going to the house of Galdós. Don Benito wants to meet me and speak about music and Machaquito's daughter. I told Gregorio the tale of that *demoiselle.* She has been taken in by Don Benito's nephew —there is not a more honest and upright man alive— who met Machaquito in Bilbao years ago. That was at the start of Machaquito's bullfighting career and he was doing badly, very badly in the ring. The audience wanted to kill him or nearly and he was desperate, almost suicidal. Don Benito's nephew took pity on him and

Pedro Antonio de Alarcón, author of the novel El sombrero de tres picos the inspiration of Gregorio Martínez Sierra's drama called *The Magistrate and the Miller's Wife.*

visited him at his hotel to console him. For that kindness he received the matador's thanks; his fervent friendship: revelations about his past life and lastly his daughter to look after. Thus whenever Machaquito is in Madrid he visits the house of Galdós, which has given rise to the rumour that he is Don Benito's son, *pas… du tout!…*

So. The *demoiselle* studies music and *voilà* that is why they want me to meet her...

I will tell you about the visit soon.

Now I must finish.

Veuillez agréer, Madame, les respectueux hommages de votre dévoué.

D. Manué

Un peu trop longue la lettre, n'est-ce pas?

MANUEL DE FALLA
Letter to María Martínez Sierra
[Madrid, 2 February 1916]

MARÍA: *Mille fois merci* for your last letter which arrived the day before yesterday. You cannot imagine what a marvellous time I had reading it because of the wonderful humour it contains...

The only thing that I feel sorry about is that your throat is not cured yet. Mean throat! But God will wish that the remains of your illness pass quickly and hopefully in your next letter you will be able to tell me that you are completely recovered.

I need not mention how much you were in our minds yesterday, and when you get back we will repeat the majestic banquet. It took place in my room —the only room in the house with space for eight people— yet still lacking the extension that comfort would demand. As well as Gregorio, my cousin María del Carmen, Matos and Lara came.

After lunch I played all that I have written for the Drama: introduction of the Magistrate, two of Frasquita's ladies and the grape scene. Of the last I had made two versions and the first was unanimously chosen. Up to now all goes well, let us hope the rest is as good! Gregorio is angered that I listen to his congratulations of my music without objecting or blushing. That made me laugh a lot. The explanation is simply that I do not think that they deserve congratulations at all, even though it makes me very happy that my humble work is to his taste.

To answer your questions *je vous* tell *Madame* that I do not consider Maestro Turina's suite any more or less scholarly than the rest of his work. But this has nothing to do with whether I like it or not. I definitely like it, as I told you, and I think that I will like it even more when I hear it again. At the moment the Maestro in going through one of his friendly periods: he is agreeable, affectionate, cheerful and communicative. He is a good man and we can work on correcting his vices. Good heavens it cannot be so difficult.

When I reproached him for not having replied to my last letters he made his habitual *sourire de lapin* and until the next time.

But, I insist, he is a good fellow and he will soon repent.

MANUEL DE FALLA
Letter to María Martínez Sierra
[Madrid, 15 February 1916]

Score of The Magistrate and the Miller's Wife.

CHÈRE madame et amie:

Je suppose que vous aurez reçu mes deux lettres adressées à Paris. I, however, have only received *la votre à S. Sebastien. Heureusement* I feel calm about your journey, which I heard had been all right in your telegram the day before yesterday. I hope I will be given more detailed news soon. *Je les souhaite bien.* Did you go straight to Paris from S. Sebastian? The date of the telegram makes me think not.

I am also in the midst of a telegram correspondence with Gregorio. I have sent him *trois dépêches* over the last twenty four hours. They are all about the *Ballets russes.* Diaghilev told me yesterday that he wants to take his ballet to Barcelona. I believe that this is an excellent financial opportunity (even more so for Serrano) and considering that taking Gregorio along with me would avoid a correspondence from interfering with his *saison,* I telegraphed him. The rest you will find out from him. I will be happy if the affair sees the light as I consider it a safe bet. I have never seen the Real theatre like it was today. There was not one free seat. Another thing, which I told you I was afraid would happen, I will have to make important changes to the second scene of the *Magistrate* because it has been made more *choreographic.* This is correct, so much so, that I do not mind having to work on the composition again. This means that there will be two versions: the original (which will stay as it is, for comic theatre groups) and the choreographed, which is for the Russians. They still have not finished making changes. The only thing that seems clear at the moment is that I will have to compose a long finale, developing the fight scene and even, perhaps, making room for the Miller there, who comes back chased by the Magistrate's constables.

To answer your second question, the one about *Love the Magician, je dois vous dire, Madame, que j'ai touché les droits de 6 représentations,* I seem to remember.

Pastora has behaved badly again. What are we going to do! She is sure to do the same again on the South American tournée.

Gregorio is still searching for a way to flesh out the text of the piece so that it can be produced in normal theatres. The audition at the *Nacional* will take place in the last two weeks of March.

I hope you have received my last two letters (the last on Saturday) sent to the Reina Victoria Theatre, like this one.

The cuckoo's song is very amusing. Gregorio gave it to me on Sunday. Do you think it is a good idea to hear, right after this song, the cuckoo clock on stage singing a duet with the bird which sings the news?

The first production of *The Magistrate and the Miller's Wife*, Eslava Theatre Madrid, 7th of April 1917. Pantomime farce inspired by some incidents from Alarcón's novel. It was acted by Luisa Puchol as "The miller's wife", Ricardo de la Vega as "The magistrate" and Pedro Sepúlveda as "The miller". The orchestra, consisting of musicians from the Madrid Philharmonic Orchestra, was conducted by Joaquín Turina. Amorós and Blancas did the stage designs and the costumes were by Rafael Penagos.

I have to finish now to send this letter. *La suite à la prochaine lettre.* I am meeting Gregorio at the Lion d'or later.

Marvellous weather.

Nothing new. All goes well, thank God.

My family send you warm regards.

Admirable the last *Modern woman...*

I have run out of time.

Mille amitiés de votre devoué

D. Manué

Does censorship exist in Melilla? I ask because your envelope looked as if it had been opened and resealed on one side in such a way that the glue had stuck a little to the letter.

À bientôt!

Nin, who is in Barcelona seems to have obtained his passport and tells me that as soon as he reaches Paris he will be at your service.

MANUEL DE FALLA
Letter to María Martínez Sierra
[Madrid, 8 June 1917]

THE IDEA of composing *The Three-cornered Hat* based on Pedro Antonio de Alarcón's famous novel, inspired by the popular romance of *The Magistrate and the Miller's Wife*, had pursued Falla for many years. So much so, that when he asked Fernández Shaw to write a libretto for the opera he planned to send to the competition at the Academy of Fine Arts, they hesitated about whether to do *La vida breve, The Three-cornered Hat* or *Paolo and Francesca.* They decided to leave the decision to luck. They wrote each title on a piece of paper and placed them in a hat. *La vida breve* was picked. Falla's initial aim was to compose *The Three-cornered Hat* as a lyrical piece as opposed to a ballet. But the writer's heirs could not grant permission for the novel to be set to music and produced on stage because this was forbidden by a clause in the testament.

JAIME PAHISSA

"The miller's" arrest, *The Magistrate and the Miller's Wife*, Teatro Eslava, Madrid, 1917.

PLOT: Consists of poking fun of the old magistrate of the city of Guadix in Andalusia, who flirts amorously with the miller's beautiful wife. She pretends to respond to his courtship, up to the point in which he finds himself in an embarrassing situation and the old gallant becomes the laughing stock of the villagers who egged him on him, whilst the miller and his wife profess steadfast love.

ENCOURAGED by the great success of *Love the Magician*, we looked for the subject for a drama. Thus came into being what later became a ballet and was and is shown throughout Europe and America with the title *The Three-cornered Hat*.

The choice of a story was always the most difficult part of working with Falla, who did not allow even the slightest shadow of doubt to fall over the sixth commandment and who had decided —unhappy dreamer— never to write a single note which paid service to sensual sin. We were inspired not so much by Alarcón's enjoyable short novel *El sombrero de tres picos* as by the popular romance *The Magistrate and the Miller's Wife*,

which was undeniably used by the novelist as his starting point. In folk literature there are themes of such lush vitality that they are open to all kinds of interpretations and yet, in every case, they retain their original liveliness.

There were no travels for this collaboration. The theme is Andalusian, but the piece was entirely composed in Madrid and the revision was made on a good sounding Rönich piano. When I had decided to buy a piano Joaquín Turina, admirable pianist and very choosy in questions of the instrument, had recommended the Rönich. The drama was produced in this form at the Eslava Theatre, very competently acted by the members of the Martínez Sierra company.

The score was also for a small orchestra —seventeen instruments plus a piano—. The Madrid audience were amused and entertained by it, but at the same time Diaghilev was passing through Madrid with his Russian Ballet on their first visit to the Spanish capital.

Diaghilev, wise and great admirer, attended a number of performances of our drama and realised the enormous success that it could achieve in ballet form. Diaghilev was stubborn and impatient. Driven by his imperious will, both composer and librettist began working once more. The libretto had to be modified somewhat to bring choreographied ensemble dances into the picture and to provide the principle dancer —on that occasion Léonide Massine— with the "love dance" which every vedette of Terpsichore art needs to shine. Falla had to arrange the piece for a full-size orchestra, add the

"Farruca" so wonderfully performed by Massine, and to compose the splendid finale, a mosaic of folk theme crowned by a triumphant *jota*.

There is no need to mention the success of the *The Three-cornered Hat* which was choreographed and danced by Massine —who studied Flamenco dances in depth and who admits to having found many beautiful poses in bullfighting— and designed and costumed by Picasso. Anyone interested in theatrical music will know that within a few months the work had earned the category of a "classic" and since then has been placed in the annals of great ballets such as *Petrushka* and *Schéhérazade*.

Incidentally, that first visit of the Russian ballet to Madrid gave me the opportunity to get to know Stravinsky, who accompanied Diaghilev on that excursion.

Quite often, whilst we were putting the final touches to *The Three-cornered Hat*, he came to our house with Diaghilev and Massine, and with his boyish humour (he still looked like one) and the modesty of a great artist —only the mediocre ones are vain— he was quite prepared to sit at the piano and generously delight us with his inspiration and his equally prodigious technique. He was in the midst of composing a *Village Wedding* and thus I was granted the privilege of hearing the piece long before it was played in public. With his simplicity, unaffected by the knowledge of his own worth, with his unchangeable optimism and his relaxed and naturally affectionate conduct he was very similar to two other illustrious composers, Maurice Ravel and Joaquín Turina, and struck a sharp contrast to Manuel de Falla's inherent sadness and distrustful pessimism.

MARÍA MARTÍNEZ SIERRA

Ernest Ansermet, Serge Diaghilev, Igor Stravinsky and Serge Prokofiev.

THE THREE-CORNERED HAT

Serge Diaghilev's Russian Ballet company during their European tour of *The Three-cornered Hat.*

WHEN *THE MAGISTRATE AND THE MILLER'S WIFE* WAS FIRST PRODUCED, SERGE DIAGHILEV WAS VISITING MADRID WITH HIS BALLET COMPANY. IMPRESSED BY THE WORK, HE ASKED FALLA TO TRANSFORM IT INTO A BALLET. AS SOON AS A CONTRACT WAS DRAWN UP FALLA BEGAN AT ONCE TO WORK ON EXTENDING AND ADAPTING THE PIECE TO FIT THE NEW STAGE VERSION FOR THE RUSSIAN BALLET. THE FIRST WORLD WAR DELAYED THE PREMIÈRE PLANNED FOR 1917. MEANWHILE, FALLA WORKED ON THE UNFINISHED *FUEGO FATUO*. WITH WAR OVER THE PREMIÈRE WAS ARRANGED FOR LONDON IN 1919. FALLA INTENSIFIED HIS CLOSE WORKING RELATIONSHIP WITH PABLO PICASSO WHO PREPARED THE COSTUMES AND STAGE DESIGN. THE PREMIÈRE TOOK PLACE AT THE ALHAMBRA THEATRE IN LONDON ON THE 22ND OF JULY 1919 WITH CHOREOGRAPHY BY LÉONIDE MASSINE AND CONDUCTED BY ERNEST ANSERMET.

Score of The Three-cornered Hat.

Manuel de Falla and Léonide Massine in the gardens of the Alhambra in Granada.

Manuel de Falla and Léonide Massine in the Lions courtyard at the Alhambra in Granada.

ON VARIOUS occasions Diaghilev had spoken to Falla about the possibility of composing a work for his famous "Russian Ballet" company. Diaghilev's first idea was to produce *Nights in the Gardens of Spain* as a ballet. The idea had also occured to Martínez Sierra. With this aim in mind they travelled to Granada to see at close quarters the place in which the action of the work developed. There in the Alhambra, Diaghilev's oriental fantasies began to envisage the scene of the ballet: a party at night in the gardens of the Generalife... the ladies covered by expensive Manilan shawls... but the men in tuxedos... And other scenes in a similar vein. Falla, however, was not convinced by the idea and did not see how his music, conceived and carried out with such precise orchestral detail and such ethereal poetry could adapt itself to the rhythm of some theatrical dances. He would not be convinced even though they pleaded him and Stravinsky himself pointed out that *Petrushka* had started out as a piano concert.

The fact is that that idea went no further, but Falla did promise Diaghilev to write a ballet especially for him and he told him about his plans to compose one based on the book *El sombrero de tres picos*. Diaghilev was thrilled by the idea, and lost no time drawing up a contract between himself, Martínez Sierra (as librettist) and Falla. But that was at the height of the First World War, and the difficulties it implied for an artistic company of an international nature meant that Diaghilev was not able to produce the new piece. For this reason he gave Martínez Sierra permission to stage it, not as a ballet but as a drama under the title *The Magistrate and the*

Miller's Wife. This is how the curtain went up on it at the Eslava Theatre in Madrid. It included some musical numbers written for chamber Orchestra. Turina conducted, and Ricardo Vega played the part of the magistrate, better —said Falla— than anyone has ever managed to since. Afterwards, Martínez Sierra's company showed *The Magistrate and the Miller's Wife* in a number of Spanish cities; I remember seeing it at the Teatro Novedades in Barcelona. When Falla saw the performance he noticed that in order to make it into a ballet he would have to cut out certain parts —the development was too drawn out— and add others. Falla set to work and if he took longer to finish *The Three-cornered Hat* than other pieces it was because he wasted many hours and days composing the unfortunate *El fuego fatuo* and because he had already begun *Master Peter's Puppet Show*.

Diaghilev's problems had reached new proportions. He was denied entry into France and England because of his nationality —the recent revolution in Russia had brought isolated peace with Germany— and the Italian frontier was also closed to him, so he had no other choice than to make the best of Spain. Moreover, his financial situation was very complicated and difficult, which made it hard to find enterprises willing to engage his company. Falla went to visit him at his room in the Palace Hotel in Madrid and found him at the end of his tether.

"I'm ruined" —Diaghilev told him— "What will become of me! There's only one way out: I'll go to a monastery."

Despite of the contradiction which is suggested by a resolution so out of keeping for a man like Diaghilev who, in many respects, led such an unusual life, one should bear in mind that deep down all Russians are profoundly religious; Stravinsky for example.

But Falla had gone to speak to him in order to find a solution to his present state. And he found one. He looked for a lawyer who managed to sort out his situation and arrange an excellent deal with an entrepreneur. The lawyer was Leopoldo Matos. In recognition, Falla dedicated to him *The Three-cornered Hat*. With his affairs sorted out Diaghilev was able to start work with his company once again and Falla on his composition. Diaghilev intended, because of war restrictions, to organise a reduced company and produce ballets for small orchestras which were simple to stage. Thus Falla, as mentioned earlier, began to arrange a pared-down version of *The Magistrate* for a tiny orchestra. But gradually he had to arrange for it to be played by a full-size orchestra as the war drew to a close and Diaghilev made ready to produce the ballets with all their previous elements and splendour. That is why the orchestra for *The Three-cornered Hat* is slowly filled out, from the small "chamber-like" group at the beginning to the huge orchestra that play the *jota* at the end.

JAIME PAHISSA

Portrait of Manuel de Falla by Larionov.

FALLA AND DIAGHILEV WRITE

DEAR FRIEND:

By now you should have received my missive in reply to yours and thus know how pleased I am about the good news and that I am prepared to be in London with the music on the 15th of June.

I place my trust in your wise planning concerning everything related to the journey: I cannot leave without making arrangements for my absence here at home. I also have to withdraw from some engagements and leave my classes. The cost of the journey, scenery and costumes has to be added to all this...

Forgive me for speaking about these *mishaps*, I do so by virtue of our long friendship.

I think that the casting has been magnificent and I think the same about the choice of our painter collaborator... I remember very vividly that day —in the Palace— when we spoke with Picasso about *The Magistrate* and I am thrilled to have him with us. Please send him, and Massine as well, my warmest regards.

Did you receive the postcard I sent a few months ago? Afterwards I suffered the blow of losing my father and I have been ill and unable to leave the house for a couple of months. Nothing serious, but a great nuisance.

My most affectionate regards yours

MANUEL DE FALLA
Letter to Serge Diaghilev
[Madrid, 30 April 1919]

You might have heard that I am composing a piece —almost completed— for Princesse de Polignac's theatre.

Your telegram took nine or ten days to reach me. I thought I should warn you.

MY DEAR friend:

First and foremost receive my deepest sympathy. I know how very dear your family are to you and your misfortune has affected all of us. I think that after winter it would do you some good to leave Spain and come to visit us for a while.

Tell me what you think about this trip, in other words, what you need. Take into account that I am not very rich and act like a good friend in your calculations. You will see that in the programme for this season I have introduced a novelty in our performances. They are "Symphonic Interludes". They went down well in London and the music is proving as popular as the performance. Therefore I would be very pleased if you could play your *Nocturnes* —you would have to play them 3 or 4 times, because we play the *Interludes* every session and we have to keep all the punters happy.

I would also like you to play *Triana* and another brilliant piece from Albéniz's *Iberia* (whose title slips my mind), orchestrated by Arbós. Please, could you ask him for me and bring me the material which I would send back after the London season. Naturally he has to give it to us in an absolutely acceptable condition as it is not for the ballet, but for the symphonic interludes.

As far as your ballet *The Three-cornered Hat* is concerned we have come up with the following: as there is going to be a handsome curtain by Picasso which will be seen before the ballet commences it would be a good idea to play a short overture and we thought that one of your three pieces for piano called *Andalusia* would be very appropriate —if there is no orchestral version, could you write one? In a tone which corresponds to the beginning of the Ballet. It is one of your most beautiful works and it would fit perfectly.

Picasso agrees that it would be very typical to add voices to some of the dance numbers such as the *jota*, the *farruca*, etc., he thinks it is very Spanish.

Could you take charge of bringing me the material for orchestra, which will be conducted by Ansermet? Could you also come to an agreement about the material with the authors' society as is stipulated in your contract? Nothing else.

Massine is choreographing the ballet and Picasso is making wonderful set designs. You will like it a lot. Awaiting your reply my most affectionate regards yours

S. DIAGHILEV

P.S. Massine asks me if you can bring him 30 pairs of castanets, 15 first class ones and 15 ordinary ones. Tell me how much they cost you.

SERGE DIAGHILEV
Letter to Manuel de Falla
[London, 10 May 1919]

MY DEAR friend:

Heartfelt thanks for your kind words concerning the misfortune which has afflicted me...

The day before your letter arrived I received the programme of your season (with the photo of Granada which I was very pleased to see again) and I am longing to see all that Massine and Picasso have done with the ballet.

You can count on me for the *Nocturnes* whose title is *Nights in the Gardens of Spain*.

In reply to what you have so kindly asked, I calculate that in order to undertake the journey —taking into account the circumstances which I mentioned in my last letter— I would need 1,700 pesetas (not francs, because of the exchange). As far as the rest is concerned we can speak in London and, as always, I trust your friendship..

I saw Arbós and spoke to him about *Triana* and *El Puerto*. He answered that though he was very happy that you wanted to play them he is afraid that he is not able to send you them, firstly because at present he has only got material enough for his orchestra on tour and secondly because he has already been asked once or twice to play them in London, but has turned all offers down as he hopes to present them himself when he has finished arranging the other pieces from *Iberia* included in his suite.

He will write to you about all this, but what he is prepared to play is *Catalonia*, orchestrated by Albéniz himself.

We can speak about the short overture for Picasso's curtain in London. I have an idea for this which I would like to try out during the rehearsals.

I was very pleased to hear that Ansermet is with you.

Picasso is right: it would be very typical to add the human voice at some points; but I think that cries, *olés* etc,. shouted by the dancers themselves, would be better than singing, don't you? I asked about the price of the castanets: 4 ptas for good quality ones and 2 ptas for the ordinary ones (the discount depends on the number of pairs you buy).

I will arrange orchestral material with the General Authors' Society and bring it with me, along with the *Nocturnes* and the castanets. Permit me to advise you to send an invitation to Martínez Sierra so that he and his wife can attend the ballet's première. It would make me very happy. That, dear friend, is everything for the moment, and awaiting good news receive my sincere and affectionate regards yours

MANUEL DE FALLA
Letter to Serge Diaghilev
[Madrid, 24 May 1919]

THEATRE NATIONAL
OPÉRA

VENDREDI 23 JANVIER 1920
Rideau à 21 heures

Ballets Russes

ARTISTES

Thamar **KARSAVINA**

Vera **CARALLI**   Lubov **TCHERNICHEVA**

Léonide **MASSINE**

Lydia **SOKOLOVA**   Joséphine **CECCHETTI**

Vera **NEMCHINOVA**   Alexandra **WASILEVSKA**

Leokadia **KLEMENTOVICZ**   Hilda **BEWICKE**

Veceslaw **SVOBODA**   Stanislas **IDZIKOVSKY**

Nicolas **KREMNEFF**   Léon **WOIZIKOVSKY**

Nicolas **ZVEREFF**   Jean **JASVINSKY**

Félia **RADINA**

Le Maître Enrico **CECCHETTI**
et le Corps de Ballet

CHANT

Mlle Zoia **ROSOVSKA**

Régisseur général : **Serge GRIGORIEFF**

PAPILLONS

Chorégraphie de FOKINE - Décor de DOBOUJINSKI

Musique de SCHUMANN

LE TRICORNE (Création à Paris)

Chorégraphie de L. MASSINE - Décors de P. PICASSO

Musique de Manuel DE FALLA

CONTES RUSSES

Chorégraphie de L. MASSINE - Décor de M. LARIONOW

Musique de LIADOV

L'Orchestre sera dirigé par **M. Gabriel GROVLEZ**

Samedi 24 Janv.	Dimanche 25 Janv.	Lundi 26 Janv.	Mardi 27 Janv.
FAUST	BALLETS RUSSES	SALOMÉ - GOYESCAS	BALLETS RUSSES

Le bureau de location est ouvert de 10 h. à midi et de 13 h. 1/2 à 18 h., rue Auber, dans le bâtiment de l'Opéra

Léonide Massine as the "Miller", Théâtre National de l'Opéra, Paris, 1920. (Photo Lynn Garrafola, New York).

Polunin Album, photographs taken at the Covent Garden workshops, London, while the curtain of *The Three-cornered Hat* was made in 1919. (© RMN–SPADEM).

IT WAS in Madrid that we met Félix Fernández. Diaghilev had first seen him dancing in a square in Seville, and had come to the conclusion that he was the most brilliant Spanish male dancer of his day. He was now dancing on the stage of a café in a back street of Madrid, where working people used to go. Diaghilev must have been in some doubt whether this fiery, ignorant boy would be able to work and fit in with his highly disciplined company, but he took the risk and engaged him.

The employment of Félix was the first step towards the realisation of the great Spanish ballet which Massine intended to create, though at the time neither Diaghilev nor Massine can have known exactly what form it would take. The essential was that Massine and the company should learn to perform Spanish steps in a Spanish way; and Massine in particular had to master the grammar of the Spanish dance before he could work out his choreography. At this stage Diaghilev and Massine probably saw Félix as the eventual star of their Spanish ballet, for if they had only needed a professor, it would surely have been more reasonable to engage an older man with experience of teaching.

As Massine learned more of the secrets of this very special art and grew more sure of himself, and as poor Félix's unstable nature became apparent, so, I suppose, they gradually came to visualise Massine as the hero of the ballet. One thing is certain: Félix joined the company in the confident expectation that Diaghilev intended to make him a world-famous star.

LYDIA SOKOLOVA

From left to right: Serge Diaghilev, Vladimir Polunin and Pablo Picasso in the workshop where the scenery for The Three-cornered Hat was painted, London, 1919. (© RMN–SPADEM).

Programme of The Three-cornered Hat. Lydia Lopokova in the rôle of "the Miller's wife".

WHEN WE had sailed from Barcelona to South America in 1917, leaving the "lucky few" behind, Diaghilev had seen in a Madrid theatre a short work which he was to transform into Le Tricorne. This was a mimed play written by the writer Martínez Sierra with music by Manuel de Falla, based on a nineteenth century novel El Sombrero de Tres Picos by Alarcón. Diaghilev liked this piece so much that he arranged for de Falla to fill it out with new numbers and rescore it for a larger orchestra. Rehearsing separate dances with a piano often gives a dancer very little idea of the true beauty of the score, and I remember how thrilled I was when we heard de Falla's joyful music played by the full orchestra. De Falla was a sweet person but he looked like a timid little official. It was wonderful to think that a quiet little man I knew with an umbrella and a black-and-white straw boater could have given birth to this explosion of melody and rhythm. I found the music of Le Tricorne so exhilarating that I preferred dancing it even to watching it.

LYDIA SOKOLOVA

Programme of the première of The Three-cornered Hat, London, 1919.

Lydia Sokolova in the rôle of "the Miller's wife".

Copy of The Three-cornered Hat, London, J. & W. Chester, 1921.

Costumes by Pablo Picasso.

Vera Nemchinova and Léonide Massine as the "Miller's wife" and the "Miller".

DE FALLA, great musician, gentle and unassuming, reminiscent of an El Greco portrait, did not think it derogatory to play at our rehearsals. A magnificent pianist, he had delighted Rouché, director of the Paris Opera, with his rendering of the score of *The Three-cornered Hat*. On another occasion he had played for me alone the score of his ballet, *L'Amor Brujo*.

Although it was indeed presumptuous of me to sum up a composer then at the height of his creative power, de Falla always seemed to me a happy genius nurtured from the vital sources of his own country. Though his work is of international importance, he will remain a magnificent example of the intensely national artist.

Pablo Picasso in his daring search for new expression has never lost sight of that consummate mastery of line, and while many would laugh at his bolder experiments and say that they, too, could make patchwork pictures, he alone possessed that precise, strong and delicate inflection of line which seemed to be lost with Ingres. He also had an absolute sense of the stage and its requirements, the abbreviated and strong formula of composition and a neo-romanticism far away from the sentimental. At the time of the rehearsals he had completed all the costumes save mine, and he would come and watch me dance. The costume he finally evolved was a supreme masterpiece of pink silk and black lace of the simplest shape —a symbol more than an ethnographical reproduction of a national costume.

On the first performance of *The Three-cornered Hat* Diaghilev welcomed me with a wreath that bore the inscription "In celebration of the day on which you returned to your Father's embrace."

TAMARA KARSAVINA

Costume by Picasso for the "Magistrate".

Pablo Picasso. Sketch for the scenery of *The Three-cornered Hat*, 1919.

de la Manga (of the sleeve), because he would have been less like Don Quixote if the translator had translated "Mancha" by "Tache" (spot) rather than "Manche" or, in other words, if he had tried to preserve the native name of Don Quixote's region, instead of Frenchifying it. The influence of time, takes effect for the foreigner in a space; for this reason, in a sense the foreigner, like posterity, stands before a work of art.

Sculpture, painting and music, are translated in space, carrying their surroundings with them; they are so internationalist, so cosmopolitan, that the native quality is brought to play in them, which in native art is played by universal qualities.

Pablo Picasso. Early study for the scenery of *The Three-cornered Hat*, 1919.

the première of his danceable *The Three-cornered Hat* was a real accomplishment.

Falla approaches Spanish musical themes from the perspective of the international artistic vanguards. He is off now to an Andalusian farmhouse to finish the music for his *Master Peter's Puppet Show*, which we will hear in Paris next winter.

The music box, I mean Falla's head, is bald; and baldness is a very ordinary symbol of all men. The success of *The Three-cornered Hat* is that Falla has put Alarcón's *Sombrero de Tres Picos* on his music box. Alarcón was much less universally literate than Galdós.

CORPUS BARGA

FALLA'S BALD PATCH
AND *THE THREE-CORNERED HAT*

IT IS strange that native art is nearly always the most intellectual and natural. Literature and painting are usually native arts whereas sculpture, painting, music are generally cosmopolitan ones.

In literature there is always something which cannot be translated from one language to another. The space of architecture cannot be translated; it is still impossible to shift light (according to today's physicists this light should not be represented figuratively by a straight line. This light can be weighed —so physicists say—; but it remains the undefinable part of architecture).

A translated book is a new book. An architectural style seen under a different light only remains unchanged for the learned. The influence of the environment on architecture is, generally, posthumous. If you put León cathedral in Chartres it would end up looking more like Chartres cathedral than that of León.

Literature, in order to overcome this, considers it essential to find a universal quality or, in other words, some virtue which imbues it with a strength that goes beyond language and the tragic moment arrives when language, which is most important, loses its value and the poor native, literature, transcends...

Architecture has the same universal quality; the great styles are universal equations which are not able to resolve the unknown native value. Typical Arabian architecture does not belong to either the Arabs or Arabia; it is the embodiment of universality, in a literal or spiritual sense and in an architectural or material sense, steeped in native air. What I said about León cathedral can be applied analogically and to the same effect to the Cordova mosque. It is very likely that if one moved the Omar mosque to the Cordovan mountain range it would not have to be painted blue, but could be orange; likewise in French, Don Quixote need not be Don Quixote de la Mancha, i.e of the spot, but rather Don Quixote

Léonide Massine as the "Miller".

In Spain people say:

"What a shame that Galdos' work isn't universally interesting!"

Zuloaga, not long ago, speaking about recent Spanish painting, lamented:

"There is nothing Spanish, nothing which is 'ours'; only Solana..."

Julio Antonio, who was a sculptor open to all influences, died looking for an Iberian style.

Manuel de Falla is a post-Wagnerian composer and, consequently, Russophile for that Russian music which aims to surpass Wagner. His position will become clear by naming two of his admirers: Debussy and Stravinsky. In Paris, he is the best known Spanish composer, and

Historical recording of *The Three-cornered Hat*.

Léonide Massine and Tamara Karsavina.

Pablo Picasso. Costume for the "Miller's wife".

Programme of the première of *The Three-cornered Hat,* **the Alhambra Theatre, London, 1919.**

M. S. Idzikovsky as the "Magistrate".

AT THE opening of the ballet, Leon mimed the role of the grotesque old Governor. Picasso gave him a fantastic make-up, with dabs of the same blue which was used in the costumes of his bodyguard of policemen. During rehearsals I greatly enjoyed stamping away on top of the little bridge and pushing the Governor over the side to see him fall on a mattress and change his coat for one with stripes of black American cloth on it, so that when he reappeared it looked as if he were dripping wet. A day or two before the first night, Diaghilev, with his keen eye for effect, decided that he did not like the finale, which was performed in small groups, so Massine rearranged it.

The new finale had far more mass excitement; and the climax, during which the Governor's effigy was tossed on a blanket to the abandoned laughter of the villagers was a great moment of ballet. We had one full-dress rehearsal and the ballet was danced without a hitch. *Le Tricorne* was an immediate success: de Falla and Picasso had made their stage début in England with a bang.

LYDIA SOKOLOVA

POUR LE TOMBEAU DE CLAUDE DEBUSSY

THIS SHORT WORK WAS COMPOSED FOR GUITAR IN GRANADA IN AUGUST 1920, TO MARK THE DEATH OF CLAUDE DEBUSSY. IT WAS COMMISSIONED BY HENRI PRUNIÈRES FOR THE COMMEMORATIVE EDITION WHICH *LA REVUE MUSICALE* DEDICATED TO THE MEMORY OF THE FRENCH COMPOSER. IT WAS PUBLISHED ALONGSIDE OTHER HOMAGES WRITTEN BY DUKAS, ROUSELL, MALIPIERO, GOOSENS, BARTOK, SCHMITT, STRAVINSKY, RAVEL AND SATIE. AN ESSAY BY FALLA ON "DEBUSSY AND SPAIN" APPEARED IN THE SAME PUBLICATION.

PROBABLY WRITTEN FOR THE GUITARIST MIGUEL LLOBET, WHO PLAYED IT FOR THE FIRST TIME, IT WAS LATTER INTERPRETED BY MARIE LOUISE HENRI CASADESUS ON HARP-LUTE AT THE SALLE DES AGRICULTEURS IN PARIS ON THE 24TH OF JANUARY 1921. FALLA ARRANGED THE VERSION FOR PIANO IN SEPTEMBER 1920. IT WAS PUBLISHED BY J. & W. CHESTER OF LONDON IN 1926.

Portrait of Miguel Llobet by José María López Mezquita and caricature of Debussy, 1913.

MIGUEL LLOBET had often asked Falla to compose him a piece for guitar. Falla granted Llobet's wish. Debussy had died. One day, at a concert, Falla bumped into Henri Prunières, who told him he was going to devote an issue of his *Revue Musicale* to Debussy and asked Falla to write an article. Falla would have preferred to make a musical contribution. Prunières petition worried him; rather than write an article he would have liked to have expressed his affection towards Debussy through music; but he did not know what kind of music to compose. In the end he wrote the article and the composition. Regarding the latter, he had just one idea: he wanted the piece to finish with Debussy's *Soirée dans Grenade*. Then the idea came to him that he could compose something for guitar, which would satisfy both the *Revue Musicale* and Llobet. So, while passing through Barcelona, on his way to Granada from Paris, he told Llobet:

"I know what I'm going to do now."

Falla set to work by studying guitar method in order to learn all its properties, just as he had studied other instruments following Dukas' advice, and fifteen days later Llobet received to his great surprise (he knew how slowly and meticulously Falla worked) the composition *Pour le Tombeau de Claude Debussy*, which has since become a part of the repertory of all concert guitarists.

JAIME PAHISSA

WE KNOW how much modern music owes to Debussy, from this point of view as well as many others. However, I am not, of course, referring to the servile imitators of the eminent composer, but rather to the direct and indirect consequences of his work, to the feeling of emulation it has stirred up, to the unfortunate prejudices it has destroyed once and for all.

Spain has greatly benefitted from this combination. We might say that, to a certain degree, Debussy had taken to new lengths our knowledge of the modal possibilities of our music already revealed in our teacher Felipe Pedrell's essays. But while the Spanish composer to a large extent uses authentic popular material in his music, the French master avoids them and creates a music of his own, selecting only the parts which have inspired him and only the essence of the fundamental elements. This working method, always praiseworthy among native composers (unless precise documentary use is jus-

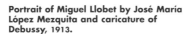

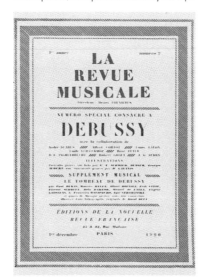

tified) acquires still greater value when practised by those who write music which is, as it were, foreign to them. There is another interesting fact regarding certain harmonic phenomena which occur in the particular texture of Debussy's music. These phenomena are played in their most pure state on the guitar by villagers in Andalusia as if it were the most natural thing in the world. It is curious that Spanish composers had neglected those effects, even despised them as barbaric, or adapted them to the old musical procedures, until Debussy taught how they should be used.

The results were immediate: the twelve admirable jewels left to us by Isaac Albéniz under the title *Iberia* are enough to show it.

I could certainly say a lot more about Claude Debussy and Spain, but this modest study is just the outline of another, more complete, in which I shall also deal with everything that our country and our music have inspired in foreign composers, from Domenico Scarlatti, whom Joaquín Nin claims for Spain, to Maurice Ravel.

But now I want to proclaim loudly that, if Debussy has used Spain as the keystone of one of the most beautiful facets in his work, he has paid us back so generously that it is Spain who is today his debtor.

MANUEL DE FALLA

Score of *Pour le tombeau de Debussy*.

FANTASIA BÆTICA

FALLA, RUBINSTEIN, ANSERMET AND STRAVINSKY KEPT CLOSE CONTACT OFTEN COLLABORATING TOGETHER. THE PROBLEMS CAUSED BY THE WAR IN EUROPE LEFT COMPOSERS IN A HAZARDOUS FINANCIAL SITUATION. THE ONLY PLACES THAT COMPOSERS WERE ABLE TO FIND STAGES AND FEES WORTHY OF THE MUSICIANS WERE BARCELONA AND MADRID, IN SPAIN, BUENOS AIRES AND SOME CITIES OF THE U.S.A. THE PIANIST ARTHUR RUBINSTEIN WAS VERY POPULAR AND HIS FINANCIAL SITUATION QUITE FAVOURABLE, MAINLY AS A RESULT OF HIS LATIN AMERICAN TOURS. WHILE GOOD FORTUNE SHONE ON HIM HE DID NOT FORGET HIS FRIENDS AND, THROUGH FALLA, HELPED YOUNG STRAVINSKY BY SENDING HIM SOME MONEY ON THE PRETEXT OF COMPOSING A WORK FOR HIM. HE ALSO ASKED FALLA FOR A PIECE WHICH HE COMPOSED IN 1919 AND DEDICATED TO HIS BENEFACTOR. THE *FANTASIA BÆTICA* FOR PIANO WAS FIRST PLAYED ON THE 20TH OF FEBRUARY 1920 BY RUBINSTEIN IN NEW YORK.

Cover of the *Fantasia Bætica* published by J. & W. Chester, London.

MANUEL DE FALLA came to see me at the Palace Hotel in Madrid with a folder. This contained the work I had commissioned a long time ago. He smiled at me shyly. "It's a bit long. I've written it in the same spirit as *Love the Magician* which you liked so much. But at the same time I have given thought to you and your way of playing. Please accept this manuscript of *Fantasia Bætica*. I dedicate it to you with my friendship and gratitude for the respect you have shown for my work." With a certain solemnity we approached the piano. He placed the priceless manuscript on the music rest and he played it to me with a lot of difficulty, stopping here and there to point out certain passages to me. Afterwards I sat at the piano and tried to decipher it. It was no easy task. The piece raised quite a few technical problems with its stylised flamenco, its complicated imitation of the guitar and perhaps with a *glissandi* or two too many. I thanked Falla warmly and promised to learn it. I decided to present it at a concert as soon as possible, in a suitable city in the Spanish provinces. We celebrated the event over cocoa in "La Mallorquina".

ARTHUR RUBINSTEIN

HERE IS the story about how the composition of *Fantasia Bætica* originated. It happened during the 1914 war. The celebrated pianist Arthur Rubinstein had begun to climb the road to success. One day, while Rubinstein was staying in Madrid, Falla received a letter from Maestro Ansermet from Geneva, telling him that Stravinsky, who was also living in the Swiss city at that time, was suffering financial hardships, and he asked Falla to pass the news on to Rubinstein that he was in Madrid. Falla did so, and Rubinstein, who had always been very generous, immediately gave him a large cheque to send to Ansermet to give to Stravinsky, and in order to justify the donation and be tactful, he commissioned a com-

position from him. Rubinstein then did the same for Falla: he paid him an amount of money in return for a piano composition. The composition was *Fantasia Bætica*. He did it quite quickly and when Rubinstein returned from a tour, three or four months later, Falla showed him the finished piece. Rubinstein was delighted and wanted to perform the piece a few days later at some concerts that he was going to play in Barcelona. Falla promptly set to work and produced a definitive version. But Rubinstein did not have time to study it sufficiently for the Barcelona concerts, and he played it later for the first time in New York. After performing it in a few other cities he stopped playing it. But the piece which Stravinsky composed for him, the *Piano Rag-music*, was never played by him. It seems that Rubinstein said that he did not understand it, and did not even know how to play it.

Later on, when then war was over, Falla bumped into Rubinstein, near Versailles, in the house of an Italian prince. While they were leaving Rubinstein asked Falla to write him a piano piece to which Falla responded that he had already written him one, the *Fantasia Bætica*, which he never played, and that he had no desire to write any more piano pieces, which, in fact, he has not done. Rubinstein apologised, saying that it was too long and giving other such reasons. Then Falla told him that he wanted to make a transcription of the *Fantasia Bætica* for piano and orchestra, which Rubinstein thought was a very good idea. Cools had the same opinion when he was told the idea. However, Falla never carried out his plan.

JAIME PAHISSA

Arthur Rubinstein. [To my friend Manuel de Falla with my deepest admiration and friendship, 1919.]

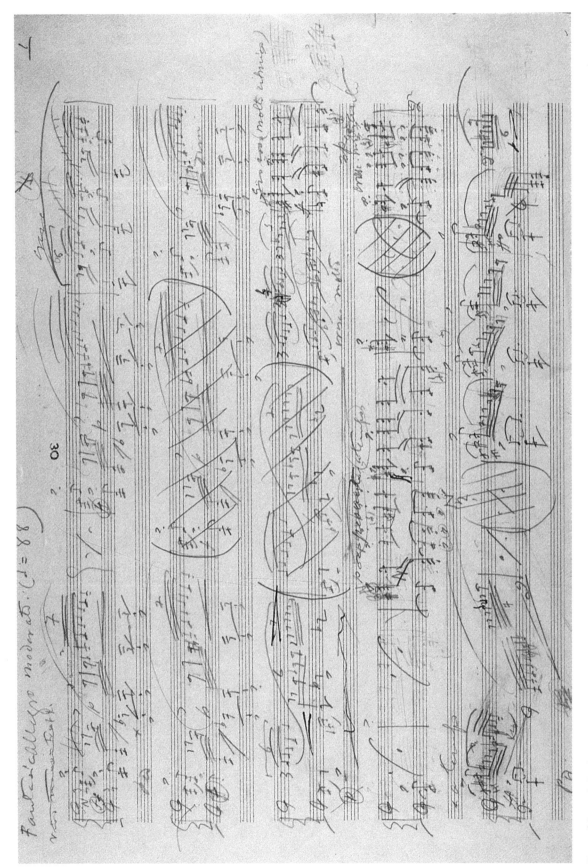

Score of Fantasia Bætica.

MANUEL DE
FALLA'S
PHYSICAL TRAINING
ROUTINE

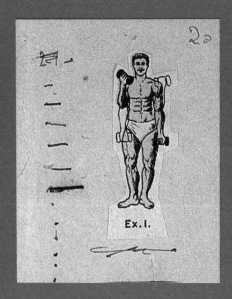

Ex.1.

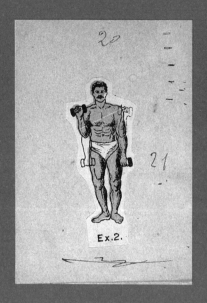

Ex.2.

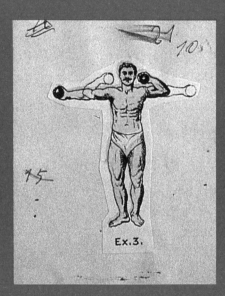

Ex.3.

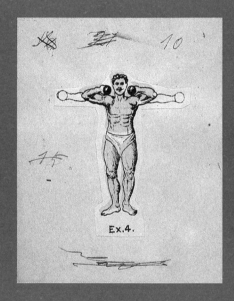

Ex.4.

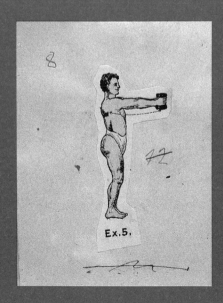

Ex.5.

Ex.6.

12

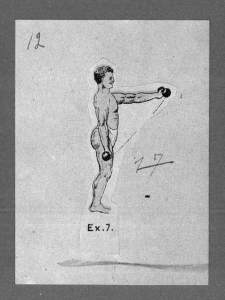

Ex. 7.

50

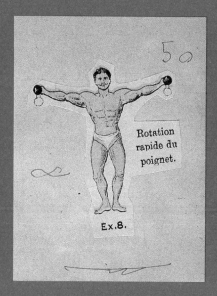

Rotation rapide du poignet.

Ex. 8.

25

Imprimer l'haltère un mouvement de rotation en saisissent par une extrémité

Ex. 9 & 10.

12

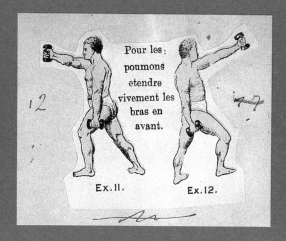

Pour les poumons etendre vivement les bras en avant.

Ex. 11.   Ex. 12.

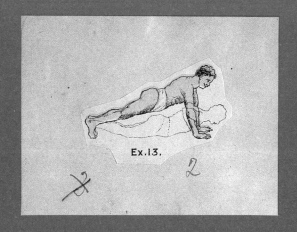

Ex. 13.

2

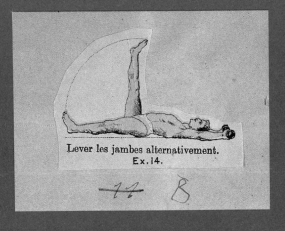

Lever les jambes alternativement.
Ex. 14.

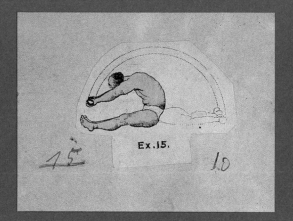

Ex. 15.

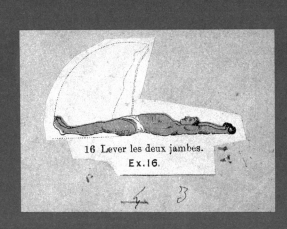

16 Lever les deux jambes.
Ex. 16.

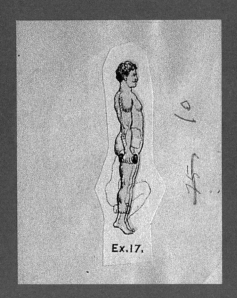

Ex. 17.

Exercice analogue à celui
No. 17, mais les pieds écar-
tés de 30 centimetres et les
talons à plat sur le plancher.
Ex. 18

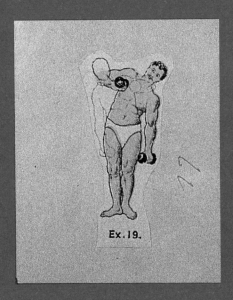

Ex. 19.

WITH J. B. TREND IN GRANADA, 1927.

THE FIRST TIME I met Don Manuel de Falla was on a blustering September evening at the "Villa Carmona" on the Alhambra Hill. It was the first suggestion of autumn. The tops of the Duke of Wellington's elm trees swayed in the high wind, and the pomegranate under which we were dining dropped pips in luscious, sticky envelopes on to the tablecloth. Suddenly there was a burst of rain, and every man seized his bread, plate and glass and ran for the house; I never realised the possibilities of a romantic situation so thoroughly as when I trod lightly on a rotten quince which was lying on the garden path. Sr. de Falla described the whole episode as a mixture of *La soirée de Grenade* and *Jardins sous la pluie*; but the setting was, he added, more thoroughly Spanish than Debussy could have known, for his acquaintance with Granada was derived from books and picture postcards of the Alhambra which Sr. de Falla had shown him.

It was always with a sense of relief that I went into Charles V's palace, a noble example of real architecture. And then Sr. de Falla with Sr. Vázquez Díaz, one of the most modern of Spanish painters, took me at night. The moon was waning, but it showed about half, and covered everything with an intense, queer light which was now violet, now greenish, but emphatically not white. The atmosphere seemed friendly, familiar, not strange and uncomfortable as in the daytime. The long tank in the Court of Myrtles stretched away into an uncertain distance; and a man with a lantern passed slowly under the arches in front of the Hall of the Ambassadors. Then I realized what had happened. The atmosphere of the Alhambra at night is the atmosphere of opera. The man moving under the arches with a lantern is the figure of countless operas, and he showed me that to understand the Alhambra as Sr. de Falla does, you must receive it in the state of mind in which you go to an

opera-house. Wherever we went the effect was the same.

Sr. de Falla, however, enabled me to increase my imaginative perception of Granada by introducing me to its music and its guitars, not so much in folk-songs, nor yet in the gypsy entertainments got up for strangers, but in cultivated music played in private houses and gardens.

One evening Sr. de Falla took me to a house just outside the Alhambra. In the *patio* the fountain had been muffled with a towel, but not altogether silenced; there was a light murmur of water running into the tank. Don Ángel Barrios, who is part composer of the charming Goyesque opera *El Avapiés*, sat there collarless and comfortable with a guitar across his knee. He had tuned it in flats so that in some odd way it harmonized with the running water, and was extemporizing with amazing resource and variety. Then his father joined us, and Sr. de Falla asked him if he could remember any old songs. The old gentleman sat there with eyes half closed, while the guitar kept up a constantly varied "till ready," chiefly in D flat and in B flat minor, sliding down with the characteristic "false relation" to F major. Now and again he lifted up his voice and sang one of those queer, wavering melodies of *cante flamenco*, with their strange rhythms and flourishes characteristic of Andalucía, while Sr. Barrios accompanied, sometimes thrumming simple chords, sometimes producing a sort of orchestral "melodrama," sometimes playing a counterpoint, sometimes treating the song as a recitative and punctuating it with staccato chords. Sr. de Falla wrote down those which pleased him, or those which it was possible to express in staff-notation, for one of the best of them was full of "neutral thirds and sixths" –intervals unknown and inexpressible in modern music.

My most memorable *Soirée de Grenade* was one in which music had a large share. In honour of the Maestro there had been a concert at the Arts Club, at which the instruments had been a trio of guitar, Spanish lute and bandore.

But the memorable part of the evening began when the concert was over, and we were taken to a *Carmen* (a villa and garden), in one of the highest parts of the town, facing the Alhambra Hill. It was an enchanting place, and the word may be used deliberately because the enchantment had been most carefully planned, and art had made the utmost use of the natural possibilities and beauties of the situation. The *Carmen*, which belongs to D. Fernando Vilches Jiménez, is built on the site of one occupied in the seventeenth century by the painter Alonso Cano. A wide verandah runs along the front, and the garden falls away below, at first in terraces, then in a gradual slope. Half a dozen slender cypresses planted close together shelter one end of the house from the sun. The stone work is covered, but not hidden, by plants in pots, creepers, oranges, pomegranates and quinces. The musicians took their "strange lutes" to a carefully chosen spot on the terrace, out of

NEWLY ARRIVED IN GRANADA, *STANDING AND FROM LEFT TO RIGHT,* THE
WATERCOLOURIST SOLLMANS, DANIEL VÁZQUEZ DÍAZ AND MANUEL DE
FALLA *AND SEATED,* MARÍA DEL CARMEN DE FALLA, EVE EGGERHOLM DE
VÁZQUEZ DÍAZ, ÁNGEL BARRIOS AND AN UNIDENTIFIED GENTLEMEN.

sight of the verandah, and by the side of the pool so that the
utmost resonance might be obtained; and there they played part
of their programme over again. Some of our admiration may have
been due to the unconscious and inevitable influence of the beauty of the night, and to the enthusiasm we all felt for Maestro Falla.
But the experience of the exceptional moment had not altogether
laid reason to sleep, and one was able to a certain extent to clarify
one's impressions by analysis. In the concert room it had been
clear that the trio was able to interpret music in such a way that its
intimate structure was plainly revealed and the beauty or inade-
quacy of its workmanship easy to gauge. Here, in the "strange
delight" of the garden, I realised how immensely the emotional
and musical resources of guitar, lute and bandore are enchanted
by the open air. It was not a case of romantic *Nachtmusik* or sentimental association, as of Bach fugues played in a darkened college
chapel. There was no uncertain glimmer of star-light, but a serene
and marvellous radiance. There was nothing mysterious about it;
the whole thing was most carefully staged. The hidden musicians,
the tall thin cypresses, the masses of foliage and the indistinct
scents which came from it, the light trickle of water even, were all
carefully considered, and stage-managed with great skill by our
host, Sr. Vilches. We felt that we were witnessing one of the best
and most effectively produced operas which it was possible to
imagine. Sr. de Falla, of course, has long realized what sort of
music and what instruments are most suited to the gardens of
Spain, as some people in England have learnt that the music most
expressive for an English garden is to be found in unaccompanied
madrigals.

Before leaving the *Carmen,* our host made us follow him
upstairs to another verandah, just below the roof. Here we were
above the tops of the cypresses, and a vast panorama presented

itself: the curved backs of the Sierra Nevada, the shadowy outline
of the Alhambra Hill and its palaces, the greenish violet of the
white walls bathed in moonlight with the rose-coloured blotches
of the not too frequent lamps, the distant chimes, the bells to reg-
ulate irrigation, the gentle murmur of falling water. We shouted
for the music of de Falla. And then, when the musicians had
played till they were tired, a poet recited in a ringing voice an ode
to the city of Granada. His voice rose as image succeeded image
and his astonishing flow of rhetoric fell upon the stillness. What
did it matter, he concluded, that the glories of the Alhambra were
departed if it were possible to live again such nights as this, equal
to, if not surpassing, any of the Thousand and One! He ended, and
"the silence surged softly backwards." Then a clock struck four,
and we stumbled down into the town over the ungainly cobbles
and climbed up to the Alhambra under the Duke of Wellington's
elm-trees.

Moorish art is only made intelligible by moonlight; Granada is
only explained by its gardens and its guitars. The daytime is for
reading or writing in a garden, or for painting in the Generalife. Sr.
de Falla spent the greater part of the morning at work, though
at luncheon he would surprise us with new combinations of
mules and dili-
gences to go to
the Sierra Nevada.
He planned one
glorious excursion.
Mounted on asses,
followed by spare
asses and asses
laden with cold *tor-
tillas, boquerone*s,
pimientos, bread
and enormous *da-
majuanas* of wine,
we were to go into
the heart of the
mountains; and
there "in the thin
clear mirk of dawn"
or the starry radi-
ance of night, the
muleteers would
sing *coplas,* and de

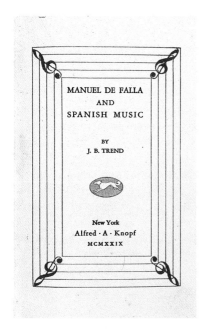

Falla would afterwards weave his exquisitely planned, firmly con-
structed movements about what we heard. The music is being
written, but the excursion remained a plan.

J. B. TREND

PORTRAIT BY PICASSO, 9TH OF JUNE 1920.

[1] PORTRAIT OF MANUEL DE FALLA BY
VÁZQUEZ DÍAZ. [2] THE GUITARIST
ANTONIO BARRIOS, *EL POLINARIO*, BY
SANTIAGO RUSIÑOL AND [3] BY JOHN
SINGER SARGENT. [4] *TABERNA DEL
POLINARIO*, OIL PAINTING BY J. SÁBADA,
1898 AND [5] VILLA CARMONA, THE GUEST
HOUSE WHERE THE COMPOSER STAYED
ON HIS VISIT TO GRANADA.

HOWEVER, I remember to the last detail, how our first meeting with him went, a meeting which was attended by almost all the people from our "retreat".

In calle Real de la Alhambra, that ugly modern street which runs from the bottom of the Santa María de la Alhambra's church up to the Tower of the Captive where some antique shops and photographic and souvenir shops for tourists are located, there was a tavern owned by Don Antonio Barrios, better known by his nickname "*El Polinario*". "*El Polinario*" had three extraordinary virtues –rare in a tavern owner– which were discovered by the great expert in wines, men and landscapes, Santiago Rusiñol: Don Antonio did not water down the wine, he knew how to recognise art, especially painting, and he was a outstanding singer of Flamenco. His son Ángel –whose dark moorish features, tanned face and thick, round lips inspired our nickname for him 'Maestro Picorreondo' (Big Lips)–, was an accomplished guitar player as well as a modest composer. In his youth 'Maestro Picorreondo' had organised a quintet of guitars and *bandurrias* –the "Albéniz Quintet"– which had made a magnificent and triumphant tour of all the European capitals a few years before the outbreak of the First World War, but gradually problems brought by success and romance started to break the group up. One of the members of the group settled in Saint Petersburg in the arms of a duchess; and soon after the others went similar ways, apart from Ángel Barrios who returned to Granada with an enhanced artistic vocation and thorough training as a composer. His symphonic poem *Cantos de mi tierra*, was good enough to be included in the programmes of the Madrid Symphonic Orchestra; his opera *El Avapíes*, was produced at the Teatro Real. But most of the time he was a great guitarist and a popular tavern tender like his father.

A tavern such as this, governed by two artists and situated in the very heart of the Alhambra was bound to become a meeting place for artists from Spain and the rest of the world visiting Granada. Artists, in particular, stopped off at "*Polinario's*" tavern, after a long tour of Spain or after a work trip of exploration and inquiry, to relax and converse, and they all left the popular tavern tender a momento, a sketch, a drawing or a painting, as well as signing the tavern visitors book whose frontispiece had been painted by Rusiñol and whose first inscription was by Rodrigo Soriano. With those momentos the tavern tender had built up one of the most complete, substantial and welcoming private museums of modern art imaginable in his lounge and it was here that Don Antonio's and Ángel's friends gathered to exchange ideas and recollections, drink wine and hear them play and sing. That was during Winter or when the weather was cold because in hot weather, the meetings were held in the garden, in the shade of an enormous tree, among the beds of periwinkles and myrtles. Ángel would begin to pluck his guitar, everyone became silent, and when he reached the right point of emotion Don Antonio would start to sing.

One summer's night we had gathered in the garden under the tree and, to appreciate the bewitching nature of the music as purely as possible, we had turned off the lights. Someone rang at the door and Ángel went to open. But at that time, with the tavern being closed, it could only be friends or relations. However, he was confronted by a group of people he did not recognise, strangers and artists, one of whom spoke to him to explain that they had heard the music and singing and had decided to ring and ask if they could come in to listen. To justify their petition they told him their names. They were: the painter Vázquez Díaz and his wife, a sculptor from Sweden or Norway, Gustavo Bacarissas the landscape painter from Algeciras, a strange fellow, Alejandro Mackinglay, a hispano-Argentinian writer of dramas in French verse and his wife a Russian Tzarist emmigrant, and finally another man and a woman who had modestly remained until last, but whose name reverberated through all of us like a bell:

"Manuel de Falla... María del Carmen Falla..."

We could not believe it.

"Falla!... You're Falla?"

But it was true. That humble, physically insignificant man, dressed in a cheap dark suit and that woman who

had passed the frontier into old age and whose face resembled like a chick pea seen through a magnifying
glass, were the composer of *Nights in the Gardens of
Spain*, *La vida breve*, *The Three-cornered Hat*... and his
sister, his inseparable and attentive companion. The
presence of the composer obviously contradicted the
idea we had, in our provincial and youthful minds, about
what a world famous and recognised artist should look
like. The visit could not have been more welcome and
that night's *medias granadinas* and flamencan *malagueñas* were sung by Don Antonio with greater solemnity
and emotion than ever, because Ángel's fingers trembled
when he began to pluck the strings and Don Antonio
looked at the visitor out of the corner of his eye uncertain perhaps of being able to give his song sufficient
vigour and expression.

Afterwards Falla explained that, apart from seeing
Granada once again, his visit was a kind of exploration
to see if he could find a small well-located and cheap
house to rent, as he had the intention of settling down
here. He needed that peaceful retreat to work and to re-
cover from the losses he had suffered when his publisher
had gone bankrupt and to reduce his already minimal
spending. (When we thought of that dignified poverty
and were reminded of the vast quarterly sums that some
composers of light lyrics and pornographic *zarzuelas*
earned in authors rights we were very disheartened. But
this always seems to be the fate of art and artists.) It goes
without saying that, the next day, Falla was accepted as
our friend, as if we had know him for years, and we set
about looking for the cheap house he had in mind. We
found it, of course.

JOSÉ MORA GUARNIDO

ANTONIO BARRIOS AND HIS SONS, AMONG OTHERS, WITH HIS FLAMENCO CIRCLE.

5

GRANADA

1920-1929

The *carmen* of Antequeruela Alta. Easter Week in Seville and the *Saeta*. Ignacio Zuloaga. The *Cante Jondo* competition. Federico García Lorca. The *Cristobitas* (puppet) theatre. Ernesto Halffter. The composers of 27. The Andalusian Chambre Orchestra. *Master Peter's Puppet Show*. Homages on his fiftieth birthday. Wanda Landowska. Darius Milhaud.

Granada - Alhambra - Vista general

C H R O N O L O G Y

1920. ■ HE SETTLED IN GRANADA IN THE *CARMEN* OF SANTA ENGRACIA. ■ HEALTH PROBLEMS.

1921. ■ IN JANUARY IGNACIO ZULOAGA VISITED HIM. ■ AT THE END OF FEBRUARY FALLA AND HIS SISTER MOVED TO THE *CARMEN* OF ANTEQUERUELA, Nº. 11, WHICH BECAME THEIR DEFINITIVE HOME IN THE CITY. ■ HE RECEIVED VARIOUS VISITORS, MIGUEL LLOBET AMONG THEM. ■ HIS CIRCLE INCLUDED FERNANDO DE LOS RÍOS, HERMENEGILDO LANZ, MIGUEL CERÓN, FERNANDO VÍLCHEZ, RAÚL CARAZO, FEDERICO GARCÍA LORCA, ANDRÉS SEGOVIA AND OTHERS. ■ IN MAY HE TRAVELLED TO PARIS AND LONDON WHERE HE SAW HIS FRIEND GEORGES JEAN-AUBRY AGAIN. ■ IN AUGUST HE COMPOSED THE *FANFARE POUR UNE FÊTE* COMMISSIONED BY THE ENGLISH MAGAZINE *FANFARE*. ■ HE CONTINUED TO WORK FOR THE PRINCESSE DE POLIGNAC ON AN EPISODE FROM *DON QUIXOTE, MASTER PETER'S PUPPET SHOW.* ■ HE ARRANGED SUITES Nº. 1 AND 2 FROM *THE THREE–CORNERED HAT* AND A PIANOLA VERSION OF THE PIECE.

1922. ■ TOGETHER WITH IGNACIO ZULOAGA AND HIS FRIENDS FROM GRANADA, FEDERICA GARCÍA LORCA, HERMENEGILDO LANZ, MIGUEL CERÓN, MANUEL JOFRÉ AND OTHERS, HE STARTED TO ORGANISE A *CANTE JONDO* COMPETITION IN ORDER TO RECUPERATE PRIMITIVE ANDALUSIAN SONG. ON THE 19TH OF FEBRUARY, AT THE ARTISTIC CENTRE, FEDERICO GARCÍA LORCA READ HIS LECTURE "HISTORICAL AND ARTISTIC IMPORTANCE OF THE PRIMITIVE ANDALUSIAN SONG CALLED *CANTE JONDO*". ANDRÉS SEGOVIA PLAYED FOUR CONCERTS IN THE TINY THEATRE OF THE ALHAMBRA PALACE HOTEL. THE LAST EVENT TO ANNOUNCE THE COMPETITION WAS ALSO HELD HERE AND A TEXT BY FALLA WAS READ. ANDRÉS SEGOVIA PLAYED AND MANUEL JOFRÉ AND GARCÍA LORCA READ A POEM. ■ IN MARCH FALLA COMPOSED HIS *CANTO A LOS REMEROS DEL VOLGA*, FOR PIANO, A PIECE DEDICATED TO RUSSIAN REFUGEES UNDER THE AUSPICES OF THE LEAGUE OF NATIONS. ■ DURING EASTER WEEK FALLA TRAVELLED TO SEVILLE ACCOMPANIED BY ALFONSO REYES. HE CONTACTED THE SEVILLE MUSICIANS SEGISMUNDO ROMERO AND EDUARDO TORRES. ■ THE *CANTE JONDO* COMPETITION TOOK PLACE ON THE 13TH AND 14TH OF JUNE. IT GAVE RISE TO A CONTROVERSY ON THE SUBJECT AND BROUGHT MANY ARTISTS AND INTELLECTUALS TOGETHER. ■ ON THE 27TH OF JULY, KURT SCHINDLER, WHILE VISITING GRANADA, PLAYED A CONCERT WITH FALLA AND SINGER URSULA GRENVILLE AT THE ARTISTIC CENTRE. ■ WANDA LANDOWSKA VISITED GRANADA, PLAYED SOME CONCERTS AT THE ALHAMBRA PALACE HOTEL AND STUDIED FALLA'S SKETCHES FOR *MASTER PETER'S PUPPET SHOW* WITH HIM. ■ ON THE 2ND OF DECEMBER, GUITARIST EMILIO PUJOL PLAYED *POUR LE TOMBEAU DE CLAUDE DEBUSSY* FOR THE FIRST TIME AT THE PARIS CONSERVATORY. ■ FELIPE PEDRELL DIED IN BARCELONA.

1923. ■ ON THE 6TH OF JANUARY, FALLA, HERMENEGILDO LANZ AND FEDERICO GARCÍA LORCA ORGANISED A PUNCH AND JUDY STYLE PUPPET SHOW IN LORCA'S HOUSE. ■ EXCURSIONS IN SEARCH OF POPULAR SONG IN THE COUNTRYSIDE OF GRANADA. ■ ON THE 23RD AND 24TH OF MARCH THE CONCERT VERSION OF *MASTER PETER'S PUPPET SHOW* WAS PERFORMED FOR THE FIRST TIME IN SEVILLE WITH AN ESPECIALLY CHOSEN ORCHESTRA CONDUCTED BY FALLA. MEANWHILE IN PARIS AND GRANADA, MANUEL ÁNGELES ORTIZ AND HERMENEGILDO LANZ WORKED ON THE SCENERY AND PUPPETS FOR THE NEXT SHOW IN THE PRINCESSE DE POLIGNAC'S SALON. ■ IN MID-APRIL FALLA SET OFF ON A TOUR OF VARIOUS EUROPEAN CAPITALS. HE RETURNED AT THE END OF MAY TO PREPARE, WORKING EXTREMALY HARD, THE PREMIÈRE OF *MASTER PETER'S PUPPET SHOW,* WHICH TOOK PLACE ON THE 25TH OF JUNE. THE ORCHESTRA WAS CONDUCTED BY WLADIMIR GOLSCHMANN AND WANDA LANDOWSKA PLAYED THE HARPSICHORD. ■ IN OCTOBER A FIRST VERSION OF *PSYCHÉ* WAS NEARLY FINISHED. ■ IN NOVEMBER, IN PARIS, HE CONDUCTED THE FIRST PUBLIC PERFORMANCE OF *MASTER PETER'S PUPPET SHOW.* ■ HE WORKED WITH FEDERICO GARCÍA LORCA ON THE PIECE *LOLA LA COMEDIANTA*, A PROJECT WHICH WAS NEVER FINISHED.

1924. ■ THE ANDALUSIAN CHAMBER ORCHESTRA (LA ORQUESTA BÉTICA DE CÁMARA) OF SEVILLE WAS SET UP AT FALLA'S REQUEST AND WITH THE COLLABORATION OF SEGISMUNDO ROMERO AND EDUARDO TORRES. FALLA WORKED IN CONSTANT CONTACT WITH THEM TO PREPARE THE ORCHESTRA'S FIRST CONCERT IN SEVILLE. ■ ON THE 28TH OF MARCH THE CONCERT VERSION OF *MASTER PETER'S PUPPET SHOW* WAS PLAYED FOR THE FIRST TIME IN MADRID AT THE TEATRO DE LA COMEDIA. ■ ERNESTO HALFFTER SPENT SOME TIME IN GRANADA TO PREPARE THE PIECES HE WAS GOING TO CONDUCT WITH THE ANDALUSIAN ORCHESTRA IN SEVILLE ON THE 11TH OF JUNE. ■ FALLA SPENT A FEW DAYS IN MALAGA WORKING IN ORDER TO ESCAPE THE NOISE OF LOUDSPEAKERS IN GRANADA DURING THE CORPUS CHRISTI. ■ AT THE BEGINNING OF SEPTEMBER HE FINISHED THE COMPOSITION *PSYCHÉ* BASED ON A POEM BY G. JEAN-AUBRY, AND HE DIRECTED HIS ATTENTION TO ALTERATIONS FOR THE NEW STAGE VERSION OF *MASTER PETER'S PUPPET SHOW*, WITH MANUEL ÁNGELES ORTIZ AND HERMENEGILDO LANZ. ■ HE WORKED ON *LA CELESTINA* BY PEDRELL.

1925. ■ THE PREMIÈRE OF THE NEW STAGE VERSION OF *MASTER PETER'S PUPPET SHOW* WAS SHOWN ON THE 30TH OF JANUARY IN SEVILLE AT THE TEATRO SAN FERNANDO, PLAYED BY THE ANDALUSIAN CHAMBER ORCHESTRA. ■ THE PREMIÈRE OF *PSYCHÉ* TOOK PLACE ON THE 9TH OF FEBRUARY AS PART OF A CONCERT DEDICATED TO FALLA AT THE PALAU DE LA MÚSICA CATALANA IN BARCELONA. THE ANDALUSIAN ORCHESTRA WAS CONDUCTED BY BOTH ERNESTO HALFFTER AND FALLA. ■ GERARDO DIEGO VISITED HIM IN GRANADA. ■ ON THE 22ND OF MAY THE NEW VERSION OF *LOVE THE MAGICIAN*, IN ONE ACT, WAS PRODUCED IN PARIS AT THE TRIANON LYRIQUE, WITH ANTONIA MERCÉ "LA ARGENTINA" AND VICENTE ESCUDERO, DIRECTED BY FALLA. ■ HIS ORCHESTRAL REVISION OF THE "OVERTURE" FROM ROSSINI'S *THE BARBER OF SEVILLE*, AND HIS ADAPTATION OF DEBUSSY'S *PRÉLUDE À L'APRÈS-MIDI D'UN FAUNE* WERE PLAYED BY THE ANDALUSIAN ORCHESTRA IN SEVILLE CONDUCTED BY ERNESTO HALFFTER. ■ IN NOVEMBER HIS HEALTH DETERIORATED ONCE AGAIN.

1926. ■ PREMIÈRE OF *MASTER PETER'S PUPPET SHOW* IN NEW YORK. ■ IN JUNE HE ATTENDED AND SUPERVISED THE STAGE PRODUCTION DESIGNED FOR THE WORK IN ZURICH AS PART OF THE ISCM FESTIVAL (INTERNATIONAL SOCIETY OF CONTEMPORARY MUSIC). HE TRAVELLED ACCOMPANIED BY MIGUEL LLOBET AND JUAN GISBERT. ■ MANUEL DE FALLA STARTED TO THINK ABOUT COMPOSING A PIECE BASED ON VERDAGUER'S *ATLÁNTIDA*. ■ JUAN RAMÓN JIMÉNEZ WROTE HIS LYRICAL PORTRAIT OF FALLA WHICH HE WOULD LATER INCLUDE IN *OLVIDOS DE GRANADA*. ■ IN SPRING, TO CELEBRATE FALLA'S FIFTIETH BIRTHDAY, THE PARIS COMIC OPERA ORGANISED A SEASON OF HIS WORKS. THESE INCLUDED *MASTER PETER'S PUPPET SHOW* WITH SCENERY BY IGNACIO ZULOAGA AND PUPPETS BY MAXIME DE TOMÁS. BOTH FALLA AND ZULOAGA COLLABORATED ON THE PRODUCTION. ■ FALLA FINISHED HIS *CONCERTO*, WHICH WAS PLAYED FOR THE FIRST TIME ON THE 5TH OF NOVEMBER AT THE PALAU IN BARCELONA, CONDUCTED BY PAU CASALS AND MANUEL DE FALLA AND FEATURING WANDA LANDOWSKA, (TO WHOM THE PIECE WAS DEDICATED) AT THE HARPSICHORD. ■ ON THE 14TH OF DECEMBER THE ANDALUSIAN ORCHESTRA, ALONG WITH CONCHITA BADÍA AND FRANK MARSHALL, PAID TRIBUTE TO FALLA WITH A CONCERT IN SEVILLE. THE CITY OF SEVILLE GRANTED HIM HONORARY CITIZENSHIP. ■ THE CITY OF CADIZ PAID HOMAGE TO HIM ON THE 17TH AND 18TH OF DECEMBER AND GRANTED HIM HONORARY CITIZENSHIP.

1927. ■ HONORARY CITIZENSHIP WAS BESTOWED UPON HIM IN GRANADA AND HE WAS PAID HOMAGE TO IN A CONCERT ON THE 8TH AND 9TH OF FEBRUARY. ■ ON THE 28TH OF FEBRUARY HE WAS NAMED HONORARY CITIZEN OF GUADIX. ■ BARCELONA RENDERED HIM HOMAGE WITH A SERIES OF CONCERTS: ON THE 17TH OF MARCH, A FALLA FESTIVAL DIRECTED BY THE PAU CASALS ORCHESTRA AND, ON THE 20TH, A FESTIVAL OF CATALONIAN MUSIC WAS HELD IN HIS HONOUR AT THE LICEO. ■ ON THE 24TH OF MARCH FALLA PAID HOMAGE, WITH VARIOUS FRIENDS, TO ENRIQUE GRANADOS AT THE VERY PLACE IN THE PORT OF BARCELONA WHERE THEY SAID FAREWELL IN 1915. ■ PARIS PAID HOMAGE TO FALLA WITH A MUSICAL EVENING ON THE 14TH OF MAY AT THE SALLE PLEYEL. IN THIS TRIBUTE THE *SONNET TO CORDOVA* BY LUIS DE GÓNGORA, SET TO MUSIC BY FALLA TO CELEBRATE THE POET'S THIRD CENTENARY, WAS FIRST PERFORMED AND THE TWO VERSIONS OF HIS *CONCERTO*, FOR PIANO AND HARPSICHORD, WERE PLAYED. THE FRENCH GOVERNMENT AWARDED HIM THE LEGION OF HONOUR. ■ FOR THE CORPUS CHRISTI CELEBRATIONS IN GRANADA HE COMPOSED A PIECE OF INCIDENTAL MUSIC BASED ON CALDERÓN DE LA BARCA'S *AUTO SACRAMENTAL*, *THE GREAT THEATRE OF THE WORLD*. ■ ON THE 22ND OF JUNE, *MASTER PETER'S PUPPET SHOW* AND HIS CONCERT WERE PRODUCED AT THE AEOLIAN HALL IN LONDON. ■ SCULPTOR JUAN CRISTÓBAL FINISHED HIS BUST OF MANUEL DE FALLA. ■ J. & W. CHESTER PUBLISHED *PSYCHÉ*. ■ THE MADRID CITY COUNCIL ADDED THEIR OWN HOMAGE TO THE OTHERS HELD THROUGHOUT THE YEAR. ON THE 3RD OF NOVEMBER THEY HELD A RECEPTION AT THE CITY HALL AND ON THE 5TH THEY CELEBRATED A FALLA FESTIVAL AT THE PALACIO DE LA MÚSICA, AT WHICH HIS *HARPSICHORD CONCERTO* WAS PLAYED. ■ THE ATENEO OF GRANADA ORGANISED A TRIBUTE TO SCARLATTI AT WHICH FALLA PLAYED SCARLATTI'S PIANO *SONATAS*.

1928. ■ IN MARCH HE VISITED PARIS TO SUPERVISE ANTONIA MERCÉ'S PRODUCTION OF *LOVE THE MAGICIAN*, WITH COSTUMES DESIGNED BY GUSTAVO BACARISAS. ■ HE SUFFERED AN EYE INFECTION WHICH PREVENTED HIM FROM READING AND WRITING. ■ ON THE 12TH OF SEPTEMBER HE TRAVELLED TO SIENNA, ACCOMPANIED BY JUAN GISBERT AND PEDRO BAUCHS, TO PLAY HIS CONCERT. ON HIS WAY BACK HE VISITED BARCELONA. ■ MAURICE RAVEL VISITED FALLA IN GRANADA AT THE END OF OCTOBER. ■ THE PARISIAN PUBLISHER MAX ESCHIG ISSUED HIS *HARPSICHORD CONCERTO*.

1929. ■ MANUEL DE FALLA TURNED DOWN THE MEMBERSHIP HE WAS OFFERED AT THE ACADEMY OF FINE ARTS AS IT MEANT THE EXCLUSION OF THE COMPOSER CONRADO DEL CAMPO. ■ JOSÉ MARÍA SERT VISITED FALLA AT THE BEGINNING OF JUNE. THEY BOTH DECIDED AGAINST FORCING THE PREMIÈRE OF *ATLÁNTIDA* WHICH WAS SCHEDULED TO BE PERFORMED AT THE INTERNATIONAL EXHIBITIONS IN SEVILLE AND BARCELONA. ■ ON THE 4TH OF AUGUST A CONCERT WAS PLAYED BY FALLA AND NIRVA DEL RÍO AT THE THEATRE OF THE PALACE HOTEL. ■ HIS BROTHER GERMÁN MARRIED IN PARIS. ■ FEDERICO GARCÍA LORCA'S *ODE TO THE BLESSED SACRAMENT OF THE ALTAR* WAS PUBLISHED. ■ FALLA WORKED ON "FIRE IN THE PYRENEES" AN EPISODE FROM *ATLÁNTIDA* .

CARMEN OF SANTA ENGRACIA, HIS FIRST HOUSE IN GRANADA.

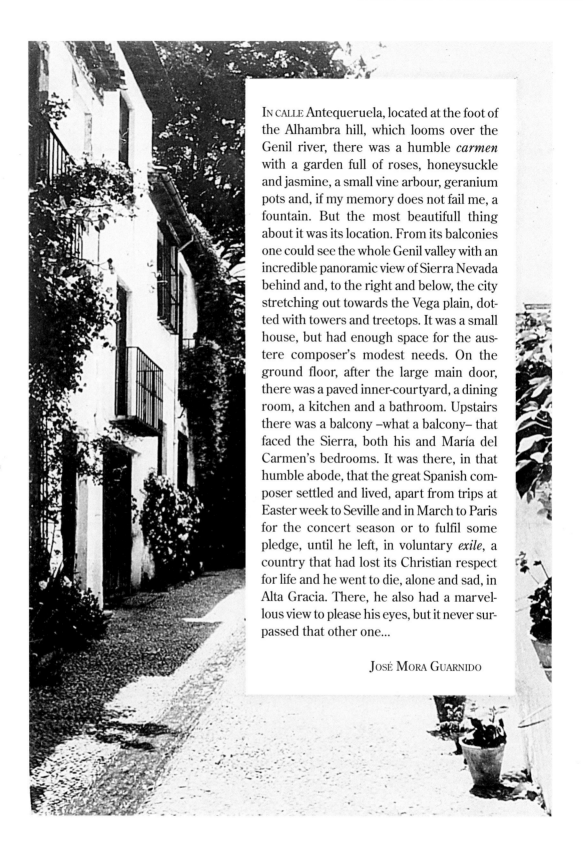

IN CALLE Antequeruela, located at the foot of the Alhambra hill, which looms over the Genil river, there was a humble *carmen* with a garden full of roses, honeysuckle and jasmine, a small vine arbour, geranium pots and, if my memory does not fail me, a fountain. But the most beautifull thing about it was its location. From its balconies one could see the whole Genil valley with an incredible panoramic view of Sierra Nevada behind and, to the right and below, the city stretching out towards the Vega plain, dotted with towers and treetops. It was a small house, but had enough space for the austere composer's modest needs. On the ground floor, after the large main door, there was a paved inner-courtyard, a dining room, a kitchen and a bathroom. Upstairs there was a balcony –what a balcony– that faced the Sierra, both his and María del Carmen's bedrooms. It was there, in that humble abode, that the great Spanish composer settled and lived, apart from trips at Easter week to Seville and in March to Paris for the concert season or to fulfil some pledge, until he left, in voluntary *exile*, a country that had lost its Christian respect for life and he went to die, alone and sad, in Alta Gracia. There, he also had a marvellous view to please his eyes, but it never surpassed that other one...

JOSÉ MORA GUARNIDO

FALLA DID not like us to call him "Maestro", a title that he considered far too pretentious –a title which, in his opinion, given its symbolic value, could only fittingly be referred to Christ– and neither did he speak about music as a noble profession, but rather as a craft, a trade –"those of us who work in the music trade...". His sister called him "Manolo", but we, always respectful, called him Don Manuel.

When he finished his tea, Don Manuel went on to the ritual ceremony of the cigarette, which he performed, like everything he did, in a disciplined, methodical and coordinated manner. He took one out from the box where María del Carmen kept his cigarettes which she made by rolling a smooth tobacco (Prince Albert) in special papers. Then he tore off one end of the cigarette and pushed in a small cardboard cylinder which he filled with a small ball of cotton–wool using a tooth–pick and, once this filter had been prepared, he lit up. After smoking, he invited us to the lounge and sat down at the piano; the rest of us made ourselves as comfortable as we could, we always outnumbered the seats and some of us had to squat and sit cross–legged on the floor, like children in family photos.

JOSÉ MORA GUARNIDO

MANUEL DE FALLA'S *CARMEN* IN Nº. 11,
◄ CALLE ANTEQUERUELA ALTA,
GRANADA.

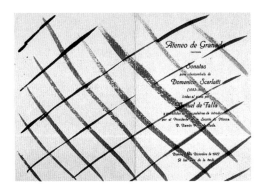
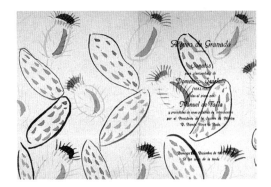

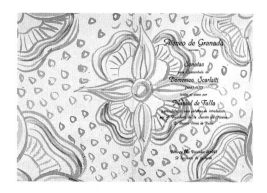
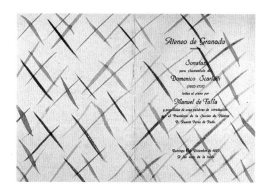

PROGRAMME OF THE HOMAGE TO DOMÉNICO SCARLATTI HELD AT THE ATENEO OF
GRANADA IN 1927, FOR WHICH FALLA PLAYED THE *SONATAS*. THE PROGRAMME WAS
PROBABLY HAND-PAINTED BY HERMENEGILDO LANZ.

WHEN FALLA –a magnificent pianist– sat down to play, he was never selfish, he was generous. He liked to search the shelf of sheet music which was within hands reach and choose fragments that had been mentioned earlier during the conversation. But he was particularly fond of harpsichord music and of French and Italian harpsichordists –Couperin Le Grand, Scarlatti, Rameau, etc.– later he would enter the thick forest of Bach and Mozart, or of the group of *The Five* and, if it had some bearing on his work, he did not scorn the use of fragments by contemporary composers. Only on rare occasions, when we insisted, would he deign to play his own compositions, but never, the ones he was composing. These he barely mentioned at all. I was part of the small group for which he played fragments from *Master Peter's Puppet Show,* which he was working on at that time, because he wanted our advice about which phrases he could cut, without appreciably mutilating the text, to find a precise adhesion between word and rhythm to avoid making the recitatives drag. After playing all our requests and when it was time to leave (we always left late because time just flew by) he played us a kind of inframusical ablution, to relieve us –he said– from the load he had made us bear during the session, interpreting with a funny display of virtuosity, in the midst of our laughter and a truly raucous gabble of improvised tremolos and arpegios, the *Habanera* by Iradier or *Carnaval de Venecia.*

JOSÉ MORA GUARNIDO

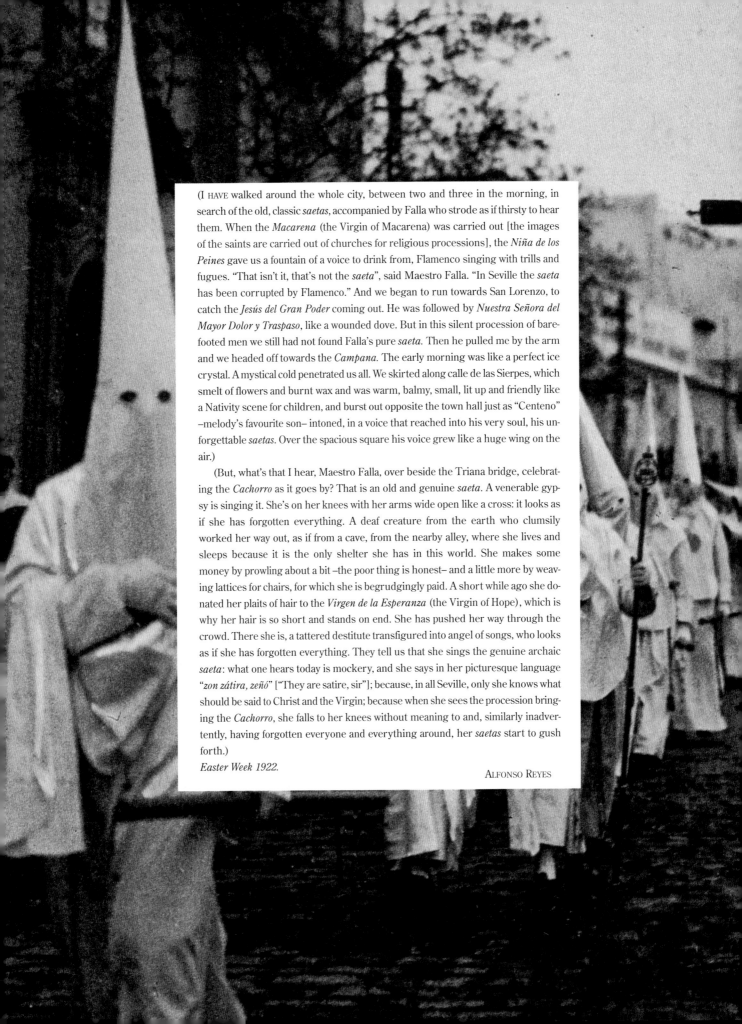

(I HAVE walked around the whole city, between two and three in the morning, in search of the old, classic *saetas*, accompanied by Falla who strode as if thirsty to hear them. When the *Macarena* (the Virgin of Macarena) was carried out [the images of the saints are carried out of churches for religious processions], the *Niña de los Peines* gave us a fountain of a voice to drink from, Flamenco singing with trills and fugues. "That isn't it, that's not the *saeta*", said Maestro Falla. "In Seville the *saeta* has been corrupted by Flamenco." And we began to run towards San Lorenzo, to catch the *Jesús del Gran Poder* coming out. He was followed by *Nuestra Señora del Mayor Dolor y Traspaso*, like a wounded dove. But in this silent procession of barefooted men we still had not found Falla's pure *saeta*. Then he pulled me by the arm and we headed off towards the *Campana*. The early morning was like a perfect ice crystal. A mystical cold penetrated us all. We skirted along calle de las Sierpes, which smelt of flowers and burnt wax and was warm, balmy, small, lit up and friendly like a Nativity scene for children, and burst out opposite the town hall just as "Centeno" –melody's favourite son– intoned, in a voice that reached into his very soul, his unforgettable *saetas*. Over the spacious square his voice grew like a huge wing on the air.)

(But, what's that I hear, Maestro Falla, over beside the Triana bridge, celebrating the *Cachorro* as it goes by? That is an old and genuine *saeta*. A venerable gypsy is singing it. She's on her knees with her arms wide open like a cross: it looks as if she has forgotten everything. A deaf creature from the earth who clumsily worked her way out, as if from a cave, from the nearby alley, where she lives and sleeps because it is the only shelter she has in this world. She makes some money by prowling about a bit –the poor thing is honest– and a little more by weaving lattices for chairs, for which she is begrudgingly paid. A short while ago she donated her plaits of hair to the *Virgen de la Esperanza* (the Virgin of Hope), which is why her hair is so short and stands on end. She has pushed her way through the crowd. There she is, a tattered destitute transfigured into angel of songs, who looks as if she has forgotten everything. They tell us that she sings the genuine archaic *saeta*: what one hears today is mockery, and she says in her picturesque language "*zon zátira, zeñó*" ["They are satire, sir"]; because, in all Seville, only she knows what should be said to Christ and the Virgin; because when she sees the procession bringing the *Cachorro*, she falls to her knees without meaning to and, similarly inadvertently, having forgotten everyone and everything around, her *saetas* start to gush forth.)

Easter Week 1922.

ALFONSO REYES

Falla and Zuloaga write

DEAR Don Ignacio:

You cannot imagine how pleased I was to hear how fondly you remember your visit to Granada and that you plan to come back soon! I suppose that the letter I sent a few days ago has been forwarded to you from Madrid. Among other things, I mentioned that my sister has carried out your assignment to the *Virgen de las Angustias* (the Virgin of Anguish). Afterwards they brought the twelve handled pots which you ordered and I await your instructions to send them on.

I still think enthusiastically about our plans.

A thousand thanks for your arrangements and news about *La Faraónica*. Let us hope she will return to the fold soon.

I have written to my cousin to convey your fine judgements on his painting. He is mad with joy, and as he is one of your most fervent admirers he begs me to introduce him to you so that he can call on you in Paris. As I am sure of your kindness I am going to send him to you and I hope that you will forgive any difficulties this may cause. I do so because I am sure he will profit enormously from such a visit. I know what it is like from my own experience.

Yesterday it snowed a little here. I thought a lot about how much you would have loved to see the view of the Sierra and the Albaicín covered by snow. It was really wonderful. What about the photographs? Please do not forget about them.

We send your daughter our warm regards, and my sister sends you more of the same.

With all my affection your devoted friend,

MANUEL DE FALLA
Letter to Ignacio Zuloaga
[Granada, 6 February 1921]

DEAR Falla:

I have not written before because I had a thousand things waiting to be seen to. The memory of that blessed land is always in my thoughts an haunts me. It is cold and rainy here and the sky is the colour of lead.

You can imagine how we feel at the moment. How I envy you! That is the philosophy of life.

I will happily receive your cousin and will do what I can for him.

"La Faraónica" is definitely coming next week; when she arrives I will talk to Carré (at the Comic Opera).

I have given orders for you to be sent the *Memoirs of Captain Contreras*.

MANUEL DE FALLA BY IGNACIO ZULOAGA.

Regarding Alonso Cano, I will send everything soon. I enclose a photograph. Lucía will send you the rest. Could you find space, somewhere in your house, to keep my pots, so that when I go next I can collect them myself.

I dream about our plan.

I have written something about it. I will send it to you when it has ripenned.

Here art has become decadent. I believe that the damned war has atrophied many minds.

Everyone speaks about you with enthusiasm and veneration.

Best wishes to your sister and your friend Barrios.

Affectionately yours,

IGNACIO ZULOAGA
Letter to Manuel de Falla
[Paris, 12 February 1921]

DEAR Don Ignacio:

We have now settled into our new villa and are arranging it following your *precious* indications in the truest sense of the word. You will soon see how well the matted skirting board and pots (which we painted as you suggested) have turned out. When are you coming? I have to spend May between Paris and London but, God willing, I will be back in Granada at the beginning of June which, as we told you, is the best time of year in this part of the country. I eagerly await your return and the chance to discuss our plans and ideas; I am anxious to know what you have written about them. If you can, do not hesitate to send me any ideas because, apart from being impatient to hear them, they could help me to start developing my own ideas.

The photograph you sent me is excellent! A thousand thanks for this, and for the others you said Lucía will send us. Meanwhile, both my sister and I send Lucía our warmest regards.

I also thank you for offering to speak to Carré about the "La Faraónica"-*Love the Magician* affair and for the generosity with which you responded to the news of my cousin's visit, who I suppose will have been to see you.

Following your instructions we have packed your pots safely away until you are ready to come and collect them.

Will you be in Paris at the beginning of May?

It would be wonderful if you were because then I could go to see you as soon as I arrived. Affectionately, and with all the esteem and admiration of your devoted friend,

MANUEL DE FALLA
Letter to Ignacio Zuloaga
[Granada, 20 March 1921]

The Competition of *Cante Jondo*

AT THAT TIME Falla had organised the first competition of *cante jondo* in Granada in June 1922. Zuloaga and Ramón [Gómez de la Serna] assisted Falla in the artistic and literary aspects and Don Antonio Chacón and Ramón Montoya in guitar aspects.

Falla wanted, and suceeded in stopping the decadence of *cante*, which was in an abysmal state at that time.The great singers had been forgotten and the only prevalent songs were a few unbearable flamenco-like light lyrics, a few effeminate *colombianas* and a whole series of trivial and warbling *fandangos*, each new one more ridiculous than the last. No one knew how to listen to *tonás*, or *deblas*, or the *martinetes*, or the *siguiriyas*, or the *caña*, or the *polo*, or the *serranas* with their prelude of *liviana*. Falla was very severe and eliminated all the present day folk singers who only knew how to sing rowdy songs from the Sacromonte caves and songs from the neighbourhood courtyard.

At the festival Manolo Torres and a boy called Manolo Caracol, who won a prize, sang. There was also a seventy-two year old man, called *"Tenazas"*, who had walked all the way from Puente Genil to Granada, smoking a pipe and holding a pipe-cleaner, who brought tears to the eyes of Chacón and Montoya when he sang, in the first round of the contest, the *Cabales de Silverio*.

Federico [García Lorca] had found an old woman begging in the Albaicín, and she was the only one to begin the *serranas* singing the *liviana* that was thought to be lost. At that time Federico was exploring villages in the mountains and gathering old folk songs from old men and women, to which he put some poetic and musical order. These delighted Falla enormously when at night we gathered at his *carmen*. The *cante jondo* festival was a great success for all those involved, and mainly for me, because I made friends with the professors, registered at the University of Granada and finished my studies there in September.

EDGAR NEVILLE

I HAVE HEARD various competitions of *Cante jondo* in Seville and Sanlúcar and there were two winners. I liked the old man, but the boy. Well, at the moment I am completely disorientated. Do you think it comes from Delhi? Or are we just being silly?

JOAQUÍN TURINA
Letter to Manuel de Falla
[Madrid, 7 October 1922]

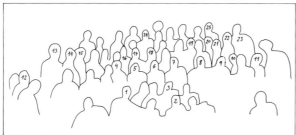

THOSE PRESENT AT THE BANQUET IN FALLA'S HONOUR HELD AT THE CASINO PALACE IN GRANADA. AMONG
OTHERS: *1.* NICOLÁS MARÍA LÓPEZ DÍAZ DE LOS REYES. *2.* JOSÉ MARÍA RODRÍGUEZ ACOSTA. *3.* JUAN MARÍA
GALLEGO BURÍN. *4.* SANTIAGO RUSIÑOL. *5.* URSULA GRENVILLE. *6.* MANUEL DE FALLA. *7.* LEIGHT HENRY.
8. IGNACIO ZULOAGA. *9.* RAMÓN GÓMEZ DE LA SERNA. *10.* FEDERICO GARCÍA LORCA. *11.* MELCHOR FERNÁNDEZ
ALMAGRO. *12.* KURT SCHINDLER (URSULA GRENVILLE'S HUSBAND). *13.* ANTONIO LÓPEZ SANCHO. *14.* ÁNGEL
BARRIOS. *15.* CONSTANTINO RUIZ CARNERO. *16.* AGUILERA. *17.* EDGAR NEVILLE. *18.* NARCISO DE LA FUENTE.
19. MAURICIO LEGENDRE. *20.* VALENTÍN ÁLVAREZ DE CIENFUEGOS. *21.* THE BULLFIGHTER CAGANCHO.
22. ANTONIO GALLEGO BURÍN. *23.* JOSÉ GARCÍA CARRILLO. *24.* J. B. TREND. *25.* JOSÉ ACOSTA MEDINA.

A B O U T   C A N T E   J O N D O

THIS NAME is given to a group of Andalusian songs, of which we believe the so–called *siguiriya gitana* to be the genuine type. Other varieties stem from this which are still alive among the people –the *polo*, the *martinete*, the *soleares*– which, of great quality stand out among the broad group of songs which common people call *flamenco*.

Strictly speaking, this name should only be given to the modern group of songs called *malagueñas, granadinas, rondeñas* (the last one is the root of the other two), *sevillanas, peteneras*, etc. All these varieties can only be considered a consequence of the aforementioned group.

Given that the *siguiriya gitana* is the characteristic song of the *cante jondo* group, before underlining its purely musical value, we would like to point out that it is perhaps the only European song which preserves in all its purity –in structure as well as style– the highest qualities of the primitive song of oriental people.

Likewise, one should remember that an essential quality of pure Andalusian *cante* is to avoid any imitation of a concert or theatrical style and one must bear in mind that a competitor is not a singer but a *cantaor*.

The *cantaor* should not be discouraged if he is told that in certain notes he is out of tune. This is not considered an obstacle by the true connoisseur of Andalusian *cante*.

It should also be remembered that a great vocal range, that is, a voice that embraces many notes, is necessary for *cante jondo*, but can be detrimental to its stylistic purity if used improperly.

MANUEL DE FALLA

COVER OF THE MANUSCRIPT OF FEDERICO GARCÍA LORCA'S LECTURE. DRAWING BY GALLEGO BURÍN.

'

MAESTRO: your epic telegram filled with joy, really cheered us up. We all knew that you were one of the worthy few because this is reflected in your painting. However, after your terms of support, we have the satisfaction of having found our Pope; and from this day on, if we feel attached to you with constant admiration and new gratitude, we are also sure that you will not abandon us and will guide us in affairs of the heart. Whatever we do, you will hear about it first.

In this reply, protracted a few days by the delays inevitably involved in the meeting of a Conclave, I wish to express, if words can express subtle semi-tones, the very complicated feelings, from which deep admiration and gratitude for you have risen to fill my heart.

Long live the honest men!

Miguel Cerón, Manuel de Falla, Fernando Vílchez, Fernando de los Ríos, Franco Vergara, Manuel Jofré, Federico García Lorca, Miguel Sánchez, A. Ortega Molina and H. Giner de los Ríos.

MANUEL DE FALLA
Letter to Ignacio Zuloaga
[Granada, 24 January 1922]

DEAR Don Ignacio:

From my telegram and letter, which you should have received by now, you can imagine the great enthusiasm which met your response to our petition. This enthusiasm was renewed by what you wrote about our situation (we can call it this now) in your last letter, which I did not answer earlier as I wanted to give you all possible information on the person you refer to. All that I was able to find out is favourable, apart from on one point which I was not able to resolve: the reason why he stopped being an ordinary soldier (or seaman). Nevertheless, he appears to be a serious and well-intentioned young man and his friends, who I have consulted confidentially, do not interpret this fact badly. It seems that he has resigned voluntarily. I, however, do not know him personally. If I receive any more enlightening information I will contact you right away.

Let us turn to the competition. I enclose a copy of the application form which must be handed in at the council offices next week. This will go together with your telegram, an *important* document, in the hope that the wonderful example you give there will be enough to convince them to provide us with what we request.

The signatories of the document include, among others: Pérez de Ayala, Díez-canedo, Arbós, Turina, Salazar, Conrado del Campo, Juan Ramón Jiménez, Salvador, Rodríguez Acosta, Óscar Esplá, Alfonso Reyes, Pérez Casas... and we are still waiting to add the most important ones, such as Pedrell, Azorín, etc. Of course we must make sure that Chacón is on the jury and we should choose the most reliable people in Seville, Jerez and Cadiz to help us with publicity. I really think that this is going to be something truly magical and unforgettable.

Imagine what you are going to do to the San Nicolás square!

Yours affectionately and with gratitude, your devoted,

MANUEL DE FALLA
Letter to Ignacio Zuloaga
[Granada, 3 february 1922]

DEAR Falla:

The fun document signed by all of you arrived and it pleases me enormously to hear that you are so full of enthusiasm to get this celebration of renewal and glorification of *jondo* (or *hondo*) art underway.

As I already stated in my telegram, you can count on me because I am even more excited about it than you are.

Here everyone has found out about the sensational event and many artist and people (who are not artists) have decided to go.

When everything is finally settled you must send me photographs of the place where the celebration is to take place with everything to be seen in the background because I have already thought about the form and outline it should take.

I think that there should be room for everything there, playing, singing and dancing; because so many of the guitarists in this country convey emotions like real artists (without knowing anything about music). This makes me think that when one is an artist it *is sufficient* to know the means of expression. All the rest is *decadence*.

One day while talking to a gypsy guitarist, he asked me what kind of playing moved me most. I replied: when *falsetas* are played with the pickering finger (without bending the hand) and, above all, using the 4th and 5th and the bass string and that Llobet and Segovia's playing style did not interest me.

He answered: "My God, this *payo** can really talk."

IGNACIO ZULOAGA
Letter to Manuel de Falla
[Paris, 5 February 1922]

**Payo*, word used by gypsies to refer to non-gypsies.
[*Translator's Note.*]

FOR TWO UNFORGETTABLE nights, at the Plaza de los Aljibes in the Alhambra, decorated by a group of artists directed by Ignacio Zuloaga, who lit the tall surrounding towers with red flares that reflected and flooded over the rectangle of seats and boxes, a great multitude gathered to listen with respect and emotion to the *cantaores* who, accompanied by their respective guitarists, filed past the central platform. A jury, presided over by Falla and for which the *cantaor* Don Antonio Chacón acted as technical advisor, arbitrated the event, deciding each performer's score. A conclave of music critics from every corner of the globe was designated a special box, next to another for the national and international press. The authenticity of the songs and the marking of the popular artists assembled there was done with strict impartiality.

It was there that Federico [García Lorca] met Manuel Torres the "*siguiriya*" singer, "great Andalusian artist", "the man who carries culture in his blood", intuitively understanding the strength of those dark sounds, the cardinal representative of the mysterious power of expression and feeling from the feet upwards known as "*duende*". There we all got to see Bermúdez, the old and miserable Lazarus of *cante jondo*, an epic poet who felt cornered and mummified because no one understands his songs anymore, and who came all the way from the province of Seville on

IN THE TWO MONTHS preceding the competition, we went in search of non-professional *cantaores*. To tell the truth, this "we" is inappropriate because the real searcher was Don Manuel Jofré (R.I.P.) amazing amateur guitar player and a close friend of mine. He introduced us to these strange taciturn creatures, one by one, after having driven them out of their hidden dens. (None of them wanted to participate in the competition.) It was also he who accompanied this or that singer on the guitar at the meetings we held to arrange the competition. On consecutive days he brought before us, among others, a retired smuggler, whose name I forget, "Paquillo of Gaz", the prominent *siguiriya* singer and uncle of "Frasquito Yerbagüena", inventor of the *media granadina*.

One night we heard a somewhat deaf old hat maker from the shop Tule y Plancha called Crespo sing *soleares*. I must underline, so what follows can be understood, that a such halo of goodness, honesty and nobility radiated from him, that only a fool would suspect him of trickery. Perhaps his deafness contributed to the impression he made on us. An absent minded and remote expression, proverbial among deaf people, marked his conversation with long pauses. As always, there was only a group of six or seven of us at the meeting. One of us –a friend of Falla's and of the rest of us who later became an academic and a minister– asked Crespo innocently, in one of the silent intervals between songs:

"What do you think about while you sing." To which came the reply, which is worth recording in bronze. "Women... sadness... About my son dying... my only son... the only one left to me... my friend Gálvez... and myself..." "*Cantemos por siguiriyas!*"

Later, after the echo of his last words died away, Falla, who had listened to him, pale and still as a stone, in which only his eyes burnt like steel, bowed his head and made the sign of the cross in amazement. After a long silence, we said goodbye to each other and separated in deep thought.

The fact is, that the competition itself did not achieve very much, neither from the point of view of what it set out to do, nor from the point of view of pure art. Hardly anyone noticed this. Least of all the renowned critics, artists and writers who came from all over attracted by Falla's prestige. These illustrious foreigners seemed to be carried away and really amazed by so much beauty and exoticism. Whilst, Don Manuel simply smiled and kept his true feelings to himself.

THE PEOPLE AT THE COMPETITION BY LÓPEZ SANCHO IN A CARICATURE OF THE TIME: *1.* DIEGO BERMÚDEZ, *EL TÍO TENAZAS. 2.* RAMÓN MONTOYA SALAZAR. *3.* JOAQUÍN CUADROS. *4.* PASTORA PAVÓN, *LA NIÑA DE LOS PEINES. 5.* VALENTÍN FELIP DURÁN. *6. EL NIÑO DEL BARBERO. 7. LA NIÑA DE LA AGUADERA. 8.* ANDRÉS SEGOVIA. *9.* JOSÉ RUIZ ALMODÓVAR. *10.* JOSÉ SÁNCHEZ PUERTAS. *11.* RUPERTO MARTÍNEZ RIOBOÓ. *12.* ANTONIO LÓPEZ SANCHO. *13.* IGNACIO ZULOAGA. *14.* JOSÉ GARCÍA CARRILLO. *15.* FERNANDO VÍLCHEZ. *16.* MANUEL DE FALLA. *17.* VICENTE LEÓN CALLEJAS. *18.* FEDERICO GARCÍA LORCA. *19.* HERMENEGILDO LANZ. *20.* JOSÉ MARTÍNEZ RIOBOÓ. *21.* LUIS RIOBOÓ. *22.* RAMÓN MARTÍNEZ RIOBOÓ. *23.* SANTIAGO RUSIÑOL. *24.* ANTONIO ORTEGA MOLINA. *25.* JOSÉ CARAZO. *26.* ROGELIO ROBLES POZO. *27.* FRANCISCO VERGARA CARDONA. *28.* FERNANDO DE LOS RÍOS. *29.* SANTOS MARTÍNEZ. *30.* MIGUEL CERÓN RUBIO. *31.* RAMÓN CARAZO.

Jealous competitors made old Bermúdez, the only pure *cantaor,* drunk before his performance. When he began to sing the wonderful *soleares* by Silverio "Correo de Vélez"... and, repeated it, countless times, without ever going further than the first part. But, because no one knew anything about *cante jondo*, they applauded him riotously.

Back then he was known as "El Tenazas", and now they call him "Dieguito el de Morón". With the money he won from the competition (which in 1922 was a sizeable sum) he decided to live in style, lodging at the Posada de las Tablas guest house. He lived there for some months while waiting to see if the record company Odeón would pay him few pesetas to make some recordings, which Falla and I were negotiating. In the meantime, every afternoon, he came up to my studio (I was trying my hand at sculpture at the time) and, once in a while, as I sculpted, he would break into song. That was "El Tenazas" (God save him) with his short, wizened body and a face that sent friends fleeing, his expres-

sion as serious as an undertaker's. He only had one lung because, back in his youth, someone had stabbed him in the other. In fact, as far as his physical aspect was concerned, combined with his age –he was well into his eighties– he was the opposite of Don Juan. Well, one afternoon as he silently watched me working with the clay, he began to tell me in a shy hushed voice: "I've left the guest house... and I've paid a room in Realejo... 'cos I've got me a woman." Seeing my stupified expression, he added: "No, no!... I need someone to take care of me." A few days later I told Falla the story and I still remember how he laughed. With that laugh of his, which was almosty completely inaudible, but which resonated in my spirit like a waterfall.

MIGUEL CERÓN

On another occasion I went to Granada to see the supreme *cante jondo* tournament. Zuloaga and Falla, who were waiting for me at the station, made me promise to speak at the solemn celebration that evening, in the wood of the Alhambra.

"We need you to speak, to explain what it's all about, to fight the hostility of those who believe that this competition should never have been held."

"All right," I said, "I'll speak. My only condition is that you cover my legs during the *tablado*: a small table covered with a Manilan tablecloth.

Now I had given my word, but when I realised the magnitude of the event and saw a proud and flamenco people gathered in the Plaza de los Aljibes of the Alhambra, I felt like the victim who disappears into the bowls of a factory, sacrificed to the high aims of the business.

"Fairies of the wood, ladies and gentlemen," I began and carried on in this salutory tone to address the stars and, in second place, the men who, in deep despair, can only raise their spirits when they sing *cante jondo*.

The eyes of the flamencos listening to me were full of dislike and the men drank tall glasses of *manzanilla*, not the first, but the second, which made the great sea of people a little choppy. I reacted quickly then, and said: "I always travel with a five minute speech, a half hour speech and a two and a half hour speech... The most appropriate for this evening is the five minute one, and for that reason I shall retire at once, after having praised the mission of those who have quoted hardened preachers and survivors of something as disturbing in effect as the noise a stone makes when it falls in the deepest well."

A sherry I drank, hidden from view with the commission behind the gypsies perched on the stage, quenched my thirst.

While I drank it a gentleman approached me and said:

"You're lucky to have escaped so lightly... There was an oaf beside me who pointed his pistol at you and kept asking us: Well? Shall I kill him now?"

RAMÓN GÓMEZ DE LA SERNA

PROGRAME OF THE *CANTE JONDO* COMPETITION WITH TEXTS BY FALLA AND DRAWINGS BY MANUEL ÁNGELES ORTIZ.

foot in the hope of finding someone to listen to him again. In his seventies, short-sighted and with one lung swallowed by the scar of a stab wound, a mummy who haunts Andalusian taverns, he still has a voice like thunder and the profound wisdom of a genuine *cantaor*. At the audition in which he sang a *serrana*, a copla which has the solemnity and seriousness of a dirge and the reiteration of a ritual, the effect was astonishing.

In my flock there was,
In my flock there was,
In my flock there was...
   A she-lamb,
   A she-lamb,
   A she-lamb...
From too much stroking,
From too much stroking,
From too much stroking...
   She turned a wild beast,
   She turned a wild beast,
   She turned a wild beast...

On hearing that Don Antonio Chacón, the great master of *cante*, was absolutely bewildered and crossed himself exclaiming:

"Bless my soul, what a thing I am hearing!"

It was as if the preacher of an old and forgotten creed had suddenly found his Messiah alive and well.

JOSÉ MORA GUARNIDO

FALLA WITH, *FROM LEFT TO RIGHT*, ADOLFO SALAZAR, ÁNGEL BARRIOS, FEDERICO GARCÍA
LORCA, AND *IN FRONT*, FRANCISCO GARCÍA LORCA, IN THE VAULTS OF THE ALHAMBRA.

The *Cristobicas* Theatre

THE FOLLOWING year Falla faced a different kind of problem. This time it had nothing to do with an artistic treasure in danger of being buried by the tide of progress and unscrupulous degeneration. It was a much smaller affair of a personal nature, related to the fate of his own work. Don Manuel was finishing his *Master Peter's Puppet Show* and had reached the decisive moment of sorting out its staging.

Chance has it that not many people know how this work by Falla came into being and as his scruples, which prevented him from revealing any details even to those closest to him, are not so prevalent now, I think the time has come to shed some light on the matter. The Princesse de Polignac (the "*Madame Machine à coudre*," as Debussy called her) had commissioned from the three great composers of the time –Ravel, Stravinsky, Falla– a few small concert pieces, to present them as exclusive firsts at a party in her Parisian palace and with the guarantee that they would not be shown in any other venue for a year. The other two composers complied strictly with the task. But Falla's project grew and grew the more he thought about it. He had intended to make a brief commentary on an episode in *Don Quixote* and when he focussed his attention on that episode, he found that it did not fit in with the terms of his commission, but he had developed a liking and enthusiasm for the project. He outlined his problem to the occasional entrepreneur and proposed, without making any change at all to his fees, that she should cover the costs imposed by the expanded project. The princess accepted.

Now another problem emerged. Now that he had a new idea for a stage piece with the participation of actors, now that the presence of a puppet show was necessary, what could be done about characterising Don Quixote? How could this symbolic man be embodied by the physique, not always adequate, of a corpulent, fat, unsuitable tenor or baritone? How could he solve this problem? The best thing to do would be to completely get rid of the human figures replacing them with puppets, in other words, a kind of double puppet show using characters of distinct sizes. But, how would this work in practice?

A trial performance became indispensable. The precedent of traditional puppet shows was not sufficient. Then Federico suggested that they hold the rehearsal at his house, setting up a puppet show which he was going to do for the children of some friends at the Epiphany celebrations. Thus Lorca's first *Teatro de Cristobicas* was born, which began as no more than the transformation of the puppet shows of Spanish Fairs (Cristóbal in Andalusian and Bululú in Galician) into a more sensible vein.

JOSÉ MORA GUARNIDO

PROGRAMME OF THE PERFORMANCE OF THE PLAY, *MISTERIO DE LOS REYES MAGOS*, ORGANISED BY LORCA WITH THE HELP OF FALLA AT THE PIANO AND HERMENEGILDO LANZ, WHO MADE THE SCENERY.

IN THE ALPUJARRA MOUNTAINS IN SEARCH OF POPULAR SONG, WITH ANTONIO LUNA, FEDERICO GARCÍA LORCA AND JOSÉ SEGURA.

DEAREST DON MANUÉ (colon)

I am thrilled about the idea of the trip to the Alpujarras. I am really looking forward to making some *Cristobicas* [puppets] full of Andalusian nature and enchanting popular character.

I think that we should do this seriously; the slapstick puppet show is perfect for doing highly original songs.

We must create the tragedy (never fully praised) of the Knight of the flute and the mosquito of the trumpet, the wild idyll of Don Cristóbal and Señora Rosita, the death of Pepe-Hillo in the plaza in Madrid and other farces of our own invention. Then we will have to borrow romances [Spanish ballads] about crimes and one of the miracles of the *Virgen del Carmen* (Virgin of Carmen) which speaks about fish and the waves of the sea. If we go to the Alpujarras we should take some moorish story, Aben-Humeya's for example, along with us too. All we have to do is add a little love to the story and we can procure a clean sinless *art*, and not an *upstart*.

When are you going to come here? In town the other day there was a chap with some *cristobicas* who *had a real go* at the audience in a truly Aristophanic manner.

Manolito and you can fashion some precious things and Mora, who is very familiar with the low folk romances, will prove very useful. As you well know, I am prepared to do anything, apart from sending telegrams!

Thank you very much for my father's congratulations. Regards and lots more from my mother and sister for María del Carmen and there go the affectionate wishes of your ever devoted friend.

Come and visit me!

FEDERICO GARCÍA LORCA

Letter to Manuel de Falla

FEDERICO GARCÍA LORCA, RAFAEL AGUADO, ANTONIO LUNA, JOSÉ SEGURA AND MANUEL DE FALLA IN THE ALPUJARRA.

CURTAIN AND SCENERY OF THE SMALL DE *CRISTOBICAS* THEATRE.

COMPOSITIONS

Appendix III

MASTER PETER'S PUPPET SHOW

HARPSICHORD CONCERTO

Score of Master Peter's Puppet Show.

MASTER PETER'S PUPPET SHOW

AFTER BEING COMMISSIONED BY THE PRINCESSE DE POLIGNAC, AT THE END OF 1918, TO WRITE A COMPOSITION TO BE PERFORMED AT HER PARISIAN SALON MANUEL DE FALLA STARTED TO CONSIDER A THEME BASED ON AN EPISODE IN *DON QUIXOTE*. THE THEME IS FOUND IN CHAPTERS XXV AND XXVI IN WHICH A PUPPET SHOW PLAYS A SPECIAL RÔLE. FALLA WORKED ON CERVANTES' TEXT, MAKING THE CHANGES HE CONSIDERED APPROPRIATE. THE COMPOSITION OF THE PIECE DRIFTED ON FOR SOME YEARS, FROM 1919 TO 1923, AND MANUEL DE FALLA WORKED ON ITS EVERY ASPECT, INCLUDING ITS STAGING. THE SLAPSTICK PUPPET SHOW HE HAD SET UP WITH FEDERICO GARCÍA LORCA AND HERMENEGILDO LANZ IN 1923 PROVIDED A USEFUL EXPERIENCE. *MASTER PETER'S PUPPET SHOW* INCLUDES PERFORMANCES BY THE PUPPETS AND THE ACTORS.

FOR THE FIRST PERFORMANCE OF THE WORK AT THE PRINCESSE DE POLIGNAC'S PALACE IN PARIS, MANUEL ÁNGELES ORTIZ COLLABORATED WITH HIM IN BUILDING THE PROSCENIUM ARCH AND THE CURTAIN OF THE PORTABLE STAGE, HERMENEGILDO PAINTED THE PUPPETS' FACES AND HERNANDO VIÑES, ALONG WITH MANUEL ÁNGELES ORTIZ, DESIGNED THE COSTUMES AND SCENERY. HECTOR DUFRANNE INTERPRETED "DON QUIXOTE", THOMAS SELIGNAC WAS "MASTER PETER" AND MANUEL GARCÍA AND AMPARITO PERIS WERE "TRUJAMÁN". THE ORCHESTRA WAS CONDUCTED BY WLADIMIR GOLSCHMANN WITH WANDA LANDOWSKA AT THE HARPSICHORD AND MME. HENRI-CASADESUS AT THE HARP-LUTE.

Letter to Manuel de Falla from the Princesse de Polignac, requesting a short orchestral piece for small orchestra as part of the repertory of compositions being prepared for performance at the salon of her palace in Paris. Saint Jean de Luz, 25 October 1918.

The Princesse de Polignac.

THE PRINCESSE DE Polignac, a very wealthy woman, wanted to produce some puppet shows at her palace in Paris. She commissioned works from Stravinsky, Erik Satie and Falla. Stravinsky composed *Renard*; Satie, *Socrates*; but neither of these were performed at the palace of that lady. Diaghilev produced *Renard* as a ballet for just one season, without repeating it afterwards. *Socrates* was presented at a concert. Only Falla's work was shown at the Princesse de Polignac's theatre.

Falla received notification of this in Madrid, shortly after the end of the First World War, at the beginning of 1919. He was very interested in the idea, more from an artistic point of view than a financial one, because it was common knowledge that the Princess' immense fortune was reflected in the splendour of her way of life, but not in the generosity of her gifts. Falla was worried about what to do: he could not find a subject. The idea finally came to him one night, a time when inspiration usually

occurs, that there could be nothing more suitable for a theatre of marionettes than the scene of the puppets in *Master Peter's Puppet Show* in *Don Quixote*. Thus, taking Cervantes' novel in his hands he began to make his own version, cutting out this and that and adding others, but always using the text of *Don Quixote*. He started to compose the music with great enthusiasm, as he always did after taking a decision, because he has never been able to work from scratch. He began, as with all his compositions, by searching for materials which referred to the character of the work, with the aim of documenting and enhancing the substance of the theme. He studied the music of the classical Spanish period (15th and 16th century) in Pedrell's eminent work, *Hispaniae Schola Musica Sacra*, and the organography and folk music of the period. Then he decided to use three styles:

First: the towncryer, that characteristic cry heard in the streets of Spanish villages: the song of the nightwatchman; the hawking of street vendors; the declamation of a man who in a half-sung, half-recited tune, tells a story about bandits or a famous and terrifying crime, depending on the scene before him. He points to this scene —painted on a fabric stretched between two metal bars and hanging from a wooden pole, like a standard— with a stick held in his hand, as he explains it. Those cries that we heard as children have almost disappeared today. But as an adult in Madrid, while he was starting the composition of *Master Peter*, Falla could still hear a man who, surrounded by a group of entranced children on a piece of open ground in the Salamanca district, told one of those stories with the horribly fascinating illustrations painted on fabric.

Second: evocative music, Spanish Romantic music, medieval music, all in his own idiosyncratic style, like Don Gayferos' ride to rescue Melisenda.

Third: the period in which the action takes place, the music that Don Quixote sings at the end of the piece.

He channelled all his efforts into composing *Master Peter*. He finished it in Granada.

JAIME PAHISSA

Marionettes by Hermenegildo Lanz for Federico García Lorca's Puppet Show.

IN *MASTER PETER'S* Puppet Show, finished in 1920 and based on a well-known episode of *Don Quixote*, Falla revealed for the first time his new creativity which, up to the present time, still represents the high point of modern Spanish music. The purification of elements, common to Falla's previous compositions, the simplification of method and of the material resources employed, is taken to its limits in *Master Peter*, which uses the human voice and a simplified orchestration. He gathered together a group of musicians in Seville for the first performance of his work in the city. As an outcome of this and because of Falla's opinion about the instrumental execution of classical scores and the point of balance between earlier orchestras and Viennese classicism, this group of musicians was shaped into an orchestra which Falla called "Andalusian Chamber Orchestra", immediately placing his disciple Ernesto Halffter on the conductor's podium. That orchestra was really an achievement of Falla, and for that reason I have drawn attention to it here: It was the living embodiment of his ideas and of the concepts expressed in his compositions and constantly repeated in his conversations and in his rare, but notable, essays.

ADOLFO SALAZAR

Programme of the first concert performance of *Master Peter's Puppet Show*, conducted by Manuel de Falla, Seville, 24th of March 1923.

J. J. VINEGRA INTERVIEWS MIGUEL CERÓN ABOUT MANUEL DE FALLA

COULDN'T YOU tell me just one more anecdote about your friend's life?

—Falla had been staying in Seville for a few days when I arrived to help with the première of *Master Peter's Puppet Show*. We only spent a moment together that afternoon. After the concert that evening, when I left the theatre, without attempting to see him, I wan-dered around Seville's silent and deserted streets until dawn. As I had left Granada very early that morning and felt quite tired, I decided to go to bed. But, just as I was dropping off, I was startled by a strange noise. In the adjacent room which was divided from mine by a sliding door, someone had turned the light on. Then I clearly heard the "shuga–shuga" of my neighbour brushing his teeth, he was brushing the enamel off them by the sound of it. After the scrubbing noise it was the turn of his throat, "glug–glug", once, twice, he went on gargling endlessly. This concert lasted for almost an hour and then it was time for the nose. Sniffing, snorting and sneezing. I was so tired that not even all this could have kept me awake, had it not been for the racket made, every two or three minutes, by a mouthful of water as it hit the brass wash basin.

—Who on earth was your neighbour? I asked him.

And Don Miguel answered with a smile:

—The last thing I could have imagined was that Falla could be making those noises so late at night; back then I wasn't familiar with his peculiar repertory on the rules of hygiene —and after a pause he carried on. I hardly slept a wink and the next morning they came to wake me because Falla was waiting to have breakfast with me. Instead of congratulating him on the concert of the previous night, I began to rant and rave about my neighbour's conduct and all the other people with Falla at the table agreed with me. I don't remember exactly what I said, but I do recall referring to the throat gargler as "a stupid idiot". When I had finished my speech, which was applauded by those gathered there, Falla, who was in an excellent mood, his eyes shining with happiness, speared a fritter (which he had ordered because he knew I liked them) as if with a baton and ended the gesture with these words: "My dear Miguel, forgive me, but I am the stupid idiot who didn't let you sleep." And in the midst of everyone's surprise he dunked the fritter in his coffee.

DEAR HERMENEGILDO:

I believe that you will be pleased to hear that the Princesse de Polignac —as the result of our conversation— would like you to make the heads and hands (in the way you know) of the puppets for *Master Peter* (the première will take place at her house on the 8th of June), as well as a sketch for the decoration of the second scene, in other words Melisenda's tower.

Mme. de Polignac invites you (with all expenses

paid, that is to say, the cost of the journey and accommodation in Paris) to come a few days before the première and stay until the production finishes its run. Imagine how happy it makes me to think that we can carry on in Paris the slapstick puppet work we began in Granada. Manolo Ortiz who is also collaborating on *Master Peter*, wrote to you telling you the exact measurments of the heads:

They are:

1. Don Quixote (bigger than the rest).
2. Master Peter.
3. The boy who explains the action (Trujamán).
4. Sancho Panza.
5. The innkeeper.
6. The student.
7. The page.
8. The man with the lances and halberds.

In the second scene we see the tower of homage of the Sansueña fortress, and in the background, distant lands. Melisenda appears leaning out of one of the tower's balconies. A richly and soberly dressed moor —King Marsilio— makes various appearances on one of the castle's outer passageways, which one supposes will lead to the tower of homage.

Melisenda is surprised by a moor who plants a kiss right on her lips. King Marsilio orders the moor's arrest (King Marsilio's Guard). As you will remember, I want both the scenery and the characters (rough textual outline) of this scene to be inspired by the frescoes in the Palace of Justice (colour, clothing, etc.). Nevertheless, in this case, there is no need follow Cervantes indications about Melisenda's moorish apparel.

There is no need for me to suggest you read the two chapters of the second part of *Don Quixote* which are concerned more or less with *Master Peter*...

Nothing else because it is nearly two o'clock in the morning and I am terribly tired and still have to go home. So...

Best wishes for Fernando and more for you from your faithful friend,

MANUEL DE FALLA
Letter to Hermenegildo Lanz
[Paris, 28 April 1923]

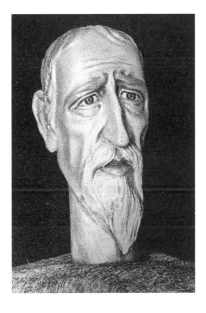

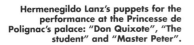

Hermenegildo Lanz's puppets for the performance at the Princesse de Polignac's palace: "Don Quixote", "The student" and "Master Peter".

FALLA LIVED in Granada, in calle Antequeruela, with his sister María del Carmen and a cat called Confucius.

In that environment, Falla told me some details of the rehearsals which were underway in Paris for the first performance of *Master Peter's Puppet Show*. The stage adaptation of two chapters from the second part of Don Quixote into a musical plot which combined liturgical music, medieval romances and 16th and 17th century Castillian music in the same theatre. Manuel de Falla's most complete and successful composition.

This indisputable masterpiece —"Devout tribute to the glory of Miguel de Cervantes dedicated to Madame la Princesse de Polignac" was what was written on the score— was produced for the first time in the Princess' salon.

Joaquín Peinado and Hernando Viñes told me that at the first performance of *Master Peter's Puppet Show* the puppets were handled by friends of Falla, including Ricardo Viñes, Hernando, the guitarist Emilio Pujol and his wife.

The scenery was painted by Manolo Ángeles Ortiz and Hermenegildo Lanz.

Manuel de Falla did not let anything go unnoticed at rehearsals, but his severe and perfectionist nature was complemented by a friendly spirit of camaraderie, enthusiasm and good humour.

They all felt the greatest respect for Don Manuel, but lamented and joked about the complete disinterest shown towards them by the Princesse de Polignac who when she retired in the evening, knowing full well that the preparation of puppets and scenery would carry on until much later, did not even think to offer them a glass of water.

"Tomorrow I'll bring you some lovely sandwiches," said Don Manuel.

"And I'll bring beer," added Ricardo Viñes.

The piece was finally performed and raised enormous curiosity in the musical world.

MARIO VERDAGUER

ON THE 25TH of June 1923 *Master Peter's Puppet Show* was performed for the first time at the palace of the Princesse de Polignac. It was executed by Golschmann's concert orchestra, conducted by that Maestro, with Wanda Landowska on the harpsichord.

The idea of using a harpsichord in the orchestra of *Master Peter* had occurred to Falla during a trip to Toledo one Easter Week. While there he visited the house

The première of *Master Peter's Puppet Show*, at the salon of the Princesse de Polignac, Paris, 25th of June 1923.

of Don Ángel Vegué y Goldoni, a Fine Arts professor, who possessed an impressive collection of antique keyboard instruments, among them various harpsichords and clavichords*. Falla played the one that was in the best condition. The slightly archaic character of its sound gave him the idea that it would be appropriate to use it in *Master Peter*. That is why a harpsichord appears in the orchestra. The reason why Wanda Landowska interpreted this part at the première is as follows. This artist had demonstrated, on many occasions, a great desire to go to Granada. To grant her wish Falla managed to persuade the Philharmonic Society of Granada to engage her to play a concert, which was, in reality, a posthumous concert because the Society had just dissolved. For this reason Wanda Landowska often visited Falla's house in Granada and, naturally, they spoke about *Master Peter* which Falla was composing at the time. On other previous occasions Wanda Landowska had asked him to com-

pose her a concert for harpsichord and orchestra. So when she heard *Master Peter* and saw that there was a part for harpsichord she told him that she wanted to play it at the première. And that is what happened.

When *La vida breve* was being shown for the first time in Brussels, Falla attended the second night. On his journey back to Paris he was accompanied by the singer Salignac. Falla asked him if he would like to sing in *Master Peter*, which he accepted while, at the same time, offering his help in searching for other singers. He found Dufranne and Amparito Peris, a very musical girl who did so well that she was taken on by the Comic Opera to interpret another child rôle. They sang it in Spanish and they said that they felt so comfortable singing it in the original language that when they had to sing in French again they found it much more difficult. The same performers sang *Master Peter* when it was first produced in London, apart from the part of the child, which was performed very adequately by Vera Janakopulos. Here too, it was sung in Spanish.

The following artists took part in the première of *Master Peter*: Dufranne as Don Quixote; Salignac as Mas-

Curtain by Manuel Ángeles Ortiz.

ter Peter; and Manuel García and Amparito Peris as Trujamán. The scenery and the puppet designs were done by Manuel Ángeles Ortiz.

The performance at the house of the Princesse de Polignac was a huge success. Both the stage and the composer were showered in roses. The audience enjoyed the piece so much that they called for it to be repeated. But the interpreters did not want to, giving the excuse that it might not turn out so well a second time. The true reason, however, is that the Princess had not invited them to the grand supper afterwards to which she treated the

---

* "El Ventanillo": A house in Toledo beside the Tagus river, which was rented by Ángel Vegué y Goldoni, A. García Solalinde, Alfonso Reyes, José Moreno Villa and Américo Castro. [*Editor's Note*]

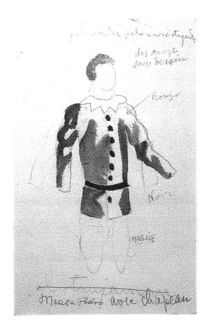

"Master Peter", "Trujamán", "The innkeeper", "The page", "The student" and "The man with the lances and halberds", costumes by Manuel Ángeles Ortiz.

distinguished guests who had attended the show. Neither did she invite Falla. It was a great success, with heaps of roses and flowers, but at the end of the show he was kicked out like a servant. Wanda Landowska forgot her fine lace handkerchief and the Princess returned it to her inside a beautiful shellac box, but Wanda, upset by the indifference she had been shown by not being invited, kept her handkerchief and sent the box back. The Princess' behaviour during the days of preparation and the première of *Master Peter* at the palace is completely bewildering because she was such a lover of the

arts and, in particular, music. To the extent that she never once offered Falla anything to eat; and if he needed a soft drink or a coffee, he had to ask someone to bring him one from outside; and on one occasion Wanda Landowska brought him some sandwiches in case he needed them. However, the Princess invited Falla to the supper she held after the première of Stravinsky's *Les Noces*. It is clear that she considered those who worked an inferior class.

JAIME PAHISSA

MY DEAR FRIEND:

I have been informed by the publishers Chester that *Master Peter* is almost ready to be shown and have taken advantage of the first post to send you enclosed some notes about the vocal execution. These are the same ones that have been sent to Chester to be translated into English and French and published alongside the music.

I also send you brief indication guidelines for the placement and distribution of the orchestra. As you can see, the harpsichord has to be placed in front of the other string instruments. The number of strings should be as follows:

Two first violins.

Two second violins.

Two violas.

One cello.

One double bass.

Only in this manner can the sound of the harpsichord be balanced with the rest of the orchestra.

If you cannot use a large size harpsichord (a theatre or church one) it would be better to use a *piano-forte*, with pedal, and the hammers covered with leather. You must take the lid off completely (I would advise the same whether using a *harpsichord* or a *piano-forte*) and in case the lid cannot be removed, the instrument should be placed in such a way that the lid does not obstruct the sound waves from reaching the audience freely. I think you will see what I mean.

The orchestral playing should be, in general, *very nervous and energetic*, and the musicians must follow all the indications to the letter. With a conductor like Adrián Bonet and with your priceless advice, for you know the work so well, I am confident that the interpretation will be magnificent. Please do me the favour of passing on my regards to Bonet.

How sorry I am not to be able to be with you at the première!

My best wishes for Mr. Dent, yours affectionately your friend,

MANUEL DE FALLA
Letter to J. B. Trend
[Granada, 2 October 1924]

NOTES ABOUT THE VOCAL EXECUTION

The vocal style of the three main singers must strictly avoid any kind of theatrical mannerisms.

The part of *Don Quixote* should be sung with a noble tone, which will contribute both to the ridiculous and the sublime, exaggerating the interpretation of the musical indications even in the smallest details. A nervous, energetic and agile voice rich in expressive nuances will be indispensable for the correct execution of this part.

For the part of *Master Peter*, the artist should try to avoid all excessively lyrical expressions, adopting instead the most vivid or intense musical diction according to the tone demanded by each dramatic situation.

He must be able to capture the picaresque and humorous nature of the character, without clowning, but by being purposefully comic.

The part of *Trujamán* demands a nasal and some-

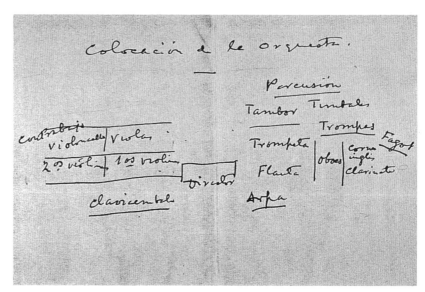

Falla's note indicating the placement of the orchestra.

what forced voice: that of a child street hawker; coarsely expressive and, consequently, exempt from lyrical inflexion. This part should be sung by a child, and if one cannot be found, by a woman (a high mezzo-soprano) who shall simulate the afore mentioned vocal quality and expressive character.

Letter to Manuel de Falla from Joaquín Nin commenting on the première of *Master Peter's Puppet Show*, "There is no need to repeat what I have told you a thousand times; everything that you do is impressive; absolutely definitive, believe me. Last night was one of those nights which will be written about in books: *Master Peter* will mark a period in our history... ", 1923.

MANOLO will write to you about the form the scenery is to take. We intend to simplify it a lot to give a greater impression of a *Puppet show*.

The scenery of the Melisenda scene, for example, could consist of the tower, etc, (like in the photo) built; and of a tree with a backdrop giving the effect of distance. The same with the rest. The puppet stage would not be right in front of the audience, but at a slight angle, so in order to let the audience follow the action it will have to be enacted as close as possible to the proscenium. In this way the big puppets (the bad characters) will be seen in profile and not from behind as occurred in Paris.

MANUEL DE FALLA
Letter to Hermenegildo Lanz
[Granada, 27 August 1924]

Stage designs by Manuel Ángeles Ortiz (*above*) and by Hernando Viñes.

Première of *Master Peter's Puppet Show*, conducted by Mendelberg, Amsterdam, 26th of April 1926. (*On the left*: Luis Buñuel.)

DURING THE first years I spent in Paris, when I knew practically only other Spanish people, I barely heard about the Surrealists. One night, as I passed in front of the "Closerie des Lilas", I saw some broken glass on the floor. At a celebratory dinner for Madame Rachilde, two Surrealists —I don't remember who they were— insulted and slapped her, which lead to a general row.

To tell the truth, at first I wasn't very interested in Surrealism. I had written a piece about ten pages long entitled, quite simply, *Hamlet* which we acted ourselves in the basement of the "Sélect". Those were my first steps towards being a director.

At the end of 1926 a great opportunity came my way. Hernando Viñes was the nephew of the famed pianist Ricardo Viñes, who had discovered Erik Satie.

At that time, Amsterdam had two grand orchestral ensembles, among the best in Europe. The first had just finished a very successful season with Stravinsky's *A Soldier's Tale*. The second of those ensembles was conducted by the great Mengelberg. In order to compete with the other orchestra they wanted to present *Master Peter's Puppet Show*, a short piece by Manuel de Falla, based on an episode in *Don Quixote*, to close a concert. They were looking for a stage director.

Ricardo Viñes knew Mengelberg. Thanks to *Hamlet* I had a reference, though, in truth, quite a meagre one. But they offered me the stage direction and I accepted.

I had to work with a world famous conductor and some outstanding singers. We rehearsed for fifteen days in Paris, at Hernando's house. *Master Peter* is, in reality, a marionettes' puppet theatre. Theoretically all of the characters are puppets dubbed by singers' voices. I had the idea of introducing four characters of flesh and blood, wearing masks, who attended the spectacle of Master Peter and occasionally took part in the action, also dubbed by the singers in the orchestra pit. Of course, I gave these four non-speaking parts to my friends. Peinado was the innkeeper and my cousin, Rafael Saura, was "Don Quixote". I also gave a part to Cossío, another painter.

We gave three or four performances in Amsterdam to packed houses. The first night I forgot to prepare the lights. You couldn't see a thing. After hours of hard work, helped by an electrician, I was able to have everything ready for the second performance, which went off without a hitch.

LUIS BUÑUEL

A moment from the performance of *Master Peter's Puppet Show*, Amsterdam, 1926.

Stage design by Manuel Ángeles Ortiz for the performance in Amsterdam.

DEAR DON MANUÉ: All my best wishes to congratulate you on the success of *Master Peter* in Amsterdam. My friend Luis Buñuel is going to direct it, and I hear that the young painters Bores and Cossío are involved as well. I am sure that they will do their utmost to ensure all goes well. Goodbye Don Manuel, regards to María del Carmen and my warmest wishes, yours,

FEDERICO GARCÍA LORCA
Letter to Manuel de Falla

Stage design and puppets by Manuel Ángeles Ortiz and Hernando Viñes.

A moment from the performance of *Master Peter's Puppet Show*, Amsterdam, 1926. Francisco Cossío as "Sancho Panza", Rafael Saura as "Don Quixote" and Juan Esplandiu as "Trujamán".

Stage design by Manuel Ángeles Ortiz, Amsterdam, 1926.

Self portrait by Ignacio Zuloaga.

Portrait of Sancho Panza by Ignacio Zuloaga for *Master Peter's Puppet Show*, 1926.

IN THE SPRING of 1926, to celebrate the fiftieth anniversary of the birth of Falla, the Comic Opera of Paris organised performances of his compositions: *La vida breve, Love the Magician* and *Master Peter*.

For this performance of *Master Peter*, Zuloaga painted the scenery and his brother-in-law Maxime de Thomás built the puppets out of wood, flat, cut-outs. Zuloaga and Falla took part in the first performances, Zuloaga in the part of Sancho, and Falla as the innkeeper. A few days later the direction of the Comic Opera played a joke on them by sending them five francs each for their work and a memo informing them that it was satisfied with

the way in which they had handled their rôles and encouraged them to keep at it because, with time, they could go far.

JAIME PAHISSA

MY DEAR Falla: Believe me that neither my article nor my dedication has been able to pay you what I owe you for being allowed to hear *Master Peter*—it is the only one that will remain here in Spain if the Yankies go on taking away *Retablos* (altarpieces) from our churches. For me Zurich was an unforgettable moment. I have a true love for *Don Quixote*—as you will have noticed from my book— and I was overawed to hear him sing it sung. You are, my dear Falla, the only person who has ever been able to make him sing. All we can do is speak —well or badly— about him. But you, and you alone, have made him sing from the bottom of his heart as well as speaking. That day confirmed my old idea that music is the purest of all the arts, the one that affects human emotions most directly. I had a clear, instinctive feeling that day that human substance is to music what clay is to sculpture. I envy you your art, as you can see, in every sense of the word.

Do you remember that poem by Río that I read you a long time ago in your room in Granada?

It is going to be published very soon along with other poems, sonnets and romances, the last of which is the title of the book: *La fuente serena*.

I will certainly send it to you.

Here I am spending a few free days skating with the girls and my wife. We are at an altitude of 1,200 metres and it will snow without a break until March. At the end of the month I return to Geneva and will spend February between Brussels, London and Paris. When are we going to hear your latest piece in Geneva? And when is *Master Peter* going there?

My wife asks me to send you and your sister her tender regards which I second. Your ever dutiful friend,

SALVADOR DE MADARIAGA
Letter to Manuel de Falla
[Gstaad, 19 May 1927]

Manuel de Falla shakes hands with Don Quixote, Venice, 1932.

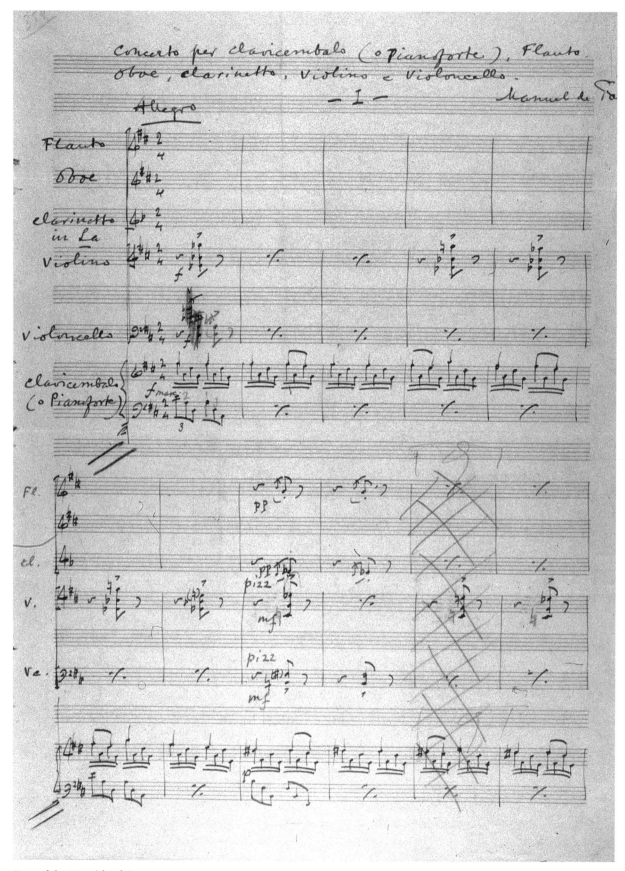

Score of the *Harpsichord Concerto*.

HARPSICHORD CONCERTO

MANUEL DE FALLA'S RELATIONSHIP WITH WANDA LANDOWSKA AND HIS PLEDGE TO REINSTATE THE HARP-SICHORD, AN INSTRUMENT WHICH HAD BEEN IGNORED AT THE BEGINNING OF THE 20TH CENTURY AND WAS RECUPERATED FOR MODERN MUSIC BY POULENC AND FALLA, AS WELL AS AN INTEREST IN COMPOSERS LIKE SCARLATTI, LED HIM TO WRITE ONE OF THIS CENTURY'S MOST IMPORTANT COMPOSI-TIONS.

FALLA WORKED ON THE *CONCERTO* BETWEEN 1923 AND 1926. IT WAS FIRST PLAYED IN BARCELONA, AT THE PALAU DE LA MÚSICA CATALANA, ON THE 5TH OF NOVEMBER 1926 BY WANDA LANDOWSKA, TO WHOM THE WORK IS DEDICATED AND WAS CONDUCTED BY FALLA.

An emblem showing Wanda Landowska at the harpsichord.

Wanda Landowska's emblem.

Wanda Landowska. ("To my dear, revered friend, to Manuel, Wanda. Evaux, 25 August 1924.")

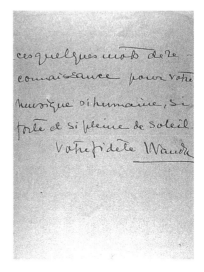

Recording of the *Harpsichord Concerto*.

MY GREAT and wonderful friend:

Your *Concerto* is a masterpiece. I am trembling with joy and happiness. I work day and night and the only thing I can think about is how to find the *authentic* and *perfect* stress to remain faithful to you.

I will write to you from here in a few days to request some explanations. Meanwhile I send you these words of thanks for your music which is so human, strong and full of sunlight.

Your faithful

WANDA LANDOWSKA
Letter to Manuel de Falla
[21 September 1926]

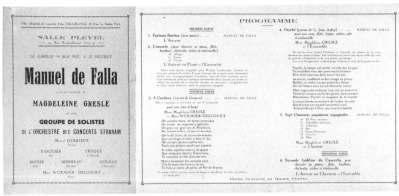

Programme of the première of the *Concerto*, played by Falla, part of the tribute which the Salle Pleyel in Paris paid to the composer to celebrate his fiftieth birthday.

Recording the *Concerto*, Paris, 1927.

WE WERE all anxious and worried. Wanda Landowska who had just arrived expressly from Paris was quite tired and had hardly touched her difficult solo part. The rest of the musicians, though excellent interpreters, could not work wonders. The composer controlled his nerves by smoking cigarettes and waited impatiently.

The rehearsal began. Everyone made a superhuman effort, but the disproportion between the difficulties of the work and the preliminary work necessary to overcome them became clear to the anguished composer on whose clean and shiny head droplets of sweat began to form.

Falla gave all that he could and more. His good nature kept his lips sealed and prevented him from uttering a word of complaint, but his eyes blazed with indignation, like Mose's saintly wrath.

Shortly afterwards the concert began. Casals conducted the "Last Dance" from *The Three-Cornered Hat* and *Nights in the Gardens of Spain* which Falla played with the combination of utmost precision and exquisite taste and elegance that characterised his own personal style. The second part was devoted to the *Concerto*, and

the third to *Master Peter's Puppet Show*. Both of them were conducted by the composer.

On the afternoon of the following day I had an appointment with the Maestro at Marshall's house. Falla was not at all satisfied with the interpretation of the work and wanted us to read it carefully in *petit comité* before I wrote my article. Accompanying him and Marshall were Maestro Llongueras and Minister Higini Anglés. We talked about the concert. The audience had applauded the composer but was far from having understood his music which could only be given substance with a perfect execution . "You have seen a simulacrum of my *Concerto*", Falla told me.

We began a slow, fruitful and delicious reading session. I felt as if I was in a hermitage because, in spite of the differences in character and environment, there was something that unified the two places: Falla's music heard in privacy, far from the mundane tumult of applause and the formal atmosphere of the concert hall, in other words, sheltered on his spiritual haven.

JUAN MARÍA THOMAS

THE MUSIC of *Master Peter* (with its distinct styles, depending on whether it is referring to "real" characters or to the ficticious characters of the romance of Don Gayferos and Melisenda or to the characters Don Quixote dreams about) makes quite clear reference, which could be specified by analysis, to Spanish primitive religious, romantic and popular music, and to old Spanish court music. However the elements from which the *Concerto* is built are more abstract, more difficult to pinpoint than the others because they are more personal and intense. In other words, they repeat Falla's evolving process which I pointed out earlier with reference to Spanish popular music. Compare, for example, the primitive religious atmosphere of the *Concerto* (the beginning of the "Lento") with the fifth scene of *Master Peter*, where Melisenda makes her appearance in the tower.

Schematism and brevity are two essential qualities of this work, in which the focus is on the intensity and speed of the impression. The trained musician will be able to see this more clearly by reading the score than by reading anything an article can tell him. Thematic schematism, treated with a minimal level of development, to the imperative extent to maintain melodic substance, leads to a schematism of form. There is never the slightest attempt to fill out or embellish the instrumental parts, and they seem extremely frugal. Even the softness of the "tessitura" of the instruments is avoided, resulting in a general timbre of old sounding music played on crude and harsh original instruments. The plentitude of polyphony is avoided and naturally it follows that the instruments, in this antiquated mixture, work in octaves, kept separate by this peculiar timbre; their fusion is avoided and they maintain the colour of their instrumental independence. In other words, the instruments begin a canon-like imitation in harsh harmonic intervals, which accentuates the similarity of this music to Berruguete's sculptures and, at times, to certain decorations found in gothic cathedrals in Spain, whose appeal rests notoriously on their attractive harshness and precise detail.

ADOLFO SALAZAR

COMPOSITIONS

Appendix IV

PSYCHÉ

SONNET TO CORDOVA

BALLAD OF MAJORCA

POUR LE TOMBEAU DE PAUL DUKAS

FANFARE

HOMENAJES

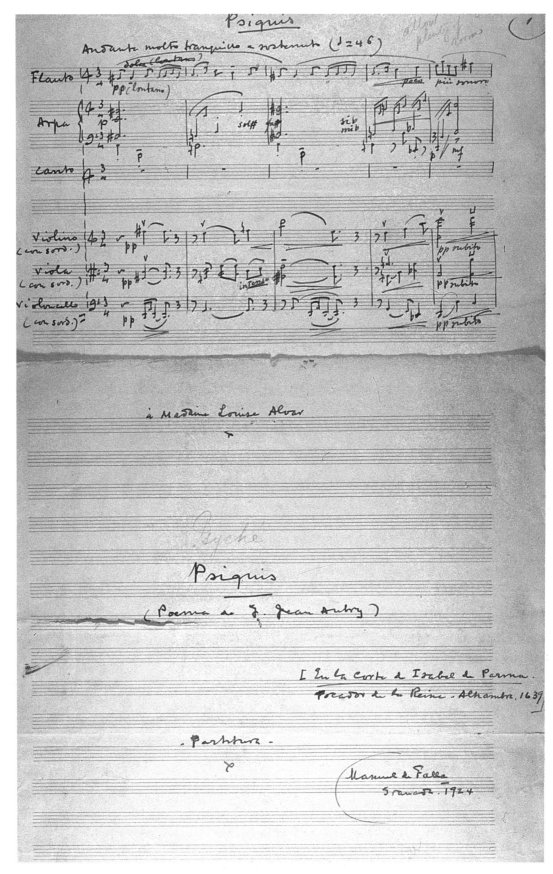

Score of Psyché.

PSYCHÉ

THIS COMPOSITION, PERFORMED ON THE 9TH OF FEBRUARY 1925 AT THE PALAU DE LA MÚSICA CATALANA IN BARCELONA, CAME ABOUT BECAUSE OF THE FRIENDSHIP BETWEEN THE COMPOSER AND CRITIC AND COMPOSER GEORGES JEAN-AUBRY. FALLA WAS VERY ENTHUSIASTIC ABOUT THE MUSICALITY OF SOME OF JEAN AUBRY'S POEMS, AND PLEDGED HIMSELF TO SET ONE OF THEM TO MUSIC. HOWEVER, SEVERAL YEARS WENT BY BEFORE HE REALLY BEGAN TO WORK FULLY ON THE COMPOSITION. BY OCTOBER 1923 THE WORK WAS ALMOST FINISHED AND IN SEPTEMBER 1924 HE COMPLETED THIS MUSICAL POEM COMPOSED FOR FLUTE, HARP, VIOLIN, CELLO AND MEZZO-SOPRANO.

Manuel de Falla with G. Jean-Aubry, *on Falla's left*; Salvador de Madariaga and other guests at Mme. Alvar's house in London, June 1921.

PSYCHÉ

Psyché! Ta lampe est morte; éveille-toi. Le jour
Te considère avec des yeux noyès d'amour,
Et le désir nouveau de te servir encore.

Le miroir, confident de ton visage en pleurs,
Reflète, ce matin, lac pur parmi des fleurs,
Un ciel laiteux ainsi qu'une éternelle aurore.

Midi s'approche et danse, ivre sur ses pieds d'or.
Tends lui les bras, sèche tes pleurs; dans un essor
Abandonne, Psyché, la langueur de ta couche.

L'oiseau chante au sommet de l'arbre; le soleil
Souris d'aise en voyant l'universel éveil,
Et le printemps s'étire, une rose à la bouche.

G. JEAN AUBRY

THESE ARE, my dear Jean, the few lines about our *Psyché* which you requested.

"In 1639, Philip V and his wife, Isabelle of Parma, lived in the Alhambra Palace. I composed *Psyché* imagining it as a small court concert held in the Queen's Boudoir, which is a tall tower (with a splendid view) decorated on the inside in the style of that period. The style of the music is also from that time (18th century Spanish court music), or, at least, how I imagine that music to be...

The ladies of the court play and sing for her about a mythological theme which we know was very fashionable at that time. You already know the instruments: flute, harp, violin (viola) and cello (muted).

The original score is thirteen pages long and that is everything for the moment.

I have just suffered that awful dizziness I felt at the Paris première. So, as you can see, it was not just me worrying.

Thank goodness that I feel better now. But my doctor has forbidden me any excessive effort because, in his opinion, over working is what causes these dizzy spells.

Now I am trying to find someone who can help with my business correspondence so that I can spend as much time as possible on composing which I feel more enthusiastic about than ever.

You will soon receive the translation of Lorca. Naturally your name should appear in any concert of *Psyché*.

I am impatient to read your article in *Musical Quarterly*. I need not remind you how much I am looking forward to your hispanic journey: *Lusitania, Baetica*. We will go on some beautiful walks around the Alhambra and we will talk about many things my dear Jean!

Your Manuel.

My sister sends you her regards. I was happy to hear that Mrs. Alvar has returned safely to London. Her letter was very moving and I will write to her soon. Meanwhile please give her my warmest regards.

MANUEL DE FALLA
Letter to G. Jean Aubry
[Granada, 29 September 1924]

Cover of the edition of *Psyché*, London, J. & W. Chester, 1927.

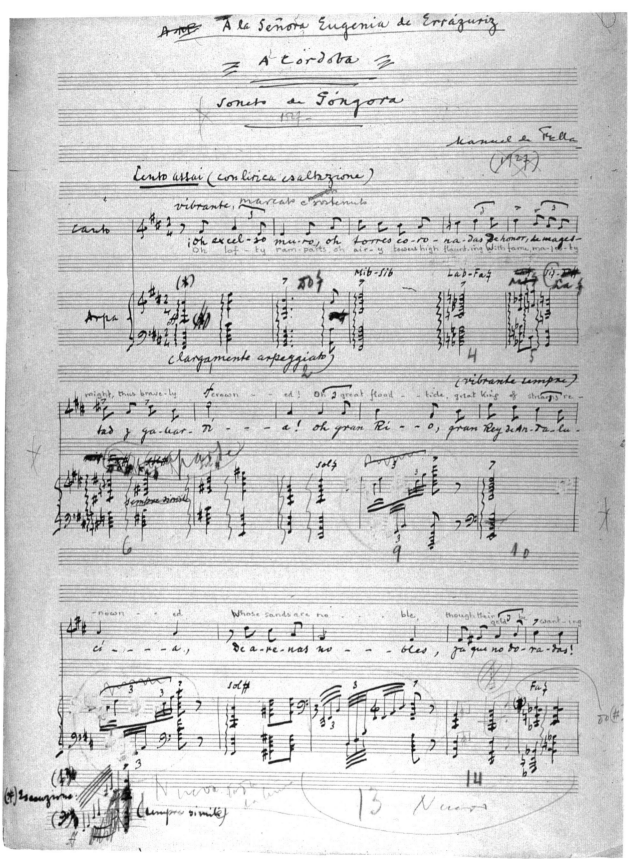

Score of *Sonnet to Cordova*.

SONNET TO CORDOVA

IN 1927 A GROUP OF YOUNG POETS DECIDED TO ORGANISE A NATIONAL HOMAGE TO DON LUIS DE GÓNGORA TO CELEBRATE THE THIRD CENTENARY OF HIS DEATH. FEDERICO GARCÍA LORCA AND GERARDO DIEGO REQUESTED FALLA'S COLLABORATION IN THE EVENTS ARRANGED FOR THE CELEBRATION AND FALLA COMPOSED A WORK BASED ON THE SONNET "A CÓRDOBA" AND SENT A FEW BARS OF IT TO BE PUBLISHED IN THE SPECIAL ISSUE OF THE MALAGA BASED MAGAZINE *LITORAL* DEDICATED TO GÓNGORA. THE *SONNET TO CORDOVA*, WRITTEN FOR SOPRANO AND HARP OR PIANO WAS FIRST PERFORMED AT THE SALLE PLEYEL IN PARIS ON THE 14TH OF MAY 1927. IT WAS LATER PUBLISHED BY THE OXFORD UNIVERSITY PRESS.

MY DEAR and respected friend: With some delay I answer your pleasant letter. I spent last month away from home too; I picked your letter up in Madrid on my way to Gijón, where I arrived a few days ago. I passed on your news and questions to the friends of Góngora. It seems that the Halffter brothers have almost finished, or perhaps by now they will have completed, their works for Góngora. We have spoken about holding a private party (by invitation) to air them before they are used for the Góngora homage on the 24th of May. That would be excellent.

As regards publication, the friends decided to negotiate with the *Revista de Occidente*. Of course, the copyright will have to be registered all the same. I propose a simpler idea —a limited programme— a musical album with original facsimile reproductions. The drawings we have received from Picasso, Gris and other young Spanish painters could be published in the same volume. It depends on the original received. It would be better to publish the music printed, but this might be difficult for the magazine to do unless it had more material. E. Halffter had the idea of making a large size foreign edi-

**"To Cordova. Sonnet by Góngora",
Manuel de Falla's contribution to the
tribute organised by the magazine
Litoral, October 1927.**

tion (Eschig) with the collaboration of Ravel, Prokofiev and Honneger. I think it is a wonderful idea and we will have to produce it if those composers are willing, and provided it does not interfere with the more modestly formatted (facsimile or print) Spanish homage.

The important thing is that the music gets done, because even if it is delayed the publication will appear sooner or later. All that we need to do now is give the concert this month. Accept my friends and my warmest thanks in advance for your collaboration which I am anxiously awaiting.

Now one more request: Could I be so bold as to ask you to send me a facsimile of the original copy of your *Sonnet* or, if that is impossible, a fragment (or a sketch)? If you can send it to me here then I can forward photographs of all the pages right away to Madrid and can keep the original safe with me. I still do not know who is going to be in charge of finalising the concert and publication details. I am writing to Madrid today to see if we can sort this out.

Many thanks as well for the coming arrangement about *Psyché* and the *Concerto*.

I am going to publish the *Via Crucis* soon, with a few minor corrections.

Say hello to your sister from me. Your humble servant and your ever faithful and grateful friend,

GERARDO DIEGO
Letter to Manuel de Falla
[Gijón, 3 May 1927]

MY DEAR friend: I was very pleased to receive your letter as I left for Paris, where on the 14th of May Góngora's *Sonnet* was played for the first time. Afterwards it was sung at another of my concerts in London, and after the Paris première the "Oxford University Press" asked me if they could publish it. During the negotiations I told them about the publishing possibility (in a manuscript copy) which you had mentioned to me, and they agreed to give permission as long as it appears after the Oxford version. I have not sent them the music yet, and that is why you have not received it either. But as some friends of *Litoral* asked me a few days ago for something for the Góngora issue they are preparing (in which I know you are collaborating) I have sent them the first two verses of the work, which is all the circumstances allow me to publish. So, I wanted to tell you not to be surprised if they publish it, which I suppose they will. I will send you the complete manuscript (or a photo of it) when Oxford have finished with it, and I take this opportunity to say what a pleasure it will be to send it to you.

Psyché and the *Concerto* are going to be released in autumn, and you will be among the first to receive it.

I was delighted to hear that you are going to publish *Via Crucis*. What have you published by Góngora?

Your friend, sincerely,

MANUEL DE FALLA
Letter to Gerardo Diego
[Granada, 15 August 1927]

**Cover of the magazine *Litoral*, issue
dedicated in honour of Don Luis de
Góngora, Málaga, October 1927.**

**Drawing by Juan Gris for the issue in
honour of Góngora, *Litoral*, Málaga,
October 1927.**

DEAR DON Manuel: I earnestly wish you a prosperous and fruitful 1928 and a happy Saint's day. Please pass on my best wishes to your sister María del Carmen.

You should have received *Carmen,* and I suppose —inmodestly— that you have liked it. I will gladly send you all the issues.

I look forward impatiently to seeing your new works printed. I saw the first verses of the *Sonnet* in *Litoral.*

I apologise for *Lola'*s indiscretion; it is her duty and cannot be avoided.

I repeat my heartfelt felicitations, your respectful friend

GERARDO DIEGO
Letter to Manuel de Falla
[Santander, 30 December 1927]

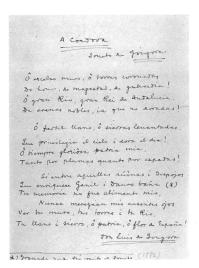

A page of "To Cordova" by Luis de Góngora, copied in Manuel de Falla's handwriting.

Cover of *Lola,* "*Carmen'*s friend and supplement", about the third centenary of Góngora, 1927.

MY DEAR friend:

Thanks for your letter and for *Carmen* and *Lola'*s visit (so "Spanish" and so... "witty"). Yes, I definitely did like them! And I am very thankful for your kindness in offering to send me the coming issues, but please do not deprive me of the pleasure of being included among your suscribers. I found what you called *Lola'*s indiscretion (my "conversion") very funny. Though my devotion to Don Luis is hardly new, it is true that until recently it was far from being unconditional...

Ever since your letter and the magazine arrived, I have wanted to reply; but... what a way to live. I have a horrible lack of time (what can we do about it?) and even more so now that I am making travel arrangements. I tell you all this to justify my silence and the brevity of this letter. I would be so happy to be able to have a long chat with you about *Orfeo, Carmen,* the anthology... and so much more. If I can I will write from Paris. Will we see each other in Madrid when I get back? I hope to be there by mid-April. Then you will receive the *Sonnet.* The "pocket" edition of *Psyché* is not ready yet, but I hope they decide to publish it. Up until now they have only published the complete "material".

Happy new year (a little late perhaps), and my thanks for everything.

Your true friend,

MANUEL DE FALLA
Letter to Gerardo Diego
[Granada, 8 February 1928]

FALLA'S CONVERSION

Federico García Lorca has informed us about Falla's conversion to Gongorism. Our pleas had been met with a painful silence. Falla was no friend of Góngora; influenced no doubt by the popular image —completely unfair— of Góngora, he probably thought him to be a bore, and too practical. Nevertheless, Lorca did not give up hope. One day he managed to get the Maestro to read some of Góngora's letters in the Foulché Delbosc edition. The following day he found Falla absorbed by Góngora. "Magnificent, magnificent. What a fellow! What a great mind! What an artist! And the same thing happens to him as to our artists. The same misunderstanding of the purity and strength of his art." Now all he had to do was choose a text. The "Cordova's Sonnet" written in Granada. Falla has also written his music in Granada. Now Góngora's verses will sing triumphantly the whole world over. "Because Cordova", explains Falla "is Roman, as Don Luis saw it, and not Arabian. All the allusions in his Sonnet are Roman and Christian."

A few days ago a group of Falla's and Góngora's friends had supper together. The Maestro warmly congratulated Dámaso Alonso on his prologue and version of *Soledades.* "Of course. *Soledades* is the landscape of Andalusia and Spain. If it wasn't for those seals..."

GERARDO DIEGO

BALLAD OF MAJORCA

FALLA COMPOSED THIS CHORAL PIECE DURING HIS FIRST VISIT TO PALMA DE MALLORCA IN 1933 THE *CAPELLA CLASSICA* WHICH WAS DIRECTED BY HIS FRIEND THE MINISTER JUAN MARÍA THOMAS. HE BASED HIS WORK ON A TEXT BY JACINTO VERDAGUER AND ON A THEME TAKEN FROM THE SECOND "BALLAD IN F MAJOR OP.38" BY F. CHOPIN. THE *BALLAD OF MAJORCA* WAS FIRST SUNG AT THE CARTHUSIAN MONASTERY OF VALLDEMOSA ON THE 21ST OF MAY 1933 AS PART OF THE FESTIVALS DEDICATED TO CHOPIN.

To come back to the 1933 Festival [dedicated to Chopin], I would say that, as Falla was unable to offer Chopin his great work complete, he decided to honour his memory with a small fragment of the same poem by Verdaguer to which he applied the best and most adequate music that he could wish for: Chopin's own music, masterfully adapted, with the tribute of a few minor personal touches, which in no way impaired the whole. Moreover, music that Chopin had composed there, within the walls of the monastery. Such is the choral version that it was simply called *Chopin Song* back then. The following year after Falla had finished the definitive version, he called it *Ballad of Majorca* adopting the title used by Verdaguer to describe that charming fragment of his vast poem.

JUAN MARÍA THOMAS

Manuel de Falla with the minister Juan María Thomas and the members of the *Capella Classica*, Majorca, 1933.

The première of the *Ballad of Majorca* was the greatest achievement of the 1933 festivals. The audience was full of foreign composers and critics. As well as the personal participation of Manuel de Falla, the *Capella Classica*, the pianist Copeland and the Madrid Symphony Orchestra, we heard a brilliant performance by the *Association des Jeunes Musiciens Polonais à Paris* founded by its president the composer Felix R. Labunski. They sang a choral fragment of an interesting *Polish Cantata* based on an old Polish text by Jan Kochanowsky. We also heard the pianist Jerzy Sulikowsky; the singer Jadwiga Hennert and the violonist Grazyna Bacewicz who only took part in the concerts in Palma. The *Capella*, as well as singing the *Ballad of Majorca* and Labunsky's *Cantata*, let us hear the splendid compositions of the Polish polyphonists Gomolka and Zielensky, bringing the programme to an end with Palestrina's Credo of the *Missa Papae Marcelli*.

The musicians and music lovers who filled the immense corridor of the monastery on that rainy May afternoon honoured Don Manuel with such an ovation that he was obliged to repeat the *Ballad*. There was nothing in the programme, but rumour had it that Don Manuel would conduct the première. However, as the draught in the corridor was as harmful to Don Manuel as the damp atmosphere of the cellar, he decided to stay in one of the cells during the concert, hoping to come out to conduct the chorus if the weather improved. It did not improve and, for this reason, he only came out at the end to thank the audience applause.

JUAN MARÍA THOMAS

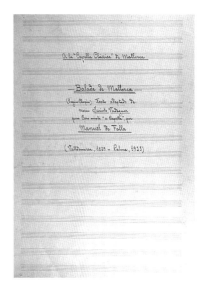

Score of *Ballad of Majorca*.

Pour le Tombeau
de Paul DUKAS

MANUEL de FALLA

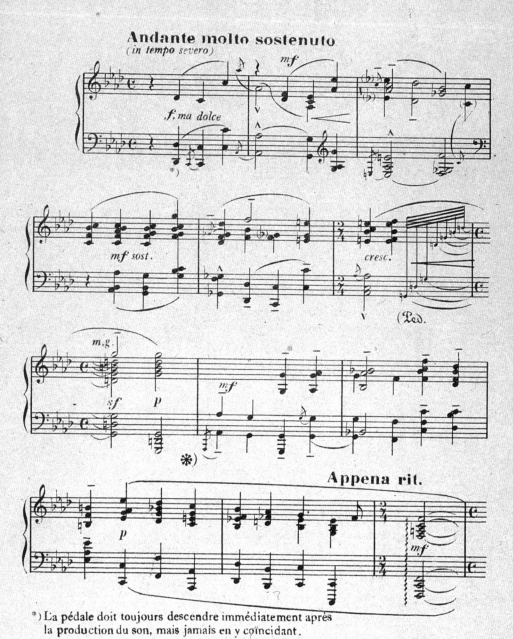

*) La pédale doit toujours descendre immédiatement après la production du son, mais jamais en y coïncidant.

Score of *Pour le tombeau de Paul Dukas.*

POUR LE TOMBEAU DE PAUL DUKAS

THIS PIANO COMPOSITION WAS WRITTEN IN GRANADA IN DECEMBER 1935, A FEW MONTHS AFTER THE DEATH OF HIS FRIEND AND MAESTRO PAUL DUKAS. THIS WORK, LIKE HIS HOMAGE TO CLAUDE DEBUSSY, WAS PUBLISHED BY *LA REVUE MUSICALE*, PARIS, 1936. IT WAS FIRST PLAYED BY THE YOUNG PIANIST JOAQUÍN NIN CULMELL.

DEAR Leopoldo:

I was pleased to receive your letter, as I had begun to worry about your not replying to the one I sent you in October. Did it reach you? If not I can send you the copy I kept. Since then I have hardly been able to do the work I told you about because another musical task that is thankfully finished now obliged me to make the sacrifice of abandoning it. I am referring to my contribution to the "*Tombeau de Dukas*" which *La Revue Musicale* is going to publish; an unavoidable collaboration because of the many and true tokens of kindness I owe Dukas, whom I shall never forget. It has been a great loss, both the man and the admirable artist.

When will I see you in this part of Antequeruela? We have so many things to speak about, those you mention in your letter, among others!

We send you all our warmest wishes for peace and health in the new year. With these wishes receive my affectionate regards,

MANUEL DE FALLA
Letter to Leopoldo Matos
[Granada, 10 January 1936]

THE HOMAGE to Dukas is an orchestration which appeared in the supplement of *La Revue Musicale* of Paris, May-June 1936 issue , with the title *Le tombeau de Dukas*. Falla's composition for piano appears alongside other compositions of lesser musical importance and emotional intensity. It is a full solemn piece as moving as a funeral service. The deep friendship which had brought them together had caused a theme from Dukas' *sonata* to pervade the notes of this work. The words "*Spes vitae*" appeared in Latin beside the title in the programme of the première.

JAIME PAHISSA

Paul Dukas.

Cover of the homage to Dukas, *La Revue Musicale*, Paris, May-June, 1936.

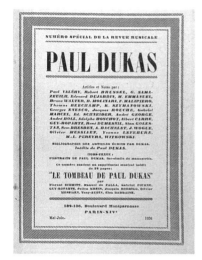

Cover of *La Revue Musicale* on Dukas' death.

FANFARE

THE *FANFARE*, DEDICATED TO ARBÓS, WAS COMPOSED DURING HIS STAY IN PALMA DE MALLORCA IN FEBRUARY 1934, IN ORDER TO BE PLAYED AT A CONCERT HELD TO CELEBRATE ARBÓS' SEVENTIETH BIRTHDAY. THE WORK IS BUILT AROUND THE MELODIC SEQUENCE MADE BY THE NOTES WHICH CORRESPOND TO THE INITIALS E. (ENRIQUE) F. (FERNÁNDEZ) AND THE SURNAME ARBÓS.

HOMENAJES

FALLA DECIDED TO COMPOSE A SUITE AFTER BEING INVITED BY THE COLÓN THEATRE TO CONDUCT A NUMBER OF CONCERTS IN 1939.
HE BEGAN WORK ON THE ORCHESTRATION OF HIS HOMAGES TO DEBUSSY AND DUKAS AND LATER ON FELIPE PEDRELL'S *LA CELESTINA*, WHICH HE TRANSFORMED INTO *PEDRELLIANA*. THE SUITE BEGINS WITH THE *FANFARE ON THE NAME OF ARBÓS*. THE PREMIÈRE WAS CONDUCTED BY FALLA AT THE COLÓN THEATRE IN BUENOS AIRES, IN NOVEMBER 1939.

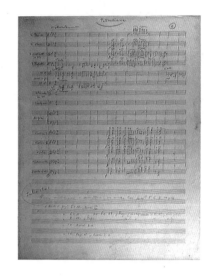

Score of *Pedrelliana* in homage to his Maestro Felipe Pedrell.

Enrique Fernández Arbós and his wife.

FALLA HAD always had the idea of paying tribute to Pedrell. When he imagined it in the form of a *"suite"* he had the idea of composing one for the composer who had been his Maestro. At the same time, with the aim of disseminating in some way the work of the almost forgotten Catalan composer, who had been the father of modern Spanish music, he decided to employ themes from *La Celestina*, the opera that Pedrell was composing when Falla had studied with him, and which had never been performed. To justify his use of various themes from *La Celestina*, and to avoid the piece being treated like an old-fashioned operatic folly, Falla used the beautiful part of the hunt at the beginning of Pedrell's opera as the backdrop to his poem *Pedrelliana*, like one of those scenes painted by Orcagna in the frescoes of the cemetery in Pisa: the presentation of "the joy of life and the sadness of death". It is the first part that Falla wants to evoke: a scene set in a pleasant and changing landscape where the men hunt while the women sing and play gracefully, seated on the grass among the flowers and shaded by tree leaves.

JAIME PAHISSA

Now let us come to *Homenajes*, or rather to those valuable lines you dedicated to them in your last card. You cannot imagine, dear Juan José, how much good they have brought me and how they have spurred me on in my work, this is one of the rewards: to see yourself judged so well by a friend —such a friend!— and to find that all one's efforts to express what the heart feels are not in vain. What you felt when you heard *Pedrelliana* (which agrees with what Enrique Bullrich told me in an earlier letter) is not just due to the love with which the piece has been composed, but mainly to the pure beauty of the music which is essentially, *entirely* Pedrell's music. What has brought me most satisfaction is to have been able to make people listen to an almost unknown and clumsily judged music so that they can begin to appreciate it, even if only in part.

MANUEL DE FALLA
Letter to Juan José Castro
[Alta Gracia, 8 February 1946]

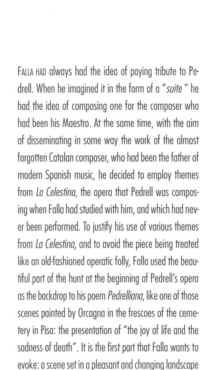

Score of *Fanfare* in honour of Enrique Fernández Arbós.

THE FALLA FAMILY'S happiest memories are linked to celebrations at home, like Christmas, for example. They always came to our house for dinner and sang christmas carols afterwards. Don Manuel and Federico, one of them at the piano and the other accompanying with a din of pot lids, drums, rattles, and clinkink forks against the bottle of "el Mono" anis. I think we sang quite well, that we were not bad at all...

After these funny songs we went to the Midnight Mass, at Las Tomasas Church in the Albaicín district. The Albaicín was whiter than ever and the nuns' chapel was pretty and charming. Falla's absorption in the mass was as thrilling and sincere as his happy and innocent youthful abandon had been moments earlier. He felt everything with the same intensity and there was a moment for everything. Falla never built himself an ivory tower. He was friends with everyone: one-eyed Paco, the wafer vendor, who was so refined and affected that he only sold wafers at the Alhambra and the university, was one of Don Manuel's friends whose visits were always entertaining...

MANUEL DE FALLA, HIS SISTER MARÍA DEL CARMEN, ANDRÉS SEGOVIA AND EMILIA LLANOS.

I also remember another great event during the Epiphany holiday, when Federico's puppet show *Los títeres de cachiporra* for two speakers was shown in my house. Falla loved conducting the small orchestra he had formed. After that Stravinsky's *A Soldier's Tale* was played in my house for the first time. Falla's understanding of Federico was very deep at such times. It was at this time that they went touring around villages –Federico more than Falla because, of course, he was younger– gathering popular songs. I do not like anecdotes, but I think that this one is worth telling: Falla would not be convinced that the song *Las tres hojas* that Federico had found and harmonized was an original popular song... I think that he considered it to be too much like one of his and thought that Federico had written it. "Don Federico" (they always referred to each other most respectfully) "this is your work" he insisted... In the end they had to go to Alfarque so that the old woman who had sung the song to Federico could do the same for Falla. We went on a lot of excursions because my father lent us his car whenever Don Manuel wanted...

ISABEL GARCÍA LORCA

Lola la comedianta

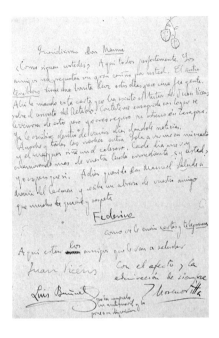

DEAREST DON *MANUÉ*:

How are you? We are all well here. My friends all ask after you. The *dark den* is beautifully lit these days, but full of ugly people. I am sending you the letter which Juan Vicens' tutor wrote about the *Master Peter* affair. Tell me as soon as possible what you think about the idea, but I think it will certainly be performed in Zaragoza. I will write to you in a few days time with more news.

Last night, like every night, *Lola* came to visit me in my bedroom and the marquis got into a fight with the coach driver. With each passing day my love for our pretty comedienne grows. Do you feel the same? I hope so. Goodbye dear Don Manuel. My regards to María del Carmen. All my love and respect, your affectionate friend.

FEDERICO.

As you can see I am sending you *letters* and *telegrams*.

Here are some friends who want to say hello.

JUAN VICENS.

With all my affection and admiration,

J. MORENO VILLA.

LUIS BUÑUEL,

Who has bought a car and puts it at your service.

FEDERICO GARCÍA LORCA
Letter to Manuel de Falla

FALLA PLANNED TO SET *LOLA LA COMEDIANTA*, BY FEDERICO GARCÍA LORCA, TO MUSIC. LORCA'S MANUSCRIPT WITH FALLA'S NOTES.

HE WENT to Granada in search of silence and time, and Granada afforded him sufficient harmony and eternity. A passerby on Antequeruela Alta peering through the lush vegetation of the upper garden might chance to see a clean small black figure with white edges like a black piano key standing on end, or a harsh, torn twilight the colour of brick dust, reddened by the sun, with airplanes circling above or a sunday group around a table (set with sherry and biscuits) in the lower garden: a romantic, slender Granada woman dressed in mourning lace, the old lady who always wears a pretty old-fashioned bonnet, a fake foreign dancer, the child Maceo with his coconut head, and some Spanish poet.

This great verve, which no one from here has been able to equal in music, was treasured by Falla, at his weekly harvest, and on his walks deep into the luxuriant waves of dense verdure on the pathways that climb the Alhambra hill, sensually embracing the harshly delicate colours, amethyst, opal and distant Sierra Nevada pink, Théophile Gautier's truth; or when he faced San Nicolás with the scarlet building blocks of the square and solid architecture of its towers, static and solitary beneath the unexpressive and successive branches of veined rich clouded evenings; or blending in front of the perennial of that unmournful cypress tree, like a cut-out against the merry new moon white of the harsh villa.

At night the echoes rise from Granada: Children's cries, bells, bleats which rise like shooting stars (we are with the great ones), a cornet, half-sung *coplas*, undulating laments; and the incessant lights of the Valley's comings and goings. There is an absolute solitude in Antequeruela, where that green balcony juts proudly out, with that green blind, with that green street lamp (in the street gutter a dead rat). And the secret corner of dramatic temptation starts to take its shape and moment where hiding in the moon's shadow roams the composer's dream the happy and satisfied after his rosary prayers are said, phantasmogorical rhythm with whispers of tempting occult, copper coloured, lost gypsy song.

JUAN RAMÓN JIMÉNEZ

Ernesto Halffter

ERNESTO HALFFTER WITH MANUEL DE FALLA IN GRANADA. HALFFTER WAS
FALLA'S DISCIPLE IN THE FIELD OF COMPOSITION. THEY WORKED CLOSELY
TOGETHER ON THE ANDALUSIAN CHAMBER ORCHESTRA PROJECT.

WORK with absolute faith and pursue without
hesitation of any kind your manner of feeling
music. This is the only way you will take full
advantage of the extraordinary gift you have been
blessed with. You also have the advantage of being
close to Adolfo [Salazar], whose advice has been
and will continue to be of great use. In my opinion,
I reiterate what I already told you and Adolfo: I am
at your disposal and will gladly look with critical
interest at any music that you compose and care to
send me.

MANUEL DE FALLA
Letter to Ernesto Halffter
[Granada, 6th of August 1923]

CARICATURE OF ERNESTO HALFFTER
BY FRESNO.

The composers of 1927

ALBÉNIZ had his imitators, but has left no disciples. That is natural. Disciples spring from inner principles. His imitators were dazzled by the splendor of the surface, which in Albéniz has wonderful reflections. But it is through Falla that the teaching, that vital factor which is gradually raising our "provincial" departure point to a universal level, must continue. The process has just begun, and even though we are quick to learn, it has not had time to reach everyone's ears yet. It still lacks the necessary explanations, the struggle and discussions which are its test; but for a hardened critic there is no need for more evidence.

Falla's supremacy in Spanish modern music is an accepted fact among young Spanish and foreign people. Even though all his work is prepared with a steadfastness and skill which bears the hallmarks of genius, it was with one of his recent creations, *Master Peter's Puppet Show*, that he chose to surround himself with inexperienced people whilst the rest of Spain's most notorious composers appeared consumed by the sterility of their own personali-

ADOLFO SALAZAR BY VÁZQUEZ DÍAZ

ties, which have some foliage, but lack fruit. What we could call the "Falla School" has started to emerge with an extraordinary vitality.

His strength of personality finds a staunch ally in Ernesto Halffter, his favourite student, who is exquisitely talented and has a technical perfection of the highest rank.

ADOLFO SALAZAR

JULIÁN BAUTISTA, RODOLFO HALFFTER, GUSTAVO PITTALUGA, FERNANDO REMACHA AND SALVADOR BACARISSE TOGETHER AT MADRID'S UNIÓN RADIO, IN THE 1930'S.

THE GREATEST PRAISE that anyone can give me for these songs, is to have found a certain connection between them and your work, which has been my guide and incentive at all times, as it is for all Spanish composers of my generation and the next. We all consider ourselves, to an degree, your spiritual disciples, even though we have not had the good fortune to receive your council which of course, would have been of immense use and incalculable value to us.

JULIÁN BAUTISTA
Letter to Manuel de Falla
[Buenos Aires, 13th of January 1943]

The Andalusian chamber Orchestra, 1923

1

2

3

4

THE ANDALUSIAN CHAMBER ORCHESTRA 1 EMERGED AFTER PLAYING THE FIRST CONCERT VERSION OF *MASTER PETER'S PUPPET SHOW* IN SEVILLE AND WAS THE PRODUCT OF THE EFFORT AND ENTHUSIASM OF THE CELLIST SEGISMUNDO ROMERO 2 , THE CHOIR MASTER EDUARDO TORRES AND MANUEL DE FALLA. ON FALLA'S REQUEST BOTH HE AND ERNESTO HALFFTER SHARED THE TASK OF CONDUCTING. THE OFFICIAL PREMIÈRE TOOK PLACE ON THE 11TH OF JUNE 1924 AT THE LLORÉNS THEATRE IN SEVILLE, AND MANUEL DE FALLA WROTE THE INTRODUCTORY LEAFLET 4 HE ALSO ARRANGED SOME CLASSICAL WORKS, AND MUSICIANS SUCH AS ROSA GARCÍA ASCOTT, ADOLFO SALAZAR AND ERNESTO HALFFTER COMPOSED PIECES FOR THIS ORCHESTRA. THE EMBLEM 3 WAS DESIGNED BY HERMENEGILDO LANZ

Master Peter's Puppet Show

[SEE *COMPOSITIONS*, APPENDIX III, PAGE 171]

PROGRAMME OF THE CONCERT PERFORMANCE OF
MASTER PETER'S PUPPET SHOW PLAYED BY THE
ANDALUSIAN CHAMBER ORCHESTRA, SEVILLE, 1923.

PROGRAMME OF THE PERFORMANCE GIVEN AT
PRINCESSE DE POLIGNAC'S HOUSE, PARIS, 1923.
PAINTING BY HERNANDO VIÑES.

MARIONETTES BY OTTO MORACH FOR THE 1926 ZURICH PRODUCTION OF *MASTER PETER'S PUPPET SHOW*.

I AM completely devoted to music. It
is something that one has to
experience and have inside oneself,
because the shaping of a musical
work is a bit like the creation of a
living creature. It needs time. One
watches it take shape in so natural a
manner... Music is so mysterious! I
think music is the youngest art and
in two or three centuries time it will
become clear that we are only just
beginning.

Social life becomes more
complicated day by day, which is why
the artist must isolate himself. Music,
unlike painting, has no primitive
artists: 18th century music is only
relatively primitive and its values
were forgotten or despised until the
end of the 19th century.

MANUEL DE FALLA

GRANADA is the place where I work, but unfortunately I travel too much, and one always wastes time travelling. To prepare myself to work, once a year I isolate myself in a small town in Andalusia and, for ten to twelve days, I do not utter a word to a soul.

•

The essential elements of music, its source of inspiration, are nations and people. I am against music which is based on authentic folklore documents; I believe, on the contrary, that one must be inspired by natural living sources and use the substance of sonority and rhythm, not their outward appearance. In Andalusian music, for instance, one must delve very deeply indeed to avoid caricaturing it.

•

I believe in the beautiful usefulness of music from a social point of view. One should not create it selfishly, for oneself, but for others... Yes, to work for the public without compromising, that is the question and my constant concern. One has to be worthy of one's innermost ideal and express it, prise it out. It is a substance which must be extracted, even if it is a difficult and painful task, and then the effort must be concealed, as though it were a very balanced musical improvisation, accomplished with the simplest and surest of means.

MANUEL DE FALLA

Homages on his fiftieth birthday

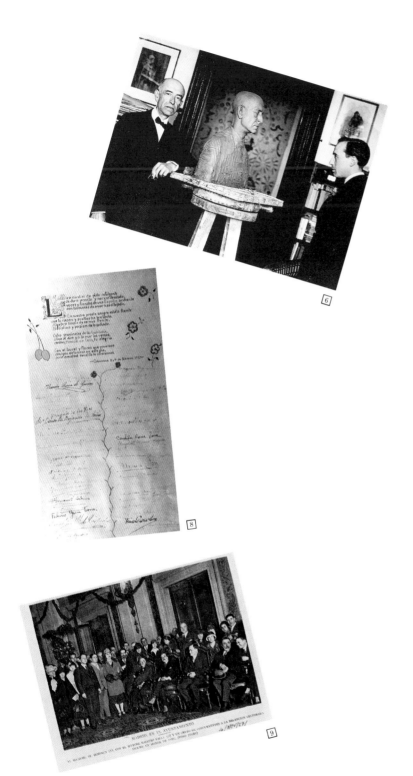

BETWEEN 1926-27 ON THE OCCASION OF HIS FIFTIETH BIRTHDAY HE BEGAN TO RECEIVE RECOGNITION FROM WHAT CITIES HE CONSIDERED "HIS CITIES".
IN DECEMBER 1926 THE UNVEILING OF A COMMEMORATIVE PLAQUE 1 IN CADIZ ON THE HOUSE WHERE HE WAS BORN; 2 ON THE 17TH OF THE SAME MONTH, A BANQUET HELD BY THE TOWN CORPORATION IN THE MEETING ROOM OF THE TOWN HALL, AFTER WHICH HE WAS GIVEN THE FREEDOM OF THE CITY 3 ; GRAND THEATRE FALLA 4 WHERE A FEW DAYS LATER A CONCERT WAS PLAYED BY THE ANDALUSIAN CHAMBER ORCHESTRA CONDUCTED BY FALLA, WHO INTERPRETED HIS OWN COMPOSITIONS; 5 THE MAYOR OF SEVILLE PRESENTED HIM WITH A SCROLL WHICH PROCLAIMED HIM HONOURARY CITIZEN OF THE CITY; 6 WITH THE SCULPTOR JUAN CRISTOBAL AND THE BUST OF FALLA COMMISSIONED BY THE GRANADA TOWN COUNCIL IN 1927; 7 THE SCROLL PAINTED BY HERMENEGILDO LANZ DECLARING HIM HONORARY CITIZEN OF GRANADA; 8 FIRST PAGE OF THE BOOK OF AUTOGRAPHS PUBLISHED SPECIALLY FOR THE OCCASION, WITH DRAWINGS BY FEDERICO GARCÍA LORCA; 9 ON THE 3RD OF NOVEMBER 1927, THE MADRID CITY COUNCIL HELD A RECEPTION IN HIS HONOUR, WHERE THIS PHOTOGRAPH, PUBLISHED IN *LA ESFERA* ON THE 12TH OF THE SAME MONTH, WAS TAKEN.

MONSERRAT, BARCELONA, MARCH 1927.

A CELEBRATION IN THE STUDIO OF THE PAINTER OLAGUER JUNYET.
BARCELONA, 10-XI-1926.
MANUEL DE FALLA BETWEEN THE SINGER CONCHITA BADÍA AND
THE PIANIST FRANK MARSHALL.

YEARS LATER, Catalonia was to show him early recognition and constant admiration. Barcelona paid tribute to him, dedicated festivals to his work, and he was at all times treated affectionately by its inhabitants. Everyone admired him and had the highest opinion of him, even the most uncompromising enemies of the image of the Castilian Spain dominated and absorbed the Catalan spirit. He was seen by all as a valuable composer: by the men of the left who ruled the government of Catalonia –the cultural attaché Ventura Gasol and president Francisco Maciá who gave him proof of their admiration– as well as by the right-wing Catalans, the powerful members of the "Lliga de Catalunya", and finally by the musicians and intellectuals of "Orfeó Catalá". As a small example of the general esteem in which the Catalan people held him, I will mention a short anecdote. One day he caught a taxi home with the pianist Frank Marshall, disciple and continuer of Granados' piano school. When they arrived and he was going to pay, the driver would not accept money, saying that the honour of driving Falla was sufficient payment. It turned out that it was the same driver who had taken Falla –along with others including Frank Marshall and the critic Rafael Moragas– to the end of Barcelona's harbour breakwater where they threw a crown into the sea to commemorate the anniversary of Granados' death in the waters of the Channel. The driver had recognised Falla.

JAIME PAHISSA

[1] AT THE END OF HIS STAY IN BARCELONA, FALLA EXPRESSED THE WISH TO
MEET APELES MESTRES WHOSE TALES HE HAD READ IN HIS CHILDHOOD. HE
WENT TO VISIT MESTRES AT HIS HOME. THE PHOTOGRAPH BEARING THE
FOLLOWING DEDICATION DATES FROM THIS VISIT: "DEAR FRIEND AND MAESTRO:
A THOUSAND THANKS FOR YOUR CONCERN, AND GLADLY ACCEDING TO YOUR
WISH –NOW THAT YOU ARE COMPLETELY RECOVERED– YOURS A HUMBLE
GARDENER WHO LOVES YOU AS MUCH AS HE ADMIRES YOU, APELES MESTRES.
BARCELONA, 31ST OF JANUARY 1928"; [2] COVER, INSIDE PAGE AND PROGRAMME
OF THE FALLA FESTIVAL DIRECTED BY PAU CASALS, AT THE BARCELONA LICEO
ON THE 5TH OF NOVEMBER 1926; [3] SURROUNDED BY THE ARTISTS WHO
PARTICIPATED IN A CONCERT HELD IN HIS HONOUR AT THE SALA PARÉS IN
BARCELONA ON THE 10TH OF NOVEMBER 1926.

Wanda Landowska in Granada

WANDA LANDOWSKA played two concerts in Granada during her visit. This praiseworthy artist knows exactly how to express the life of the music she likes and how to bring this music, so far-removed from us in time, close to us in ideas and emotions. At her concerts, instead of conveying a boring air of erudite purity, so difficult to avoid with ancient music, Wanda Landowska transforms them into events of purely artistic pleasure. The uncommon gifts she has been blessed with are notably emphasized in the richness of the harpsichord and the charm of her recordings. One cannot reach this level just by feeling and loving music: one must live it.

In another aspect too one can say that Wanda Landowska *orchestrates* the pieces she executes: she knows how to convert her harpsichord into something rather like a stringed organ. Her concert programme consisted of works by Bach, François Couperin (whose *Vielleur* seems to announce Mussorgsky), Daquin, Haendel, Pachelbel, Pasquini, Purcell, Rameau, Domenico Scarlatti (as well as a delectable *Bourrée d'Auvergne* composed by Wanda Landowska herself based on folk motifs), played gracefully by the eminent artist for the failing Philharmonic Society, with the charitable excuse of seeing it resusitated...

FROM LEFT TO RIGHT, FRANCISCO GARCÍA LORCA, ANTONIO LUNA, MARÍA DEL CARMEN DE FALLA, FEDERICO GARCÍA LORCA, WANDA LANDOWSKA, MANUEL DE FALLA AND JOSÉ SEGURA; *AND BELOW,* WITH WANDA LANDOWSKA IN ANTEQUERUELA.

While we were up at the Alhambra hill we asked Wanda to play the music of past centuries, and imagined the figure of Isabelle of Parma, in the *Queen's boudoir* of the Arabian palace, playing the *Variaciones sobre el canto del caballero* by Félix Antonio de Cabezón on her harpsichord.

MANUEL DE FALLA

Darius Mihaud

IT WAS freezing cold and pouring with rain when we arrived in Granada. Manuel de Falla was waiting for us at the station, wrapped in a thick overcoat and with a scarf covering his face. This moved me even more when I heard about the precarious state of his health. He drove us to our hotel. The balcony in our room looked out over the woods which covered the Alhambra hill. When it stopped raining the intoxicating fragrance of jasmine from that ocean of perfumed verdure invaded the room and hundreds of nightingales began to sing their lost song. The silhouette of Charles V's unfinished palace stood out against this backdrop of fragrances and bird song. On the following morning, Manuel de Falla called on us to take us to visit the Alhambra and the Generalife. These marvellous works of architecture are built in such an incredible setting that our enthusiasm was divided between the Arabian design which covered the walls and the breathtaking views that we saw from the windows. To accompany us to his house in Antequeruela Alta, where he had invited us for lunch, Falla led us past a hill inhabited by gypsies who lived in caves dug out in the rock. As we approached, children and old men gathered around us with their arms outstretched. Typical images were to be seen everywhere: full skirts, long shawls, carnations stuck on the top of large ornamental combs. A strumming of guitar chords could be heard mixed with the *Cante Jondo cantaores'* gruff and wonderful voices and the marvellous smell of safron, tomato and garlic wafted from every corner... The three of us walked on under a lead sun. Only a few roads crossed ours, raising clouds of dust which obliged Falla to cover his mouth with an enormous handkerchief and hide behind a thicket until the atmosphere had recovered its purity. Falla lived with his sister in a charming little white house. They served us a delicious lunch of cheese fritters, fish croquettes and jam pastries. We sat for a long time at the table chatting, a little weakened by the heat which came off the lit stove and warmed our calves in spite of the early spring. Afterwards Falla showed us the room where he worked, where he composed *Atlántida*. When I had begun to compose *Christopher Columbus*, he warned me that Christopher Columbus would be one of the supporting characters in his next work. I responded that I did not mind, because Christopher Columbus was the very basis of my opera. My admiration for Falla and this situation in particular spurred me to dedicate my work to him. After lunch we went for a long outing by landau: Then, we parted.

DARIUS MILHAUD

In Granada with Manuel de Falla

EVERY VISIT, not only to Granada, but to Spain, should finish on the slope of the hill that climbs to the Alhambra, where the route of the faltering tram that was such a source of mirth to Mr. Henry de

beautiful woven borders around these whitewashed rooms, or the exquisite finish of even the most insignificant nail, with an iron head, forged and fashioned, from which the things were hung.

Montherlant comes to an end. But, nowadays perhaps, seeing the exiled congeniality of the last refuges which that hill preserves in the world, he *would laugh* less at this vehicle in which a village woman who has just given her customers their washed clothes greets us further along with a "God keep you!" which we doubt that any washer woman from Angoulême –the region which Mr. Montherlant compares with Granada– has ever used to greet a foreigner.

But it is not for the pleasure of taking this tram that the traveller should go up the Alhambra hill in it: it is for the pleasure of taking it back down. The last stop is, to put it this way, Manuel de Falla's little house.

His house did not surprise me. I had already seen it. Yes, I must have seen it in some primitive artist's painting, an angelical garden, that view of white rooms with their well-arranged waxed furniture giving an appearance of wisdom and purity and an overall look of care and hope as if it belonged in the background of somebody's *Annunciation*.

When one of my friends visited the Maestro at his house he was amazed at such simplicity –he was heard to describe it with another word–. Luxury must indeed have perverted our taste! Everything in this great artist's house which has been chosen with the most exquisite discernment. It was just that my friend, used to the ostentatious glitter of rich luxury apartments, did not notice the

The only opulence to be found in this charming dwelling, apart from rare books and some old editions of music, is in its flowers. There are flowers everywhere, an assembly of colours with the unaffected arrangement of convent chapels.

The author of *Love the Magician* lives in this seraphic picture, which looks over the Sierra Nevada and Granada's paradisical flood plain. Those amiable snobs who consider him a master of eroticism (there are some people who think that the *Fire Dance* is a kind of lascivious ritual) would be very surprised.

However, Falla's fervour is to love what a flame to a bonfire: the bright but impalpable combustion of pure essences, the step from subtlety to absolute immateriality.

The reason that there are some people who cannot perceive this exciting *transitus* in the music of the composer from Granada –though he was born in Cadiz we attribute him the home town of his choice– and if some "singe their fingers" it is because they too are part of the dark and cumbersome material which feeds the fire.

As regards us, if they told us that Falla had been seen abducted from life in a chariot of fire to the heavens, like Elijah, we would not raise an eyebrow. In fact, I would say, that as the composer grows older, he is preparing for this miracle. His face, so thin now, is more and more consumed. One cannot live in this fervour with impunity.

Nothing could be further from the common possibilities of understanding. When Valéry, using all the devices of precise and lucid language, explains the state of intellection, we have to work hard to follow him. What would it be like to capture this latent and constant combustion in which a fervent person lives?

Imagine for a moment the extreme awareness that overcomes us, for example, when faced by danger, the consciousness which

lated recluse, sheltered from the world, they would be completely mistaken. Never has the expression "*sonorous echo*" applied to an artist been more apt or more *literally* correct. Oh, if only Manuel de Falla's communication with the outside world were solely aesthetical! If only he knew how to remain impassive! But he cannot. I have seen the great artist incapable of working because he had

suddenly awakes and is heightened throughout our entire being, this state *in which everything is important*; now try transposing this "trance" to a normal state, creating the normal fabric of time from it: we would more or less have the essence of an existence similar to that of the famous composer.

In an age in which, like it or not, the great majority of hours slip into the past without being remembered, ending up on the pile of ashes, Manuel de Falla has accomplished the feat of not doing anything automatically. Writing a letter, ordering a book, sending a bill, all of these are "consciously lived" moments for him or in a less pedantic layman's terms, moments which *serve God*. This is no other than that form of saintliness understood by the great Saint Teresa when she said to her flock: *the Lord moves among our daily bread.*

We could mention the many other ways that the illustrious composer serves God which, if not more noble, are at least closer to the word of the gospel. But his notable modesty would not forgive us. Suffice it to say that in the poor areas of the Albaicín, in olden times the district of the Moorish nobility which like fallen queens has retained something sovereign in its sad state, if you simply mention that you are *Manuel de Falla's friend* you cannot pass by the poor and sick wretches because of the reflection of veneration and universal gratitude that they attach to your undeserving person.

If, after this, anyone imagines him withdrawn, living in his iso-

heard about some misfortune which did not concern him in the least. His friends have seen him double up in pain and fall ill because of the atrocious picture the newspapers drew of starvation in China. These distant suffering and miseries, all the world's grief, crucify him. Falla's art immolates this gospel love of all creatures; he consumes his strength on this burning and tremendous fraternity. He finds this completely natural and he would reproach comfortable or simply salutary reclusion as abominable selfishness.

Faced with a soul of such high ideals and with a conscience which gives priority to the human before any other interest, even artistic, one feels a mixture of veneration and pity. In one's thoughts one starts to protect the fragile creature who is torn by such noble torments; one starts to yearn for the advent of justice and happiness which will enable him to do his work.

What does it matter if a few confused people only hear the call of earthly love in his music! Perhaps, through this, some day a spark of the other love will appear in their hearts. But on this day, however, the call of God reaches them; on this day, they will at last have understood Falla's music.

MATHILDE POMÈS

I DO not need to tell you, who knows me so well, the differences that
separate us as regards the theme of your *Oda.* If I were to work on it I would
go about the task in a humble attitude, hoping that all humanity could be
deified by virtue of the Sacrament.

   Along with this, the gifts: gold, frankincense and myrrh. *Pure;
unadulterated...*

   You understand me, Federico, forgive me if I displease you in any way. I
would be very sorry!...

   Of course, like all your work, it has a beauty and an unarguably apt use of
expression; but I cannot hide from you –as I might do from someone else–
my precise impression. That would go against the friendship and loyalty I
owe you. Moreover, I put my faith in the definitive version and in the rest of
the poem.

MANUEL DE FALLA
Letter to Federico García Lorca
[Granada, 9 February 1929]

EDITION OF THE "ODE TO THE BLESSED SACRAMENT OF THE ALTAR" IN THE MAGAZINE *REVISTA DE OCCIDENTE.*

6
GRANADA
1930-1939

Antonia mercé, "*La Argentina*". Fernando
de los Ríos. On the island of Majorca. Rosa
García Ascott. José Bergamín. Jacques Maritain. Roland Manuel. Ramiro de Maeztu.
Manuel Azaña. José María Pemán. Spanish
civil war. Farewell. Departure for Buenos
Aires.

GRANADA — La Alhambra desde el Paseo de los Tristes

C H R O N O L O G Y

1930. ■ THE ITALIAN COMPOSER H. CASELLA VISITED FALLA IN GRANADA. ■ IN DECEMBER FALLA TRAVELLED TO CADIZ TO CONDUCT A CONCERT AT THE THEATRE WHICH BEARS HIS NAME. HE WENT ON AN EXCURSION TO SANCTI PETRI, INSPIRED BY *ATLÁNTIDA*, WHERE THE RUINS OF THE TEMPLE OF HERCULES ARE THOUGHT TO BE FOUND.

1931. ■ HE TRAVELLED TO LONDON TO CONDUCT *MASTER PETER'S PUPPPET SHOW* FOR BBC RADIO. ■ 14TH OF APRIL, PROCLAMATION OF THE SPANISH 2ND REPUBLIC. ■ ON THE 14TH OF MAY, AFTER THE DESTRUCTION OF CHURCHES AND CONVENTS IN GRANADA, HE SENT A TELEGRAM OF PROTEST TO THE PRESIDENT OF THE REPUBLIC, NICETO ALCALÁ ZAMORA, AND WROTE TO HIS FRIEND FERNANDO DE LOS RÍOS, A GOVERNMENT MINISTER, DEMANDING URGENT ACTION. ■ HE WAS NAMED DIRECTOR OF THE NATIONAL COMMITTEE OF MUSIC.

1932. ■ THE CONFRONTATION BETWEEN STATE AND CHURCH INTENSIFIED. MANUEL DE FALLA IN A STATE OF DESPERATION WROTE HIS WILL IN FEBRUARY. ■ ON THE 3RD OF SEPTEMBER HE PARTICIPATED IN THE OPENING CONCERT OF THE SAN TELMO MUSEUM IN SAN SEBASTIAN. HE CONDUCTED *MASTER PETER'S PUPPPET SHOW* AND SPENT A LOT OF TIME WITH HIS FRIENDS IGNACIO ZULOAGA AND JOSÉ MARÍA SERT. HIS FIRST EXPRESSIVE VERSIONS OF CHORAL WORKS BY CLASSICAL SPANISH COMPOSERS DATE FROM THIS PERIOD. ■ HE TRAVELLED TO VENICE WITH PEDRO SEGURA AND ANDRÉS SEGOVIA, TO ATTEND A FESTIVAL OF THE ISCM AT WHICH *MASTER PETER'S PUPPPET SHOW* WAS PERFORMED. ■ ON HIS WAY BACK HE SPENT A FEW DAYS IN BARCELONA, WHERE A FALLA FESTIVAL WAS HELD BY THE ASSOCIATION OF MUSIC "DA CAMERA" ON THE 13TH OF DECEMBER IN THE PALAU DE LA MÚSICA. ■ HE CORRESPONDED WITH JACQUES MARITAIN ABOUT THE SITUATION AND THE RESPONSIBILITY OF CHRISTIANS AT THAT MOMENT OF CRISIS. ■ THE OXFORD UNIVERSITY PRESS PUBLISHED *SONNET TO CORDOVA.*

1933. ■ HE SPENT SOME TIME WITH HIS SISTER IN MAJORCA ESCAPING THE NOISE IN GRANADA. MINISTER THOMAS, CHOIR MASTER OF THE CAPELLA CLASSICA FOUND FALLA A SUITABLY QUIET PLACE TO WORK. HE COMPOSED THE *BALLAD OF MAJORCA* WHICH WAS FIRST PERFORMED ON THE 21ST OF MAY IN VALLDEMOSA BY THE CAPELLA CLASSICA. ■ PROBLEMS AROSE WITH HIS PUBLISHERS CHESTER OVER AUTHORS' RIGHTS, WHICH WORSENED A FEW YEARS LATER. ■ ON THE 19TH OF NOVEMBER, FALLA EXERCISED HIS RIGHT TO VOTE FOR THE FIRST TIME IN HIS LIFE IN THE ELECTIONS IN GRANADA. ■ HE TRAVELLED TO BARCELONA WHERE HE GAVE A CONCERT OF HIS COMPOSITIONS AT THE LICEO. ■ HE RETURNED TO PALMA DE MALLORCA. ■ *CRUZ Y RAYA*, OF WHICH FALLA WAS A FOUNDING MEMBER, WAS PUBLISHED.

1934. ■ IN FEBRUARY HE COMPOSED *FANFARE ON THE NAME OF ARBÓS*, TO COMMEMORATE THE SEVENTIETH BIRTHDAY OF HIS FRIEND, WHICH WAS PLAYED ON THE 28TH OF MARCH AT THE CALDERÓN THEATRE IN MADRID, CONDUCTED BY ARBÓS HIMSELF. ■ HE RECEIVED NEWS OF THE GREAT PUBLIC ACCLAIM RECEIVED BY ANTONIA MERCÉ'S PRODUCTION OF *LOVE THE MAGICIAN* IN MADRID WITH THE PARTICIPATION OF VICENTE ESCUDERO, PASTORA IMPERIO AND MIGUEL DE MOLINA. ■ IN JUNE HE ABANDONED MAJORCA AND RETURNED TO GRANADA. ■ IN NOVEMBER HE EXPRESSED HIS ANXIETY ONCE AGAIN ABOUT THE SOCIO-POLITICAL SITUATION OF SPAIN. ■ HE WAS NAMED A MEMBER OF THE FRENCH INSTITUTE.

1935. ■ FALLA'S DIFFERENCES WITH JOSÉ BERGAMÍN ON THE DIRECTION THAT THE MAGAZINE *CRUZ Y RAYA* (OF WHICH HE HAD BEEN FOUNDER AND COLLABORATOR) WAS TAKING, RESULTED IN THE BREAKING-OFF IN THEIR RELATIONS. ■ HIS FRIEND PAUL DUKAS DIED IN PARIS. ■ IN JULY, FALLA EXPRESSED HIS FEARS ABOUT THE POSSIBILITY OF A WAR WHICH HE FELT IN THE AIR. ■ ON THE 9TH OF AUGUST HE MADE AN ADDITION TO HIS WILL. ■ INCIDENTAL MUSIC FOR THE *AUTO SACRAMENTAL* BY LOPE DE VEGA, *LA VUELTA A EGIPTO.* ■ HE COMPOSED THE PIANO PIECE *POUR LE TOMBEAU DE PAUL DUKAS* WHICH WAS FINISHED IN DECEMBER.

1936. ■ *POUR LE TOMBEAU DE PAUL DUKAS* WAS PUBLISHED IN THE MAY-JUNE ISSUE OF *LA REVUE MUSICALE*, OF PARIS. ■ THE SPANISH CIVIL WAR BROKE OUT. AFTER THE MILITARY UPRISING A PROCESS OF CRUEL REPRESSION BEGAN IN GRANADA. ON HEARING THAT HIS FRIEND FEDERICO GARCÍA LORCA HAD BEEN ARRESTED FALLA PRESENTED HIMSELF AT THE CIVIL GOVERNMENT, RISKING HIS OWN SAFETY, IN ORDER TO ATTEMPT TO SAVE HIM. FALLA SUFFERED A FINAL BLOW WHEN HE HEARD THAT LORCA HAD BEEN PUT TO DEATH. HE ISOLATED HIMSELF IN HIS HOUSE IN ANTEQUERUELA ENGAGED IN WORK AND PRAYER. ■ IN NOVEMBER HE MADE A DÉMARCHE TO HELP HIS FRIEND HERMENEGILDO LANZ, WHO WAS HELD UNDER SUSPICION BY THE NEW REGIME.

1937. ■ HIS STATE OF HEALTH WAS DELICATE, HE COULD HARDLY WALK. ■ HE RECEIVED A VISIT FROM JOSÉ MARÍA PEMÁN WHO HAD AN IDEA FOR A JOINT PIECE WHICH FALLA TURNED DOWN. ■ THE NATIONALISTS CONTINUED TO PRESSURE HIM AND FALLA COMPOSED A *WAR ANTHEM* BASED ON A PIECE BY FELIPE PEDRELL. ■ HE ONLY RECEIVED VISITS FROM NEIGHBOURS AND FRIENDS WHO BECAME HIS NEW CIRCLE: LANZ, BORRAJO, GHYS, PÉREZ RODA, RUIZ AZNAR, LUIS JIMÉNEZ AND MIGUEL CERÓN. ■ AT THE END OF THE YEAR HIS FRIEND MAURICE RAVEL DIED IN PARIS.

1938. ■ ON THE 1ST OF JANUARY THE GOVERNMENT OF THE NATIONALIST ZONE SET UP THE SPANISH INSTITUTE IN SALAMANCA NAMING FALLA ITS PRESIDENT WITHOUT HAVING FORMERLY CONSULTED HIM. WITH JOSÉ MARÍA PEMÁN'S HELP FALLA DID NOT GIVE UP UNTIL HE MANAGED TO GET HIS RESIGNATION ACCEPTED. ■ ON THE 25TH OF MAY HE WROTE TO A FRIEND IN ARGENTINA WITH THE IDEA OF SPENDING SOME TIME IN THAT COUNTRY.

1939. ■ IN MARCH HIS "NOTES ABOUT RAVEL" DEDICATED TO ROLAND MANUEL AND MAURICE DELAGE, WERE PUBLISHED IN *LA REVUE MUSICALE* OF PARIS. ■ HE SPENT SUMMER IN ZUBIA, A VILLAGE NEAR GRANADA, WORKING ON HIS *HOMENAJES* FOR THEIR COMING PREMIÈRE IN ARGENTINA, WHERE HE HAD BEEN INVITED TO CONDUCT A NUMBER OF CONCERTS. ■ ON THE 28TH OF SEPTEMBER HE LEFT GRANADA WITH HIS SISTER MARÍA DEL CARMEN, HEADING FOR BARCELONA WHERE, ON THE 2ND OF OCTOBER, THEY BOARDED A SHIP BOUND FOR BUENOS AIRES.

Falla's imaginary life

FALLA DOES NOT live in a city, but on its outskirts. His little house is clean and clear. It is surrounded by laurel trees, cypresses, jasmine. The cypress trees raise their sharp peaks above the undergrowth of the rest of the trees. The sand in the garden hardly ever crunches, inopportune visitors rarely crunch the yellow sand of the central avenue underfoot. Hardly anyone knows that in this bright walled, white-washed house lives a great composer. This is because the composer does not live in the present, an age of journalists and curious fans, but in the 16th century or, even earlier, in the 12th century. The laurels, the cypresses, the roses are the same that were here in the 12th century. The whitened walls were exactly the same in that century as they are now. Only an artist in this house, alone in the peace and quiet, can cre-

ate the illusion that the same thing still lives inside him, in both periods, the same today, in the 20th century, as in the 12th century. The only things change are the world's vain worries and as Falla is not subject to these worries, his life is "unpresent". As "unpresent" as the fine, subtle, fluttering music so full of spirituality that Falla writes on the staved lines.

There have been a number of major events in Falla's life: once the composer was sitting on the shore of a wide and gently flowing river, watching the water run by. The river was the one that the noble Spanish poet, Garcilaso, called the "divine river", in other words, the Danube. Falla cannot remember exactly how long he was there on the banks of the Danube; he remembers that he has been on the shores of many rivers, but that never before had he experienced, like

this time, the sensation of the current of time which carries things away. Another major event in the composer's life occurred one day when he reached the peak of a mountain one day to see the sun rise. At that moment he lost his sense of time as well. Watching the dawn light break over the mountain penetrated deep into the composer's sensitivity. The third noteworthy moment in Falla's life happened one night when, being unable to sleep, he got out of bed and gazed at a star from the garden. The composer was not familiar with the star which was glowing very brightly. Everything was silent, when suddenly in the distance, a dog began to bark. It sounded as if this distant echo, wept for some reason; the bark was sad and plaintive. While everything slept and the dog barked, the far off star shone with mysterious brightness in the infinite firmament. Per-

haps the star no longer existed: Its heavenly light, extinguished, had ceased to shine centuries ago, and it was now that it reached us. The composer observed the splendour, which came from a star that no longer lit up the immense universe, with yearning. On returning to his room Falla began to compose. He wrote the beginning of one of his most beautiful pieces: His hand ran quickly and feverishly over the lined paper. The lives of conquerors, financiers, apostles of this or that belief, are full of such resounding events: A composer who lives among the laurels and the cypresses has had no more than these. With just these alone his life is brimming over with spirituality.

AZORÍN

Antonia Mercé, *"La Argentina"*

POSTCARD FROM *"LA ARGENTINA"* TO
MANUEL DE FALLA: "DEAR FRIEND: A
THOUSAND GREETINGS FROM HERE. I
THINK I AM GOING TO WORK VERY WELL
HERE. I KNOW THAT YOU HAVE MANY
VERY GOOD FRIENDS HERE AND YOU ARE
ONE OF MINE. WOULD YOU BE KIND
ENOUGH TO SEND ME SOME LETTERS OF
RECOMMENDATION? I WOULD BE VERY
GRATEFUL. TO BE OF SERVICE TO YOU IN
ANY WAY, JUST ASK. MY ADDRESS IS
CRÉDIT LYONNAIS. SERVICE DES
ACCRÉDITÉS. BOULEVARD DES ITALIENS. I
LOOK FORWARD TO HEARING FROM YOU.
YOUR GOOD FRIEND, ARGENTINA";
COSTUME DESIGNS FOR THE CHARACTER
"SALUD" IN *LA VIDA BREVE*, AND *ON THE
PREVIOUS PAGE*, ANTONIA MERCÉ, *"LA
ARGENTINA"* PHOTOGRAPHED WEARING
THE SAME COSTUME, PARIS, 1930.

Falla writes to Fernando de los Ríos

My VERY dear friend:

Doubtlessly I have not explained myself very well in my letter. If you still have it, you will be able to see my position very clearly; but personal, dramatic conflict, prevents me from revealing everything I hinted at.

What horrible things have happened since then! Your valuable letter arrived while I was experiencing one of the most horrible moments of despair and desperation in my life. You will have an idea of what happened from our telegram, which moreover reflected an absolute and spontaneous concurrence of viewpoints. The horrible blasphemies freely uttered in the street over the last couple of days, gave a most clear indication of what was to follow. The events here are conducted coldly, without masses, or outward passion. I am absolutely convinced that if you had been in Granada, your great moral authority would have been enough to prevent them.

Of course, I have seen the shady element which is always involved in these movements and those *who take advantage* and attempt to divert worthy currents of indignation to completely different ends.

Among other residues, the events have left an impression of helplessness which, added to the attitude of a certain, infamous section of the population, makes some religious people fear for their personal safety. They have told me their fears, knowing the friendship which happily unites us, so that I might draw your attention to them.

I still remember that in our last conversation last Autumn, your exact words to me were: *"we must bring the gospel to Spain"*, and your wish, which gave me so much hope for the present future, comes to mind every time that the Spanish state officially confirm their rationalism or their anti-religious concept. I speak to you, Fernando, as I would do to a beloved brother. I want to open my heart, which is bursting with bitterness, to you.

With all my fond affection,

MANUEL DE FALLA
Letter to Fernando de los Ríos
[Granada, 19 June 1931]

My DEAR FRIEND:

I have always taken the utmost care not to do or say anything that could belittle in the slightest detail Spain's prestige to the eyes of a foreigner. But I am amazed to see that in a touristic city, such as Granada, foreigners have witnessed and comment on, with evident damage to the national prestige which many of us had tried so conscientiously to maintain intact, the unpunished violence which has been comitted there without any military or political reason to justify it. Last night, in spite of the measure taken at last, the San Nicolás church was still burning to the ground, while someone rang the bells unashamedly...Spain is pitiful, and between one and another they are going to keep on destroying it!

I am not judging, nor am I the right person to do so, where the blame of what has happened should lie, I only wish to refer to them and the grevious impression they have had on thousands of people with clear consciences, and I am sure that yours too is deeply shaken by such abominable crimes.

You know perfectly well what my ideals are, that they go beyond political limits, and it is my heart's desire that the injustice suffered by the population and their needs be alleviated and put to right. I am one of the first to condemn the senseless political-military movement which has given rise to the events in question; as well as the senselessness of what has happened in Granada, where that movement has not the least support. It is tragic that, to all appearances, those who should upkeep law and order have sat back, and only at the very end have they attempted to give the impression that they exist. I tell you all this, not only to give a dear friend trustworthy information, but also to a man responsible to the government of Spain, and as a protest (respectfully, but with the noble indignation of a Christian, a Spaniard and as an artist) to all of those who like you share this tremendous responsibility. My conscience and my honour oblige me to do so. On the contrary I would hold myself, to a certain degree, responsible too for the "acquiescence" which has facilitated countless irreparable and punishable deeds. I am so sincere in what I say that, as I write to you, I feel my conscience free itself from the weight which oppresses it, because it is my firm belief that in the present chaotic situation, silence means complicity with evil. I wish to do everything in my power to prevent the repetition of such evil. Can you believe that yesterday some people tried to incite the destruction of the Alhambra Palace?...

I want to finish by assuring you that, as always, I have spoken to you with "my heart on my sleeve" following your insistent requests that I should do so. Likewise –from the bottom of our hearts– we have thought about you and your family and the dreadful misfortune you have suffered with the loss of your sister (who is in God's grace), endorsing once again the deep feelings we expressed in our telegram.

Your sincere and faithful friend,

MANUEL DE FALLA
Letter to Fernando de los Ríos
[Granada, 13 August 1932]

On the island of Majorca, 1933-1934

I SPENT THREE afternoons a week helping him with his correspondence. It was not easy or quick to perform this task to the entire satifaction of a man who weighed words like a severe and meticulous administrator of ideas. Sometimes we spent ages to write a simple telegram to a friend. How should it end? "The word regards is not very expressive", said Don Manuel. "Let us put *affectionate regards*" I suggested. "I don't like the *affectionate*". "*Fond*? Would be too much". That day the telegram was settled with a "sincere regards" or something similar. Even more complicated were letters which might be misinterpreted or distort his opinion, especially when answering publishers or concert organisers to whom, he said, one must put everything very clearly and that even then they often understood things which had nothing to do with what you wanted to tell them.

On such occasions our descent down the small stairways was done in a most original manner. Chatting calmly, Don Manuel scanned the steps with a look. When he had located one of the many banana or orange peels which the children and soldiers often left in the middle of the path, he charged it, using his walking stick like a lance, without mercy until he had managed to clear it off the path and prevent any fractured legs or arms. Having put the town to rights (which the town council usually left as it was) he said to me smiling: "Who knows how many falls we are avoiding!... The prevention of big accidents can be achieved through small measures... as long as they are applied in time."

JUAN MARÍA THOMAS

WITH THE MINISTER JUAN MARÍA THOMAS AND ALFRED CORTOT AMONG OTHERS.

HOUSE IN THE GÉNOVA DISTRICT WHERE HE LIVED DURING HIS STAY IN PALMA DE MALLORCA.

CONCERT WITH THE MADRID SYMPHONIC
ORCHESTRA IN PALMA DE MALLORCA, 1933.

MANUEL DE FALLA WITH THE MINISTER THOMAS
AND THE CAPELLA CLASSICA OF MAJORCA.

EVERY MORNING, at the same time, a black car drove past. It was driven by a chauffeur who wore a black uniform and whose face was red rather than white. In spite of this, his features bore a slightly characteristic similarity to those of a corpse. Another man, also dressed in black, always sat beside him. And though the other man's physiognomy was frank, generous and gentlemanly, there was still something about him that reminded one of the chauffeur. The first meeting between this vehicle and Don Manuel proved an unpleasant surprise for the composer. Just before midday, he was on his way home, walking quickly, as he was in the habit of doing, rapt and absorbed in a composition. On one of the bends in the road he suddenly found himself face to face with the car which braked swiftly and in almost the same instant let sound the notes of its "polyphonic" horn. They were the notes of the theme of the *Fifth Symphony*, the tragic Beethovian call of fate!

Don Manuel, who saw the car's two occupants for the first time, was completely overwhelmed. From that moment on when, every day at the same time, he heard the "horn of death", his nerves were set on edge and he was unavoidably overcome by the most disagreeable sensation. But, a week after he had told me about what had happened, with all the details, I met him, in the afternoon, glowing with joy. "Did you know", he said to me "the horn no longer plays the fateful theme? They have banished a note. What's more they don't play it when they go past the house any longer. You hear it in the distance, like an echo..." So then I explained what had happened. It turned out that the car belonged to my friend Don José, director of the Provincial Hospital and a music lover, which meant that as soon as I had stated our case, he took action to remedy the situation.

JUAN MARÍA THOMAS

THE DOCTORS Don Virgilio and Don Vicente introduced him to the outstanding painter
Maroussia Valero. She was preparing an exhibition of her work at the Costa Gallery and
wanted to celebrate the occasion by painting
a portrait of Don Manuel who, day by day, became more stubbornly confined to his inner
asylum and showed increasing aversion to
any kind of exhibition. It took a colossal effort to win his consent to pose merely for one session.

He did so simply to humour his friends. The portrait proved to be, in some
respects, a masterpiece. Some people found his expression hard and lacking that Franciscan
goodness which marked the composer's features. But in my opinion, that is precisely its best
quality. It reflected explicitly Don Manuel's state of mind during those days and on that occasion. It was a faithful portrait of a man who was so in love with truth that, without afore-
thought, he could never hide his feelings and they were clearly reflected in his face whether
he was silent or speaking.

JUAN MARÍA THOMAS

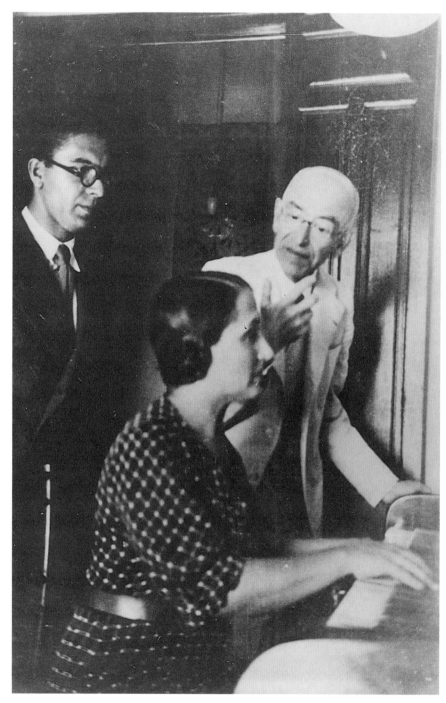

WITH ROSA GARCÍA ASCOTT, AND HER HUSBAND JESÚS BAL Y GAY, GRANADA, SEPTEMBER, 1935.

Rosa García Ascott

I CAN still imagine her sitting at the piano, next to the balcony of the high flat in calle Bailén where the García Ascotts lived with little Rosa, his favourite disciple, the only one, I be-

"FOR HER DEAR TEACHER FROM ROSA, WHO IS PROUD TO BE HIS DISCIPLE. 8-V-1917".

lieve, he ever had. The balcony looked out over a vivid Guadarrama landscape. I can still imagine her playing and singing and almost dancing the English verses of Chueca's famous *zarzuela Cádiz*. She did it very funnily and with blithe enjoyment. I never discovered whether or not she helped the superb Madrid born composer to write his scores. I know that Falla liked to be called a *zarzuelero* composer, because he was one. And he was among the best: Chueca, Chapí, Bretón, Gerónimo Giménez... His masterful *Love the Magician* deserves a place alongside *La Revoltosa, La Chavala, La Verbena de la Paloma, La Gran Vía, La Boda* and *El Baile de Luis Alonso...* light theatrical works, but great at the concert hall. However, always a *zarzuelero*: the living *zarzuela*, little burning bush from which God pronounced his mysterious *adsun* "Here I am". Saint Manuel de Falla was there listening to him. But like every saint he had to converse with the Devil because, according to the gospel, "faith is for the ear and the ear for the word of God". Music too is for the ear and can steal our faith, the divine word, if the Devil has his way.

JOSÉ BERGAMÍN

MY LITTLE Rosa:

I am writing to you on Manuel's behalf, who is so busy at the moment that he does not have time to fulfil his desire to do so. He asks me to tell you how pleased he is to hear you are going to play the *Concert*. Have you heard Kastaner play it? Manolo was told that he is not very sure rhythmically and that he is not very audible. Is that true? He tells me that you should play it on a piano with the register of a harpsichord like the one he used when he played it in Madrid.

This can be easily arranged (if you give them some notice) in Madrid and Barcelona and can be applied to any upright piano.

The movements of the second and third part of the records are not, unfortunately, exact. They must be speeded up a little. He would be grateful if you could tell Pittaluga this when he studies the instruments, also please send him Manuel's regards.

With reference to Manuel's previous letter (*Nights...*) he asks me to tell you to read it again, as he thinks you have not fully understood the reasons he gave you.

He also tells me how much he longs to hear the *Concert*, to see you both, and to hear your work. He sends you his warmest wishes.

We do not know anything about what you told us about *Master Peter* with puppets. Who is doing it? It is extremely difficult!

MANUEL DE FALLA

Letter to Rosa García Ascott written by Carmen de Falla, no date.

Falla and Bergamín write

MY DEAR FRIEND:

Much as I would always like to write to you about happy things, unfortunately, it is not sufficient "always" to achieve what I have in mind. This has been one of the reasons for my prolonged silence. Since I received the copies of your book *La cabeza a pájaros* which you had the kindness and fellowship to dedicate to María del Carmen and myself, I have wished to send you my sincere thanks, both for your present and for the many "profound" and clear things which, among others less clear, it contains. But at the same time I had to speak to you about an affair which is not at all pleasant, and I did not wish to do so before thoroughly examining it in order to avoid, not just possible unfairness on my part, but also a possible shock on your part. However, the months have passed by as I awaited the appropriate and correct moment which, much to my dismay, never presented itself. You cannot imagine what my life has become. I have so little free time that sometimes I have the sensation that life is virtually over for me. I do not complain; there must be a reason for it to be like this, and the only thing to do is "follow the current" after vainly exhausting the resources which are available to our poor human means to prevent it. I tell you all this to justify my silence and to make it clear that it was caused by your silence, also prolonged and lamented. I took advantage of my last stay with Alfonso Valdecasas in Granada to beg him to tell you some of this along with other "commmissions"

related to the magazine, and at that time I decided to confirm what Alfonso had said to you; but, once again, I was obliged to postpone sending a letter. In this manner time has slipped away until I received the *Almanaque de Cruz y Raya*, which I thank you for sending, but which has left me with such a bitter impression, in spite of the beautiful and admirable things which it contains, or perhaps precisely because of them...

With an affection which honours me, you have asked me often to speak my mind, and that is what I am going to do: I think that, as a whole, the *Almanaque de Cruz y Raya* is *monstruous* in the literal sense of the word. You will not have noticed this while you were compiling it, and I, for my part, do not wish to judge the reasons which have brought about this wrong, which, moreover, does not come as a great surprise considering the "angle" the magazine has taken recently. The only thing I should add to what I have said, which will probably come as no surprise to you, given the extreme point which things have reached and the lack of exact fairness (and the excess of bad intentions) with which the public tend to see and interpret what they are given, is that I can no longer go on, not even in the modest position that befits those of us who simply appear as the magazine's founders. I say this thinking about and referring to the very *next* issue. Being sincere in the friendship I profess for you, I write to you with apologies for the upset I may cause you, but my conscience demands I do so quickly and decisively. This is not a simple question of scruples: It is nothing more than upholding the second commandment of God's law in

its most essential meaning, even though it is not the most commonly applied. What more need I add to one who has such a sensitive understanding?...

Forgive me for the bad moments –I regret them I assure you– which reading this letter may cause you, and I send you my affectionate regards and my faithful friendship,

MANUEL DE FALLA
Letter to José Bergamín
[Granada, 16 February 1935]

COVER PAGE OF THE MAGAZINE
CRUZ Y RAYA, MADRID, 1933.

MY EVER DEAR AND RESPECTED FRIEND:

Your letter arrived on the same day that I left for Paris to give a conference about Lope, at the Hispanic Studies Department of the University. I got back on Sunday evening, but do not wish to leave you without an answer, at length, before entering the labyrinth of tasks which, like you, according to your letter, almost completely absorb my time.

Certainly enough, your letter has caused me

great distress; even more so because it was unexpected. I knew nothing of the commissions which you gave to Valdecasas for me, as I hardly had time to see him: through no fault of his, because he asked me to meet him a number of times, but because of the constant burden of work weighing on me.

I have read and reread your letter. I looked for some reason therein, some motive to explain your decision. I have not found them. Instead of these, I read statements which deeply upset me because of the suppositions on which they are undoubtedly founded, which you have decided are not worth naming. Thus, I have to content myself, solely, with the fact that you have examined your motives thoroughly, without being told what they are. The sorrow and sadness I feel are not just the result of you distancing yourself from me, but rather the fact that you have not thought fit to give me any explanation in this respect. Forgive me then, that now I give you my own reasons, without knowing whether or not they have any bearing upon the reasons for your decision.

Of course your name, and all the others, the entire list of *founders*, will disappear from the magazine from issue 22, corresponding to January –and consequently, *before* the date on which your letter arrived– my first notification of your wish. It has always been my opinion that this list does not imply, in any manner, direct or indirect responsibility for those who appear in the magazine, but rather their desire and my honour to maintain a historical fact: that we started and founded it all together. I repeatedly refused to take charge of it; and if I have accepted to do so at last it is because I felt it was my unavoidable duty to do so. But accepting too exclusive a responsibility for any mistakes I might make. I do not understand why, if you think that mistakes have been committed, you did not inform me beforehand; and even now, you let me know that there are mistakes but you do not tell me where. I make this deduction, a very serious one, from your letter: *that I took the name of God in vain*. Well then, from the very beginning when the magazine was initiated, I refused to run or collaborate in it at all if it was to be a *closed* Catholic confessional magazine: because, for

me, that would have been to take God's name in vain. That is how I expressed it in the introduction which met with enthusiastic support. My position, in general terms, is in keeping with advice of Pope Pius IX; that is, not to make a Catholic magazine, because this implies searching for refuge in the guise of the Church; instead of defending it, but on the contrary: that we Catholics should produce a magazine which, with all modesty and decision, would prove spontaneous, naturally defending those spiritual principles which, for us Catholics, coincide –in life, history and culture– with liberty and with the personal and human independence of our faith and its real and public practice.

But... to make a magazine. Substantive. With literature, philosophy, scientific research, art... and seriousness. With all the spiritual activities of thought, independent and compatible with religious activities and faith –and of hope and charity. My clumsiness, my personal insignificance, have, in your opinion, killed the idea. My aims, even though you do not say so –you do not even say it yourself because of the great respect you have for me, much greater than I deserve– my aims have served, once more, to continue to pave the way to hell. I cannot say it. Its effect on my constantly troubled conscience is no light matter. But the work is there. Why do you not tell me clearly where the evil lies and the nature

A PAGE FROM THE MAGAZINE *CRUZ Y RAYA.*

of the errors? I will then be able to remedy those of the magazine and my own alike.

But you, who know the veneration with wich I regard you, abandon me saying simply: "I cannot go on at your side because I cannot take God's name in vain'. It implies that I do. Then you add as the sole explanation for these *terrible words*: "In my opinion the Almanac is *monstrous*, although this does not shock me considering the *angle* the magazine has taken".

I draw your attention to this. If you have examined your statements in order to avoid being unfair to me, according to what you say, how can you ignore the injustice you do me with your decision to refuse to tell me what your motives are, when you knew full well the pain it would inflict upon me?

Nevertheless, I am going to attempt to explain to you or to myself the way you may have interpreted truly or falsely the direction in which the magazine is moving; and the *monstrous* almanac. So once you hear it you may respond if you so wish.

The magazine, in accordance with its aims, has commissioned and published collaborations which, whether in their own right or on account of their authors, were of such undeniably high poetic, aesthetic, literary, scientific and moral worth that the magazine took shape on its own accord as a magazine of "open and independent collaborations". At the same time, I wanted it to reveal significant aspects of our present-day lives that demonstrated our agreement or disagreement on account of their personal or public implications, in short, our criticism of the complex and difficult modern life in Spain and the rest of the world. For this reason, in the section entitled "*Cristal del Tiempo*", a number of general aspects were included. Not as many as I had wished for, but not so few either. But I myself wrote a series of brief critical commentaries, whose coherence with my conduct I believe evident. I am not so sure of their accuracy, but they were sincere in this sense. At the same time, in the section "*Criba*" a permanent commentary was introduced on the principle aspects of books or publications or events taken from daily newspapers. Our aim was to give our *yes* or our *no*, our *cruz* (cross) or our *raya* (dash). But I always, at all times –in my writings as with everything– upheld the staunch pledge and noble virtue not to take the holy name of God in vain, nor his Church nor Christ. Furthermore with the excuse of those very short sections "*La espada y la pared*" and "*Las cosas claras*", etc..., I wanted to give short pieces of *advice* in both cases, with texts of such a clear nature that they accomplished, and I think this was almost always achieved, their pure epigrammatic aim. Perhaps from these small pieces of brief advice, periodically published in the magazine, came the idea of an extended piece of "Advice" which I published this year in the form of the almanac, in an effort of enormous concentration, selection and supervision, which took up a month of my time, driven by honesty rather than modesty. In this, my "Advice" –you could not know the effort it cost me when you condemned it– I employed with more determination than ever my constant idea of penetrating the wavering spirit of Spanish readers with the most truthful and honourable words of our faith. I did this in such a way that the *appearance* and *staging*, as Calderón would say of the spectacle of human life, scarcely revealed the merciful, compassionate and charitable Christian purpose. In order to achieve this I took a shortcut: beauty and poetry. I do not know whether I have been successful. You think not. Your opinion is a great source of distress to me.

I took down my scaffolding from the almanac once I had set it up. But you cannot ignore its coherence, its sense: nor as its deep "*jonda*" authenticity. It does contain monstrous things but its monstrousness is confined to its labyrinth". It is a dream of life and the world in which you can find the *mirror* and the *enigma* with which the Christians since Saint Paul, have explained everything. But with the desire, constantly present in me and perhaps exaggerated, to elude any hint of pedantry. For this reason, I am not the kind of person who enjoys those repulsive confessional spectacles at

all (for Saint Augustine the word *confession* signified and signifies exactly the opposite of any Rosseauism, whoever may use it, including that used by that poor grotesque histrionic father, Laburu, whom the great lack of Spanish ecclesiastical authority allows to speak instead of silencing him as it should do). No, I prefer to speak my truth with jest. It is a question of style.

You consider this dangerous. For me the most dangerous thing is not to do something when we understand it should be done like that. I have simply done this *as God has made me feel it should be done*. I do so, because I remember by heart the words of Saint Augustine who said: "the greatest danger lies in understanding without action".

Perhaps for this reason, for me, the finished work –the *artefact* for scholars– in the absolute independence of its creation, does not have any responsibility or indirect connection whether moral, political or religious: it is an instrument which can be neither good or bad, it is simply an instrument. The moral, political and religious responsibility does not rest with its author –as our too little known friar Juan de Santo Tomás believed– but with he who uses it; and it rests with the author, and anyone else, when he uses it. There is no need for me to push the point which is pure Thomism, and which you are very familiar with. This is, philosophically, our strictest orthodoxy.

But you, who have a personal relationship with me, know that my whole life, and more so now, is a fabric woven of constant suffering and anxieties. That the only secret of my existence is this pain of glimpsing, of trying to follow for an inkling, without ever attaining it entirely, the path of Christ. There is not a single particle of my life, in body or soul, that does not aggrieve me constantly in this sense, like a regret; with the thought of death that has haunted me since my childhood; with the fact that my whole life and faith are constantly shadowed by the permanent torment of my conscience... For all this, I thank God, as it makes me feel that He has not left me completely aside.

Is it possible that you, a believer, who have been an example for me (to what extent I will not indulge so as not to offend your modesty) reproach me for the *literary game* of concealing, *not out of human respect but out of divine respect*, those feelings which only the purest act of

charity can communicate to us.

If I were such a saint or a sinner like Saint John or Lope, of course I would do and say, but this is a very different way of doing and saying. What more do you want me to do if I do not even know if I am saying what I want, jumping the abyss of action which is so difficult for me?

Lastly, and though in this respect I do not fear your disagreement, I want you to know my profound and true repugnance for the entire world of official Spanish Catholics (Gilson would call them institutionalists) because of their hypocrisy and political trickery or nonsense, which is turning our holy Church into a contemptible profit market or dividing it into factions. Because of the corrupted and corruptive decomposition of clericism. Because of all that filthy masquerade of vile interests and passions which are disguised as Catholic religion to exploit nationwide superstition and poor pious people. In short, because of anything which takes blatant advantage of Christ's cross, from a shop window to a book cover to a voting paper. I ask you to rage against all this the great gale of your inspiring words. Because I, a pitiful sinner, unworthy, can do nothing, but wait, tempering my nerves with hope and with desperation bearing witness to so many lies, so much ignominious and nauseating decay, which are cynically bandied about between us Catholics. I have to point out to you that in Spain everything that is rightly described as CEDA [Spanish Confederation of Independent right-wing Associations] will probably lead to positivist literacy with the sewer influences of Lerouxism and masonery, etc, etc.

My dearly respected and true friend, forgive me if not everything in this letter appears to be aimed entirely at clearing up any mistakes that the circumstances, distance, silence or who knows what, have placed between us.

But I do not wish to, nor should, conceal from you the bitterness which among so many other things –I say this today, with the taste of ash still in my mouth– must reach you with this letter because of the great and unexpected injury yours brought me.

Your ever faithful and devoted friend,

JOSÉ BERGAMÍN
Letter to Manuel de Falla
[Madrid, 6 March 1935]

ALBERT LOLTRONIERI,
LEOPOLDO TORRES BALBÁS,
MANUEL DE FALLA, ARTURO
BONUCCI AND ALFREDO
CASELLA IN THE ALHAMBRA,
1930.
ALFREDO CASELLA, ITALIAN
COMPOSER (TURIN, 1883 -
ROME, 1947) WAS ONE OF THE
REPRESENTATIVES OF 20TH
CENTURY MUSICAL
RENOVATION IN HIS
COUNTRY. HE HAD A CLOSE
FRIENDSHIP WITH FALLA,
SHARED BY THEIR FELLOW
FRIEND AND COLLEAGUE
GIAN FRANCESCO MALIPIERO.

LIKE OTHER great composers (Wagner and Ravel for instance), Falla is by no means a tall man. His appearance is one hundred percent Andalusian, and he seems drawn from one of El Greco's paintings. He has high forehead, dark eyes, a straight nose and an aesthetic but, at the same time, passionate expression. His face looks like the face of a both a country man and a old monk and he has an extraordinary nobility of manners, a sweet voice with a hopelessly Spanish accent to make it even more personal. These are the physical characteristics of the man, one of the greatest composers in Spain at the present time, and one of the most admired in the rest of the world.

ALFREDO CASELLA

FROM HIS restless retreat in the Alhambra in Granada, a lonely figure, consumed by love and faith has, however, shown us the way. Manuel de Falla's song, harsh and wise like passion, discreet, secret, precise, and gradually transfigured in a desert of prayer, makes an eternal spring issue from the rock. Leaning initially towards blunt violence, however, which tends towards what is picturesque in folk melodies, the Falla of *Master Peter's Puppet Show* tames, like an ascetic speaking with birds, the universe of poetry. He is too exceptional a composer for the philosopher, trying to explain the leaps of intelligence in a false age, to unravel his lesson. Another lonely figure, who has also set an important example, answers him.

JACQUES MARITAIN

AT LAST, I would like to tell you how moved I was to read the letter you sent to the Seville newspaper in response to mine. What hope your intellectual persuasion (about certain Catholic aspects) gave me. I already knew this, since the time I had the enormous pleasure of first conversing with you both.

In this time of bitter responsibility for the Latin Christians of Europe and America, your voice can and must be raised to show us the way. Especially so in Spain where the religion of the majority needs the purification which we find in such an exemplary manner in France.

MANUEL DE FALLA
Letter to Jacques Maritain
[Granada, 4th of October 1932]

WITH ROLAND MANUEL AND MAURICE DELAGE IN GRANADA; BIOGRAPHY OF MANUEL DE FALLA WRITTEN BY ROLAND MANUEL AND PUBLISHED IN PARIS, 1930. ROLAND MANUEL (PARIS, 1891-1966), WAS A COMPOSER AND CRITIC WHO FORMED PART OF THE GREAT MUSICAL MOVEMENT THAT FOLLOWED THE IDEAS OF DEBUSSY. CLOSE TO RAVEL, AMONG OTHERS, HE MET FALLA IN HIS YOUTH AND BECAME HIS RESPECTED FRIEND AND BIOGRAPHER.

THE LAST time I saw him was in 1935, a year before the civil war. His delicate health obliged him to live the life of a recluse and he rarely went out apart from going to mass in an old worn-out cabriolet. On the other hand, he was too absorbed in his own dreams to feel any need of leaving his "villa", on a hill behind the Alhambra, and his little garden, from where one could see Granada's entire vast flowering valley, which poets compared to the Damascus plain.

When I visited Falla at his house in 1935, it was the first time I had seen him for years. During this time, his face had wasted away and was even more emaciated. I still remembered him just as I had found him in 1921, still full of the passion of his creations, the wild *Fire Dance* and *The Three-cornered Hat*, an intellectual levelling himself against a throng of Andalusian demons. Now he looked like an ascetic monk, whose life was spent between meditation in his cell and reverie in his garden. Now his only ambition was peace and seclusion.

WALTER STARKIE

Falla writes to Ramiro de Maeztu

DEAR SIR:

As Don Manuel de Falla is presently convalescing from a serious illness, which has put his life in danger, and as the doctors have forbidden him any exertion, including speaking and writing letters, he has asked me to reply to your letter of the 8th of this month, by reproducing in brief the conversation we had concerning it.

Don Manuel de Falla is very sorry that he cannot agree on many points in your letter. In his opinion, the Revolution was not fundamentally the work of writers and philosophers, but rather the result of the fact that Catholics had forgotten their principles of justice and love, which are essential to Christian belief. For this reason God permitted the revolutionary scourge, in order to teach and punish all of us, and to purify and clear the air, as Maritain puts it in one of his works. For Don Manuel de Falla, the only solution for this is not a conservative counter-revolution, which would certainly retain the execrable, but rather another deeper and more noble revolution, guided by the love of God, above all things, and of our neighbour, as you would have him love you. Until this comes about it is useless to resort to tradition, a word which excercises an almost magical effect on some sections of the Spanish population and with which they try to explain and justify everything. Don Manuel de Falla believes that there is only one consistently truthful and worthwhile tradition, the eternal tradition of the word of God; any other is imperfect and impure and should be constantly corrected and purified, because every age demands new solutions and more generosity and love for our fellows. What does not conform to this represents nationalist traditionalism which will finish, like any exaggerated nationalism, by opposing Christ's genuine teachings.

MANUEL DE FALLA
Letter to Ramiro de Maeztu, written
by María del Carmen de Falla,
dictated by her brother Manuel
[Granada, 8 July 1936]

Falla writes to Manuel Azaña

MY DISTINGUISHED friend,

I take this opportunity to sincerely congratulate you on your rise to the Presidency of the Republic and to express a heartfelt desire, shared by many Spaniards: that these bitter times come to an end in which Spanish Christians have suffered the destruction of temples, in which public and collective blasphemies have gone unpunished –commencing with the most horrendous insults against the Holy Name of God, revered up to now over the centuries and by all the educated and ignorant people of this land– and in which people who consecrated their lives to charity have been martyred. Thus I beg you, not just as President of the Republic but as a man of fine literary sensibility whom I consider my friend, to help us at this difficult time by exercising your supreme authority.

With this hope I write you this letter, the first in a long time, because of a serious illness caused by these sacriligous events, which has endangered my life. Rest assured that I speak to you solely as a Catholic, free from any political (which I have never had) or purely humanistic interest, which I have always considered reprehensible.

Sincerely wishing you, as a good Christian and a faithful friend, every success with your presidential work. I gladly send you my respect and affection,

MANUEL DE FALLA
Letter to Manuel Azaña
[Granada, 23 May 1936]

José María Pemán and the Civil War

DEAR AND ADMIRED MAESTRO:

Over the last few days I have been working on the lyrics for your *War Anthem* and here are the verses I have written, as absolutely *monstrous* as you told me to make them. I enclose a typed version and another at the foot of the musical notation. In order to *test it* I had it sung by a chorus of the Academia de Santa Cecilia and was very pleased with the result.

Now, you have the last word. I will be here until Wednesday the 6th. I then leave for Burgos, Hotel Norte and then London. In Burgos I wanted to be able to hand in our work to General Orgaz: but I do not want to do so before you come to a decision about the lyrics.

JOSÉ MARÍA PEMÁN
Letter to Manuel de Falla
[Cadiz, 3 October 1937]

WITH JOSÉ MARÍA PEMÁN, 1937.

PAX, THE MOTTO WITH WHICH MANUEL DE FALLA HEADED HIS LETTERS IN THE YEARS LEADING UP TO THE CIVIL WAR.

MY DEAR and admired friend:

Your silence after my telegram of the 7th, as well as the absence of any news related to the honourable –and overwhelming– appointment, leads me to confirm the hope I placed in your friendship, so full of generosity, loyalty and understanding, that I might be substituted in the assignment.

I assure you, dear José María, that the reasons I gave you in my telegram to justify my plea still plague me to such an extent that not only has my recovery been notably delayed, but even my compositional work, which I resumed a few days ago, has lost the efficiency (thank God and unexpected satisfaction) with which it was being done. I believe, as I told you, that I can only aim to be of some use to our homeland by doing this work, and even more so at times like these. In short, second to God, I continue to rest my hopes with you, and this should make you see how anxiously I am waiting to receive your news, to calm my constant worry about taking responsibility for something which I know nothing about, and with which I do not wish to be involved.

Of course, as you can guess, nothing of what I am saying affects my deep and heartfelt gratitude,

MANUEL DE FALLA
Letter to José María Pemán
[Granada, 19 January 1938]

Don Manuel de Falla's departure from his house in Granada

ON THE 28th of September 1939 we gathered at Don Manuel de Falla's house at three o'clock in the afternoon: Don Manuel was leaving for Buenos Aires and his friends had come to say goodbye.

Ramón Pérez de Roda and his wife, Eugenia, María Prieto de Olóriz and one of her cousins, Emilia Morell de Gallego Burín, the mayor of Granada, Miss Emilia Llanos, a woman I did not know, Pedro Borrajo and his daughter, Luis Jiménez and the writer of this, Hermenegildo Lanz and his wife Sofía Durán de Lanz were there.

Also present was Germán Falla, his wife and daughter Maribel. On the patio there was an old lady, to whom María del Carmen Falla gave financial support, a servant and another woman from the neighbourhood.

In the small dining room of the villa, among suitcases and trunks, we chatted about María del Carmen who was not convinced by the idea of the journey and was thinking about not going. The general conversation lacked sparkle, and wit struggled among the vulgarities which were unsuited to most of the company's intelligence. There are moments in which the brain withers and words can express nothing but unfathomable nonsense.

At three thirty Don Manuel came downstairs, followed by his brother Germán and his sister-in-law. María del Carmen said goodbye to her friends kissing the women and shaking hands with the men, she conceded me the honour of an embrace... God Bless her! The emotion we were both struggling to contain experienced a moment of release, but was quickly suppressed. María del Carmen is a saint, I am like a brother to her, and she is like a mother to me. We did not exchange a word, not even goodbye. She continued to wave and got into the car with slightly tearful eyes, but with a smile on her face, like someone who is not going far and expects to be back soon.

Don Manuel followed his sister, he shook hands with everyone, and said goodbye to them all... Goodbye, see you soon! he said, with his saintly anchorite face and his expression of goodness, smiling but pale, very pale, in good spirits, however, and wanting to cheer the rest of us up. He did not take long to say farewell to those in the dining room. A few of us remained on the patio a brief moment after having said goodbye to María del Carmen. Don Manuel came up to me, I fondly hugged him and whispered weakly to his ear, "Thank you.... Thank you!" He did not embrace me and he told me that it was because he could not move his arms very easily, because of the operation which he had undergone, but he leaned his cheek against mine and I felt his emotion, not repressed like his sister's but expressed with such awful words, so profound and different to those said before that I reflect them here because they wounded me most deeply. Goodbye, until eternity, at the bottom of the sea, perhaps! Whatever Providence decides!

Goodbye... (he took his leave of the old lady, the servant and the neighbour) until eternity where we will all meet; I will be lonely at the bottom of the sea, it makes no difference, it does not matter, Whatever Providence decides!... The three ladies began to cry... No, master!... they cried and Don Manuel walking with somewhat lighter step than usual and with his face ablaze, his eyes shining and a smile on his lips, a nervous one, sat down next to his sister in the car and once there received the purest kiss of his little neice Maribel.

All of Don Manuel's friends, formerly mutual good friends, said goodbye to each other immediately, probably not to meet again...

What can we do? We will meet in afterlife!

H. Lanz

At seven o'clock in the evening on the day of the departure. In my studio.

After writing this I went to bed because I felt cold, upset and not very well during the whole afternoon. Today, a day later, after sleeping badly, and very little, I count the hours since my second father Don Manuel de Falla left me – the man who had shaped my mind– had perhaps to never see me again.

God's will be done!

HERMENEGILDO LANZ

ONE OF THE LAST PHOTOGRAPHS TAKEN
OF FALLA BEFORE HE DEPARTED FOR
ARGENTINA, IN WHICH HE APPEARS WITH
HIS BROTHER GERMÁN, HIS SISTER-IN-LAW
MARÍA LUISA LÓPEZ AND MARIBEL, THEIR
DAUGHTER.

IT WAS an afternoon at the end of
September 1939. All of his
friends were gathered together on the patio at the entrance
situated between the villa
and the house. Don Manuel
had come downstairs, said
his last farewells, and was on his
way up the hill, waving his hand in a last goodbye, while we remained in the hallway as if secretly insisting
on a past that no longer existed. And as he waved to us, he said –and these
were his last words for us–:

"Goodbye, goodbye everyone! Until the valley of Josaphat! Until the valley of Josaphat!"

LUIS JIMÉNEZ

CONFUCIUS, MANUEL DE FALLA'S CAT.

7
ARGENTINA
1939-1946

Trip to Buenos Aires. Colón Theatre. The première of *Homenajes*. The Córdoba Symphonic Orchestra. Radio el Mundo concerts. Carlos Paz Villa and Alta Gracia. Darius Milhaud and Léonide Massine write to him. Remembering Granada. Francesc Cambó. Rafael Alberti. Visitors. Falla's death and his mortal remains sent to Spain.

AERIAL VIEW OF THE CITY BUENOS AIRES.

CHRONOLOGY

1939. ■ ON THE 18TH OF OCTOBER HE REACHED THE PORT OF BUENOS AIRES ABOARD THE STEAMSHIP *NEPTUNIA* AFTER STOPPING OFF IN THE CANARY ISLANDS, RIO DE JANEIRO AND MONTEVIDEO. ■ ON THE 18TH OF NOVEMBER THE SUITE *HOMENAJES* WAS PLAYED AT THE COLÓN THEATRE IN BUENOS AIRES. ■ FRIENDSHIP WITH COMPOSER JUAN JOSÉ CASTRO AND HIS WIFE RAQUEL. ■ ON THE 20TH OF NOVEMBER, THE WAGNERIAN ASSOCIATION OF BUENOS AIRES PAID HIM HOMAGE.

1940. ■ HE SETTLED DOWN WITH HIS SISTER MARÍA DEL CARMEN IN THE CARLOS PAZ VILLA, IN THE PROVINCE OF CÓRDOBA. ■ ON THE 30TH OF MAY HE CONDUCTED A CHARITY CONCERT WITH THE CÓRDOBA SYMPHONIC ORCHESTRA. ■ HE MOVED TO THE DEL LAGO VILLA WHERE HE WAS VISITED BY ARTHUR RUBINSTEIN. ■ AT THE END OF THE YEAR HE CONDUCTED SOME CONCERTS IN BUENOS AIRES ON RADIO EL MUNDO. ■ THE WAR IN EUROPE MEANT THAT HE DID NOT RECEIVE MONEY FOR AUTHORS' RIGHTS AND HE LIVED IN FINANCIAL HARDSHIP. HIS FRIENDS HERNÁNDEZ SUÁREZ, JUAN JOSÉ CASTRO, GUIDO VALCARENGHI AND FRANCESC CAMBÓ HELPED HIM.

1941. ■ HE FELL ILL WITH A FEVER WHICH PREVENTED HIM FROM WORKING ON *ATLÁNTIDA* FOR SOME MONTHS.

1942. ■ HE RECEIVED A LETTER FROM DARIUS MILHAUD LIVING IN EXILE IN THE UNITED STATES, GIVING HIM NEWS ABOUT THEIR MUTUAL FRIENDS. ■ HE SETTLED IN ALTA GRACIA, IN THE PROVINCE OF CÓRDOBA, IN A HOUSE CALLED "LOS ESPINILLOS". ■ IN DECEMBER HE TRAVELLED TO BUENOS AIRES TO GIVE SOME CONCERTS FOR RADIO EL MUNDO.

1943. ■ HEALTH PROBLEMS. ■ FREQUENT MEETINGS IN ALTA GRACIA WITH FRANCESC CAMBÓ AND ENRIQUE LARRETA. ■ IN SPITE OF HIS POOR STATE OF HEALTH FALLA CONTINUED TO COMPOSE *ATLÁNTIDA*, MENTIONING THE POSSIBILITY OF PLAYING A VERSION AT A CONCERT.

1944. ■ JAIME PAHISSA VISITED HIM IN ALTA GRACIA AND STARTED TO WRITE HIS BIOGRAPHY, WHICH WAS PUBLISHED IN 1947. ■ HEALTH PROBLEMS ALTERNATE WITH THE PEACE OF *ATLÁNTIDA*.

1945. ■ HE WAS VISITED BY MARGARITA XIRGÚ AND BY RAFAEL ALBERTI. ■ HE TURNED DOWN AN INVITATION FROM THE SPANISH GOVERNMENT TO RETURN TO SPAIN. ■ IGNACIO ZULOAGA AND JOSÉ MARÍA SERT DIED. ■ COMPOSER SERGIO DE CASTRO COLLABORATED WITH FALLA UP UNTIL HIS DEATH.

1946. ■ ON THE 14TH OF NOVEMBER FALLA DIED IN ALTA GRACIA, A FEW DAYS BEFORE HIS SEVENTIETH BIRTHDAY. ■ ON THE 19TH OF NOVEMBER HIS FUNERAL WAS HELD IN THE CATHEDRAL OF CÓRDOBA. ■ IT WAS DECIDED TO SEND FALLA'S MORTAL REMAINS TO SPAIN. ■ ON THE 22ND OF DECEMBER HIS SISTER, MARÍA DEL CARMEN EMBARKED FOR SPAIN ACCOMPANYING THE COFFIN.

1947. ■ ON THE 9TH OF JANUARY THE BOAT REACHED CADIZ AND FALLA WAS BURIED IN THE CRYPT OF THE CATHEDRAL.

María del Carmen writes to her brother Germán

DEAREST Germán, María Luisa and Maribel:

Up to now I have not had sufficient peace of mind to write to you.

When we reached Gibraltar the passengers started to panic a little. One of the boats there started to move out towards us and had us waiting there for an hour; they dropped anchor and an English seaman boarded our boat by climbing up a rope ladder. He inspected everything and when he climbed back down to his boat, our passengers said goodbye to him uttering a "good afternoon..." in English which echoed in the air and was answered with a sardonic smile. We calmly awaited the outcome.

The beauty of Tangiers impressed us when we arrived; in the morning its houses appeared to be made of ivory and sparkled like a great display of precious stones in the evening. Our stop over was entertaining because of the wonderful goods the small boats carried. It was strange too, some boys who begged for money threw the coins they were given into the sea and then dived in to retrieve them.

One of the most exciting parts was when we reached Rio where we went ashore to see those marvellous woods, which impressed me so much that I decided our trip had been worthwhile; I can count this as one of the best moments of my life.

In Montevideo we also left the ship and were invited to eat there and given a drive round in a car afterwards. In comparison with Rio it was not very interesting. I think that it was there that a man, who knows you from Paris, Germán Elizalde, embarked on our boat. He is very affectionate and obliging with Manuel and is a singing teacher and has two very promising pupils, a Russian girl and a young Italian man, who lives here.

The concerts were magnificent, well-played, well-sung and with a truly admirable ovation. A long while afterwards –an hour or so– we left for a minor port, but there were still a group waiting there to greet Manuel and one lady rushed forward and kissed his hand. Our new friends here could not be more kind and helpful, in particular the family of Juan José Castro, the best composer here, who conducts very well and has helped Manolo a lot with the rehearsals.

Manolo is very well in spite of the enormous grind of the rehearsals, etc... His wounds have healed completely, thank goodness, and his leg is so mended that he even goes to conduct without his walking-stick and at home he often forgets where he has left it. His temperature is normal.

I am fine, thank God, but longing for some peace and quiet.

Yesterday we were invited to the house of a princess, María Pía of Bourbon, who is a charming lady, but

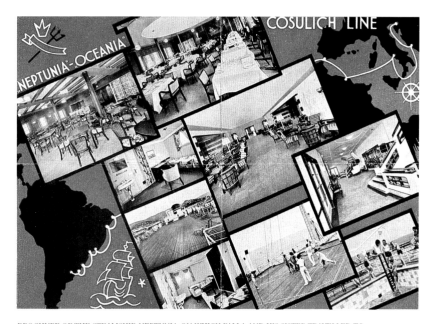

BROCHURE OF THE STEAMSHIP *NEPTUNIA*, ON WHICH FALLA AND HIS SISTER TRAVELLED TO BUENOS AIRES.

I am not ready for this kind of thing yet.

We had only just arrived when two gentlemen called me to one side to ask me some things so as not to disturb Manolo. I felt awful thinking that I might say something which he would not agree with, and moreover I felt faint being surrounded by so many people I did not know. But I was astounded when they asked me if we would like to spend a few days –before rehearsals began– in the country house of one of them. Sure enough, a few days later the man came to collect us in his car to take us to the country house, beautifully restored by one of his sons (who owned the house) who was an engineer, with bunches of carnations in all the rooms, even in the *bedrooms*, arranged with an extraordinary taste. They placed a white-gloved servant, a cook and a nice girl at our disposal to help me with whatever I desired and to keep me company. Every day the gentleman would telephone to inquire as to how we were and to send us whatever was not to be found there, and paid us short visits every two days. In short, as I was saying, the whole thing was a *paradise*; the like of which I had never seen before...

We are longing to hear about how you are. If Germán cannot find what he needs there, he should take courage and come here because, given the friends he could make and their favourable disposition towards us, he could certainly find it here. They have just appointed a man to a very good position on Manolo's

recommendation. Can Maribel write to tell us what she is doing? María Luisa, please tell us how things are *going...*

Manolo does not know that I have written to you and I am not going to tell him because he is very busy and working hard as they are rehearsing a première and it is full of mistakes; the first rehearsal was very tiresome and he barely has time to finish revising the *piece.*

Please find out about ship departures and inform us in good notice. The boat leaves tomorrow and I do not want to waste any opportunity.

All my love and affection,

MARÍA DEL CARMEN DE FALLA
Letter to Germán de Falla
[Buenos Aires, 15 December 1939]

HE ARRIVED in a quite a shocking physical condition: he was pale, weak and wasted away. He had only eyes and that wide and gentle smile, which was the essence of his warmth.

He settled, for the meantime, in a big hotel. Presently he announced that its luxurious and high class atmosphere was not what he needed. In response to the kind invitation of some friends he moved to a house in the countryside, not far from the Federal Capital. Incidentally, his journey to the country has had its small setbacks. It had recently rained there in a truly startling manner, and the road that led to the es-

THE PLAZA HOTEL IN BUENOS AIRES.

tate was full of puddles which impeded the car from reaching the house. The Maestro got into a "break" to avoid the mud, and even had to be carried by a farmhand over the last stretch until he reached firm land. Falla laughed like a child at all those vicissitudes. It was clear that the countryside made him happy. He breathed deeply the pure air of the tree plantation, and his happiness further increased when he saw the flowerbeds full of carnations, which reminded him of his villa in Granada.

His life in this place, in the company of his sister María del Carmen, was completely peaceful. "Few visitors", the doctor had advised him, "only essential ones." His friends and relatives kept to the prescription.

PEDRO MASSA

PAGE 267 ▶

COMPOSITIONS

Appendix V

ATLÁNTIDA

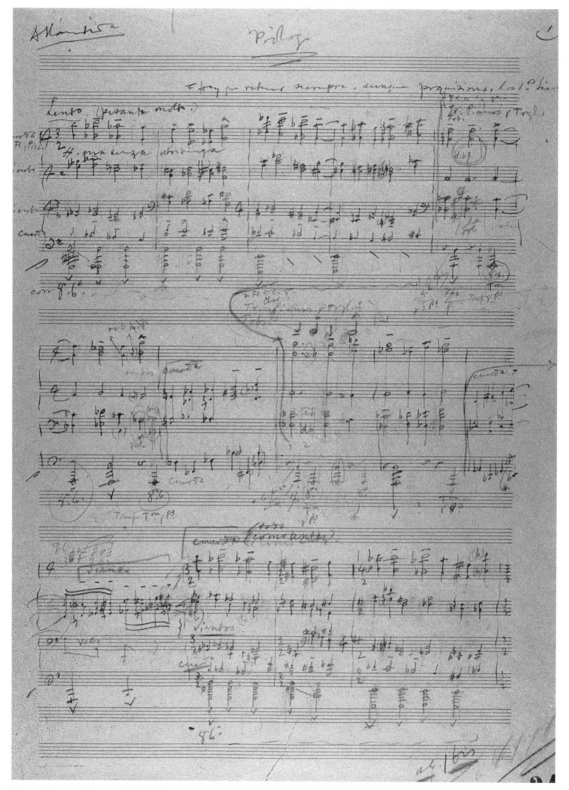

Score of the "prologue" of *Atlántida.*

ATLÁNTIDA

EVEN TODAY THIS IS STILL ONE OF THE LEAST KNOWN OF ALL OF MANUEL DE FALLA'S COMPOSITIONS. HE BEGAN WORK ON THIS THEATRICAL ORATORIO-CANTATA, WHICH WAS TO REPRESENT THE CULMINATION OF HIS LIFE AND WORK, IN ABOUT 1927, BASING IT ON A DRAMATIC POEM OF THE SAME TITLE BY JACINTO VERDAGUER. IN ORDER TO WORK ON HIS *ATLÁNTIDA* FALLA CARRRIED OUT AN IN-DEPTH STUDY OF THE CATALAN LANGUAGE AND VISITED VARIOUS PLACES IN SEARCH OF SOUNDS WHICH HE COULD EMPLOY IN THE MUSICAL TREATMENT OF THE WORK. HE SOON ESTABLISHED CONTACT WITH THE PAINTER AND STAGE DESIGNER JOSÉ MARÍA SERT TO DEVELOP THE PROJECT JOINTLY, PLANNING INITIALLY TO PRESENT THE PREMIÈRE AT THE UNIVERSAL EXHIBITIONS IN SEVILLE AND BARCELONA IN 1929.

HOWEVER, THE CRISIS OF THE 1930'S MEANT THAT COMPLETION OF THE WORK WAS DELAYED. SOON THE TIME HE SPENT WORKING ON IT BECAME THE MOST IMPORTANT THING IN HIS LIFE AND THE CAUSE OF MUCH SUFFERING OWING TO HIS POOR HEALTH.

THE TIME of the Latin-American Exhibition in Seville was approaching and the subject came up in conversation. Suddenly Sert had an idea:

"Why don't we do something for it?" Said Sert.
"*Atlántida*." Replied Falla.

The reason for this suggestion was that at that moment the fiftieth anniversary of the first modern day poem *L'Atlántida* by Jacinto Verdaguer, the great Catalan poet, was being celebrated. This was in 1926, the same year in which Falla celebrated his fiftieth birthday, which meant that the poem and the composer were the same age. Falla had read excerpts from the poem in the newspaper *El Sol*. It had been recited by Eduardo Marquina, in his own translation into Castillian Spanish, in a event held at the Spanish Academy to commemorate the day. These excerpts had fascinated Falla to such an extent that he ordered the entire poem. He thought it would be very useful for his plan and very appropriate because the affair was neither Greek nor Latin but somewhere between the two, between mythology, and the archaic times of primitive Iberia; between the Pyrenees and the Mediterranean, and between the legendary land of Gadex and the other great sea. Since his childhood his surroundings had filled his imagination with strange grandiose fancies like dark ancestral dreams. Cadiz, his home town, was at one time the Gadex of the Romans; and before that of the Iberians; and before that the lost atlantic continent, which was vaguely remembered by the Egyptians, the Phoenicians and the Greeks. The coat of arms of Cadiz showed Hercules with two pillars and the motto "*Hercules fundator*" (Hercules the founder), and he imagined the hero breaking up the land with his club and opening a channel to the immense sea. One can imagine the deep effect that reading *L'Atlántida* had on him as it brought his unfaded childhood images to life.

After Falla had relived these memories and meditated upon them in order to begin work on the composition of the poem and to translate them into music, he went to Cadiz, where the town council made him a guest

Jacinto Verdaguer, author of the dramatic poem *L'Atlántida*, which inspired Falla to compose his *Atlántida*.

of honour, which he wished to repay by giving a concert for charity. Cadiz proved highly evocative, located in a privileged spot where the Mediterranean and Europe end and facing the Atlantic and the New World! And with such a history, mixed with mythology and great historical figures: Alcides, the *Odyssey*, Phoenicia, had left their memory and age-old imprints on this beautiful and fortunate land, beneath a turquoise sun! Walking through Cadiz one can read street names like "Hercules" or "Arganthonius" and others taken from ancient Iberia. These streets were christened by Adolfo de Castro, an educated man, with a passion for pre-historic Iberian studies and in particular for Arganthonius, king of Tarshish, as well as being the author of *El Buscapiés*: a novel which was attributed to Cervantes and treated as such, even by the most respected Cervantists. Near the city, between Cadiz and Gibraltar, is the "Parsley" or "Pigeon" island which, according to Victor Bérard's research, in a book which studies the voyage of Ulysses on his return from Troy, belonged to the nymph Calypso in the *Odyssey*, and has the same vegetation and the same spring which were described by Homer.

From Cadiz Falla went to Jerez de la Frontera. There

he was accompanied by friends on excursions whose interest for him was of incalculable worth. They went to Sanlúcar de Barrameda, the port which is so closely connected with Columbus' voyages to the new continent. Following the path which leads between two lofty mountains, in some pastures which spread out to one side, they saw some oxen and cattle grazing. On their heads, between their horns and on their backs, stood some tall, graceful birds which the cattle made no attempt to remove. These birds ridded the cattle of parasites. They looked like the symbols on an Egyptian temple. These tall, grand birds really did come from Egypt: they were the beautiful ibis of the Nile which migrate every year from the eastern-most edge of the Mediterranean to beyond its western boundaries.

Afterwards they visited the ruins of the Temple of Hercules; among the dust of the earth one can still find the remains of urns and pieces of the stone from the monument, which is more than two thousand years old. Then they passed a small and pretty town: at the corner of one street they saw a marble bust depicting Hercules. The town is called Medina Sidonia: *Medina* from white Arabia; *Sidonia* from Sidon in Phoenicia.

They reached Tarifa, the point of Spain closest to Africa, at the narrowest part of the Gilbraltar Straits. They climbed the heroical and historical tower of Guzmán el Bueno. From the top they saw the sun setting between the massive neighbouring continents of Africa and Europe, as if they really were the pillars erected by Hercules to support them. The sun's rays shining through the shadows sketched by the clouds gave the impression of a biblical sky. The scene is one of epic proportions imbued with mythology, legend and remote history.

Now Falla was ready to begin work: his mind was saturated with magic and the sublime. For years it was the source of inspiration which sustained his work. A source which reflected his yearning. The proof of this is that one day, later on, with his composition underway, he was travelling through the Pyrenees on his way to Toulouse in France, and as he passed the wonderful sight at the foot of the tall and snowcapped peak of Canigó the music that he had composed for this canto of the poem came to his lips. He was pleased by this because he felt it was a worthy tribute to such majesty. Later, one night in the Carlos Paz villa in Argentina, under a deep blue sky and a clear moon that reminded him of those nights in Andalusia, he felt touched by inspiration and began to work. The next day he told his friend Doctor Carlos Quiroga Losada: "I am happy: I have written Hercules' entrance into the garden of Hesperides."

JAIME PAHISSA

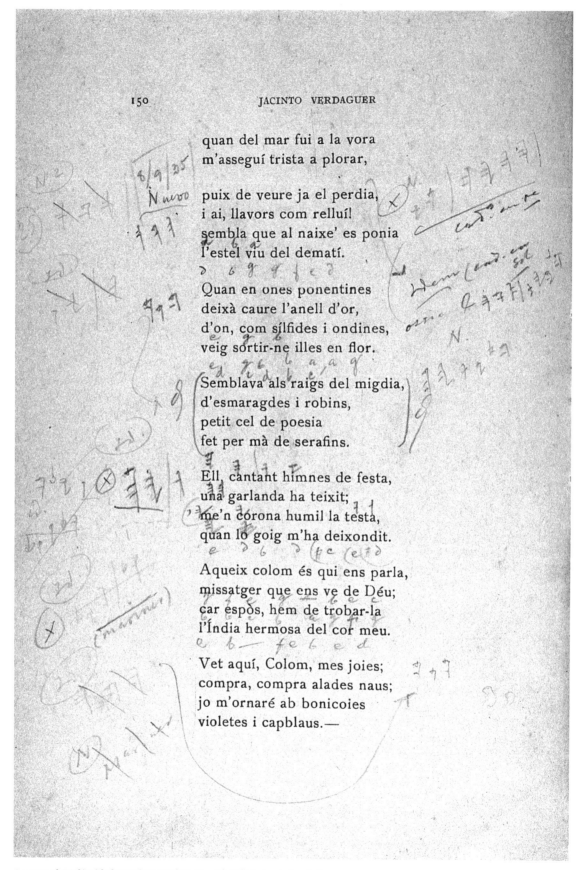

quan del mar fui a la vora
m'asseguí trista a plorar,

puix de veure ja el perdia,
i ai, llavors com relluí!
sembla que al naixe' es ponia
l'estel viu del dematí.

Quan en ones ponentines
deixà caure l'anell d'or,
d'on, com sílfides i ondines,
veig sortir-ne illes en flor.

Semblava als raigs del migdia,
d'esmaragdes i robins,
petit cel de poesia
fet per mà de serafins.

Ell, cantant himnes de festa,
una garlanda ha teixit;
me'n corona humil la testa,
quan lo goig m'ha deixondit.

Aqueix colom és qui ens parla,
missatger que ens ve de Déu;
car espòs, hem de trobar-la
l'Índia hermosa del cor meu.

Vet aquí, Colom, mes joies;
compra, compra alades naus;
jo m'ornaré ab bonicoies
violetes i capblaus.—

A page of *L'Atlántida* **by Jacinto Verdaguer, with Falla's musical notations.**

IN ONE OF my last conversations with Don Manuel de Falla he said:

"Over the last few days —two or three— I have sorted out one of the most tricky problems of *Atlántida*. Yes, I have been working on *Atlántida* —I repeat— to prove how divine providence never abandons the true believer, even if the obstacles set by destiny seem unsurmountable. The subject is a parley between Geryon, the three-headed guardian and Alcides, or Hercules. This raises a very difficult problem of expression: Geryon, who fears that Hercules has been ordered to kill him, tries to convince him not to carry out his task and tells him that beyond the sea is the island of the Hesperides, where golden apples grow, but in order to taste them he must first kill the golden serpent. At last Alcides gives in to Geryon's pleas: he turns his back on him and sets off in search of the garden of the Hesperides. In this passage the difficulty lies in expressing the mixture of adulation and fear with which Geryon tries to evade the danger that threatens him. Well then: here are the things which happen in a musical composition. At first, I had no intention of working on *Atlántida*, but I had to put the score in a place where it would be safe from the bombings and as I picked up the papers, which had lain out of sight for so long, the first thing that I saw was this passage. Incidentally, this part had been very awkward to compose and I was never satisfied with the final result, even after trying it out this way and that. But over the last few days I have completely altered it and now it is perfect, to the point that I no longer have to play it. This is partly thanks to you. Do you remember last Sunday you told me you would like to hear me play Chueca's *zarzuelas* on the piano? Well, the outcome of your request that evening was that I, with my usual insomnia, started to mentally analyse certain passages in Chueca, and that was the source of my solution. This is how I found the melodical-tonal structure which could be used to express the difficult parley between Geryon and the scornful Olympian gesture of Alcides. And it is all Wagner's fault. That wretched Wagner! I have been studying his composition recently and without realising it I applied Wagner's ideas to the declamatory style of the characters in *Atlántida*. But let it be known that I am one of this composer's greatest admirers, in the moments in which one sees the extraordinary qualities which characterise him. Recently I was reading the passage of the bird in Siegfried, in the second act. One has to admit that it is a really incredible passage: there is no better way of creating the ineffable sensation caused by a bird singing in a wood than that

shown here by Wagner. However, the scene with Fafner the dragon is tiresomely grey, monotonous and long!"

LUIS JIMÉNEZ

ANOTHER PIECE of information: one afternoon, Don Manuel, who had recently returned from Paris, if my memory serves me well, said to me: "The evening after my return from Paris I had a strange and wonderful dream. I found myself in a concert hall, on the podium, conducting an orchestra. The piece we played was more beautiful than any I have ever heard or conceived. The reason I am telling you this is because it was the beginning of *Atlántida*, that is the music that I had to write for my idea of a cantata based on Verdaguer's poem."

So, judging from this disclosure, it might be correct to state that the music of *Atlántida* was literally heard, perhaps in its compact entirety, one bright spring afternoon: a private, secret and unique hearing, but one which would launch his gigantic halo into the realms of eternity.

LUIS JIMÉNEZ

IN OCTOBER 1926 Falla the composer slowly read Jacinto Verdaguer's *L'Atlántida*. He read it relying on the French and Spanish translations.

"There's so much music in Minister Cinto's monumental *L'Atlántida*", we heard him say.

The following year, while he was in Barcelona, he informed Moragas that not only did he aim to turn Verdaguer's *L'Atlántida* into an oratorio, but that he had already begun work on composing it in Granada.

"And", added the famous composer, "I'm learning Catalan, because my oratorio is going to be in Verdaguer's Catalan. Let's hope this turns out alright, God help me."

During Lent in 1928, Manuel de Falla went to see his friend the Dean of the Association of Notaries in Barcelona, Antonio Par y Tusquets, about signing a contract with the heirs of Minister Cinto to allow the poem *L'Atlántida* to be transformed into an oratorio.

One night, while we were eating at Frank Marshall's house, along with a close friend of Falla, the businessman Juan Gisbert, we heard Falla say:

"I am dedicating *Atlántida* to Catalonia and, when the score is finished, it will be performed for the first time by the Orfeó Català with Luis Millet and his singers at the Monastery of Santa María de Ripoll."

In 1930 Moragas went to Granada with Juan Gisbert and they heard some fragments of *Atlántida* played to them by the composer.

Don Manuel had composed: "*El incendio de los Pirineos*" (The Pyrenees Fire) —the voice of the abyss, Hercules snatching Pilleus from the fire— the "*Coro de islas griegas*" (Chorus of Greek islands), "*El sueño de Isabel*" (Isabel's dream), in which Falla attained, yet again, the Castillian union of realism and mysticism.

In 1933 Luis Millet, Francisco Pujols, Miguel Llobet, Juan Gisbert and Rafael Moragas were invited by Falla to lunch at the Nouvel Hotel in calle Santa Ana.

The recurring theme of conversation was *Atlántida* which, the composer repeated, would be presented by the Orfeó Català.

In March of the same year, Moragas received a long letter from Manuel de Falla in which he wrote at length about his Oratorio.

At the end of the letter he had written:

"*A Deu siau, benvolgut Rafael, visqueu molts anys, us desitja vostre Manuel de Falla.*"

Moragas deposited the letter straight away in the Historical Archives of the City.

One imagines it is still there.

During the same year, Falla spent part of winter in Majorca, where he deepened his friendship with the illustrious Majorcan composer, Minister Juan María Thomas.

Minister Thomas has published a noteworthy book, in some respects quite basic, about Manuel de Falla. In it, Minister Thomas tells of the negotiations which were undertaken to establish that the first performance of *Atlántida* take place in Valldemosa in Majorca.

In his book, Minister Thomas mentions the effort José María Sert went to in order to produce Falla's last score in Valldemosa.

Sert managed to convince a wealthy American enthusiast to proffer a blank cheque to allow him to engage the world's most famous singers and present *Atlántida* in the United States.

Falla firmly turned down all these offers. He was not prepared to make any alteration to his former idea. He had earmarked his last composition for the Orfeó Català to be sung at the Monastery of Santa María de Ripoll.

MARIO VERDAGUER

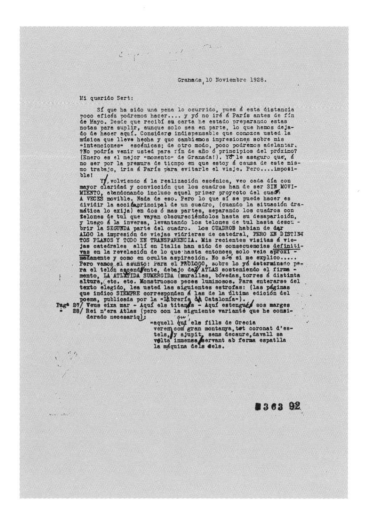

MY DEAR Sert:

Indeed, what has happened is a shame, and at this distance there is very little we can do about it... and I am not going to Paris until the end of May. Since I received your letter I have been preparing these notes to make up, if only in part, for what we have neglected to do here. I consider it essential for you to hear the music I have finished so that we can exchange views about my scenic "aims"; if not, there is not much we can do. Could you come and visit me at the end of the year or at the beginning (Granada is at its "best" in January!) of the next? I assure you that if I were not under such pressure because of this work, I would go to Paris to save you the trip. But.....it is impossible!

Coming back to the scenery, every day I become more clearly convinced that the scenes should be WITH-OUT MOVEMENT, abandoning even that initial idea of OCCA-SIONALLY movable scenes. None of that. But what we can do is divide the main action of a scene (when the dramatic situation demands it), into two or three parts, separating the scenes with a tulle curtain and blacking them out until they disappear, and afterwards the opposite, lifting the tulle curtains to reveal the second part of the scene. The scenes should allude to the old stained glass windows of a cathedral, BUT FROM MANY DIFFERENT ANGLES AND COMPLETELY TRANSPARENT. My recent visits to old cathedrals in Italy have proved highly useful in revealing what, up to then, I could only vaguely discern, like a hidden desire. I do not know if I am making myself clear... But here goes: For the PROLOGUE, over what we already decided for the rising curtain, under ATLAS supporting the firmament, ATLANTIS SUBMERGED (walls, vaults, towers of various heights, etc, etc. Monstrous luminous fish. To see what text goes here, read the following stanzas: the pages I refer to ALWAYS correspond to the most recent edition of the poem, published by the "Librería de Catalonía".)

Page 27/ *Veus eixa mar* — Aquí els titans — *Aquí estengue sos marges*

Page 28/ *Rei n'era Atlas* (but with the following alteration which I felt necessary):

"aquell qu'els fills de Grecia
verem com gran montanya, tot coronat d'estels,/
y ajupit sens decaure, davall sa volta inmensa/
servant ab ferma espatlla la máquina dels cels."

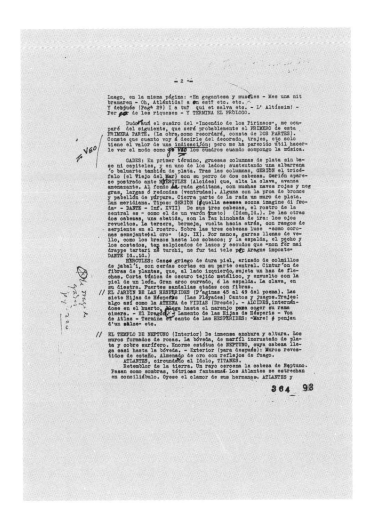

Then, further down on the same page: "*En gegantesa y muscles — mes una nit bramaren — Oh, Atlántida! a on est? etc, etc.*"

And later (page 29) *I a tu? qui et salva*, etc. —*L'Altíssim!* — *Per po de les riqueses*— END OF THE PROLOGUE.

I have not made my mind up about the scene for the "Incendio de los Pirineos", so I will jump to the next, which will probably be the FIRST of this FIRST PART (The piece, you will no doubt remember, consists of two parts). Please bear in mind that whatever I say concerning scenery, costumes etc, is only intended as an *indication*; but I found it useful in order to show you how I IMAGINE the scenes when I am composing the music.

GADES: Downstage, thick silver pillars with neither base nor head, one on each side holding up silver ramparts or a silver bastion. Behind the pillars, Geryon the three—headed (the Old Man of the Sea) with his two—headed dog. GERYON appears prostrate before HERCULES (Alcides) who, with his club raised, advances threateningly. In the distance the bay of Cadiz, with lots of big, round (pot-bellied) ships painted red and black. Some with a bronze prow and purple bunting. A silver wall encloses part of the bay. Midday light. Characteristics: GERYON (*quella sozza imagine di froda* —DANTE— Inf. XVII). One of his three heads, the middle one, is "like a honest man" (Ibid.). One of the other two is downcast and with a face swollen with rage: Its eyes roll. This third is bright red and bent back, with features like a snake's. On the heads glitter "three crowns like gold"

(Ap. IX). His clawed hands an arms are covered by hair up to his armpits: his back, his chest and flanks are so bedecked with ribbons and shields that "*non fêr mai drappe tartari ne turchi, ne fur tai tele per Aragne imposte*" (DANTE, Ibid.).

HERCULES: A Greek helmet of hardened leather, bristling with boars teeth and with a pighair crest down the middle. A belt of plant fibre which, on his left, holds a quiver of arrows. A short dark metalic—coloured tunic, covered by a lion skin. A great bow, on his back. The club in his right hand. Hard wearing sandals laced with plant fibres.

THE GARDEN OF THE HESPERIDES (pages 45 and 49 of the poem). The seven daughters of Hesperis (the pleiades). Songs and games. Costumes: Similar to those worn by

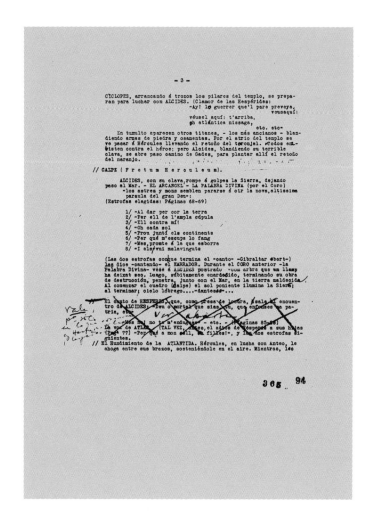

the ATHENA by PHIDIAS (Dresden). —ALCIDES enters the grove, reaches the orange tree to pick from the highest branch. —The dragon. —Lament of the daughters of Hesperis. —Voice of Atlas. —End of the song of the Hesperides: *"Mare! penjau d'un salze"* etc.

THE TEMPLE OF NEPTUNE (Inside). Enormous width and height. The walls are formed out of the rocks. The vaulted ceiling is made of marble encrusted with silver and copper containing gold. An enormous statue of NEPTUNE, whose head reaches the vaulted ceiling. Exterior (for later): walls are coated with tin. Golden battlements with reflections like fire.

ATLANTES, surrounding the idol, TITANS.

The ground shakes. A bolt of lightening decapitates Neptune. Dismal phantoms pass like shadows. The AT-

LANTES approach each other to hold council. The clamour of their sisters is heard. The ATLANTES and the CYCLOPS tear out pieces of the pillars from the temple. They prepare for the fight against ALCIDES. (Clamour of the Hesperides):

"Ay! lo guerrer que'l pare preveya, veusaquí.
veusel aquí. t'arriba,
oh atlántica nissaga, etc, etc."

In the tumult other titans appear, —the most ancient— brandishing weapons made of stone and skeletons. Hercules can be seen passing the temple vestibule carrying a newly sprouting fruit tree. They all fall upon the hero, but Alcides, brandishing his terrible club, clears his way through to Gades (Cadiz), to plant the sprouting orange tree there.

CALPE (Fretum Herculeum)

ALCIDES, with his club breaks the mountains, opening a breach to the sea. THE ARCHANGEL. —THE DIVINE WORD (by the Chorus).

"los astres y mons semblen parase á oir la nova, altissima paraula del gran Deu":

(Cosend stanzas: pages 68—69)

1/ "Al dar per cor la terra

2/ "Per ell de l'ampla cúpula

3/ "Ell contra mí!

4/ "Oh cada sol

5/ "Prou juntí els continents

6/ "Per qué m'escups lo fang

7/ "Mes, promte á la que esborra

8/ "I els vui malavinguts

(The two stanzas which end the "canto" —Gibral-

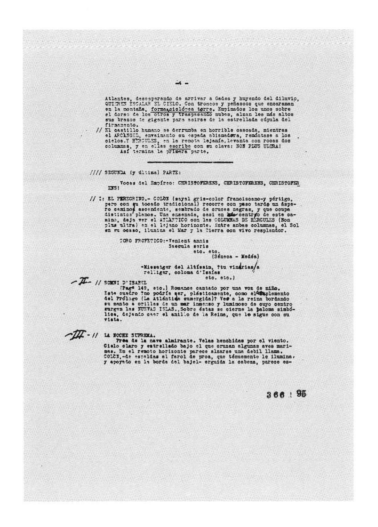

tar obert—) The NARRATOR sings them. During the previous CHORUS —the Divine Word— ALCIDES is prostrated "*com arbre que un llamp ha deixat sec.* Then, suddenly aroused, finishing his work of destruction, he reaches by sea the accursed land. To begin the scene (Calpe) a setting sun illuminates the Sierra, to finish it: gloomy sky…Dantesque…

The sinking of ATLANTIS. Hercules fights against Anteus, he strangles him holding him up in the air. Meanwhile, the Atlantes, desperate to reach Gades and fleeing the flood, WANT TO CLIMB TO HEAVEN. They place tree trunks and boulders on the mountaintop to form a tower. Perched on each others shoulders they reach beyond the clouds to stretch out their giant hands to hold the starred vault of the firmament.

The human tower falls down in a horrible human cascade, while the ARCHANGEL, sheathing his abysmal word, rises once more to heaven. HERCULES in the distance erects two pillars from rocks, and inscribes on them with his club: NON PLUS ULTRA!

End of the first part.

SECOND (and last) PART:

Heavenly Voices : CHRISTOFERENS, CHRISTOFERENS, CHRISTOFERENS!

I: THE PILGRIM. —COLUMBUS (grey coloured Franciscan sack-cloth and a staff, but wearing Columbus' hat) walks slowly up the steep uneven path, full of black crosses,

which rises on different levels. A bay, almost in the centre of this path allows one to see the ATLANTIC ocean with HERCULES' PILLARS (*Non plus ultra*) on the distant horizon. Between both pillars the setting sun lights the sea and the earth with vivid intensity.

PROPHETIC CHORUS: —*Veniant annis*
Saeculaseris,
etc, etc.
(Seneca -*Medea*)
Missatger del Altíssim, tu vindrias a relligar, coloma d'Isaías,
etc, etc.

II: *SOMNI D'ISABEL.*
(Page 148, etc.) Romance sung by a child's voice.

— 5 —

cruzar évidamente el Cielo y el Mar immensos.
CORO MISTICO: -Credidi, propter quod locutus sum:-etc.
    (Ps.115)

  -Non timebo millia populi
    (Id. III-6)

  -Ecce Deus, salvator meus,
    (Is. XII-2)

  Himno: -Ave Maria Stella-

  VOCES PROFETICAS: -Qui sunt isti, qui ut nubes volant, et quasi columbas etc. etc.
    -Me amis insulae expectant, etc.
    (Is.LX.8-9)

// IV (y último). EL DESCUBRIMIENTO
  La Tierra de América. Bosque espléndido (¿de altisimas
palmeras?) en la costa. Al fondo, las proas de las tres Cara-
belas con sus Capitanes (barba poblada; ricos trajes y armas)
y sus gentes; todos de rodillas y en actitud de adoración.
En la nave del centro -la -Santa María-, COLON, revestido de
las insignias de Almirante, erguido y como transfigurado, con
los brazos en cruz sobre el pecho. A su lado, un Capitán de
bandera, de rodillas, sostiene, enhiesto, el Pendón Real de
Fernando e Isabel.
  Una espesa nube envuelve la visión. Luego, gradualmente,
la nube se disipa, descubriendo una inmensa Catedral. Los ár-
boles (¿palmeras?) del bosque se han convertido en altas co-
lumnas, pero los bajeles siguen ocupando el fondo, y cuantos
llenan sus proas conservan la misma primera actitud. Los se-
pulcros del templo (la Catedral Hispánica) se han abierto, y
aparecen, resucitando, los héroes ibéricos: los Capitanes, los
Navegantes, los Santos y los Reyes de gloriosa historia.
  VOCES DEL EMPIREO - VOCES DE LA TIERRA: -Hosanna in excelsis. Benedictus qui venit in nomine Domine. HOSANNA IN ALTISSI-
MUS!
    et. est. etc.

  Y por hoy he terminado, querido Sert, tres días después de em-
pezar la carta... Después de leer estas notas (que le comunico
MUY RESERVADAMENTE) usted me dirá lo que de ellas piensa con
relación á su trabajo. Pero puedo asegurarle que corresponden
exactamente al mío. Insisto en que creo indispensable que nos
veamos, tanto para determinar todo como para que oiga usted lo
que llevo hecho, que es bastante, aunque aún me quede muchísimo

367   96

Could this scene not be in physical form a complement to the Prologue (Atlantis submerged)? I imagine the Queen sowing her mantle by the shores of an immense bright sea in the middle of which the NEW ISLANDS emerge. Over these islands flies the symbolic dove that drops the Queen's ring, which she follows with her gaze.

III: THE SUPREME NIGHT.

The prow of the flagship. Sails billowing in the wind. A clear and starry sky under which no sea birds cross. On the distant horizon a weak flame seems to rise up. COLUMBUS —his back to the prow lamp, which illuminates him dimly and leaning on the board of the boat— his head held high seems to study avidly the immense Sky and Sea.

MYSTIC CHORUS: —*Credidi, propter quod locutus sum*, etc (page 115).

—*Non timebo millis populi.* (Ibid. III—6)

—*Ecce Deus, salvator meus.* (Ibid. XII-2)

Hymn: —*Ave Maria Stella.*

PROPHETIC VOICES: —*Qui sunt isti, qui ut nubes volant, et quasi columbas* etc, etc.

—*Me amis insulae expectant*, etc. (Ibid. LX. 8-9)

IV (and last). THE DISCOVERY

The Land of America. Splendid wood (of very tall palm trees?) on the coast. In the background, the prows of the three caravels with their Captains (bushy beard; rich clothes and weapons) and their crew; all kneeling in a reverence. In the ship that is in the centre: the Santa María: COLUMBUS with the insignia of an admiral standing upright and as if transfigured with his arms crossed over his chest. Beside him, a flag Captain, kneeling, holds up high Fernando and Isabel's Royal Standard.

A thick cloud covers the vision. Afterwards, the cloud gradually disipates to reveal a huge Cathedral. The trees (palm trees?) in the wood have been transformed into tall pillars, but the ships are still in the background, and all of the people filling their prows maintain the same position as before. The tombs in the temple (the Hispanic Cathedral) have opened, and the Iberian heroes are resuscitated and appear: the Captains, the Navigators, the Saints and the Kings of glorious history.

VOICES FROM HEAVEN — VOICES FROM EARTH:

—*Hosanna in excelsis. Benedictus qui venet in*

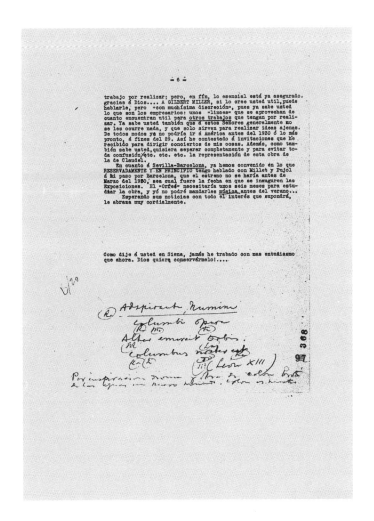

nomine Domine. HOSANNA IN ALTISSIMUS! etc, etc, etc.

And I have finished for today, dear Sert, three days after I started the letter... After reading these notes (which I communicate to you VERY CONFIDENTIALLY). You can tell me what you think about them with respect to your work. But I can assure you that they correspond exactly to mine. I insist that I consider it indispensible that we see each other, both to fix everything and for you to hear what I have already done, which is rather a lot, even if I still have loads of work to do; but, in short, the essential part is already secured, thank God... If you think that it will prove useful you can speak to GILBERT MILLER, but "with the greatest discretion" because you know what producers are like: "lynxes" who take advantage of whatever they find convenient for other productions they have in mind. You know as well that in general these gentlemen do not have many original ideas, and they are only of use to realise other people's ideas. Anyway I would not be able to go to America before 1930 or at the soonest at the end of 1929. I have replied thus to the invitations I have received to conduct concerts of my works. Moreover, as you also know, I would like to completely separate, to avoid any confusion, etc, etc, etc, the performance of this piece from the one by Claudel.

Concerning Seville - Barcelona, we already agreed about what I had said CONFIDENTIALLY AND IN THEORY to Millet and Pujol while I was in Barcelona: that the première cannot take place before 1930, whatever the opening date might be for the Exhibitions. The "*Orfeó*" will need at least six months to rehearse the piece, and I would not be able to send them the music before summer...

Looking forward with great interest to hearing from you, my sincere wishes.

As I told you in Sienna, I have never worked more enthusiastically than now. God help me keep it up!...

MANUEL DE FALLA
Letter to José María Sert
[Granada, 10 November 1928]

Manuel de Falla disembarks on the Sancti Petri Island, Cadiz, accompanied by José María Pemán, 1930.

IN SEARCH OF THE TEMPLE OF HERCULES
(FALLA THE COMPOSER AND HIS *ATLÁNTIDA*)

THE GREAT Cadiz born composer Manuel de Falla is writing a choral poem based on the *Atlántida* by Minister Jacinto Verdaguer.

He came from Granada to Cadiz to conduct a concert. He stayed in Cadiz for a few days and he used them to soak up the noise of the Ocean. Every morning and afternoon he went to the beach and watched and listened, in silence, to the whispering waves as they approached him: minute after minute... He never had enough.

"I prefer the murmur of gentle waves lapping the shore: not the sound of those that crash against the breakwaters and walls. That is the sea's dialogue with stone. Whereas the first is the monologue of a lonely sea which was there when the world was created and will be there when it ends..."

Falla told us this on the "La Barrosa" beach, a perfect blue bay, sheltered by pine trees, while he ate a plate of fried prawns. We decided to have lunch on the beach before we embarked on a boat trip to the small island of Sancti Petri.

The island of Sancti Petri is some twenty minutes by boat from the mainland. Against the dusk, its rocks resemble the fearful silhouette of a whale. On the island there is an uninhabited castle and a lighthouse. Why did we go to visit the island of Sancti Petri? I think it is easy to guess: we went in search of the Temple of Hercules...

Falla wanted to see for himself the place where the famous temple, dedicated to the hero of his poem, had been built. Rumour has it that the Temple of Hercules was built on the island of Sancti Petri. For some archaeologists this seems probable and, for others, doubtful. But poets and composers prefer not to dispute its location.

We boarded the small steam boat of a nearby fishing port. It had a tall and pointed prow, with a red-cut water, suitably evocative and decorative for our mission.

During our voyage, one of the passengers, an expert in Cadiz archaeology, explained the theory of Tarshish and Atlantis. The German archaeologist Shulten searched in vain for the rich and legendary Tarshish among the dunes and palm trees of the Doñana reserve. The characteristics of the geographical location of Tarshish described during the journey of old Rufo Festo Aviene (the two islands and four openings to the sea), are in general more applicable to Cadiz than Doñana, bearing in mind the position of the sea in this region in olden times. Tarshish was here, a world trade centre: where ships mentioned in the Bible came for tin.

But, later, the Phoenicians conquered the beautiful and peaceful kingdom whose laws were written in verse. Laws in verse do nothing to help protect a kingdom against foreign invasion. The Phoenicians, in order to hide the news of their rich conquest of the tin empire from greedy nations, propagated the fable that the legendary kingdom, whose fame would stretch to the Orient, was not there; that it was an enchanted kingdom which, in former times, had been located in the middle of the Atlantic Ocean, until the waves had covered it. As a result of this the legend of Atlantis emerged, retold later, so wonderfully, by Plato. In other words, the origin of Atlantis was a bluff, employed for trade reasons; a bit like the false news released nowadays to keep the peseta down.

But Falla was not satisfied with this explanation. He wanted poetry to mix with science in relation to Atlantis and he was sorry that archaeology had to be so disrespectful with Plato. But this is of no matter. In this duel, poetic truth is always the final victor. Don Quixote is truer than the *Conde Duque de Olivares* (Count Duke of Olivares). I comforted the Maestro:

"Don't worry, Don Manuel. In the end *Atlántida* (Atlantis) will be exactly like Plato, Verdaguer and you have always wanted it to be."

We jumped from the steam boat into a rowing boat. We rowed over the famous "hull-breaking" stones (the temple aslars?), where two years ago a diver had fished out a bronze statue. Then we arrived at Sancti Petri. There is no pier on the island. One has to draw the boat up on the beach. The rower, with his feet in the water, took us from the boat, in his arms, strengthened by the magnificent exercise of rowing, and transported us, through the air, like puppets, to the sand. This was a primitive and mythological scene. Falla's small and trembling body, stood uncertainly at the prow of the boat, before giving himself over to the strong man. He asked innocently:

"Do you think he will be able to manage with me?"

The voice of one of the group answered:

"Maestro: He could manage with Wagner, but I don't know if he can manage with you."

The old fort of Sancti Petri and the island on which it is built, are half demolished by the sea's biting attacks. On the part facing the southern storms there is an enormous riff and inside one can see the different layers of the formation of the island. It is like a brief geological compendium. One of these layers, which is black like "humus", is the one in which archaeological discoveries are invariably made. Easy to excavate, one could almost say, especially prepared by the National Tourist Board to meet the demands of archaeological activities. Urns, carved stones, earrings and necklaces have been brought

out of this layer. Rumour has it that they are remains from the Temple of Hercules.

We wanted to share, for an instant, the gloriously intoxicating experience of the rebirth of objects which is what archaeological excavation is. That intoxication, so masterfully described by d'Annunzio, in which "an antique and violent life" is relived. We dug a little into the black earth, and almost at once we pulled out a slightly curved piece of china. A fine, smooth, feminine piece, red like a September holidaymaker's skin. The archaeologist explained that it might be the piece of a funerary urn of the Temple of Hercules. The temple was in Tarshish, and Tarshish is the origin of Atlantis. Thus, in a moment, Falla, stroking the fine clay shell, extended the slight curve towards noble and florid dreams...

The enigmatic antique piece made him loquacious, like Don Quixote with his handful of acorns. He spoke to us lovingly and enthusiastically about his planned composition: the entrance of Hercules, the fire in the Pyrenees, the chant in Barcelona, the song of the seven Pleiades; Hercules the victor, running to Spain with the uppermost branch of the golden orange tree; the rupture of the Strait of Gibraltar. Then, about the Atlantes, forming a human tower to climb to heaven. When they reached the top, the voice of God was heard. Falla shivered as he said it (can you imagine the immense pledge to perfection and care implied by the words "God is heard" for a composer of Falla's artistic integrity?). "And the voice of God", continued Falla, "began the famous Verdaguerian verse: 'Atlantes: you must perish ...'"

Falla broke off. The noise of the sea could be heard. Then he finished with striking simplicity:

"I want the chorus to sing that part kneeling..."

We went back to the boat. Sancti Petri stood out against tragic clouds, which seemed to fight a naval battle in the twilight. The sun started to set.

"They say that old Poseidon", the archaeologist told us, "came to Cadiz to watch the sun set on the Atlantic. He had been told that as the sun sank into the waves, it hissed tremendously like molten iron when it is submerged in water. He went to Cadiz and watched the sun go down, but they say he heard nothing."

Neither did we hear the sun hiss as it set on that memorable afternoon when, accompanying the great Andalusian composer and master of strange harmonies, I went in search of the Temple of Hercules.

JOSÉ MARÍA PEMÁN

THE ORIGIN OF FALLA'S *ATLÁNTIDA*, "CANTATA FOR ORCHESTRA, SOLOISTS AND CHOIR"

I OFTEN LIVED with the composer Felipe Pedrell, because of the great friendship he had with my father, that bordered on familiarity. Pedrell spent long periods in our country house where he wrote some of his works, among them the opera *La Celestina*, which is not well

Juan Gisbert and his son with Felipe Pedrell.

known. He witnessed my birth, and I his death. During this time I had the opportunity to learn many things about music, because all his conversations centred on the same theme. In his house I saw many composers, who received his wise lessons, file past, among them Manuel de Falla, whom he singled out, admired and for whom he professed great esteem on account of his talent and unaffected personal conduct. In one of my conversations with Pedrell, I perfectly remember him telling me that the only one of them he thought I should continue with in the way I had been doing, was with Don Manuel de Falla. That is what I did, following his advice and habits, and that is how my friendship with Manuel de Falla, most kind and close until his death, came about. Manuel de Falla was Pedrell's favourite student, for whom he professed a deep fondness because, as well as his musical talent, he possessed a great humanitarian feeling and exceptional goodness. In this manner I became such good friends with Don Manuel that, on his travels abroad, I was often the only person to accompany him to the first nights. Only once he was accompanied by his sister María del Carmen. Not one of those who today boast to have

been his friend ever accompanied him, to the point that when he departed for Buenos Aires with his sister, on the 2nd of October 1939, the only people who went to the port to see the ship off were my late wife, my daughter Carmen and I; no one else. Don Manuel carried a folder which contained *Atlántida*; when asked to show his passport he handed the folder to my daughter, telling her: "Don't lose this, Carmen. Lose yourself rather than lose it."

First suggestion

When the Festival of the International Society of Contemporary Music, held in Zurich in 1926 finished we went to Milan. On the train we spoke about countless things, among them how he had made *La vida breve* and *Love the Magician* for Andalusia; *The Three-cornered Hat* for Aragon, and *Master Peter's Puppet Show* for Castile. He was very interested in the idea of composing something for Catalonia, which he loved deeply, in response to the continual tokens of affection and kindness he had been given in Barcelona. And though Pedrell had encouraged him to compose an opera about the life of Raimundo Lulio, that did not conform to his rules of conduct because Lulio's life had been somewhat unorthodox. It was at that moment that I suggested he do *Atlántida*, and he answered that even though he had heard of it, he had not read it and neither could he do so because, on the one hand, he did not have a copy and, on the other, he did not speak Catalan.

I answered him that I would sort everything out. When we both arrived back in Spain, we separated in Barcelona and he went on to Granada. The first thing I did was to send him a copy of *L'Atlántida*, and a short while later he asked me to send him a Catalan-Spanish dictionary from the time of Minister Jacinto Verdaguer. The only one that existed was the Labernia one, and immediately I set to work to try to find him a copy. After a long search, I was able to find one, which I sent him without losing any time. At this moment he began composing it. A few months went by and we went to Paris, in order to celebrate Manuel de Falla's fiftieth birthday. At the Comic Opera they organised some events with programmes of his compositions: *La vida breve*, *Love the Magician* and *Master Peter's Puppet Show*. On this journey we were accompanied by Marshall. While we were eating at a restaurant Falla announced that he had begun *Atlántida*.

The Hesperides play with the golden oranges

On the various visits I made to Granada we always exchanged impressions about the work. I remember that during one visit he asked me to explain the meaning of

the word "*jull*" which is in the "second canto" of "The orchard of the Hesperides", verse number 34, because he could not find it in the Labernia Dictionary. I explained that it was the word used by children when jumping a skipping rope, when they want to go faster. He told me that in Andalusia they used the word "*tocino*", and as he said this he glowed with joy because he assured me he had the feeling that the music would speed up from that moment on. During another trip when I visited Antequeruela Alta, where he lived, a new servant who did not recognise me opened the door while Don Manuel was playing the piano. I sat in the garden and waited for him to finish playing the piano; then, after we had greeted each other, he asked me if I had been waiting for long, and I replied that I had been waiting all the time he was playing. He asked me what I thought about the music I had overheard, and I told him that it sounded like a children's game. Then he told me that it was the part that describes the Hesperides playing with the golden oranges in the orchard.

Interview with the maestro Millet

On one of the trips that Don Manuel made to Barcelona, he was very interested in the idea of holding an interview with Luis Millet. I accompanied him to the Palau de la Música, where they spoke for a good while. Millet asked him how he had dealt with the choral part of *Atlántida*. He explained in technical terms how he had written it, and I vividly remember the reply he received: "Holy Mary", exclaimed Millet, putting his hands to his head expressively: "I'll need four months to rehearse the choral part". During the same visit, when the painter José María Sert was at Marshall's house, he played all the music he had composed. It had a surprising effect. We also went with Sert to the Gran Teatro del Liceo to study what form the stage designs for the piece should take. I have details of all that was spoken there.

A long while afterwards, he visited Barcelona once again, the last time before leaving for America. In my house he played all that he had composed (which was not a great deal more than on the previous visit), on the piano that had belonged to Pedrell, which he was very fond of asking me to take note of the duration in minutes of each fragment.

Manuel de Falla's letters

On the 6th of October 1927 Falla wrote me a letter asking me for the following: "I am going to allow myself to ask you to do me another favour, dear Don Juan, as it is very urgent. Could you send me another copy of *Atlántida* by Verdaguer. If there is an edition in Catalan which includes a translation into Castilian Spanish, as I am led to believe, this would be the best. Perhaps each version (the original and the translation) is published separately. Perhaps it only exists in Catalan, if this is the case I would still like you to send me it, as I cannot wait for it to appear in both languages. In short: I leave the affair in your capable hands." A few days later I found the edition he wanted and sent it off straight away and he carried on working using this copy. This is the same edition which Halffter is working with today. On the 18th of October of the same year the following reply arrived: "You cannot imagine how grateful I am for the kindness and efficiency with which you have responded to my request. You have bettered all my hopes by sending me such a pretty and curious edition of the poem translated into Castilian Spanish."

An improvised stave

Of the many anecdotes that I could tell, one of the most curious ones is the following: on one of the trips he made to Barcelona a long time before I went to wait for him in Valencia, we caught the express train together, which stopped for a long spell in Cambrils because the engine had to be filled with water. While we were there a poor man came round begging for money, playing a small recorder, a fact which interested Falla enormously, so much so that he took out his mileage book and noted down what he heard. A few years later, after he had commenced writing *Atlántida*, he told me that he had used those melodies in the composition.

On my recent trip to Milan I had the pleasure of spending quite some time with Don Manuel's only disciple, my great friend Halffter, who played the whole of *Atlántida*, now that it is completely finished, at the piano. Words do not exist to describe the magnitude of the piece. It has been orchestrated from beginning to end, and there are only a few last touches to be made before it is published by the firm Ricordi.

The piece starts off with a prologue, with Atlantis "submerged" and a *Himno Hipánicus* for choir and orchestra. The first part consists of "The Pyrenees fire" and the "Canticle for Barcelona", which is a marvellous hymn, completely choral. The second part is longer: "Hercules and Geryon", "The orchard of the Hesperides", "The dragon", "The Atlantes in the Temple of Neptune", "Hercules pursued", "*Gades Anteo*", "*Fretum Herculeum*", "The divine voice", "The sinking" and "*Non plus ultra*". The third part is made up by "The pilgrim", "Isabel's dream", "The caravels", "Praise the sea" and "The supreme night", the verge of discovery, end of the piece.

I went to the publishers Ricordi with Halffter to visit the director general, the engineer Guido Valcarengui, a very intelligent and pleasant man, who also speaks

Manuel de Falla with Juan Gisbert.

fluent Spanish, which was an advantage because we had a long and very interesting conversation. We spoke about the première of *Atlántida* and, even though it would have been better for him to arrange it for Italy he agreed, after the many reasons we gave him, that it should be produced beforehand in Barcelona, at the Gran Teatro del Liceo, with the "Orfeó Catalá", Victoria de los Ángeles and if possible the baritone Manuel Ausensi, along with

other singers, which are called for in the work, to play the various characters in the cantata. After this a concert of the main parts would be held in Cadiz and then at the Scala in Milan.

Juan Gisbert

SOMETIMES Falla spoke to me about his gigantic composition which had completely absorbed him for years: *Atlántida*. He told little bits about some of the themes he had just finished working on; I had the impression that this was a remarkable work, perhaps more important than any other he had composed. It was a two hour long oratorio in which, in his opinion, choral parts played the most important rôle. It was a kind of canticle of two worlds, a mystical cantata based on the story of a city covered by the sea. Falla spoke to me and to other friends, in particular Juan José Castro, about *Atlántida*, but he did not show any of us a single sheet of the score. This is why the piece has become shrouded in such mystery since his death and even today, seven years, no one has been able to cast any light on it.

It did not surprise us that Manuel de Falla felt deeply attracted by this material. There are many reasons which verified this in a broader sense: Falla was born in Cadiz, a city that plays a fundamental part in Verdaguer's poem; Falla was a hundred percent Spanish, from a nation which would occupy a strategic position in the world, after the sinking of Atlantis, as it became the frontier of two continents. But all this was beside the point because Falla felt attracted to *Atlántida* principally as a creative artist and this legend —which the world has spoken about for a couple of centuries and will carry on speaking about— struck a note quite logically with his imagination. The theme of *Atlántida* had the same strength as the events which Richard Wagner put on stage in his *Nibelungs Ring* cycle.

KURT PAHLEN

These photographs of the Macchu-Picchu ruins, Cuzco, Peru, deeply impressed Manuel de Falla, who asked me for some copies because, in his opinion, they were the only thing that really resembled Atlantis and the scenography which he had imagined for his composition. When he saw the breathtaking photograph *(reproduced on the right)* he said over and over again: "That is Atlantis! That is Atlantis!" The other photograph reminded him of the foundations of the famous tower which was raised by the Atlantes. (An explanatory note written by Sergio de Castro about the photographs which he gave Manuel de Falla a few months before the composer's death.)

ERNESTO HALFFTER SPEAKS ABOUT *ATLÁNTIDA*

WE HAVE proof of the many years Falla devoted to his composition *Atlántida* here in his manuscripts. They reveal the point which the composer's work had reached. On one page one can see when he began composing *Atlántida*, the 29th of December 1928; another page is dated the 8th of July 1946 and corresponds to the "aria del Pirineo" in the first part of the work. These are probably the last pages written by Falla. This means, evidently, that Falla worked for almost eighteen years to complete his effort. I am convinced that Falla had a clear idea of the finished work, and I can show this by reference to various conversations and even to the letters which he wrote me. For example: in a conversation with José María Sert (who was going to be the designer of the scenery and costumes of *Atlántida*), he told me that he had heard the entire piece played by Falla on the piano. Moreover, the last letter that I received from the composer a month before he died said textually: "I am doing everything I can to try to finish my poor *Atlántida* which has been interrupted so often because of my health." Falla had such a sincere and precise nature and what he was trying to tell me with these words was that the majority of the piece was finished. It is obvious, contrary to the opinion expressed by some people, that Falla wanted to give his work a scenic form; this has been testified to by his conversations with me and others, and as well by written documents. The contract signed on the 12th of January 1929 between Manuel de Falla represented by Juan Gisbert Padró, and Verdaguer's heirs, stipulates that permission be given "for a musical and theatrical adaptation" of the poem *Atlántida*.

If this is not sufficient proof, we also have the correspondence between Manuel de Falla and José María Sert, in which Falla explains his ideas about the theatrical representation of the piece to the eminent Spanish painter. We have, for example, Falla's letter to Sert dated the 10th of November 1928, which is an enormously important document, because not only does Falla give a general scenic overview, but he also refers to costume details, etc.

Falla died on the 14th of November 1946. In 1954, after Falla's heirs had turned down various composers' proposals to finish the piece, they insisted that I finish *Atlántida*. I was, in fact, Falla's only student and the com-

Ernesto Halffter, at Mme Alvar's house in London, 1921.

poser had named me conductor of the Andalusian Orchestra, founded by him in 1923, when I was seventeen years old. He placed such trust in me that I was sent to conduct in London, Buenos Aires, Germany and France and he set me very tricky tasks such as the orchestration of *Seven Popular Songs* and the *Fantasia Bætica*. He trusted me implicitly throughout his life. The proof of this is that he sent me a copy of the original manuscript of his orchestral "suite" from *Homenajes*, so that I could conduct its European première. Thus, it was quite natural that his heirs should trust me with the enormous responsibility of finishing *Atlántida*. For my part, I accepted, feeling excited and touched, because I consider that Falla's *Atlántida* was his most universal piece. It would be a genuine crime to leave unfinished a work that contains such a great amount of musical material. I felt truly obliged to finish *Atlántida* because I was linked to the composer by filial affection and also because I wanted it to be heard.

The task, naturally, has been an arduous one. I had

to search for an understanding of Falla's aims and make an effort to be up to the task of joining myself to that quintessential music which was worthy of Falla's last composition.

I wanted to take into account the following considerations about the content of *Atlántida*.

1. In *Atlántida*, the musical elements which Falla considered eternal and which connect him to the world of tonal music dominate. Without denying the cultural interest of dodecaphonic experiments, he preserved "tonality" as the fundamental base of the music.

2. In Falla, contrary to what is generally thought, folk elements are a stimulus which the composer uses by taking themes and transforming them into stylistically evolved forms. For example, in "Isabel's dream" the departure point is a mixture of two folk songs: a theme from Granada and a Catalan folk song. But the musical creation has all the hallmarks of Falla.

3. Falla based his last composition on the modes of the great Spanish age of polyphony. Falla, who was deeply religious, a true example of Christian humility, abstained from writing sacred music, fearing that he would not be able to express his mystical beliefs. However, he was concerned by the low standard of religious music in Spain and wanted *Atlántida* to show what sacred music could and should express. One should consider the beautiful choirs particularly in "Praise the sea" based on a text by Alfonso the Wise and which refers musically to the 11th and 12th century style.

4. Falla wanted *Atlántida* to be part of the "mystery" tradition or the tradition of sacred medieval representation which is more extended in Spain than in any other country with the famous "*autos sacramentales*" of the Golden Age; thus, he wanted a secular and religious representation performed in the church or in the public square for all the population.

Of Falla's total output *Atlántida* rates as his most universal creation which is beyond any limitations and any national or stylistic debates. In it, Falla tried to sum up his last lesson of truth to what had always been his ideals; ideals which were tonal as regards musical language and Christian as regards his spiritual ideology. That is the lesson he wanted to give with *Atlántida*: to show younger generations that it is possible to achieve a new expression in the continuity of tradition which allows man to find himself in the consciousness of his destiny.

E.H.

WHEN FALLA DIED IN NOVEMBER 1946, MANY MANUSCRIPTS, WITH A NUMBER OF FINISHED PARTS, THE
FRUIT OF INTENSE WORK, WERE DISCOVERED. ERNESTO HALFFTER, WHO HAD BEEN THE COMPOSER'S
STUDENT IN THE 1920'S, WAS COMMISSIONED TO DO THE FINAL VERSION WHICH WAS FIRST PER-
FORMED AT THE GRAN TEATRO DEL LICEO, IN A CONCERT VERSION, ON THE 24TH OF NOVEMBER 1961,
AND IN THE STAGE VERSION AT THE SCALA IN MILAN IN 1962.

**Inauguration of the National Music Auditorium in Madrid, 27th of October 1988,
with an interpretation of *Atlántida* and programme from the first performance
on 24th of November 1961 at the Gran Teatro del Liceo in Barcelona.**

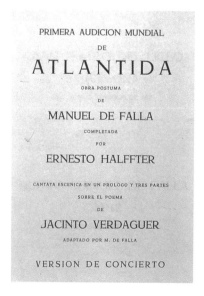

F R A N C I S
POULENC

talks about

M A N U E L   D E
FALLA

CONVERSATION WITH
STÉPHANE AUDEL IN 1963

From left to right: Francis Poulenc, Valentine Hugo, J. Hugo, Jean Cocteau, Darius Milhaud and George Auric.

STÉPHANE AUDEL.– *We have evoked Erik Satie and Max Jacob. We have disclosed the duality of poet and composer, and above all their mysticism. Platonic in Satie and Christian in Jacob, but profoundly sincere in both cases.*

I warn you: Today I'm going to question you about the mysticism of Manuel de Falla, a subject which might seem disconcerting at first because Falla remains, to the majority, the marvellous conjurer of legendary Spain, the land of Love the Magician, *of* La vida breve *and of* The Three-cornered Hat.

This Spain is very different to the Spain of Theresa of Ávila, or of Saint Ignatius of Loyola. Every Spaniard carries in his blood a fervent religiosity, but I would like you to explain to me the reasons which made you state that Manuel de Falla was a great mystic.

FRANCIS POULENC.– Well, approaching Falla about his mysticism is an ambitious way of tackling the subject, but that stance, though a little abrupt, doesn't make me uncomfortable, and I have nothing against it myself.

In the first place there has never been country more full of violent contradictions than Spain. In Spain you can pray with all your might to the Virgin, burn a forest of candles to her honour and go off to kill your rival immediately after.

The false image of Spain is that of sun, oranges, guitars and Granada's shawls and flowers.

As in bullfights, the arena is divided into two parts: Sun and shade. There is a "sun" Spain and a "shade" Spain.

These two areas mix at times in an unpredictable manner. Earlier you mentioned Saint Theresa of Ávila; well, did you know that Saint Theresa advised her Carmelites to dance to the tune of guitars and castanets, to keep body and soul healthy? The Spanish Carmelites keep this tradition which came from that time.

In a recent French translation of the book *The Foundations of Saint Theresa of Ávila*, one can admire the beautiful photographs by Yvonne Chevalier. Inside a convent one sees a number of young Carmelites, with castanets in their hands, dancing to a tune played by the prioress on the guitar.

Once this principle of contrasts has been demonstrated, we can more easily admit that Falla's mysticism is juxtaposed to the picturesque aspect which characterises him. What is most admirable in Falla is precisely the fact that his picturesque side is never on the surface, as it is with

painter Ignacio Zuloaga, but rather hidden deep in his flesh, as it is with Goya. Yes, Falla was a great mystic, and the last image I have of him is of a man, or better, of one of Zurbarán's Friars, praying in a church in Venice.

S. A.– *Why, in Venice?*

F. P.– In Venice, because that was where I saw Falla for the last time, in September 1932.

I had gone to Venice for the première of my *Concert for two pianos and orchestra,* which I composed with Jacques Février and the orchestra of the Scala of Milan.

That work had been commissioned by the Princesse de Polignac. That great lady, of American descent (her father was Singer, the sewing machine manufacturer), was throughout her life a great patron of the arts. She was friends with Chabrier, Fauré, Ravel, Richard Strauss, Stravinsky, Satie, and of course Falla, from whom she had commissioned *Master Peter's Puppet Show.*

That September I was living with Falla in the Palazzo Polignac, located on the Grand Canal; Arthur Rubinstein and other artists were lodging there as well. Its great halls were full of pianos. One day, on one of these pianos, Fauré composed his famous Venice melodies, which he dedicated to the Princess. What music we made in 1932! Among other things, I still remember vividly one morning when Arthur Rubinstein and I played *Nights in the Gardens of Spain* for Falla. I was very happy to see him again, because from the very beginning Falla had always shown me both affection and indulgence.

At the Venice Festival we gave a theatrical representation of *Master Peter's Puppet Show*; Falla and I left early every morning to attend the rehearsals, but Falla never missed his daily mass. I would be lying if I said that I was as faithful to the church every morning. When I didn't go with Falla to mass I met him later at a café near the Fenice where he usually had breakfast, after taking communion.

Falla never spoke about his faith in front of Max Jacob.

S. A.– *Never?*

F. P.– No, no, never! He lived his faith in secret and intensely. It was one morning in an Venetian café that Falla spoke to me, at length, about Pedrell, that Spanish composer, who is almost unknown outside Spain, and who played an important role in Falla's musical development when Falla went to

Madrid in 1914*. He went to Madrid because of the war. Falla always maintained that Debussy had revealed the music of Spain to him, but when he returned to his country he learnt, thanks to Pedrell, that for Spanish composers there were sources of inspiration other than Madrid's *zarzuelas*. This is what distinguishes Falla so completely from Albéniz.

S. A.– *Yes and that's often overlooked...!*

F. P.– This fact hasn't been taken sufficiently into account of yet... It is, evidently, a cultural difference. Falla was nearer to folklore and Albéniz to *zarzuela*; Felipe Pedrell did, in four volumes, for folklore, what Bartok did for Hungarian popular song; both of them concentrated on their country's authentic traditions. You can find an echo of Pedrell's very particular brand of harmonisation in "The fisherman's ballad" in Falla's *Love the Magician*, and it is even more noticeable in *Master Peter's Puppet Show*.

In Falla's conversation there was something secret and confidential. He hardly ever voiced his opinion about other contemporary compositions. He liked them, or he did not, and that was all. One could say, in fact, that his character of a dignified and reserved man, made him approve or disapprove of a work. He rarely paid any attention to technical details; and yet he had an enviable technical mastery!

Well then, it has been said that Falla was mysterious, but nothing could be further from the truth, because in reality Falla was a mystic in a pure, clear state.

He also had a very amusing side. In rehearsals he didn't get angry, he got nervous! My teacher, Ricardo Viñes, also showed this particularly Spanish trait.

A discussion between these two men would suddenly speed up to the wild rhythm of a guitar prelude!

S. A.– *Tak, tak, tak! I imagine exactly the sound you mean...*

F. P.– But, nevertheless, what calmness on the spiritual side; I'd like to tell you about one of the strangest and most miraculous days I have ever experienced. One afternoon Falla and I were all alone in the Polignac Palace; the rest of the guests had gone on a boat trip to the Lido. At about five o'clock in the evening I suggested that Falla and I go for a walk around the labyrinth of Venetian alleys, where one can get lost so easily, and even though I don't have a very good sense of direction I was able to find my way to a marvellous small church, which I had visited a few days before, and whose organ had a magnificent sound.

I have forgotten the name of the church, but I promise you, if I went back to Venice, it would not take me long to find it. Well then, it was time for the Salve Maria. I don't remember which holiday was being celebrated, but the church was entirely decorated with red damask. There was an overpowering smell of nards and incense. An organist seemed to play just for us, very well, incidentally, a piece by Frescobaldi. As soon as he entered the church Falla began to pray, and I had the impression that I no longer existed for Falla, like one of those saints who they say suddenly disappear from the eyes of the profane when they reach a state of ecstasy. After a while I decided to leave and I went up to Falla and tapped him lightly on the shoulder. He looked at me for an instant, without seeing me, and became immersed once again in his prayers. I left the church and, of course, I didn't see him again because that night he took the train while I was rehearsing at the Fenice. Falla returned to Spain. And he didn't leave again until he left for Argentina during the civil war. As I told you before, I never saw him again.

For me, the last image I have of the composer who I admired and loved... is a kind of Assumption!

S. A.– *It sounds like it. Falla ended his days in Argentina, in the small city of Córdoba. There, according to what I have been told, he lived like a saint, isolated from the world. When I was staying in Buenos Aires, some Argentinean composers confirmed that he lived in solitude, in a kind of meditative state, one could say that he followed the rules of a hermit's way of life, which corroborates your opinion of him. But, tell me, how and when did you meet Manuel de Falla?*

F. P.– Because I always have to tell you where and when I met my friends, I'll explain: I met Falla in 1918, when he returned to Paris after the 1914 war. I met him in Ricardo Viñes' house, the pianist to whom he dedicated, as you know, the *Nights in the Gardens of Spain*, and after this I saw him often because of the Russian Ballet.

That was the time at which Diaghilev, Falla and Picasso were preparing their wonderful *The Three-cornered Hat*.

*Manuel de Falla was Felipe Pedrell's student in Madrid from 1902 to 1904, before he went to Paris. [*Editor's note*]

S. A.– *But hadn't Falla lived in Paris before the 1914 war?*

F. P.– Of course! For years! Falla arrived in Paris in 1907, and he only left because of the war in 1914. He studied in Paris and got to know Debussy, Dukas, Schmitt, who later became his close friends...

S. A.– *And, no doubt, Maurice Ravel too...*

F. P.– Yes, Ravel, naturally. But let's not forget that Falla was a close friend of Debussy, and Debussy and Ravel didn't always see eye to eye...

S. A.– *Yes, that's true...*

F. P.– In fact, this was stirred up more by the Debussyists and Ravelists than by the composers themselves. Debussy was the first to recognise Falla's genius, and thanks to Debussy Falla's first compositions were published in Paris. And it was thanks to Paul Dukas that the Nice Opera, and later the Paris Comic Opera, produced *La vida breve*.

S. A.– *Do you think that Debussy had an influence on Manuel de Falla?*

F. P.– Yes, without doubt. In fact, these two composers were made to understand and admire each other mutually. They had a flawless friendship. Falla was very upset by Debussy's death. At that time, in memory of the great Frenchman, he composed that meritorious *Homage* for guitar. At the end of the work Falla quotes two bars of *Night in Granada*, and thus he paid his tribute to Debussy who, according to Falla's own admission, had guided him on the path to Spanish music.

S. A.– *Well, you dedicated your trio for piano, oboe and bassoon to Manuel de Falla, I believe?*

F. P.– Yes, I did. In 1925 I dedicated this short trio to Manuel de Falla, in order to show him, in my own way, my admiration.

S. A.– *And tell me, did Debussy ever go to Spain, to visit Falla?*

F. P.– No, no, never! The closest he probably ever got was San Sebastian. He was able to imagine Spain thanks to his remarkable intuition, and thanks to his knowledge of Albéniz, whom he greatly admired.

In Debussy's time records didn't exist, nor books about folklore. So Debussy imagined and guessed what Spain was like. Thus, his prelude for piano, *La puerta del vino*, was inspired by a post-card of Granada which Falla sent him.

S. A.– *What a sense of synthesis! This is what makes geniuses different.*

F. P.– Yes that is certainly part of being a genius.

S. A.– *Tell me, what is your favourite piece by Falla?*

F. P.– Without any doubt *Master Peter*, which I consider to be an incredible masterpiece. I don't know if I will make myself clear, but I'd like to tackle the technical aspect a little. *Master Peter* possesses a specialised form: it isn't a cantata, it isn't an oratorio, it isn't an opera. I always thought *Master Peter* was a musical object, like those works of art by the Renaissance goldsmiths, in which they connect, in an uneven and wonderful way, precious stones in a rich setting. The structure of *Master Peter* is a strange one. It is a succession of short episodes, linked by recitative passages, which end with Don Quixote's aria.

At first, it might seem to lack any order, however, a secret architecture presides over the elaboration of this masterpiece. In fact, this idea of a dominant form, which is often employed by Ravel and Bartok, has never existed in Falla's work. Look at, for example, the bacchanal ending of *Daphnis and Chloe*, and compare it with the end of *The Three-cornered Hat*. Ravel's music advances fluidly, with grandeur, whereas Falla's treads over the same spot again and again, which is the logical thing for a Spanish dance to do.

S. A.– *In short... a* zapateado!

F. P.– For example, the *Fantasia Bætica* is a rarely performed piece. It is wonderfully written for piano, but it is rarely played because it goes round in circles, whereas some parts of Albéniz's *Iberia* travel from the piano to the end of the room.

What is so marvellous about *Master Peter* is that Falla musically introduced the figure of a "presenter" of the performance acted by a child. Falla wanted this part to be sung by a child's voice, in other words, by a shrieking soprano.

Falla found his inspiration for the piece in a well-known episode of Cervantes. One night, Don Quixote stops at an inn, and after eating supper he watches a puppet show. The puppet show depicts shows the story of Melisenda, freed from the moors by Rolando, Carlomagno's nephew. Meanwhile a child announces what is going to be shown in each scene. At the end of the show, the moors depart in hot pursuit of the fugitives, at which point Don Quixote runs them through with his sword, breaking all the marionettes in this way. The truth is that the theatrical production of this piece is practically impossible, because it was conceived for the Princesse de Polignac's salon and does not adapt well to a larger stage.

This piece should be savoured at a concert, where it is really splendid. The orchestration is incredible, and the most important detail is that for the first time Falla mixes the harpsichord with the modern orchestra. At the time of its first production at the Princesse de Polignac's house, it was wonderfully interpreted... Not surprisingly, considering that it was Wanda Landowska who played the harpsichord.

S. A.– *One couldn't ask for more!*

F. P.– It was wonderful, you can take my word for it. Wanda played marvellously. She said: "well really, stop treating me like an old-fashioned woman. All the composers here should compose for me, the harpsichord isn't a museum piece."

So Falla promised her a *Harpsichord Concerto*.

He wrote it and straight afterwards I composed my *Concert champêtre* for Landowska. It was fascinating because we discovered a new Falla and a new Spain. It was no longer the Andalusia of *Love the Magician* but Castile and the Escorial....Well, it was surprising. I have to admit that the more I listen to the orchestration of *Master Peter*, the more I am fascinated by it, because I discover something new in it every time, you see, that's the miracle of SEN-SI-TIVE IN-STRU-MEN-TA-TION. One can write well, orchestrate well, but it is unusual to sense an orchestra. This is what is so surprising about Falla and Ravel. Let's take for example, *L'Enfant et les sortilèges*, by Ravel.... It begins: this conductor raises his baton, and at that moment you think, ah yes, now those marvellous oboes are going to start..., but no, that isn't it..., suddenly all that you have ever wished for comes true and the concert hall smells of countryside... this is the miracle... its wonderfuuul!

And without wishing to be poetic I think that *Master Peter* smells of Spanish wine, and of manchego cheese, that tasty Spanish cheese.

S. A.– *You've set my mouth watering, I'm dying to get my hands on some of that cheese... But let's leave gastronomy to one side or we'll never finish. Let's get back to Falla... We were speaking about his Harpsichord Concerto.*

F. P.– It is a magnificent piece, and this time indeed we find ourselves very close to Saint John of the Cross. Once again a piece written to be performed in the Escorial. The preceding one is highly disconcerting..., it is an extraordinary piece. It is a very "strange" kind of Liturgical piece.

S. A.– *This concert was dedicated to Wanda Landowska, was it not?*
F. P.– Yes.

S. A.– *So I suppose that she helped create it...*
F. P.– No, no, no, she didn't help create it, she never even played it**.

S. A.– *But why was that?*
F. P.– Falla and Wanda almost fell out over the piece. Falla worked very, very slowly, he sent the first part to Wanda, who was waiting anxiously for it. Musically she was very thrilled, but instrumentally she was disappointed. She wanted to make changes, Falla thought there were too many and he refused to alter his composition.

In the end he played it himself, around 1927 or 1928, in the old Salle Pleyel in the Opera neighbourhood.

S. A.– *It's not there anymore. It was destroyed. I wouldn't like to finish this conversation without asking you something about this posthumous manuscript which was discovered with Falla's papers, entitled* Atlántida. *Could you tell us something about this?*

F. P.– Listen, listen, *Atlántida* is an enigma, no one in the world has seen it. I am friends with both Ernesto Halffter and Roland Manuel, Falla's musicographer, but I still haven't seen the piece. Ernesto Halffter was Falla's favourite student; he has spent years trying to prepare the manuscript; which some believe was almost finished, and others barely begun. For obvious reasons I always distrust posthumous pieces, but Halffter feels a profound respect for Falla, just as Falla felt a profound esteem for Halffter. The best thing to do is to wait for the première... Until then nothing can be said...

_____
** Wanda Landowska played the première of the *Concerto* in Barcelona, in 1926. [*Editor's note*]

THE COLÓN Orchestra had the highest respect for him. None of the orchestra's professors expected him to be an accomplished conductor, but they all felt they were before an authentic composer, of sound training, with a clear opinion concerning musical questions, who knew exactly what he wanted and who had a well-defined concept of how both his music and music by others should be interpreted, even if his opinions were often diametrically opposed to the opinions of other interpreters.

KURT PAHLEN

[1] FIRST DAYS IN BUENOS AIRES; [2] WITH JUAN JOSÉ CASTRO AT A REHEARSAL OF THE CONCERTS AT THE COLÓN THEATRE [3] ; AND [4] PROGRAMME OF THE CONCERT, 1939.

1

2

WE HOPE to reach Buenos Aires by the
middle of next week. I am going to
conduct some concerts for Radio El
Mundo because, thank God, this will
not jeopardise my current state of
health, according to the doctors.

MANUEL DE FALLA
Letter to Francesc Cambó
[Alta Gracia, 1 December 1942]

AT VARIOUS MOMENTS DURING HIS STAY IN
BUENOS AIRES. ⊞ CONDUCTING THE
ORCHESTRA AT THE STUDIOS OF RADIO EL
MUNDO; ② AT THE STUDIOS OF THE RADIO
STATION, WITH ORCHESTRA DIRECTOR
ALBERTO CASTELLANO, RAQUEL AGUIRRE
DE CASTRO, MARÍA DEL CARMEN DE FALLA
AND JUAN JOSÉ CASTRO; ③ AT RADIO EL
MUNDO, WITH HIS SISTER, MARÍA DEL
CARMEN, CONCHITA BADÍA AND JUAN JOSÉ
CASTRO IN 1942; AND ④ WITH HIS SISTER
AND JUAN JOSÉ CASTRO.

CONDUCTING THE CÓRDOBA SYMPHONIC ORCHESTRA AT THE RIVERA INDARTE THEATRE IN A BENEFIT CONCERT FOR THE
VICTIMS OF THE BUENOS AIRES FLOODS, 1940.

THE CONCERTS were given in September 1939. The theatre was always sold-out and the performances were a resounding success. The programme of four concerts included works by Falla and other Spanish composers. Only
the last was devoted solely to Falla. Works by composers Morales, Victoria, Guerrero, Juan de Encina, Escobar,
Albéniz, Granados, Turina, Halffter, Óscar Esplá, Joaquín Rodrigo and one composed by myself, *Montañas de
Canigó* (which Concepción Badía sang with such deep emotion –also carried away by yearning nostalgia, the lament
of Catalan lyrics, which is even more poignant when heard in exile– which was acclaimed by the audience) appeared alongside Falla's, in these wonderful concerts.

In his work, Falla was constantly assisted by Juan José Castro who was at his side in the rehearsals, conveyed
his remarks to the orchestra, and took up the baton to conduct some of the pieces in the programme. Falla was
so accustomed to Castro's kind and efficient help, that I heard him say, after finishing a rehearsal for one of the

concerts he conducted on two previous occasions for Radio El Mundo:

"Where's Juan José?... We can't do anything without Juan José!..."

The nervousness of having to perform in public, the movement and physical effort which conducting an orchestra implies, and the pressure of so many other related factors –visits, congratulations, gifts–, brought about a relapse as Falla's illness was still uncured.

Thus his health called for precautions, and most importantly, for peace and quiet which the bustle of the city could give him, in other words, for the countryside and the mountains and their clean, bright and fresh air. For this reason his doctors have prescribed a healthy climate, and the best for his condition is the Sierra of Córdoba.

JAIME PAHISSA

RADIO EL MUNDO, 1942.

IN ONE of our encounters in Buenos Aires, the Maestro told me, in answer to my question about how things were going for him in Argentina:

"I think that all the musical motif that I have ever dreamt of are magnified here. It's as if I'm standing before an immense composition with long, unending staves."

He had a spiritual look about him at that time, and seeing at him leaning on his walking stick brought to mind the Falla I knew, his imposing gypsy-like face, which was too big for his head but showed such composure and dignity of expression that it did not matter. Hidden, timid, yellow and pale, Falla waited for his time, his dusk, because it seemed that it was in the sunset and the so-called twilight hour when he composed his profound airy music of witches' Sabbaths and cave weddings, of the echoes of the countryside in Adalusian streets, of that great fantastic peace that I remember in a street in Granada, where the landscape and the melodical notes of *cante jondo* mingled as if slipping down its steep hill, and one could see, through a grille, a hieratic and thoughtful billy goat which appeared to sit at the window of eternity. All these nuances, which evoke profundity, like tuneful nostalgia, like *ritornello* of a song which comes and goes in the wind, are what Falla collected at dusk and I will not say that they were brought by bats, because that would make what they brought seem gloomy, but I suspect, and I want others to suspect, that they were, and to see that it is not the bats that will reap the rewards of the evening confidences they have trapped.

RAMÓN GÓMEZ DE LA SERNA

ALTA GRACIA, CÓRDOBA, ARGENTINA.

THE MAESTRO'S deep religious feeling verged on mysticism. One night, his friends heard some canticles coming from his room. At first they imagined that the composer must be singing some choral pieces to amuse his sister. But he was not. What he was singing were prayers and orations which he executed with the same kind of excited enthusiasm that one would expect from a chorus of believers.

PEDRO MASSA

IN THE HEART of Argentina there is a wonderful mountainous region. Weeks and months can go by there without a single cloud disturbing the clear blue sky which covers these not very tall mountains, where numerous rivers and streams, green valleys, waterfalls and lakes are to be found. The small city Córdoba is located in the centre of this region.

Manuel de Falla travelled to Córdoba, which is located some eight hundred miles east of Buenos Aires. After spending a few days there observing the buildings, which still preserve their colonial style, and seeing how hectic modern day city life is, he decided to look for a quieter spot, finding the ideal one in the outskirts of Córdoba, next to a lake surrounded by mountains. That lake is called San Roque, and the name of the area is Carlos Paz. Small houses, hotels and guest houses can be found there. It is where carefree people spend a free days relaxing in spring and autumn, people who come from Córdoba, which is only thirty minutes away, or all the way from Buenos Aires. There are some wonderful walks around the lake and the water is dotted with many small vessels.

KURT PAHLEN

LA GRUTA, ALTA GRACIA.

WHEN THE professor told us that the composer lived in Alta Gracia, we felt something like fear. We asked him to take us to the Maestro's house to introduce us to him. The professor said that not even he had had the courage to do so. As far as we were concerned, he reminded us that we had only just learnt the treble clef and musical notes.

We prowled around near his house, aiming to casually bump into him. Once we caught a glimpse of his sister María del Carmen, which was already quite an achievement. José, the smallest of our group, said that he

could play the "Fire Dance"on the piano. This was the only piece we knew
by the composer. We had never
heard José play the piece. When we
tried to get him to play it, he told us
that he did not know it well, but that,
in the presence of its composer, he
would make an effort to play it. With
this aim in mind we attempted to approach the man we considered a iras-
cible genius.

One evening we saw his silhouette
through a window pane. He was
walking back and forth. Once in a
while we heard the sound of piano
chords. We five children were stirred
into a wild state of excitement by that
sight. Now we could boast that we
had seen him. But it seems he saw us
too and suspected something, because he opened the window and
leant out. It has always been impossible for me to remember his exact
words. He asked us what we were doing there, what we wanted. But we
did not hear him, we were looking at
his face, which had navigated on
every ocean of sound. He made us
feel ashamed to be there spying, and
we ran away. He shut the window. We
knew that behind the window, Falla
was adding the finishing touches to
Atlántida.

DANIEL MOYANO

"LOS ESPINILLOS", MANUEL DE FALLA'S HOUSE IN ALTA GRACIA.

"LOS ESPINILLOS" is the name of the chalet where Falla lives
with his good sister María del Carmen. It is located at the
highest part of the city, and the end of a broad street which
runs from the magnificent "Hotel Sierras", to his house.
This is surrounded by a rural garden that grows on firm
stony soil, with some cypresses beside the front gate, and
some pine trees behind, lots of orange trees and a few pomegranates, and numerous mimosas with their golden branches growing between aromatic herbs and wide stemmed cac-
tuses lining the wall. The archways of the sunny verandah
look out over the nearby Sierra, covered in vegetation: dark
green trees; and others, whose leaves turn yellow or slightly red in autumn and, in the midst of these, isolated black
stains made by the cypresses.

The house is comfortable and pleasant, there is nothing
lacking. But his bedroom is more Spartan than a monk's
cell: white painted walls, a window, a simple iron bed, a chair
and a table with some books on it. His work room is painted a very bright white. It contains a large table, piled high
with papers and books which are well laid out in an order-
ly fashion, and a piano, which is permanently damped –un-
evenly damped with towels– a little out of tune and unpredictable, which sounds, as Debussy would have put it, *"un
peu faux, mais, enfin, agréable"*. A wide window faces the
Sierra and on the side wall, a narrow window, which he put
there to let more air enter the room.

JAIME PAHISSA

WITH HIS SISTER MARÍA DEL CARMEN IN THE GARDEN OF "LOS ESPINILLOS".

To THIS day a simple scene is told, in which Falla and his sister were kneeling in front of the chimney trying, with great difficulty and time consuming effort, to get a fire going. In the end the two of them ended up laughing like school children and managed, at last, to get a splendid flame to burn.

They were ineffable. The night that of his resounding success at the Colón Theatre –Ortega went white watching it from a box– when a certain conductor, who told me the story, went to look for Falla and saw that Falla's sister had not dressed yet for the event. When he pointed out how little time they had left she said:

"I'm not going... My brother told me that they are going to show *Love the Magician*: it is not decent enough for my taste."

Falla's sister stayed in the hotel room, while he received an ovation which lasted exactly twenty minutes, the entire audience were *on their feet* applauding the old Maestro, the musical bullfighter, agile, short and tiny.

RAMÓN GÓMEZ DE LA SERNA

Remembering Granada

WHO HAS NOT heard of the *carmenes* of Granada? Just as Hermes was called "trimegistus" thrice greatest, the word *carmen* should denote three times beautiful. With this word, the Latin people named poetry; and it also means spell. *Carmen* in Arabic is enclosed garden. For Christians it is one of the most evocative adorations of the Mother of God.

Granada's *carmenes* are hanging gardens, in stepped terraces, like those of Babylon. In each garden there is a house. The *carmen* is an enclosure; it can be convent or harem. At times they are very humble, like the cell and orchard of a Carthusian monastery. But in them one can find peace, love and beauty; and in the quiet perhaps a certain restlessness.

Falla's fertile and chaste inspiration was harvested for years in one of these *carmenes*. Falla was quite monk-like; Carthusian because of his seclusion; Benedictine because of his assiduousness; Franciscan because of his clean gaze, limpid, of delightful ecstasy at the works of God; Carmelite, because of the pure wonder of his music. He sets one thinking about another Carmelite, Saint John of the Cross. Never have images been employed beyond feeling with more innocent, pure, crystalline and transparent expression than in the *Spiritual Canticle*. Likewise in Falla's music Andalusia's narcissistic soul and voluptuous body aspires to and pursues disembodiment and the incorporeal, without losing a jot of humanity –line, rhythm, colour, smell–.

I spoke of the Andalusian's narcissistic soul. One only has to observe the Andalusian male or female (though the male is more noticeable) at rest or in motion, but especially if they are out walking in public. He will most certainly move, even the most inexpert observer will notice it, paying far too much attention and care to the outside world, but always through and in the reflection of the inner mirror of his aesthetic imagination; he acts as he imagines one to act, or as he would like one to appear to act and tries to give his spectators a calculated effect. For example: the dancing trot of an Andalusia horse. For this reason Adalusianism is the most hackneyed, commercial, and consequently most adulterated genre. It is an export product, by means of which a false knowledge of Spain is provided for people outside the country.

Casting one's gaze, which is like casting the spirit, over the Granada flood-plain and to the top of its diaphanous Sierra another great composer and poet of Spanish prose comes to mind: Fray Luis de Granada. The landscape of Granada is one of Fray Luis' vast rhetorical sentences, evolved in a manifold and harmonious sumptuousness, from the plain to the mountain tops. If this landscape could talk it would speak with the words of Fray Luis.

John, Luis and Manuel regard the outside world as Lactance desired; as a delicate hymn in praise of the Creator. In *The Symbol of Faith*, Fray Luis writes: "What is the visible world, if not a great and marvellous book? What are the creatures of this world, so beautiful and complete, if not the guiding, illuminating letters that proclaim the skill and wisdom of their author? The beautiful creatures preach your beauty, the strong ones your strength, the great ones your greatness, the radiant ones your light, the gentle ones your tenderness and the well-ordered and abundant your marvellous providence."

It is natural that in this kind of educational nature men learn from childhood, without realising it, to be poets and composers. There, all is emotion and rhythm, gravity. Emotion and rhythm is "*cante jondo*" too. The best exponents of "*cante jondo*" are nightingales. The Nightingale and the "*cantaor*" are timid creatures: only at night in the solitude do they utter of their dense and sorrowful lament.

Once, Falla and Zuloaga wanted to resuscitate "*cante jondo*" and in order to do so they organised a nocturnal festival at the palace of Charles V in the Alhambra. The only thing that was lacking then were authentic "*cantaors*"; because "*cante jondo*" had been bastardised and seemed extinct. At last they discovered a kind of male vestal of the orphic mystery, in Puente Genil, in the province of Cordova; an old "*cantaor*", in his eighties; because in "*cante jondo*" it is not the mental powers that are important but rather emotion and ritual initiation.

If the view of Granada is impressive during the day from the Alhambra vantage point, the effect is increased at night, as if the countless rubies that a pomegranate contains within its tanned, shiny skin, almost earthenware, were scattered over the city and valley glowing like small hot coals. At this hour too the woods bleed with the intense song of the nightingale intermingled with the perfume of tuberose and jasmine.

RAMÓN PÉREZ DE AYALA

Letter from Darius Mihaud

DEAR MAESTRO and friend:

I have often thought of you since that dramatic separation; I would like to hear from you, about how you are and how your work is going because I am one of your most zealous and staunch admirers.

I have been in California with my wife and my son (he is twelve years old) since August 1940. We were lucky to be able to leave my unfortunate country in the middle of the disaster because I had composed a symphony for the fiftieth anniversary of the Chicago Concerts and was invited to conduct it. Thanks to these arrangements we were given visas right away.

I have been treated with magnificent hospitality in the United States. I give classes at Mills College, and they have built a little house for us in the college grounds.

I saw Ernesto Halffter in Lisbon before setting sail and later in Pittaluga in New York. I have news through the mediation of my mother about Poulenc, Honegger, Roland Manuel, Sauguet and Désormière. They are all well and working in Paris. Désormière is the conductor at the opera. Poulenc has produced a new ballet based on the *Fables* by La Fontaine, with scenery by André Derain. Picasso is also in Paris; he is making beautiful sculptures. They have little to do with the occupants and they see a lot of each other. They are all very courageous. Dear Lord! So much courage is needed everywhere in these cruel times.

I had the misfortune to lose my father recently. He was 88 years old. It was upsetting not to be able to bewith him during his last days and to know that my mother

was so alone. Thank God they are in Aix and do not have to see the horrors of the invasion or the catastrophic fate of the refugees on the roads. It is a comfort to know that my poor father died at home, with the doctor, and his servants who have spent so many years with us in the service of my mother and father.

All my manuscripts are in France. Here I have very few pieces and I have had to start my musical life by composing new works. For there was very little of my orchestral work in America.

Please tell your sister that we often recall the happiness of former times, of our visits to Granada and the charming welcome you both gave us.

My wife joins me in my sincere and affectionate wishes.

DARIUS MILHAUD
Letter to Manuel de Falla
[Oakland, 24 June 1942]

Francesc Cambó pays a visit

FRANCESC CAMBÓ
BY ZULOAGA.

I WAS COUNTING on the idea that the winter months in Alta Gracia would allow me to have some long talks with the Maestro Falla. I had even convinced myself that I would affectionately bully him into making considerable progress with the dramatic poem *Atlántida* which he had been working on for twelve years.... with the danger of dying without having finished it.

Falla is a gypsy, an Andalusian and an artist: three lazy elements! Perhaps one should add a fourth: his sister has loved and cared for him so much that she has helped develop his idleness. Falla has without doubt, the most exquisite –I will not say the greatest, as Strauss is still living– musical temperament of our age. There is nothing banal or common in his work, it is all pure gold... But there is so little of it! It would fit entirely into the space of one or two concerts!

Atlántida, if he keeps it up, –he says that he is doing even more than that– will give a greater volume and consistency to his work as a whole.

He told me he worked a lot last autumn and at the beginning of winter. That if he kept this rhythm up he would have the piece finished in a year or so. Could it be true? Can you trust the word of an Andalusian gypsy!

I asked him to explain his way of composing to me. This is what he told me more or less:

"When I feel inspired I work the whole day long; I work in bed, while I'm eating, while I'm given my treatment; I work at the time. My whole being is a music box and I feel the themes and the chords, I feel them combine and become clear. I live in a state of musical intoxication... And when the theme emerges with greaty clarity, I write it down."

"And the piano?" I asked him.

"I only use the piano to test the exactitude of the chord. I do not use the piano to compose. The composition is formed inside me and involves my body and soul."

What a pity that such a great artist is so lazy! He apologises for it, but he does not hide the fact. He explained how he finished the music of *The Three-cornered Hat* in Paris. Diaghilev, who was producing the ballet, did not leave him alone, night or day: his visits, telephone calls, messages, were driving Falla mad. Then he understood that his best line of defence was to work... and he worked feverishly for a few days, kept good company by a bottle of cognac.

Falla excused his laziness saying that his letter writing absorbed his time, and he showed me a dossier which contained that year's correspondence, which was much less than I send in a week. I offered to send him my secretary for a while every day in order to dispatch his unanswered mail. He was thrilled by the idea and made an appointment with her for Monday. When she visited him he told her that he needed until Thursday to think about the letters he had to dictate. On Thursday he put it off until the following week... and so on and so forth. To conclude, he never dictated a single letter.

My dear friend and great artist Manuel de Falla is a hopeless case!

FRANCESC CAMBÓ

Correspondance with Léonide Massine

DEAR FRIEND:

Owing to the huge demand for performances of *The Three-cornered Hat* in small provincial cities in the United States, I need to cut back the orchestration of the ballet so it could be played by twenty four musicians.

With this idea in mind I have approached Galaxy Music Corporation in New York, who are the representatives of Chester in this country. They have informed me that if I have your permission then they will take care of the arrangement. I had suggested that it be done by Franz Allers, who is a good composer and is very familiar with *The Three-cornered Hat*, having conducted the ballet over a number of years.

In case you prefer not to give this authorisation to your publishers but to give it solely to me and my performances, I think you can do so and that Galaxy would be even more interested in doing it this way.

I can guarantee the musical quality of the shortened version and, if you also take into account the great number of cities which will have the chance to hear *The Three-cornered Hat*, I hope that you will grant me permission and send me your prompt reply. Apart from this I would really like to make *Don Quixote* into a wonderful ballet with you. Tell me if you like the idea and, if you do, when you could have a piano version ready. We could decide on the episodes we want to use, in writing, quite quickly.

It would be wonderful if you could have a new work in a year's time.

I hope that you are in very good health and that you feel rested and ready to work once again.

I do not know if I ever told you I have a daughter, who is three and a son who was born three months ago.

Yours sincerely,

LÉONIDE MASSINE
Letter to Manuel de Falla
[New York, 16 October 1944]

DEAR FRIEND:

I received your letter and was happy to hear that you are the father of two children. I hope they grow up to be great artists like their father...!

As far as the idea of reducing the orchestration of *The Three-cornered Hat* goes, I have to admit that it does not appeal to me and Galaxy Music Corporation did very well in telling you to request my permission as a first condition. However, as it is your request I have to make an exception and I am willing to allow this orchestral arrangement, but only with the express condition *that it be used solely by you and ONLY in smaller cities where a full orchestra is not available.* Thus, following these conditions, the question of how to settle this is *yours and Galaxy's responsibility.* As regards the work, considering the trust you have in Franz Allers, Galaxy should make arrangements with him to do it; I am counting on you. Please, do not forget to write to me about how this is going and about everything else...

I too would like to do this *Don Quixote* you mentioned, but unfortunately my poor state of health over the last few years has prevented me from finishing the piece which has been interrupted so many times for the same reason, in spite of the enthusiasm I have always had in the work.

Yours sincerely,

MANUEL DE FALLA
Letter to Léonide Massine
[Alta Gracia, 12 November 1944]

Rafael Alberti visits Manuel de Falla in Alta Gracia

A LITTLE while ago, a few days in fact, some friends and I rang at the door of what was not a monastery, but a kind of recluse. It was not lost among the brown mountains of our Andalusian Cordova, as the man who lives there would have hoped, but he still keeps that hope for the not too distant future.

AT "LOS ESPINILLOS", *FROM LEFT TO RIGHT*, UNIDENTIFIED MAN, DR. CARLOS FERRER, DR. GONZÁLEZ AGUILAR, MRS GONZÁLEZ AGUILAR, DONATO COLACELLI, FALLA, HIS SISTER, RAFAEL ALBERTI AND PACO AGUILAR.

all. Don Manuel was happy. In the midst of his solitude, our visit brought and stirred –and he made no attempt to conceal the fact– the deepest waters, at the bottom of which name, Spain, which we hardly dared to utter echoed.

Our visit was celestial. A concert for Don Manuel, a can-

The mountains have a different name and the city which shelters the old angelic recluse, is pretty Alta Gracia, in the province of Cordova in the Argentinean Republic.

It was a fine morning. Cypresses, orange trees, acacias were in full bloom, and a slight breeze of violets wafted to welcome us to the solitary peace of the garden of "Los Espinillos", the recluse, the house where Manuel de Falla –Don Manuel– lived in voluntary exile, far from Granada, today the graveyard of so many things...

The sound of latches and doors as he approached and finally the eminent musician stood before us, small and bent, charming and reverent, covered by a vicuna poncho which reached his feet, the drab colour of which reminded one of a monastic serge.

"Don Manuel!"

After the little monk had hugged us affectionately, we went into the sun lounge, warm from the mountain sun and the *manzanilla* (sherry) from Sanlúcar that evoked vivid memories of Cadiz, served by María del Carmen, Falla's only and inseparable sister.

A healthy and almost infantile joy took hold of us

tata for three voices: lute, piano and poetry. We had just performed in Córdoba, but he –with his poor health to blame– had not been able to come down from his retreat to hear it. For this reason he so kindly invited us to "Los Espinillos". At one-thirty exactly. "At one-thirty exactly", his doctor González Anguilar had emphasised. That was the exact time that the doctor and his brother Paco, Donato Colacelli and I had knocked on Falla's door, knowing and respecting his concern for punctuality, his love for precision, both old characteristics in the life and work of the great Andalusian composer.

"You have to excuse the piano..." he entreated, as he looked at Paco's new lute in his hands, which was a darker shade of brown than the other one. "Apart from the damper, it is not very well tuned. Though that might not matter too much..."

And he told us, to explain his apology, that one afternoon he had attended a concert for two pianos with Ravel, after which the French composer became very serious and anxious to know which of the two performers was the best, as it had been impossible for him to tell one piano from the other.

"And it wasn't just Ravel who liked to work on an out of tune piano... Debussy like to do so as well. *Désaccordé, mais agréable*", commented Don Manuel, adding a note of humour to the apology, as he went to sit at his piano, in a bright and unaffected little room with windows that looked onto the mountains.

Now the small concert was ready:

"Invitation to a journey through sound", I read opening my enormous book, big enough for the lectern of a gothic temple, leaning it, as there was no better stand available, against the voluminous flank of a dictionary that I placed in the middle of a small table.

> "*In the beginning there was the lute.*
>
> *It came vagrant and soundful, from a journey...*"

WITH THE GUITARIST PACO AGUILAR.

Don Manuel, wrapped up in a corner, lost in his vicuna habit, bent his ivory head forward, crossed his hands over his legs, and in this attitude of acceptance –Oh the Zurbaranes in Cadiz museum!– he began to listen to the song of the lute, introduction to the cantata:

> "*... And like the palm tree, whose mast*
> *opens in an arc to the light of its green sails,*
> *passed the sea, opening its whisper*
> *of sweet leaves of the myrtles and allspice*
> *of Granada, Cordova and Seville...*"

I usually read, but I was so busy watching Don Manuel that I spoke the verses almost from memory. I can assure you, with sorrow and pride, that when the three names of the Andalusian cities were spoken a slight hint of pink colour touched the skin around his bright glasses. Nights in the gardens of Spain! The fountains of the Generalife! The jasmine and orange blossom of Cordova! The ponds and palm trees of Seville! The lute dissolved into the most limpid fountains and games invented by an anonymous Arabian Spaniard in the 16th century. Afterwards, Juan del Encina, with his heartrending canticle for the death of queen Isabel of Castile. And Diego Pisador's swaggering pavane...

The dampened sound of Falla's piano, the flowing tremor of the notes played by Cola celli, seemed to blur the voice of the lute, with a far off and drained echo, and the whole cantata sounded as if it was submerged under the transparency of a tranquil, obedient water which constantly murmured and trembled to the orders of a quill. Thus one could feel the pen lose itself as it danced amid the vapours of a misty lamentation (Purcell); twined, noisy, fugitive between shafts of light and darkness (Croft); rising suddenly in golden bubbles (Scarlatti); jumpy and twisting as if hanging from a thread (Mozart); sunken to the depths of a vast whirlpool and then rising at the next instance to a high tide of infinity (Bach).

Never had Paco Aguilar's hand plunged deeper, never had he given his lute a more remote accent, more lightness and damp lyricism. Damp, yes, because what we played that day in Alta Gracia, the home of music, for the great old Andalusian angel, whose pure life of quiet and "musical solitude" had dampened us and filled us with grace, was the water beneath the water of the cantata *engloutie*.

RAFAEL ALBERTI

MY DEAR FRIEND:

At last I am able to write to you, which I have been wanting to do ever since I read your *article* on the happy journey through sound which you shared with us during the delightful time we spent together –so reminiscent of Cadiz!

I was moved and grateful to read your *lovely* momento written with such refined wit and sincere affection and in which you spoke so highly of me. Please, believe me, Rafael I do not deserve this honour as I am very human. If there is anything good in me it is only my willpower to, whenever possible, and guided by my constant Christian convictions, cultivate my feeling of responsibility. But let us leave these serious matters aside and return to that day and all the bright and beautiful things we evoked, and which, in connection with our country, your *Marinero* –which I have read time and time again– has continued to evoke for me.

It is a shame that in the photos of that day, which I am pleased to have as a momento, I look so old. Of course that would not matter to me if it were not for the fact that I am still fully active professionally. I believe this because of the justified suspicion that people might judge the possible efficiency of my current work on the basis of the outer appearance of its author who, on the contrary, feels as young as ever *inside*. That explains my *terror* of the camera and the reason I send you a photograph which I hope reflects better times... Now I await yours, which as I told you before, I really want to have.

I have to end now I am afraid. I would have liked to have talked about more things, but I do not want to delay sending these lines any longer.

"FOR DON MANUEL DE FALLA WITH MY ADMIRATION AND GREAT AFFECTION THINKING ALWAYS OF OUR DISTANT BAY... RAFAEL ALBERTI".

With best wishes from María del Carmen, and affectionate regards from your good friend,

MANUEL DE FALLA
Letter to Rafael Alberti
[Alta Gracia, 28 September 1945]

MY DEAR DON MANUEL:

Your letter brought me much pleasure as well as your portrait, with such an affectionate dedication, which stirred up my childhood memories of sea salt, boats and pine forests. Thank you, thank you truly.

I am grateful for your kind remarks about my momento of that afternoon in Alta Gracia, which was published in *La Nación*. I would have liked to have written something more important, which could have accurately reflected all your emotion and that of those around you during that small concert, which you handled with such devotion and intimacy. After that visit, and now that I have received your portrait and letter, I feel a great sorrow which I must confess: that I was never close to you like Federico [García Lorca]; that I never saw you very often; that I cannot see you now...

RAFAEL ALBERTI
Letter to Manuel de Falla.
[Buenos Aires, 4 October 1945]

ONE DAY in the month of July 1944 I received a visit from two good friends: the well-known composer Jaime Pahissa, who had been living in Buenos Aires since the beginning of the civil war, and the radiologist Carlos Quiroga (who happened to be the brother of the famous violinist Manolo Quiroga) who had settled in Córdoba many years ago and had treated Falla for the chronic condition of the respiratory tracts. The two of them were very distressed when they told me that Falla, who lived in Alta Gracia, a province of Córdoba, was in a grievous financial situation, with hardly enough resources to see him through to the end of the month. They asked me, as the representative of the Authors Society, to write to Spain to request aid for the illustrious composer, because his modesty would never have allowed him to admit that he was needy and it was tragic that, at the end of his life, with his health sapped by an old illness, he should have to face such privations.

Without losing a moment I went to great lengths to solve that unwonted situation. I spoke with my ambassador, the Count of Bulnes, who wrote to the Minister of Foreign Affairs. For my part, I wrote to my friend Minister Ibáñez Martín, who was the head of my branch of the civil service, and to the president of the Authors Society, Don Eduardo Marquina. I asked them all to send urgent aid to the distinguished patient. A threefold petition and a threefold silence. As days went by without any news from Spain, I sent a report to the Madrid newspaper *Arriba*, for which I worked as a correspondent under the pseudonym of Íñigo de Santiago, describing the dramatic situation Don Manuel de Falla was facing. Help finally care: a few days later the ambassador received orders from the Minister to visit Falla in person. Ibáñez Martín placed me in charge of making the visit and Marquina ordered me to give Falla monthly, without any limit or condition, the amount of money he needed to be able to live comfortably. Nevertheless it must be made clear that Falla had left the administration of his authors' rights to the publishers Chester of London, and while England was at war they could not transfer any money abroad. Falla would not receive a cent

from there.

Falla had many odd habits. He lived obsessed with his poor health and paid special attention to his vitamin intake. He asked me if I knew whether any new vitamins had been added to the pharmacopoeia of those days. His plate was scarcely visible behind multitudinous medicine bottles. He also had a mania about draughts. It had to run through the house with a process which reminded one of the sluice system of the Panama Canal: firstly he shut the doors and the windows of the room he was going to occupy; then he opened the door of the adjoining room; now in this room he shut the door behind him and he opened the one which led to the next room, he repeated this procedure until he reached the dining room.

On one of my visits I arrived on Saturday and promised to come back on Sunday to say good-bye. Miss Carmen arranged the appointment for eleven o' clock. I went at the ordained time and she showered me with explanations about how, because of his delicate health, her brother had not attended mass for many weeks, though he read the Gospel. "As we trust you", she said to me "if you don't mind, stay a while and pray with us." I thanked her for the honour and so the curious religious ceremony commenced: she proceeded to remove all the objects from a large bureau and then draped a piece of white linen over it. She then placed a crucifix with a candlestick on either side which she hastened to light and finally a kind of lectern which held the Gospel. Don Manuel advanced serenely, made the sign of the cross and began to slowly read aloud the Gospel of the day. Once in a while he turned round to look at his sister and I, as we sat respectfully listening to the unusual ceremony. At the end Don Manuel turned to face the crucifix and knelt down before it with great difficulty; then he rose, turned towards us both and held his hands to us with a certain solemnity. That was a kind of urgent mass held by Don Manuel de Falla. I think that I am the only person that has ever enjoyed this rare privilege.

JOSÉ IGNACIO RAMOS

ARGENTINEAN REPUBLIC IDENTITY CARDS ISSUED TO HIM IN THE YEAR OF
HIS DEATH.

IF HIS STATE OF health is good and the weather is good as well, he attends mass at the chapel of Lourdes situated on the foothills of the Sierra opposite his house, fifteen minutes away by car, the only way he has of getting about. But if he is not able to go, he has permission to read mass in his house on obligatory days, and this is what he did. One Saturday he said to me:

"If the weather is good tomorrow we'll come and pick you up at your hotel at quarter-to-ten to go to mass at the chapel."

Sure enough, the weather the next day was marvellous: the splendid sun of Alta Gracia made one search for the shade of a tree even in winter, though at night there was a frost. At ten-to-ten the car arrived, but only with María del Carmen.

"Where's Manuel?" I asked her.

"Manolo is not very well", answered María del Carmen, "today he woke up with a temperature of 36.6 instead of his usual 36.5 and he has stayed at home." Another of the little idiosyncrasies of a great man. "We can go to mass at the village church."

We did, and when we got back to the composer's house, we found him finishing reading the mass by himself.

•

In spite of the beauty and serene peacefulness of that secluded spot, he cannot spend much time composing. Health and personal care take up five hours every day. The timetable of the house might appear completely disordered, but this is not the case: it is a delayed order. He wakes up late rather than early; he performs his ablutions, very carefully and neatly; he spends quite a while answering letters; and this done with it is now three-thirty or four and he lunches. After this he has a rest, in other words, his *siesta*; and at seven thirty he has a snack or tea (as they call it here). Then he sits down to compose until twelve o'clock at night when he stops to have supper. This organisation of the day and night hours is the cause of constant tensions among the domestic service: there is no maid who can accustom herself to this timetable and put up with it for more than a week.

I first found out about this arbitrary order the day I went

to see him at the hotel. He had invited me to lunch. I arrived at a reasonable time, at about one in the afternoon. I asked for him and was told to kindly wait a little. A little while later they asked me to go upstairs to his room because he did not eat in the dining room, but had his lunch brought to him in his room. But I saw no evidence of this. We started to speak; and in this way hours went by. I thought that perhaps they had already eaten and that I had misunderstood the in-

FALLA WITH THE COMPOSER JAIME PAHISSA, AUTHOR OF THE BIOGRAPHY *VIDA Y OBRA DE MANUEL DE FALLA* (BUENOS AIRES, 1946).

vitation. When, at about three thirty, a waiter appeared and started to lay the table I was desperately hungry because I don't usually have breakfast.

If the timetable seems a bit fanciful, so is his way of calculating it. He said to me one day: "I don't sleep much at night; after four or five hours in bed I wake up and can't get back to sleep. Last night I woke up and it must have been five-thirty, because when I looked at my watch it showed eight o'clock; but as I put it an hour fast, it would have been seven, official time, that's six, solar time; and as I had been awake for quite a while, it must have been about five-thirty."

JAIME PAHISSA

ONE OF THE LAST PHOTOGRAPHS OF MANUEL DE FALLA.

A PAGE OF HIS DIARY, IN WHICH HE MADE NOTE OF THE UPS AND DOWNS OF HIS HEALTH.

ONE MORNING the maid knocked at his door and received no answer. María del Carmen was notified and when she went into her brother's room she found him dead, as though asleep and in the midst of a peaceful dream. That was the morning of the 14th of November 1946. Nine days later Manuel de Falla would have been seventy years old, and on this occasion the world had prepared a great celebration for him. The countless articles they had written full of joy, the countless congratulations of the press the whole world over which were going to commemorate Manuel de Falla's seventieth birthday, had to be changed at the last moment into obituary notices. The concerts which were going to be played to honour him became recitals, in which Falla's music was the only thing that remained of his life.

His friends living nearby received the news at midday, and soon they began to gather around the Maestro's mortal remains; the following morning people began to arrive from Buenos Aires, converting the peaceful "Los Espinillos" into the centre of the world. Piles of telegrams, letters, wreaths, came from all over..., journalists and photographers..., a high ranking official from the Spanish Embassy claimed the body and all his belongings, in the name of his Government, in order to transport them back to Spain. Many people would have liked to have buried Falla in the New World, where he had spent the last years of his life in peace and where he was loved and admired as much as in Spain. They would also have liked to see his last composition, which he had left unfinished in Argentina, produced in Córdoba or maybe in Buenos Aires.

But María del Carmen, his only remaining relative, preferred to comply with the wishes of the Government. She wanted to return to Cadiz, which she had left at a very early age to devote her life to her brother, to be the inseparable and indispensable companion that her brother would need throughout his entire life.

The most conspicuous of all the huge piles of papers found in Falla's house were those which contained his most important composition: *Atlántida*. The first part looked as if it was almost completely finished; there were fragments of the second and the third was a series of endless sketches and notes.

They were carefully sealed up and sent with the body of Manuel de Falla, first to Córdoba and then to Buenos Aires. There they waited for a Spanish transatlantic vessel which would return his mortal remains to their homeland. Near the Spanish coast they were put aboard a warship and transported to the city of Cadiz. In the crypt of the cathedral the remains of Manuel de Falla have found eternal peace. Solemn funeral rites were celebrated to this effect.

KURT PAHLEN

1 THE FUNERAL PROCESSION AT THE CÓRDOBA CATHEDRAL, ARGENTINA; 2 THE SHIP *CABO DE BUENA ESPERANZA*, WHICH TRANSPORTED FALLA'S MORTAL REMAINS FROM BUENOS AIRES TO LAS PALMAS IN GRAN CANARIA (THE CANARY ISLANDS); 3 THE MINE-LAYER *MARTE* WHICH TRANSPORTED THEM FROM LAS PALMAS TO CADIZ; 4 FUNERAL PROCESSION FROM THE PORT TO CADIZ CATHEDRAL.

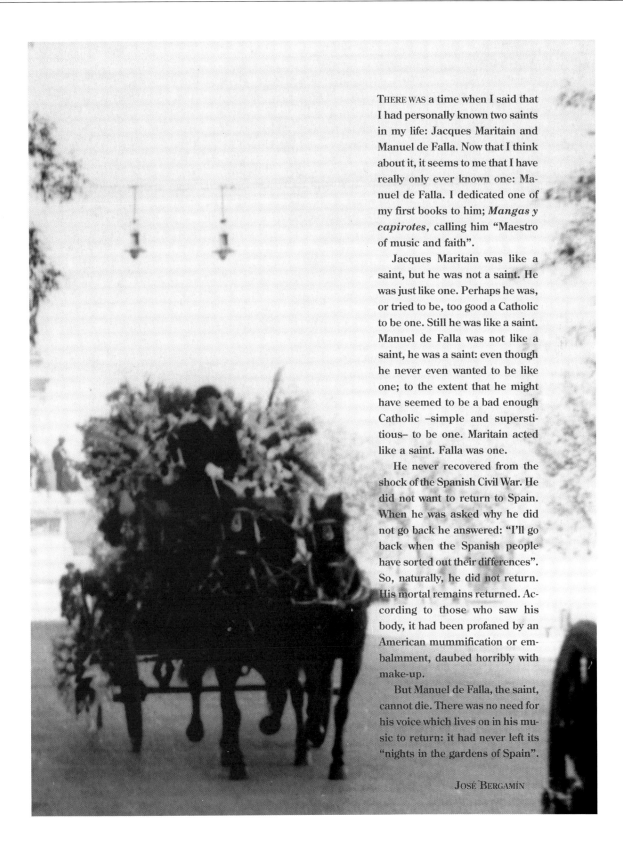

THERE WAS a time when I said that I had personally known two saints in my life: Jacques Maritain and Manuel de Falla. Now that I think about it, it seems to me that I have really only ever known one: Manuel de Falla. I dedicated one of my first books to him; *Mangas y capirotes*, calling him "Maestro of music and faith".

Jacques Maritain was like a saint, but he was not a saint. He was just like one. Perhaps he was, or tried to be, too good a Catholic to be one. Still he was like a saint. Manuel de Falla was not like a saint, he was a saint: even though he never even wanted to be like one; to the extent that he might have seemed to be a bad enough Catholic –simple and superstitious– to be one. Maritain acted like a saint. Falla was one.

He never recovered from the shock of the Spanish Civil War. He did not want to return to Spain. When he was asked why he did not go back he answered: "I'll go back when the Spanish people have sorted out their differences". So, naturally, he did not return. His mortal remains returned. According to those who saw his body, it had been profaned by an American mummification or embalmment, daubed horribly with make-up.

But Manuel de Falla, the saint, cannot die. There was no need for his voice which lives on in his music to return: it had never left its "nights in the gardens of Spain".

JOSÉ BERGAMÍN

Now I am going to visit the cathedral, closed for restoration for more than fifteen years. It is in the part of Cadiz that faces the sea with the façades of the humble houses broken and eaten away by it. For the first time in my life, I cross the threshold and enter the cathedral which reminds me of the La Salute church located at one end of the Grand Canal in Venice. I am greeted by a strong whirlpool of musty sea smells. Surprise. The old man who sells the tickets is a good pianist; I recognise him because I have seen him play at night in the hotel where I am staying. First of all I go to the museum, where I look at some huge paintings which I cannot judge because of the dim light. Then I descend to the crypt, which is beneath sea level, where one can find the mausoleum of Don Manuel de Falla, another great universal Andalusian, who died in Alta Gracia, in the Argentinean Republic. He would have liked to have stayed there, in that place with such a beautiful name. But Franco's consulate and the composer's devout sister between them decided to bring him back to Spain. Here he lies now, in the depths of Cadiz, surrounded by darting fish that disturb his rest. While I was standing there, lost in thought, contemplating Don Manuel's tomb behind the iron bars that separate it from visitors, an old guide who was leading a group of tourists stared at me for a long while, then raised his astonished arm to point at me and said: "Oh it's Albéniz!" I was absolutely amazed, and even more so when I realised, almost at once, that on that afternoon there could have been nothing more natural and fitting than for the great Catalan composer Isaac Albéniz to visit the tomb of the great Andalusian composer Manuel de Falla.

RAFAEL ALBERTI, 1987

Manuel de Falla

I N D E X E S

1. BIBLIOGRAPHICAL INDEX OF TEXTS BY MANUEL DE FALLA

2. BIBLIOGRAPHICAL INDEX OF TEXTS ABOUT MANUEL DE FALLA

3. NAMES INDEX

1. BIBLIOGRAPHICAL INDEX OF TEXTS BY MANUEL DE FALLA

THE TEXTS WHICH ARE NOT INDICATED HERE –LETTERS, MANUSCRIPTS,
NOTES...– COME FROM THE ARCHIVO MANUEL DE FALLA, IN GRANADA.

page 39
I refer... FALLA, Manuel de, *Escritos sobre música y músicos,* Madrid, Espasa Calpe, 1972, p. 58.

page 40
Pedrell was... FALLA, Manuel de, *Op. cit.*, pp. 83-85 and 91-93.

page 73
I met Ravel... FALLA, Manuel de, *Op. cit.*, pp. 130-132.

page 92
I begin to... FALLA, Manuel de, *Op. cit.*, pp. 23-25.

page 93
The Russian... FALLA, Manuel de, *Op. cit.*, pp. 25-26.

page 161
This name... FALLA, Manuel de, notes about *Cante Jondo,* 1922.

page 203
Granada is... FALLA, Manuel de, *Op. cit.*, pp. 106-107.

2. BIBLIOGRAPHICAL INDEX OF TEXTS ABOUT MANUEL DE FALLA

THE TEXTS WHICH ARE NOT INDICATED HERE –LETTERS, ARTICLES, ESSAYS,
NOTES...– COME FROM THE ARCHIVO MANUEL DE FALLA, IN GRANADA.

page 17
Cádiz was... PAHISSA, Jaime, *Vida y obra de Manuel de Falla,* Buenos Aires, Ricordi americana, S. A., 1946, p. 17.

page 18
The plaza de Mina... VINIEGRA, Juan J., *Vida íntima de Manuel de Falla y Matheu,* Cádiz, Excma. Diputación, 1966, p. 35.
At first the... PAHISSA, Jaime, *Op. cit.*, p. 23.

page 19
The children... PAHISSA, Jaime, *Op. cit.*, pp. 26-27.

page 20
Childhood and... MARTÍNEZ SIERRA, María, *Gregorio y yo,* Mexico, Gandesa, 1953, p. 121.
The Real Academia... VINIEGRA, Juan J., *Op. cit.*, p. 156.

page 22
Back again... ROLAND-MANUEL, Alexis, *Manuel de Falla,* Buenos Aires, Losada, 1945, pp. 18-19.

page 25
We lived... VINIEGRA, Juan J., *Op. cit.*, p. 47.

page 28
During the last... SALAZAR, Adolfo, *La música contemporánea en España*, Madrid, Pub. La Nave, 1930, p. 158.

page 44
At that time... VERDAGUER, Mario, *Medio siglo de vida barcelonesa*, Barcelona, Pub. Barna, 1957, p. 181.

page 53
He also got... PAHISSA, Jaime, *Op. cit.*, pp. 51-52.
And Falla recalls... PAHISSA, Jaime, *Op. cit.*, p. 190.

page 54
Around the year... TURINA, Joaquín, *Escritos*, Madrid, Alpuerto, 1982, p. 207.

page 59
At last the date... PAHISSA, Jaime, *Op. cit.*, pp. 65-67.

page 65
When Falla came to Paris... PAHISSA, Jaime, *Op. cit.*, p. 55.

page 67
Immediately after... PAHISSA, Jaime, *Op. cit.*, pp. 78-81.

page 69
Now his name takes... MARTÍNEZ SIERRA, María, *Op. cit.*, p. 119.

page 71
Falla reached Paris... PAHISSA, Jaime, *Op. cit.*, p. 65.
One day during one... MARTÍNEZ SIERRA, María, *Op. cit.*, p. 124.
When Falla returned... PAHISSA, Jaime, *Op. cit.*, pp. 99-100.

page 72
The *Nights*... PAHISSA, Jaime, *Op. cit.*, p. 104.

page 74
After Falla left... PAHISSA, Jaime, *Op. cit.*, pp. 60-61.

page 75
A weak figure... ALMAGRO SAN MARTÍN, Melchor, "Manuel de Falla", *Abc*, Madrid, 6 August 1944.

page 78
I met Manuel... MARTÍNEZ SIERRA, María, *Op. cit.*, pp. 120-125.

page 83
When he arrived... MARTÍNEZ SIERRA, María, *Op. cit.*, pp. 126-127.

page 85
One April morning... MARTÍNEZ SIERRA, María, *Op. cit.*, pp. 134-136.

page 86
At that... MARTÍNEZ SIERRA, María, *Op. cit.*, pp. 128-129.
As there... VERDAGUER, Mario, *Op. cit.*, pp. 160-161.

page 87
Usually, every morning... Martínez Sierra, María, *Op. cit.*, pp. 130-131.

page 89
The piano at... Plá, Josep, *Rusiñol y su tiempo*, Barcelona, Pub. Barna, 1942, p. 174.

page 91
In the end... Rubinstein, Arthur, *Grande est la vie*, Paris, Pub. Robert Laffont, 1980, p. 15.

page 94
It is difficult... Starkie, Walter, *Aventuras de un irlandés en España*, Madrid, Espasa Calpe, 1937, p. 226.

page 95
I saw Stravinsky... Verdaguer, Mario, *Op. cit.*, pp. 141-142.

page 98
Now Falla's... Martínez Sierra, María, *Op. cit.*, pp. 127-128.

page 104
My much longed... Rubinstein, Arthur, *Les jours de ma jeunesse*, Paris, Pub. Robert Laffont, 1973, pp. 625-627.

page 107
One day not long... Pahissa, Jaime, *Op. cit.*, pp. 91-92.
The plot... Martínez Sierra, María, *Op. cit.*, pp. 141-142.

page 108
Martínez Sierra, enthusiast... Martínez Sierra, María, *Op. cit.*, pp. 137-138.

page 109
Another curious musical... Rubinstein, Arthur, *Les jours...*, *Op. cit.*, p. 629.
The final touches... Martínez Sierra, María, *Op. cit.*, pp. 132-134.

page 115
On our travels... Martínez Sierra, María, *Op. cit.*, pp. 143 and 146.

page 116
Falla, a great... Martínez Sierra, María, *Op. cit.*, pp. 145-146.
This was not... Thomas, Juan María, *Manuel de Falla en la isla*. Palma de Mallorca, Ediciones Capella Classica, 1946, pp. 114-115.

page 119
The idea of... Pahissa, Jaime, *Op. cit.*, pp. 104-105.

page 120
Encouraged by... Martínez Sierra, María, *Op. cit.*, pp. 142-144.

page 123
On various occasions... Pahissa, Jaime, *Op. cit.*, pp. 105-107

page 128
It was in Madrid... Sokolova, Lydia, *Dancing for Diaghilev*, London, Mercury House, 1989, pp. 113-114.
When we had... Sokolova, Lydia, *Op. cit.*, p. 141.

page 129
De Falla,... Karsavina, Tamara, *Theatre Street*, New York, Heinemann, 1930, pp. 300-301.

page 131
It is strange... Corpus Barga, *El Sol*, Madrid, February, 1920.

page 132
At the opening of the ballet... Sokolova, Lydia, *Op. cit.*, p. 142.

page 133
Miguel Llobet had often... Pahissa, Jaime, *Op. cit.*, pp. 121-122.

page 135
Manuel de Falla came... Rubinstein, Arthur, *Grande est...Op. cit.*, pp. 131-132.
Here is the story... Pahissa, Jaime, *Op. cit.*, pp. 114-115.

page 141
The first time I... Trend, J. B., *A Picture of Modern Spain Men & Music*, London, Constable & Co. Ltd., 1921, pp. 237-245.

page 145
However, I remember... Mora Guarnido, José, *Federico García Lorca y su mundo*, Buenos Aires, Losada, 1958, pp. 153-156.

page 152
In calle Antequeruela... Mora Guarnido, José, *Op. cit.*, p.156.

page 153
Falla did not... Mora Guarnido, José, *Op. cit.*, p. 157.

page 155
When Falla... Mora Guarnido, José, *Op. cit.*, pp. 157-158.

page 156
I have walked... Reyes, Alfonso, *La saeta, O. C.*, volume II, Mexico, Fondo de Cultura Económica, 1986, pp. 128 and 132.

page 163
In the two months... Viniegra, Juan J., *Op. cit.*, pp. 118-119.

page 165
On another occasion..Goméz de la Serna, Ramón, *Automoribundia, 1888-1948*, Buenos Aires, Pub.Sudamericana, 1948, p. 388.

page 166
For two unforgettable... Mora Guarnido, José, *Op. cit.*, pp. 162-163.

page 169
The following... Mora Guarnido, José, *Op. cit.*, pp. 163-164.

page 173
The Princesse de... Pahissa, Jaime, *Op. cit.*, pp. 125-126.

page 174
In *Master Peter's*... Salazar, Adolfo, *Op. cit.*, pp. 177-178.
Couldn't you... Viniegra, Juan J., *Op. cit.*, pp. 120-121.

page 175
Falla lived... Verdaguer, Mario, *Op. cit.*, pp. 186-187.
On the 25th... Pahissa, Jaime, *Op. cit.*, pp. 130-132.

page 179
During the... Buñuel, Luis, *Mi último suspiro*, Barcelona, Plaza Janés, 1982, pp. 86-87.

page 180
In the spring... Pahissa, Jaime, *Op. cit.*, pp. 135-136.

page 184
We were... Thomas, Juan María, *Op. cit.*, pp. 29-35.

page 191
To come... THOMAS, Juan María, *Op. cit.*, p. 114.
The première... THOMAS, Juan María, *Op. cit.*, pp. 126-127.

page 193
The homage... PAHISSA, Jaime, *Op. cit.*, p. 158.

page 194
Falla had... PAHISSA, Jaime, *Op. cit.*, pp. 158-159.

page 195
The Falla family's... PERSIA, Jorge de, *Los últimos años de Manuel de Falla,* Madrid, S.G.A.E., 1989, p. 11.

page 197
He went to... JIMÉNEZ, Juan Ramón, "Manuel de Falla", *Olvidos de Granada*, San Juan de Puerto Rico, La Torre, 1960, pp. 37-38.

page 199
Albéniz... SALAZAR, Adolfo, *Música y músicos de hoy*, Madrid, Pub. Mundo Latino, 1928, p. 139.

page 206
Years later... PAHISSA, Jaime, *Op. cit.*, pp. 18-19.

page 209
It was... MILHAUD, Darius, *Ma vie heureuse*, Paris, Pub. Belfond, 1973, pp. 178-179.

page 210
Every visit... POMÈS, Mathilde, "'À Grenade avec Manuel de Falla", *La Revue Musicale*, Paris, year 15, nº. 145, April 1934, pp. 257-262.

page 217
Falla does not... AZORÍN, "Vida imaginaria de Falla", *La Prensa*, Buenos Aires, June 1933.

page 221
I spent three... THOMAS, Juan María, *Op. cit.*, pp. 176-177.

page 222
Every morning... THOMAS, Juan María, *Op. cit.*, pp. 301-302.

page 223
The doctors... THOMAS, Juan María, *Op. cit.*, pp. 293-295.

page 225
I can... BERGAMÍN, José, "Manuel de Falla", *Litoral*, nº. 35-36, Malaga, January-February, 1973, p. 27.

page 229
Like other... CASELLA, Alfredo, *21 + 26*, Rome, Pub. Augustea, 1931, p. 197.

page 230
From his... MARITAIN, Jacques, *Cruz y Raya*, Madrid, April 1935.

page 231
The last... STARKIE, Walter, *Espagne, Voyage musical dans le temps et l'espace*, Vol. II, Paris, Pub. René Kister, 1959, p. 150.

page 235
It was an... JIMÉNEZ, Luis, *Mi recuerdo humano de Manuel de Falla*, Granada, Universidad de Granada, 1980, pp. 28-29.

page 242
He arrived... MASSA, Pedro, "Manuel de Falla, en la Argentina", *La Prensa*, Buenos Aires.

page 245
The time... PAHISSA, Jaime, *Op. cit.*, pp. 159-162.

page 247
In one of... JIMÉNEZ, Luis, *Op. cit.*, pp. 71-73.
Another piece... JIMÉNEZ, Luis, *Op. cit.*, pp. 70-71.
In October... VERDAGUER, Mario, *Op. cit.*, pp. 188-189.

page 258
Sometimes... PAHLEN, Kurt, M*anuel de Falla*, Madrid, Editora Nacional, 1960, pp. 213 and 216.

page 267
The Colón... PAHLEN, Kurt, *Op. cit.*, p. 201.

page 270
The concerts... PAHISSA, Jaime, *Op. cit.*, pp. 179-180.

page 273
In one... GÓMEZ DE LA SERNA, Ramón, "Variaciones. La *Atlántida* de Manuel de Falla", magazine *Lyra*, Buenos Aires, 1961.

page 274
In the heart... PAHLEN, Kurt, *Op. cit.*, pp. 205-206.
The Maestro's... MASSA, Pedro, *Op. cit.*
When the professor... MOYANO, Daniel, "Tres aproximaciones a Manuel de Falla", *Liberación*, Madrid, 11 November 1984.

page 275
"Los Espinillos"... PAHISSA, Jaime, *Op. cit.*, pp. 180-181.

page 276
To this... GÓMEZ DE LA SERNA, Ramón, "Variaciones..." *Op. cit.*

page 277
Who has not... PÉREZ DE AYALA, Ramón, *Amistades y recuerdos*, Barcelona, Aedos, 1961, pp. 83-86.

page 279
I was counting... CAMBÓ, Francesc, *Meditacions, Dietari, III*, Barcelona, Pub. Alpha, 1982, pp. 1,365-1,366.

page 282
A little... ALBERTI, Rafael, "Una cantata sumergida", *La Nación*, Buenos Aires, 16 September 1945.

page 285
One day... RAMOS, José Ignacio, *Biografía de mi entorno*, Buenos Aires, Editorial Legasa, 1984, pp. 183-186.

page 287
In his state of... PAHISSA, Jaime, *Op. cit.*, p. 199.
In spite of the... PAHISSA, Jaime, *Op. cit.*, pp. 181-182.

page 290
One morning... PAHLEN, Kurt, *Op. cit.*, pp. 219-220.

page 291
There was... BERGAMÍN, José, *Op. cit.*, pp. 26-28.

page 292
Now I am... ALBERTI, Rafael, *La arboleda perdida*. Books III and IV, Barcelona, Seix Barral, 1987, pp. 228-229.

3. NAMES INDEX

A

ACOSTA MEDINA, José, *160*
ADINY-MILLIET, Ada, 49, 67
AGUADO, Rafael, *170*
AGUILAR, Paco, 282, *282*, 283, *283*
AGUILERA, *160*
AGUIRRE DE CASTRO, Raquel, *269*
AUGUSTINE, Saint, 228
ALARCÓN, Pedro Antonio de, 81, *99*, 117, *117*, 119, *119*, 120, 128, 131
ALBÉNIZ, Isaac, 28, 47, 49, 52, 53, 54, *54*, 55, 59, 65, 71, 83, 124, 133, 145, 199, 264, 265, 270, 292
ALBÉNIZ, Laura, 109
ALBERTI, Rafael, 237, 239, 282, *282*, 284, *284*
ALCALÁ ZAMORA, Niceto, 215
ALFONSO X THE WISE, 259
ALONSO, Dámaso, 190
ALVAR, Louise, 187, *187*, *259*
ÁLVAREZ DE CIENFUEGOS, Valentín, *160*
ALLERS, Franz, 281
AMADEO IST OF SAVOY, 95
AMORÓS, *119*
ÁNGELES, Victoria de los, 257
ÁNGELES ORTIZ, Manuel, 149, *165*, 173, 175, 176, *176*, *177*, 178, *178*, 180
ANSERMET, Ernest, 72, *93*, 104, *120*, 121, 124, 135
ARREGUI, 37
AUDEL, Stéphane, 261
AURIC, George, *262*
AUSENSI, Manuel, 257
AZAÑA, Manuel, 213, 232
AZORÍN, José Martínez Ruiz, 162

B

BACARISAS, Gustavo, *111*, 145, 150
BACARISSE, Salvador, *114*, *199*
BACEWICZ, Grazyna, 191
BACH, Johann Sebastian, *43*, 142, 155, 208, 283
BADÍA, Concepción, 150, *206*, *269*, 270
BAGARÍA, Luis, *53*
BAILLY, *61*
BAL Y GAY, Jesús, *224*
BARACCI, *93*
BARBIERI, Francisco Asenjo, 39
BÁRCENA, Catalina, 86
BAROJA, Ricardo, 95
BARRIOS, Ángel, 54, 82, 141, *142*, *144*, 145, 146, 158, *160*, *168*
BARRIOS, Antonio ("El Polinario"), 79, 82, 141, 145, 146, *146*
BARTOK, Béla, 133, 264, 265
BAUCHS, Pedro, 150
BAUTISTA, Julián, *199*
BÉCQUER, Gustavo Adolfo, 33
BEETHOVEN, Ludwig van, 19, 27, *43*, 74, 83, 222
BENAVENTE, 36

BENEDITO, Rafael, *108*
BÉRARD, Victor, 245
BERGAMÍN, José, 213, 215, 226, *227*
BERGES, 36
BERMÚDEZ, Diego ("el Tenazas" or "el de Morón"), 159, *163*, 164
BERRUGUETE, 184
BLANCAS, *119*
BONET, Adrián, 178
BORES, 180
BORRAJO, Pedro, 216, 234
BOLM, 104
BONUCCI, Arturo, *229*
BORRÁS, Enrique, 86
BOURBON, María Pía of, 241
BRAYER, Yves, *91*
BRETÓN DE LOS HERREROS, Tomás, *43*, *46*, 67, 225
BROCCA, 15, 22
BROOKS, Mme., 67
BUENO, Guzmán el, 245
BULNES, Conde de, 285
BULLRICH, Enrique, 194
BUÑUEL, Luis, *98*, *179*, 180, 196

C

CABEZÓN, Félix Antonio de, 208
CAGANCHO (bullfighter), *160*
CALDERÓN DE LA BARCA, Pedro, 77, 150, 228
CALVOCORESSI, M. P., 49, 52, *56*
CAMBÓ, Francesc, 237, 239, 268, 279, *279*
CAMPO, Conrado del, *93*, 95, *114*, 150, 162
CANO, Alonso, 141, 155, 158
CARACOL, Manolo, 159, 166
CARAZO, José, *163*
CARAZO, Ramón, *163*
CARAZO, Raúl, 149
CARRÉ, Albert, 61, 158
CARRÉ, Marguerite, *61*
CARRIÓN, Ambrosio, 86
CASALS, Pau, 150, 184, *207*
CASAS, Ramón, *71*
CASELLA, Alfredo, 215, *229*
CASTELLANO, Alberto, *269*
CASTRO, Adolfo de, 245
CASTRO, Américo, 176, 177
CASTRO, Cristóbal de, 33
CASTRO, Juan José, 194, 239, 241, 258, *267*, *269*, 270, 271
CASTRO, Sergio de, 237, 239, *258*
CEPEDA Y AHUMADA, Teresa de (Saint Theresa of Avila), 211, 263
CERÓN, Miguel, 149, 162, *163*, 174, 216
CERVANTES, Miguel de, 78, 173, 175, 245, 265
CLAUDEL, Paul, 253
CHABRIER, Alexis Emmanuel, 263
CHACÓN, Antonio, 159, 162, 166
CHAPÍ Y LORENTE, Ruperto, 36, *38*, 225

CHEVALIER, Yvonne, 263
CHOPIN, Frédéric, 19, *43*, 116, 191
CHUECA, Federico, 225, 247
COCTEAU, Jean, *262*
COLACELLI, Donato, 282, *282*, 283
COLLET, H., 65
COLOMBUS, Christopher, 245
COMPTA, 28
COOLS, 136
COPELAND, 191
CORTOT, Alfred, *221*
CORVINO, 95
COSSÍO, Francisco, 179, 180, *180*
COUPERIN, François, 155, 208
CRESPO, 163
CRISTÓBAL, Juan, 150, *205*
CROFT, William, 283
CUADROS, Joaquín, *163*
CUBILES, José, 71, 72, 81, 95

D

DALÍ, Salvador, *98*
D'ANNUNZIO, Gabriele, 255
DANTE, 249
DAQUIN, Louis-Claude, 208
DEBUSSY, Claude, *46*, 47, 49, 52, 53, *53*, 59, 65, 67, 74, 75, 82, 105, 131, 133, *133*, *134*, 141, 149, 150, 169, 193, 194, *230*, 264, 265, 275, 283
DEBUSSY, Emma, *53*, 67, 111
DELAGE, Maurice, 67, 216, *230*
DELAUNAY, Robert, *93*
DELAUNAY, Sonya, *93*
DENT, Edward Joseph, 178
DERAIN, André, 278
DÉSORMIÈRE, 278
D'ESPAGNAT, Georges, *56*
DIAGHILEV, Serge, 81, 82, 93, *93*, 96, 104, 119, 120, *120*, 121, *121*, 123, 124, 128, *128*, 129, 132, 173, 264, 279
DICENTA, Joaquín, 36
DIEGO, Gerardo, 150, 189, 190
DÍEZ CANEDO, Enrique, 162
D'INDY, Vincent, 54, 67
D'ORS, Eugenio, 95
DUFRANNE, Hector, 173, 176
DUKAS, Paul, 47, 49, 52, *52*, 53, 54, 55, 59, 65, 133, 184, 185, *192*, 193, *193*, 194, 215, 216, 265
DURÁN, Valentín Felip, *163*
DURÁN DE LANZ, Sofía, 234
DURAND (publisher), 65

E

EGGERHOLM, Eve, *142*, 145
ELIZALDE, Germán, 241
ENCINA, Juan del, 270, 283
ESCOBAR, 270

ESCUDERO, Vicente, 107, 111, *111,* 112, *113,* 150, 215
ESCHIG, Max, 59, 71, 72, 107, 150, 189
ESPLÁ, Óscar, 162, 189, 270
ESPLANDIÚ, Juan, *180*

F

FALLA FRANCO, José María de, 15, *18, 27, 82, 101*
FALLA MATHEU, Germán de, *27,* 49, 51, 60, 76, 102, 150, 234, *235,* 241, 242
FALLA MATHEU, María del Carmen de, 82, 102, 111, 116, *142,* 145, 153, 170, 175, 180, 190, *195,* 196, *208,* 215, 216, 225, 226, 232, 234, 239, 241, 242, 256, *269,* 274, 275, 276, *276, 278, 282, 282,* 284, 285, 287, 290
FALLA LÓPEZ, Isabel de, 234, *235,* 241, 242
FARCOUNET, 60
FAURÉ, Gabriel, 54, 263
FEDRIANI, Father, 13, 15, *26,* 45, *45*
FERNÁNDEZ, Félix, 96, 128
FERNÁNDEZ ALMAGRO, Melchor, *160*
FERNÁNDEZ ARBÓS, Enrique, 71, 72, 81, 95, 104, 107, 124, 162, 194, *194,* 215
FERNÁNDEZ BORDÁS, 49, 55
FERNÁNDEZ SHAW, Carlos, 33, *42,* 49, 52, 59, *59,* 61, *62, 83,* 119
FERNÁNDEZ SHAW, Widow of, 59, 60
FERRER, Carlos, *282*
FESTO AVIENE, Rufo, 255
FÉVRIER, Jacques, 263
FONTAINE, Jean de la, 278
FONTANALS, Manuel, *116*
FRA ANGELICO, 75
FRANCK, César, 54, 74
FRANZEN, 51
FRAY JUAN DE SANTO TOMÁS, 228
FRAY LUIS DE GRANADA, 277
FRESCOBALDI, Girolamo, 264
FRESNO, *108, 198*
FUENTE, Narciso de la, *160*
FUSTER, Francisco, *114*

G

GALLEGO BURÍN, Antonio, *160*
GALLEGO BURÍN, Juan María, *160*
GALLUZZO, Eloísa, 15, 21, *21*
GÁLVEZ, *163*
GARCÍA, Manuel, 173, 176
GARCÍA ASCOTT, Rosa, 81, 82, *200,* 213, *224,* 225, *225*
GARCÍA CARRILLO, José, *160, 163*
GARCÍA DE PAREDES, José María, *260*
GARCÍA LORCA, Federico, *98,* 147, 149, 150, 159, *160, 161,* 162, *163,* 166, 167, *168,* 169, *169, 170,* 173, *174,* 187, 189, 190, 195, *196, 205, 208,* 212, 215, 216, 284
GARCÍA LORCA, Francisco, *168, 208*
GARCÍA SOLALINDE, A., 176, 177
GASSOL, Ventura, 206

GAUTIER, Téophile, 49, 67, *67,* 197
GHYS, 216
GILSON, 228
GIMÉNEZ, Gerónimo, 225
GINER DE LOS RÍOS, H., 162
GISBERT, Juan, 150, 247, *256, 257,* 259
GODEBSKI, Cyprien, *56*
GOLSCHMANN, Wladimir, 149, 173, 175
GÓMEZ DE LA SERNA, Ramón, 159, *160,* 166, 237
GOMOLKA, 191
GÓNGORA, Luis de, 150, 189, *189,* 190, *190*
GONTCHAROVA, Natalia, *91*
GONZÁLEZ AGUILAR (Dr.), 282, *282*
GONZÁLEZ AGUILAR, Mrs. *282*
GONZÁLEZ AGUIRRE, 282
GOOSENS, Sir Eugene, 133
GOUNOD, Charles, *21*
GOYA, Francisco de, 262
GRANADOS, Enrique, 33, 49, 79, 81, 92, *92,* 150, 206, 270
GRECO, Doménikos Theotokopoulus, El, 72, 129, 229
GRENVILLE, Ursula, 149, *160*
GRENVILLE, Lillian, 60, *60*
GRIEG, Edward Hagerup, 27, 51, 53
GRIS, Juan, 189, *189*
GUSTAVINO, Carlos, 237
GUERRERO, 270

H

HAENDEL, George F., 208
HALFFTER, Ernesto, 147, 149, 150, 174, 189, 198, *198,* 199, *200,* 257, 259, *259,* 260, 266, 270, 278
HALFFTER, Rodolfo, 189, *199*
HAYDN, Joseph, 21
HENNERT, Jadwiga, 191
HENRI-CASADESUS, Marie Louise, 133, 173
HERNÁNDEZ SUÁREZ, 239
HIGINI ANGLES, 184
HOMER, 245
HONEGGER, Arthur, 189, 278
HUGO, J., *262*
HUGO, Valentine, *262*

I

IBÁÑEZ MARTÍN, 285
IDZIKOVSKY, M. S., *132*
IMPERIO, Pastora, 71, 81, 86, 91, *91,* 107, *107,* 108, *108,* 109, 110, 112, *113,* 115, 119, 215
INGRES, Jean Auguste, 129
IRADIER, Sebastian, 155
ISABEL, Princess, 55

J

JACKSON, José, 35
JACOB, Max, 263
JANAKOPULOS, Vera, 176

JEAN-AUBRY, Georges, 49, 149, 187, *187*
JIMÉNEZ, Juan Ramón, 101, 150, 162
JIMÉNEZ, Luis, 216, 234
JOFRÉ, Manuel, 149, 162, 163
JORDÁ, José María, 86
JULIO ANTONIO, 131
JUNYET, Olaguer, *206*

K

KARSAVINA, Tamara, *132*
KASTNER, Macario Santiago, 225
KOCHANOWSKY, Jan, 191
KOCHNO, Boris, *93*
KOUSSEVITZKY, Serge, *110*

L

LABUNSKY, Felix, R., 191
LAHOWSKA, Aga, *69,* 81, 82, 100
LAMBINET, 65
LANDOWSKA, Wanda, 49, 147, 149, 150, 173, 175, 176, 177, 183, *183,* 184, 208, *208,* 266
LANZ, Hermenegildo, 149, *154, 163, 169,* 173, 174, *174,* 175, *175,* 178, *200, 205,* 215, 216, 234
LAPARRA, 55
LARIONOV, Mijail, *123*
LARRA, 117
LARRETA, Enrique, 239
LEFETRURE, 51
LÉGENDRE, Maurice, *160*
LEIGHT HENRY, *160*
LEISNIER, *85*
LEÓN CALLEJAS, *163*
LERROUX, 228
LINARES, Antonio, *62*
LITZ, Franz, *43*
LLANOS, Emilia, *195,* 234
LLOBET, Miguel, 133, *133,* 149, 150, 162, 247
LLONGUERAS, Joan, 184
LÓPEZ DÍAZ DE LOS REYES, Nicolás María, *160*
LÓPEZ MEZQUITA, José María, *133*
LÓPEZ MONTALVO, María Luisa, 234, *235,* 241, 242
LÓPEZ SANCHO, Antonio, *160, 163*
LOPOKOVA, Lydia, 104, *128*
LULIO, Raimundo, 256
LUNA, Antonio, *169, 170, 208*

M

MACIÁ, Francisco, 206
MACKINGLAY, 145
MACHAQUITO, 117
MADARIAGA, Salvador de, *187*
MAEZTU, Ramiro de, 213, 232
MALIPIERO, Gian Francesco, 133, *229*
MARITAIN, Jacques, 213, 215, 230, 232, 291
MARQUINA, Eduardo, 111, 245, 285
MARSHALL, Franck, *43, 69,* 150, 184, 206, *206,* 247, 256

MARTÍNEZ RIOBOÓ, José, *163*
MARTÍNEZ RIOBOÓ, Ramón, *163*
MARTÍNEZ RIOBOÓ, Ruperto, *163*
MARTÍNEZ SIERRA, Gregorio, 47, 49, 71, 72, 79, 81, 82, *83,* 86, *87, 99,* 100, 105, 107, *107,* 108, *108,* 109, *109,* 114, *114,* 115, 116, 117, *117,* 119, 123, 124, 128
MARTÍNEZ SIERRA, María, 47, 49, 71, 72, 79, 81, 82, *83, 87, 99,* 100, 105, 107, *107, 109,* 114, 115, *115,* 116, 117, 119, 124
MASSINE, Léonide, 81, 104, 120, 121, *123,* 124, *126, 127,* 128, *129, 131,* 132, *132,* 237, 281
MATHEU ZABALA, María Jesús, 15, *18, 27,* 76, *102*
MATOS, Leopoldo, 60, 77, 117, 123, 193
MENGELBERG, 179, *179*
MERCÉ, Antonia ("La Argentina"), 107, 111, *111,* 112, *112, 113,* 150, 213, 215, *218,* 219, *219*
MESTRES, Apeles, *207*
MILHAUD, Darius, 147, *209,* 237, 239, *262,* 278, *278*
MILLER, Gilbert, 253
MILLET, Luis, 247, 253, 256
MILLIET, Paul, 49, 55, 59, *60,* 61, 71, 76
MILLIET, Mme., 76
MIRECKI, 49, 55
MISTRAL, Federico, *30*
MOLINA, Miguel de, 215
MOMPOU, Federico, 95
MONTHERLANT, Henry de, 210
MONTOYA, Ramón, *163,* 166
MORA, 170
MORACH, Otto, *201*
MORAGAS, Rafael, 81, 206, 247
MORALES, 270
MORELL DE GALLEGO BURÍN, Emilia, 234
MORENO VILLA, José, 176, 177, 196
MORILLA, Ana la, 15, 19, *19,* 21
MOUSSORGSKY, Modest Petrovich, 208
MOZART, Wolfgang Amadeus, 59, 155, 283

N

NEMCHINOVA, Vera, *129*
NEVILLE, Edgar, *160*
NIN, Joaquín, 49, 74, 92, 119, 133, *178,* 193
NIÑA DE LA AGUADERA, La, *163*
NIÑO DEL BARBERO, El, *163*

O

ODERO, Alejandro, 15, 21, 22
OLIVARES, Gaspar de Guzmán y Pimentel, Conde Duque de, 255
ORCAGNA, 194
ORGAZ, General, 233
ORTEGA MOLINA, Antonio, 162, *163*
ORTEGA Y GASSET, José, 276
ORTIZ, Manolo, 175

P

PACHELBEL, Johann, 208
PAGANINI, Nicolo, *43*
PAHISSA, Jaime, 39, 239, 285, *287*
PALESTRINA, Giovanni Pierluigi da, 191
PARENT, 54
PAR Y TUSQUETS, Antonio, 247
PARODI, Clemente, 19
PASQUINI, 208
PAVÓN, Pastora ("La Niña de los Peines"), 157, *163*
PEDRELL, Felipe, 31, 33, 39, 40, *40,* 41, 61, 81, 109, 133, 149, 162, 173, 194, *194,* 216, 237, 256, *256,* 263, 264, 266
PEINADO, Joaquín, 175, 179
PELLICER, *43*
PEMÁN, José María, 213, 216, 233, *233, 254*
PENAGOS, Rafael, *119*
PÉREZ CASAS, Bartolomé, *114,* 162
PÉREZ DE AYALA, Ramón, 162, 237
PÉREZ GALDÓS, Benito, 117, 131
PÉREZ RONDA, Eugenia, 234
PÉREZ RONDA, Ramón, 216, 234
PERIS, Amparo, 173, 176
PETIT, Abbé, 67, 73
PEYPOCH, 71
PICASSO, Pablo, 81, 82, *95, 103,* 120, 121, 124, *128,* 129, *129, 130, 131,* 132, *132, 143,* 189, 264, 278
PISADOR, Diego, 283
PITTALUGA, Gustavo, 95, *199, 225,* 278
PIUS IX, 227
PLATO, 255
POLIGNAC, Princesse de, 82, 124, 149, 169, 173, *173,* 174, 175, *175,* 176, *176,* 177, *201,* 263, 266
POLTRONIERI, Alberto, *229*
POLUNIN, Vladimir, *127, 128*
POULENC, Francis, 183, 261, *262,* 278
PRADO, Loreto, 59
PRIETO DE OLÓRIZ, María, 234
PRIETO LEDESMA, María, 31, 33, *45*
PROKOFIEV, Serge, *110, 120,* 189
PRUNIÈRES, Henry, 133
PUCHOL, Luisa, *119*
PUJOL, Emilio, 133, 149, 175, 253
PUJOLS, Francisco, 247
PURCELL, Henry, 208, 283

Q

QUIRELL, 15
QUIROGA, Manuel, 285
QUIROGA LOSADA, Carlos, 245, 285

R

RACHILDE, Mme., 179
RAMEAU, Jean Philippe, 155, 208
RAMOS, J. Ignacio, 237
RAVEL, Maurice, 47, 49, 52, *56,* 59, 65, 67, 73, *77,* 120, 133 , 150, 169, 189, 216, 229, *230,* 263,

265, 266, 282, 283
REMACHA, Fernando, *199*
REYES, Alfonso, 149, 162, 176, 177
RIMSKY-KORSAKOV, Nicolai Andreyevich, 73
RÍO, Nirva del, 150
RIOBOÓ, Luis, *163*
RÍOS, Fernando de los, 149, 162, *163,* 213, 215, 220
RIVAS, Duc de, *19*
ROBLES POZO, Rogelio, *163*
ROCAFORT, 95
RODRIGO, Joaquín, 95, 270
RODRÍGUEZ ACOSTA, José María, *160,* 162
RODRÍGUEZ Y FERNÁNDEZ, José, 35
ROLAND-MANUEL, Alexis, 19, 21, 23, 27, 28, 43, 49, 67, 213, 216, *230,* 266, 278
ROMERO, Segismundo, 149, *200*
ROS MARBÁ, Antoni, 116
ROSSINI, Giocchino Antonio, 150
ROUCHE, 129
ROUSSEAU, Jean Jacques, 228
ROUSSEL, Albert, *56,* 133
RUBINSTEIN, Arthur, 79, 81, 82, *90, 91,* 135, *135,* 237, 239, 263
RUIZ ALMODÓVAR, José, *163*
RUIZ AZNAR, 216
RUIZ CARNERO, Constantino, *160*
RUSIÑOL, Santiago, 71, *71, 72,* 81, 82, 86, *88, 144,* 145, *160, 163*

S

SÁBADA, J., *144*
SAINT-SAËNS, Charles, *43*
SALAZAR, Adolfo, 81, 95, 110, *114,* 162, *168,* 198, *199, 200*
SALIGNAC, 176
SALVADOR Y CARRERAS, Miguel, *69,* 81, *93, 114,* 162
SANCHA, F., *86*
SÁNCHEZ, Miguel, 162
SÁNCHEZ PUERTAS, José, *163*
SANDRILLE, 51
SANDRINI, 55
SANTIAGO, Íñigo de, 285
SARGENT, Joseph, 82, *144*
SATIE, Erik, 133, 173, 179, 263
SAUGUET, Henri, 278
SAURA, Rafael, 179, *180*
SCARLATTI, Domenico, *43,* 133, 150, *154,* 155, 183, 208, 283
SCHINDLER, Kurt, 149, *160*
SCHMITT, Florent, 49, 52, *56,* 67, 133, 265
SCHUBERT, Franz, 51
SCHUMANN, Robert Alexander, *43,* 51
SEGOVIA, Andrés, 149, 162, *163, 195,* 215
SEGURA, José, *169, 170,* 208
SEGURA, Pedro, 215
SELIGNAC, Thomas, 173
SELVA, Blanca, 54
SEPÚLVEDA, Pedro, *119*
SERT, José María, 150, 215, 237, 239, 245, 247, 248, 253, 255, 256, 259
SERT, Misia, 104

SÈVERAC, Déodat de, *56, 67*
SHAKESPEARE, William, 71
SHULTEN, 255
SINGER, 263
SOKOLOVA, Lydia, *128*
SOLANA, José Gutiérrez, 131
SOLLMANS, *142*
SORIANO, Rodrigo, 145
STRAUSS, Richard, 263, 279
STRAVINSKY, Igor, 49, 78, 79, 81, 82, 93, *93,* 95, *95,* 111, 120, *120,* 123, 131, 133, 135, 169, 173, 177, 179, 195, 263
SULIKOWSKY, Jerzi, 191

T

TCHAIKOVSKY, Boris, 104
THOMAS, Juan María, 191, *191,* 215, *221, 222,* 247
THOMAS, Maxime de, 150, 180
TORRE, Néstor de la, 107, 108
TORRES, Eduardo, 149, *200*
TORRES, Manolo, 159, 166
TORRES BALBÁS, Leopoldo, *229*
TRAGÓ, José, 15, 28, *28,* 33, *43*
TRUEBA, Antonio, 33
TREND, J. B., 79, 82, *141, 160,* 178
TURINA, Joaquín, 33, *47,* 69, *69,* 74, *74,* 78, 81, *83, 95, 97, 114,* 115, 117, *119,* 120, 123, 162, 270

U

UREÑA, Marquis de, 25
USANDIZAGA, José María, 83

V

VALCARENGHI, Guido, 239, 257
VALDECASAS, Alfonso, 226, 227
VALERO, Maroussia, 223, *223*
VALÉRY, Paul, 210
VAUZELLE, *85*
VÁZQUEZ DÍAZ, Daniel, 82, 141, *142, 144,* 145, *199*
VEGA, Garcilaso de la, 217
VEGA, Lope de, 215, 226, 228
VEGA, Ricardo de la, *119,* 123
VEGUÉ Y GOLDONI, Ángel, 176
VELA, Luisa, 69, *69,* 81
VELÁZQUEZ, Conchita, 112
VELÁZQUEZ, Diego, 225
VERDAGUER, Jacinto, 150, 191, 245, *245, 246,* 247, 255, 256, 258, 259
VERGARA, Franco, 162
VERGARA CARMONA, Francisco, *163*
VICENS, Juan, 196
VICTORIA, Father, 270
VÍLCHEZ JIMÉNEZ, Fernando, 141, 142, 149, 162, *163*
VILLA LOBOS, Héctor, 36
VINIEGRA, Salvador, 13, 15, 24, 25, 28, 39, 52, *52*
VIÑES, Hernando, 173, 174, 175, *178,* 179, *180, 201*
VIÑES, Ricardo, 47, 49, 52, 56, *56,* 65, *65,* 67, 71, 72, 73, 81, 95, 174, 175, 179, 264
VIVES, Amadeo, 33, 36, *36, 114*

W

WAGNER, Richard, 109, 131, 229, 247, 255, 258

WELLINGTON, 85, 141, 142

X

XIRGÚ, Margarita, 239

Y

YEPES, Juan de (Saint John of the Cross), 228, 266, 277
YERBAGÜENA, Frasquito, 163

Z

ZIELENSKY, 191
ZULOAGA, Ignacio, 49, 60, 131, 147, 149, 150, 158, *158,* 159, *160,* 162, *163,* 165, 166, 180, *180,* 215, 237, 239, 263, 277, *279*
ZURBARÁN, Francisco, 263, 283